Lecture Notes in Computer Science   **9540**

Commenced Publication in 1973
Founding and Former Series Editors:
Gerhard Goos, Juris Hartmanis, and Jan van Leeuwen

Editorial Board

More information about this series at http://www.springer.com/series/7410

Enes Pasalic · Lars R. Knudsen (Eds.)

Cryptography and Information Security in the Balkans

Second International Conference, BalkanCryptSec 2015
Koper, Slovenia, September 3–4, 2015
Revised Selected Papers

 Springer

Editors
Enes Pasalic
University of Primorska
Koper
Slovenia

Lars R. Knudsen
Technical University of Denmark
Kongens Lyngby
Denmark

ISSN 0302-9743   ISSN 1611-3349   (electronic)
Lecture Notes in Computer Science
ISBN 978-3-319-29171-0   ISBN 978-3-319-29172-7   (eBook)
DOI 10.1007/978-3-319-29172-7

Library of Congress Control Number: 2015960215

LNCS Sublibrary: SL4 – Security and Cryptology

Printed on acid-free paper

This Springer imprint is published by SpringerNature
The registered company is Springer International Publishing AG Switzerland

Preface

This volume contains the papers presented at BalkanCryptSec 2015, the Second International Conference on Cryptography and Information Security in the Balkans, held September 3–4, 2015, in Koper, Slovenia.

The call for papers was answered by 27 submissions from 15 countries. Each submission was reviewed by at least three Program Committee members. After the conference a second round of reviews was held for the revised papers. The committee decided to select 12 papers for the proceedings.

The Program Committee consisted of 28 members representing 18 countries. These members were carefully selected to represent academia and industry, as well as to include world-class experts in various research fields of interest to BalkanCryptSec.

Additionally, the workshop included three excellent invited talks and a tutorial talk. Kaisa Nyberg from Aalto University, Finland, talked about multidimensional linear attacks in a presentation entitled "Key-Variance in Statistical Cryptanalysis." Alexander Pott from Otto-von-Guericke University of Magdeburg discussed his research in a talk entitled "Almost Perfect Nonlinear and Planar Functions: A Survey of (not so) Recent Results and Open Problems." Billy Bob Brumley from Tampere University of Technology presented results, techniques, and the evolution of certain attack methods in "Software-Based Side-Channel Attacks." Enes Pasalic also held a tutorial talk titled "Constructing Boolean Functions for Stream Ciphers."

We would like to thank everyone who made the conference possible. First and foremost the authors who submitted their papers, in particular the authors of the accepted papers, and the invited speakers. The hard task of reading, commenting, debating, and finally selecting the papers for the conference fell on the Program Committee members. The Program Committee also used two external reviewers, whom we wish to thank as well.

We would also like to thank the local Organizing Committee and especially Nastja Cepak, a PhD student in cryptography at University of Primorska, for her enormous help in arranging and taking care of most of the tasks related to this conference.

This was the second annual BalkanCryptSec conference. The first one was held in 2014 thanks to Svetla Nikova and Tsonka Baicheva's idea of hosting a cryptography and security conference in the Balkans. We hope and believe the conference will continue for many years to come.

November 2015

Enes Pasalic
Lars R. Knudsen

Organization

Program Chairs

Enes Pasalic — University of Primorska, Slovenia
Lars Knudsen — Technical University of Denmark, Denmark

Steering Committee

Sedat Akleylek — Ondokuz Mayis University, Turkey
Tsonka Baicheva — Bulgarian Academy of Sciences, Sofia
Lejla Batina — Radboud University Nijmegen, The Netherlands
Vesna Dimitrova — Ss. Cyril and Methodius University, Macedonia
Zoran Đurić — University of Banja Luka, Bosnia and Herzegovina
Bogdan Groza — Politehnica University of Timisoara, Romania
Sokratis Katsikas — University of Piraeus, Greece
Miodrag Mihaljević — Serbian Academy of Sciences, Serbia
Svetla Nikova — KU Leuven, Belgium
Berna Ors — Istanbul Technical University, Turkey
Panagiotis Rizomiliotis — University of the Aegean, Greece
Ferucio Laurentiu Tiplea — Alexandru Ioan Cuza University, Romania
Tolga Yalcin — UIST St. Paul the Apostle, Macedonia

Organizing Committee

Enes Pasalic, Klavdija Kutnar, Štefko Miklavič, Nastja Cepak

PC Members

Enes Pasalic
Marko Holbl
Kaisa Nyberg
Billy Bob Brumley
Sugata Gangopadhyay
Alexander Pott
Panagiotis Rizomiliotis
Miodrag Mihaljevic
Ferucio Laurentiu Tiplea
Tsonka Baicheva
Bogdan Groza

Sedat Akleylek
Sokratis Katsikas
Paolo D'Arco
Vesselin Velichkov
Michael Scott
Claude Carlet
Dieter Gollmann
Ricardo Dahab
Frederik Vercauteren
Pante Stănică

Contents

Implementation and Verifiable Encryption

Symmetric Key Cryptography

Boolean Functions with Maximum Algebraic Immunity Based on Properties of Punctured Reed–Muller Codes

Konstantinos Limniotis[1,2]($\boxtimes$) and Nicholas Kolokotronis[3]

[1] Department of Informatics and Telecommunications,
University of Athens, 15785 Athens, Greece
klimn@di.uoa.gr
[2] Hellenic Data Protection Authority, Kifissias 1–3, 11523 Athens, Greece
klimniotis@dpa.gr
[3] Department of Informatics and Telecommunications,
University of Peloponnese, 22100 Tripolis, Greece
nkolok@uop.gr

Abstract. The construction of Boolean functions with an odd number of variables and maximum algebraic immunity is studied in this paper. Starting with any function f obtained by the Carlet–Feng construction, we develop an efficient method to properly modify f in order to provide new functions having maximum algebraic immunity. This new approach, which exploits properties of the punctured Reed–Muller codes, suffices to generate a large number of new functions with maximum algebraic immunity through swapping an arbitrary number of elements between the support of f and its complement.

1 Introduction

Algebraic attacks constitute a powerful cryptanalytic technique having received great attention over the last decade. Towards designing secure cryptosystems, the use of Boolean functions having properties like high algebraic degree, balancedness, and high nonlinearity, does not suffice to resist algebraic attacks. As a consequence, the cryptographic criterion of *algebraic immunity* (AI) was introduced to assess the strength of Boolean functions against such cryptanalytic attacks [19]. Therefore, constructing Boolean functions with the maximum possible AI is of great importance. Algebraic attacks in stream ciphers were further improved to the so–called *fast algebraic attacks* by exploiting linear relations amongst the keystream bits [10]. Hence, the behavior of cryptographic Boolean functions against fast algebraic attacks should also be considered.

This work is co–financed by the European Union (European Social Fund) and Greek national funds through the operational program "Education and Lifelong Learning" of the National Strategic Reference Framework (NSRF). Research funding program THALES: investing in knowledge society through the European Social Fund.

© Springer International Publishing Switzerland 2016
E. Pasalic and L.R. Knudsen (Eds.): BalkanCryptSec 2015, LNCS 9540, pp. 3–16, 2016.
DOI: 10.1007/978-3-319-29172-7_1

Several families of functions with maximum AI have been constructed. The first one is the *majority* function [11], which is a symmetric function; other constructions leading to symmetric or rotation–symmetric Boolean functions with maximum AI are provided in [8,23,25,27]. However, it was recently shown that almost all symmetric functions behave badly with respect to fast algebraic attacks [17]. This result has motivated many new constructions aiming at eliminating the majority function's symmetry by properly modifying its truth table [6,12,14,26]; these are called secondary constructions. In addition, new (primary) constructions of functions with maximum AI have been proposed [2,3,11]. However, all of these families suffer from low nonlinearity. An important construction proposed by Carlet and Feng [4] achieves maximum degree, high nonlinearity, and good behavior against fast algebraic attacks [16]. A construction equivalent to [4] (*see* [7]) is provided in [30], where an improved lower bound is derived on the attained nonlinearities. Another construction is presented in [28], based on the work of [29]; apart from providing functions on even number of variables with maximum AI, it further improves the lower bound on the nonlinearity of the Carlet–Feng construction. Suitable modifications of this construction have also been presented in [13,15,24,31]. In general, constructing functions having maximum AI, without sacrificing the other cryptographic criteria, still remains an active research area.

In this paper, we further study the Carlet–Feng construction, aiming at providing new functions with maximum AI. More precisely, we start from any function in *odd* number of variables with maximum AI and we prove general conditions that ensure maximum AI when many entries of a function's truth table are modified simultaneously. Subsequently, it is shown that these conditions can be applied to a function obtained via the Carlet–Feng construction, in order to get an efficient approach to properly modify f so as to ensure that the AI does not decrease. When applied to this construction, our work extends the results of [15], where the truth table of f was modified at only two positions, instead of arbitrarily many. It is also shown that other important cryptographic criteria, such as high nonlinearity, maximum algebraic degree, and good behavior against fast algebraic attacks, can be also attained.

The paper is organized as follow. The basic definitions and notation are introduced in Sect. 2, whilst Sect. 3 revisits the ideas in [15] for modifying the Carlet–Feng construction. Section 4 describes properties of functions with maximum AI, which are related to minimal codewords of the punctured Reed–Muller code RM* ($\frac{n-1}{2}, n$). Their application to the Carlet–Feng construction are treated in Sect. 5, where an algorithm for generating functions with maximum AI is developed. Finally, concluding remarks and ongoing research work are summarized in Sect. 6.

2   Preliminaries

Let $\mathbb{B}_n$ be the set of Boolean functions $f : \mathbb{F}_2^n \rightarrow \mathbb{F}_2$ on n variables, where $\mathbb{F}_2 = \{0, 1\}$ is the binary field and $\mathbb{F}_2^n$ is the n-dimensional vector space over $\mathbb{F}_2$.

Let $[n] \triangleq \{1, \ldots, n\}$ and $\boldsymbol{x} = (x_1 \cdots x_n)$; any $f \in \mathbb{B}_n$ can be uniquely expressed in its *algebraic normal form* (ANF) as [18]

$$f(\boldsymbol{x}) = \sum_{I \subseteq [n]} v_I \, \boldsymbol{x}^I, \qquad v_I \in \mathbb{F}_2 \tag{1}$$

where $\boldsymbol{x}^I = \prod_{i \in I} x_i$ (by convention $\boldsymbol{x}^{\emptyset} = 1$) and the sum is taken modulo 2. The degree of f, denoted by $\deg(f)$, is the highest number of variables that appear in a monomial of its ANF. The binary vector of length 2^n

$$\boldsymbol{f} = \big(f(0 \cdots 0) \cdots f(1 \cdots 1) \big)$$

comprised by the values of f on vectors of $\mathbb{F}_{2^n}$ lexicographically ordered, is the truth table of $f \in \mathbb{B}_n$ and the set $\mathrm{supp}(f) = \{\boldsymbol{x} \in \mathbb{F}_2^n : f(\boldsymbol{x}) \neq 0\}$ is called its support (defined for vectors in a similar manner). The function $f \in \mathbb{B}_n$ is said to be balanced if its Hamming weight $\mathrm{wt}(f) = |\mathrm{supp}(f)|$ is equal to 2^{n-1}. Note that $\mathrm{wt}(f)$ is odd if and only if $\deg(f) = n$.

Let $\mathbb{F}_{2^n}$ be an extension field of $\mathbb{F}_2$ with primitive element $\alpha \in \mathbb{F}_{2^n}$, and let $N = 2^n - 1$. Since there is a vector space isomorphism between $\mathbb{F}_2^n$ and $\mathbb{F}_{2^n}$, any $f \in \mathbb{B}_n$ is also represented by a univariate polynomial, mapping $\mathbb{F}_{2^n}$ onto $\mathbb{F}_2$

$$f(x) = \sum_{i=0}^{N} \beta_i \, x^i, \qquad \beta_i \in \mathbb{F}_{2^n} \tag{2}$$

where $\beta_{2i} = \beta_i^2$, for $i \in \mathbb{Z}_N = \{0, 1, \ldots, N-1\}$ (the indices are taken modulo N), and it holds $\beta_0, \beta_N \in \mathbb{F}_2$. A cyclotomic coset γ_t of t modulo N is defined as $\gamma_t = \{2^i t \mod N : i = 0, \ldots, n_t - 1\}$, where n_t is the least integer for which $2^{n_t} t \equiv t \pmod{N}$; the smallest element of γ_t is referred to as the coset leader, and Γ is used to denote the set of all coset leaders modulo N. Using the trace function $\mathrm{tr}_1^n(x) = x + x^2 + \cdots + x^{2^{n-1}}$, defined over $\mathbb{F}_{2^n}$, we can write (2) as (see, e.g., [20])

$$f(x) = \sum_{t \in \Gamma} \mathrm{tr}_1^{n_t} \big(A_t \, x^t \big) + \epsilon \big(1 + x^N \big) \tag{3}$$

where $A_t \in \mathbb{F}_{2^{n_t}}$ and $\epsilon = \mathrm{wt}(f) \mod 2$. Moreover, the coefficients A_t can be obtained from (3) via the following expression that defines the *discrete Fourier transform* (DFT) of the function f

$$A_t = \sum_{i=0}^{N-1} f(\alpha^i) \alpha^{-it}, \qquad t \in \mathbb{Z}_N \,. \tag{4}$$

If f has even weight, then $A_0 = \sum_{i=0}^{N-1} f(\alpha^i) = f(0)$ and its DFT coincides with the coefficients of its univariate representation; otherwise we have $\sum_{i=0}^{N-1} f(\alpha^i) \neq f(0)$ and (2) can be obtained from (3) by setting $\epsilon = 1$, as $1 + x^N$ is nonzero at $x = 0$ only. The degree of f can also be computed by its DFT; if $\mathrm{wt}(f)$ is even, then $\deg(f)$ equals the maximum weight of $t \in \mathbb{Z}_N$ for which $A_t \neq 0$.

It is well-known that if $\deg(f) \leq r$, then $\boldsymbol{f}$ is a codeword of the rth order binary Reed–Muller code $\mathrm{RM}(r, n)$ [18]. In the sequel, we utilize the punctured code $\mathrm{RM}^\star(r, n)$ of length N, which is obtained by deleting the first coordinate from the codewords of $\mathrm{RM}(r, n)$. The code $\mathrm{RM}^\star(r, n)$ is known to be cyclic having as zeros the elements α^t, for all nonzero $t \in \mathbb{Z}_N$ satisfying $\mathrm{wt}(t) < n - r$ [18].

Definition 1. *The nonlinearity of $f \in \mathbb{B}_n$ is defined to be*

$$\mathrm{nl}(f) = \min_{g \in \mathrm{RM}(1,n)} \mathrm{wt}(f + g) \,.$$

Definition 2. *A function is called an annihilator of $f \in \mathbb{B}_n$ if and only if it belongs to*

$$\mathscr{A}_f = \{g \in \mathbb{B}_n : fg = 0\} \,.$$

Definition 3. *The algebraic immunity $\mathrm{AI}(f)$ of $f \in \mathbb{B}_n$ is the least degree of all the nonzero annihilators of f and $1 + f$.*

From the work in [9,19] it is evident that a cryptographic Boolean function f should have high AI to be resistant against algebraic attacks. A well–known result is that $\mathrm{AI}(f) \leq \lceil \frac{n}{2} \rceil$, for all $f \in \mathbb{B}_n$ [9]. An important construction of maximum AI functions, the Carlet–Feng construction, is described below in an equivalent version (see [24]) that is convenient for our subsequent analysis.

Proposition 1 ([4]). *Let $n > 1$, $E = 2^{n-1} - 1$, and $f \in \mathbb{B}_n$ be defined as*

$$\mathrm{supp}(f) = \left\{ 1, \alpha, \dots, \alpha^E \right\}$$

for a primitive element $\alpha \in \mathbb{F}_{2^n}$. Then it holds $\mathrm{AI}(f) = \lceil \frac{n}{2} \rceil$.

The fast algebraic attacks are extensions of the conventional algebraic attacks whose task is to identify $g, h \in \mathbb{B}_n$, for a given function $f \in \mathbb{B}_n$, such that $fg = h$ with $\deg(g) = e < \mathrm{AI}(f)$, $\deg(h) = d$, and $e + d < n$; note that a pair (e, d) with $e + d \geq n$ always exists [10]. We say that f admits a (e, d) pair if there exist functions g, h with the aforementioned properties. Functions that have no (e, d) pair such that $e + d < n$ are called *perfect algebraic immune* [16]. Any such function has maximum AI, while the converse is not true [16,22].

3   Revisiting Secondary Constructions with Maximum AI

In [15, Algorithm 2], an algorithm is developed to modify a function f from the Carlet–Feng construction so as to retain maximum AI. The algorithm is called singleswap in the sequel and is described in Algorithm 1 (reformulated to fit our context). Algorithm 1 simply proceeds by solving a well–defined upper–triangular linear system over $\mathbb{F}_2$ by backward substitution. More precisely, recalling from [15], for any $0 \leq r < N$ each column vector $\boldsymbol{v}^r$ (see lines 5, 8 of singleswap) is given by

$$\boldsymbol{v}^r = \begin{cases} (e_r \ \cdots \ e_1 \ e_0 \ \mathbf{0}_{E-r})^T, & \text{if } r \leq E \\ (\mathbf{0}_{r-E} \ e_E \ \cdots \ e_{r-E})^T, & \text{otherwise} \end{cases} \tag{5}$$

Algorithm 1. singleswap (n, f, α^m, k)

Input: odd integer n, function $f \in \mathbb{B}_n$ with $\text{supp}(f) = \{\alpha^0, \ldots, \alpha^E\}$
    element $\alpha^m \notin \text{supp}(f)$, and integer k

1:   $S \leftarrow \varnothing$
2:   $\boldsymbol{z} \leftarrow \boldsymbol{0}$ $\triangleright$ all–zero vector of length $E + 1$
3:   $i \leftarrow E$
4:   **while** $(i \geq E - k + 1)$ **do**
5:       $z_i \leftarrow v_i^m$ $\triangleright$ from (5)
6:       **if** $i \neq E$ **then**
7:           **for** $r = i + 1, \ldots, E$ **do**
8:               $z_i \leftarrow z_i + v_i^r * z_r$
9:          **end**
10:     **end**
11:     **if** $z_i = 1$ **then**
12:         $S \leftarrow S \cup i$
13:     **end**
14:     $i \leftarrow i - 1$
15: **end**

Output: $S = \{j_1, \ldots, j_r\} \subset \{E - k + 1, \ldots, E\}$: for all $1 \leq \ell \leq r$ the function
    $g \in \mathbb{B}_n$ with $\text{supp}(g) = \text{supp}(f) \cup \{\alpha^m\} \setminus \{\alpha^{j_\ell}\}$ has maximum AI

---

where $\boldsymbol{0}_s$ is the all–zero vector of length s, E is given in Proposition 1, and $e_i \in \mathbb{F}_2$, $i = 0, \ldots, E$, are the coefficients of the polynomial

$$\prod_{i\,:\,1 \leq \text{wt}(i) \leq \frac{n-1}{2}} (x - \alpha^i)$$

whose degree is E - i.e. the generator polynomial of $\text{RM}^\star(\frac{n-1}{2}, n)$. The columns of the upper–triangular matrix associated with the above linear diagonal system are given by $\boldsymbol{v}^r$ for $r = 0, 1, \ldots, E$. The algorithm, for a given $\alpha^m \notin \text{supp}(f)$, computes all possible elements $\alpha^i \in \text{supp}(f)$ that if swapped with α^m do not decrease the AI (see the output of Algorithm 1).

Looking into the details of singleswap, the algorithm returns S with the following property: $i \in S$ if and only if $z_i = 1$, where $\boldsymbol{z}$ is the solution vector of the linear system. As also stated in [15], although the dimension of this system is $(E + 1) \times (E + 1)$, we may simply find k entries of the unknown vector $\boldsymbol{z}$, for any $k \ll 2^{n-1}$, in order to find some - and not all - of the elements of S. The algorithm computes the last k entries $z_E, \ldots, z_{E-k+1}$ in decreasing order, where the value of k can be arbitrary (as implied by the description of [15, Algorithm 2]). The above are reflected in line 4 of singleswap, where 2^{n-1} is the maximum value of k for getting all possible swaps. The overall complexity of the algorithm is $\mathcal{O}(k^2)$ [15]. Algorithm singleswap will next be used as a basis to get more functions with maximum AI starting from the Carlet–Feng construction.

4   Codewords of $\mathrm{RM}^\star(\frac{n-1}{2}, n)$ as Annihilators

In this section, we prove important results towards proceeding with the new construction of functions with maximum AI. We will next focus on functions with odd number of variables.

Proposition 2 ([1]). *If n is odd, then $f \in \mathbb{B}_n$ has maximum algebraic immunity $\frac{n+1}{2}$ if and only if f is balanced and has no nonzero annihilators of degree at most $\frac{n-1}{2}$.*

The next result summarizes [15, Proposition 6] and [15, Lemma 1], in a formulation that is more appropriate for our context.

Proposition 3 ([15]). *Let n be odd, $\alpha \in \mathbb{F}_{2^n}$ be a primitive element, and let $f \in \mathbb{B}_n$ with $\mathrm{supp}(f) = \{\alpha^{r_0}, \alpha^{r_1}, \ldots, \alpha^{r_E}\}$ have $\mathrm{AI}(f) = \frac{n+1}{2}$. Then, for all $\alpha^m \notin \mathrm{supp}(f)$, the function g with $\mathrm{supp}(g) = \mathrm{supp}(f) \cup \alpha^m$ does not have maximum algebraic immunity, whereas $g + 1$ has a unique annihilator u with $\deg(u) \le \frac{n-1}{2}$. Moreover, the function $\tilde{g}$ whose support is $\mathrm{supp}(g) \setminus \alpha^j$ satisfies $\mathrm{AI}(\tilde{g}) = \frac{n+1}{2}$ if and only if $\alpha^j \in \mathrm{supp}(u)$.*

It should be pointed out that Proposition 3, which is crucial for our subsequent analysis, holds only for n odd.

We next introduce some notation. Let $A = (a_{ij})$ be an $n \times m$ matrix; then, for any $I \subset [n]$ we denote by A_I the $|I| \times m$ matrix obtained from A by removing all rows except those whose indices belong to I; similarly, for any $J \subset [m]$ we denote by A^J the $n \times |J|$ matrix obtained from A by removing all columns except those whose indices belong to J. The matrix A_I^J is defined in a straightforward manner. We next introduce a partial ordering of polynomials h, c in the residue class ring $\mathbb{F}_2[x]/(x^N - 1)$ (see, e.g., [21, p. 25]), given by

$$h(x) = \sum_{i=0}^{N-1} h_i\, x^i \quad \text{and} \quad c(x) = \sum_{i=0}^{N-1} c_i\, x^i$$

as follows: $h \preceq c \Leftrightarrow h_i \le c_i$ for all i. Based on this ordering, a *minimal codeword* of a binary code is defined as any codeword $v(x)$ such that there is no nonzero codeword $v'(x)$ of the code with $v' \prec v$.

Remark 1. Clearly, for any non–minimal codeword $\tilde{v}(x)$ of a linear code there exist two codewords $v_1(x)$, $v_2(x)$, with disjoint supports, such that $v_1 \prec \tilde{v}$, $v_2 \prec \tilde{v}$ and $v_1 + v_2 = \tilde{v}$.

Theorem 2. *Let n be odd, $\alpha \in \mathbb{F}_{2^n}$ be a primitive element, and let $f \in \mathbb{B}_n$ be balanced with $\mathrm{supp}(f) = \{\alpha^{r_0}, \alpha^{r_1}, \ldots, \alpha^{r_E}\}$ and $r_0 = 0$. Then, $\mathrm{AI}(f) = \frac{n+1}{2}$ if and only if there is no nonzero even weight codeword $v(x)$ of the code $\mathrm{RM}^\star(\frac{n-1}{2}, n)$ such that $v(x) \preceq c(x) = 1 + x^{r_1} + \cdots + x^{r_E}$.*

Proof. Let $g \in \mathscr{A}_{1+f}$, with $g \neq 0$; note that it necessarily holds $g(0) = 0$. Let us define the vector $\mathcal{G} = (g(1)\ g(\alpha)\ \cdots\ g(\alpha^{N-1}))^T$; then, the DFT coefficients $A_0, \ldots, A_{N-1}$ of g can be computed, according to (4), by

$$
\mathcal{A} = \begin{pmatrix} 1 & 1 & \cdots & 1 \\ 1 & \alpha^{-1} & \cdots & \alpha^{-(N-1)} \\ \vdots & \vdots & & \vdots \\ 1 & \alpha^{-(N-1)} & \cdots & \alpha^{-(N-1)(N-1)} \end{pmatrix} \times \mathcal{G}
$$
$$
\triangleq \mathcal{V} \times \mathcal{G}, \tag{6}
$$

where $\mathcal{A} = (A_0\ A_1\ \cdots\ A_{N-1})^T$ and $\mathcal{V} = (v_{ij})$ is a $N \times N$ Vandermonde matrix satisfying $v_{ij} = \alpha^{-ij}$, with $i, j \in \mathbb{Z}_N$.

Let us assume that $\deg(g) \leq \frac{n-1}{2}$. Then $A_k = 0$ for any k such that $\mathrm{wt}(k) \geq \frac{n+1}{2}$; moreover, g has necessarily even weight (as otherwise we would have $\deg(g) = n$), thus leading to $A_0 = 0$ (since we have $g(0) = 0$). Consequently, due to $\mathrm{supp}(g) \subset \mathrm{supp}(f)$, we get

$$
\mathcal{V}_I^J \times \mathcal{G}_J = \mathbf{0} \tag{7}
$$

where

$$
\begin{aligned}
I &= \{l_0, \ldots, l_E\} = 0 \cup \{i \in \mathbb{Z}_N : \mathrm{wt}(i) \geq \tfrac{n+1}{2}\} \\
J &= \{r_0, \ldots, r_E\} = \{i \in \mathbb{Z}_N : \alpha^i \in \mathrm{supp}(f)\}
\end{aligned}
$$

and $\mathbf{0}$ is the all–zero column vector $\mathcal{A}_I$. Then (7) implies that the sum over $\mathbb{F}_2$ of some columns of $\mathcal{V}_I^J$ vanishes or, equivalently, there exist $c_0, \ldots, c_E \in \mathbb{F}_2$, not all zero, such that the elements $\alpha^{-l_0}, \ldots, \alpha^{-l_E}$ are the roots of the polynomial $c(x) = c_0 x^{r_0} + \cdots + c_E x^{r_E}$.

On the other hand, if there exists a nonzero $v(x) \in \mathrm{RM}^\star(\frac{n-1}{2}, n)$ with even weight, such that $v(x) \preceq c(x)$, then it is easy to see from the above that the function g with $\mathrm{supp}(g) = \{\alpha^i : x^i \prec v(x)\}$ is an annihilator of $f+1$ with degree less than $\frac{n+1}{2}$ (note that the vector $\mathcal{G}$ of such g satisfies (7)). This concludes the proof. $\qquad\square$

Remark 3. Theorem 2 leads to another proof of the fact that the Carlet–Feng construction yields functions with maximum AI; indeed, the support of this function is associated with $c(x) = 1 + x + \cdots + x^E$. Since any polynomial $v(x)$ with $v(x) \prec c(x)$ has degree less than $E+1$, we get that $v(x)$ has at most E roots over $\mathbb{F}_{2^n}$, therefore contradicting the fact that any even–weight codeword of $\mathrm{RM}^\star(\frac{n-1}{2}, n)$ has at least $E+1$ roots.

Proposition 4. *Let n be odd, $\alpha \in \mathbb{F}_{2^n}$ be a primitive element and let $f \in \mathcal{B}_n$ have $\mathrm{AI}(f) = \frac{n+1}{2}$, where $\mathrm{supp}(f) = \{\alpha^{r_0}, \ldots, \alpha^{r_E}\}$ and $r_0 = 0$. For all $\alpha^j \notin \mathrm{supp}(f)$, there exists a unique nonzero even weight codeword $v(x)$ of $\mathrm{RM}^\star(\frac{n-1}{2}, n)$ such that $v(x) \preceq c(x) = 1 + x^{r_1} + \cdots + x^{r_E} + x^j$; in addition, $v(x)$ is a minimal codeword of the code satisfying $x^j \prec v(x)$.*

Proof. Since the function g with $\mathrm{supp}(g) = \mathrm{supp}(f) \cup \alpha^j$ is not balanced, it holds $\mathrm{AI}(g) < \frac{n+1}{2}$ and, thus, Theorem 2 directly implies that there exists a codeword $v(x)$ of $\mathrm{RM}^\star(\frac{n-1}{2}, n)$ with even weight such that $v(x) \preceq c(x)$. The uniqueness of $v(x)$ is straightforward from Proposition 3 and Theorem 2 (since $v(x)$ is uniquely determined by the annihilator of g with degree less than $\frac{n+1}{2}$ and such annihilator, as Proposition 3 states, is unique). Note that $x^j \prec v(x)$ since otherwise we would have that $v(x) \preceq 1 + x^{r_1} + \cdots + x^{r_E}$, contradicting the fact that f has maximum AI (due to Theorem 2). Moreover, if $v(x)$ was not minimal, we would get that there exists a codeword v' of $\mathrm{RM}^\star(\frac{n-1}{2}, n)$ with $v' \prec c(x)$ having disjoint support with v (see Remark 1), and thus $x^j \not\prec v'(x)$ - a contradiction; hence the claim follows.   □

5   Application to the Carlet–Feng Construction

By applying Proposition 4 to the function f obtained by the Carlet–Feng construction, it is straightforward to prove the following result.

Corollary 1. *For any polynomial of the form* $c^{(j)}(x) = \sum_{i=0}^{E} x^i + x^j$, *where* $E < j < N$, *there exists exactly one nonzero even weight codeword* $v(x)$ *of* $\mathrm{RM}^\star(\frac{n-1}{2}, n)$ *with* $v(x) \preceq c^{(j)}(x)$; *necessarily* $v(x)$ *is a minimal codeword satisfying* $x^j \prec v(x)$. *In the sequel, any such codeword of* $\mathrm{RM}^\star(\frac{n-1}{2}, n)$ *is denoted as* $u_j(x)$, $j > E$.

Proposition 5. *Let* $c(x) = c_1(x) + c_2(x)$, *where we have* $c_1(x) \preceq \sum_{i=0}^{E} x^i$ *and* $c_2(x) \preceq \sum_{i=E+1}^{N-1} x^i$. *If there exists nonzero even weight codeword* $v(x)$ *of* $\mathrm{RM}^\star(\frac{n-1}{2}, n)$ *with* $v(x) \preceq c(x)$, *then* $v(x)$ *necessarily has the form*

$$v(x) = \sum_{j \in J} \delta_j\, u_j(x), \quad \delta_j \in \mathbb{F}_2 \tag{8}$$

where $J \subseteq \{E < i < N : x^i \preceq c_2(x)\}$.

Proof. Note that the existence and uniqueness of $u_j(x)$, for $E < j < N$, is straightforward from Corollary 1. Clearly, any vector of the form (8) is an even weight codeword of $\mathrm{RM}^\star(\frac{n-1}{2}, n)$. Moreover, if it also holds

$$v(x) = \sum_{j \in J} \delta_j\, u_j(x) \prec c(x)$$

then $v(x) \in \mathrm{RM}^\star(\frac{n-1}{2}, n)$ is an even weight codeword with $v(x) \prec c(x)$. We next show that there exists no other even weight codeword $v'(x)$ of $\mathrm{RM}^\star(\frac{n-1}{2}, n)$ with $v'(x) \preceq c(x)$, apart from those (if any) given above. Assume that there exists such $v'(x)$; then $v'(x) = v'_1(x) + v'_2(x)$, where $v'_1(x) \preceq c_1(x)$ and $v'_2(x) \preceq c_2(x)$. Let $J' = \{E < i < N : x^i \preceq v'_2(x)\}$; as $u' = \sum_{j \in J'} u_j(x)$ is an even weight codeword of $\mathrm{RM}^\star(\frac{n-1}{2}, n)$, we get that $u' + v'$ is also an even weight codeword of $\mathrm{RM}^\star(\frac{n-1}{2}, n)$. However, it is easy to see that $u' + v' \preceq \sum_{i=0}^{E} x^i$, which leads to $\deg(u' + v') \leq E$, contradicting the fact that $u' + v'$ has at least 2^{n-1} roots over $\mathbb{F}_{2^n}$ (see also Remark 3); this completes the proof.   □

Theorem 4. *With the notation of Proposition 5, let n be odd, $\alpha \in \mathbb{F}_{2^n}$ be a primitive element of $\mathbb{F}_{2^n}$, and let $f, g \in \mathbb{B}_n$, where f is a Carlet–Feng function and* $\mathrm{supp}(g) = \{\alpha^0, \alpha^1, \ldots, \alpha^E\} \cup A \setminus B$. *Let $A = \{\alpha^{j_1}, \ldots, \alpha^{j_r}\} \subset \mathrm{supp}(f+1)$ and $B = \{\alpha^{i_1}, \ldots, \alpha^{i_r}\} \subset \mathrm{supp}(f)$, where*

(a) $i_s \neq 0$, *for all* $1 \leq s \leq r$,
(b) $x^{i_s} \prec u_{j_s}(x)$ *for all* $1 \leq s \leq r$,
(c) $x^{i_s} \not\prec u_{j_t}(x)$ *for all* $1 \leq t \leq r$ *with* $t \neq s$.

Then $\mathrm{AI}(g) = \frac{n+1}{2}$.

Proof. Let us assume that $\mathrm{AI}(g) \leq \frac{n-1}{2}$. If $\mathrm{supp}(g) = \{\alpha^0, \alpha^{r_1}, \ldots, \alpha^{r_E}\}$, then Theorem 2 implies that there exists a nonzero even weight $v(x) \in \mathrm{RM}^\star(\frac{n-1}{2}, n)$ such that $v(x) \preceq c(x) = 1 + x^{r_1} + \cdots + x^{r_E}$. Moreover

$$v(x) = \sum_{j \in A' \subseteq \{j_1, \ldots, j_r\}} u_j(x)$$

by Proposition 5. Let $j_s \in A'$; then, since $u_{j_s}(x)$ contributes to the sum that determines $v(x)$, our hypothesis implies $x^{i_s} \prec v(x)$ - i.e. x^{i_s} appears exactly once in $\sum_{j \in A'} u_j(x)$. By the proof of Theorem 2, an annihilator of $g+1$ (the one uniquely specified by $v(x)$) evaluates to 1 at α^{i_s} - a contradiction, since $\alpha^{i_s} \in \mathrm{supp}(g+1)$. Thus, $v(x)$ is the zero codeword, which contradicts our hypothesis, and the claim follows. $\qquad \square$

Remark 5. Theorem 4 assumes that, for any given r, there exist sets A, B with the properties implied therein. However, even if this is not the case, one may reduce the value of r in order to find such appropriate sets with the desired properties. Clearly, for $r = 1$, such sets A, B always exist (it is the case of Algorithm singleswap).

Theorem 4 forms the basis to construct functions with maximum AI, having the Carlet–Feng function f as a starting point and appropriately swapping elements between $\mathrm{supp}(f)$ and $\mathrm{supp}(f+1)$. To achieve this goal, the challenging task is to determine an appropriate set B, given a set A, which in turn rests with determining $u_{j_s}(x)$ for any $j_s \in A$. However, it is next shown that the Algorithm singleswap, described in Sect. 2, suffices to determine $u_{j_s}(x)$.

Corollary 2. *Let $f \in \mathbb{B}_n$ be a Carlet–Feng function, with n odd. Let S be the set obtained by applying singleswap for arbitrary k, having as inputs the function f, and an element $\alpha^m \notin \mathrm{supp}(f)$. Then, if $j \in S$, it necessarily holds $x^j \prec u_m(x)$.*

Proof. Let $g \in \mathbb{B}_n$ with $\mathrm{supp}(g) = \mathrm{supp}(f) \cup \{\alpha^m\}$. By Proposition 3, there exists a unique $u \in \mathscr{A}_{g+1}$ with $\deg(u) \leq \frac{n-1}{2}$. Therefore, recalling the properties of $u_m(x)$ from Corollary 1 and Theorem 2, we obtain that $u(\alpha^s) = 1$ for all s if and only if $x^s \prec u_m(x)$. Let $x^j \not\prec u_m(x)$; then, we have $u(\alpha^j) = 0$. This implies that $g' \in \mathbb{B}_n$ with $\mathrm{supp}(g') = \mathrm{supp}(g+1) \cup \{\alpha^j\}$ also has u as an annihilator, contradicting the fact that g' has maximum AI as singleswap ensures. $\qquad \square$

Algorithm 2. modifyCF (n, f, M, k)

Input: odd integer n, function $f \in \mathbb{B}_n$ with $\mathrm{supp}(f) = \{\alpha^0, \ldots, \alpha^E\}$
    set $M = \{\alpha^{m_1}, \ldots, \alpha^{m_r}\} \subset \mathrm{supp}(f+1)$, and integer k
1: **for** $i = 1, \ldots, r$ **do**
2:     $S^{(i)} \leftarrow$ singleswap (n, f, α^{m_i}, k)
3: **end**
4: $S = \varnothing$
5: **for** $i = 1, \ldots, r$ **do**
6:     Choose $j_i \in S^{(i)} \setminus \bigcup_{p \neq i} S^{(p)}$ so that $\forall p \neq i$, $\exists j_i' \in S^{(p)}$ with $j_i' < j_i$
7:     $S \leftarrow S \cup \{j_i\}$
8: **end**
Output: $S = \{j_1, \ldots, j_r\} \subset \{0, 1, \ldots, E\}$: the function $g \in \mathbb{B}_n$ with
    $\mathrm{supp}(g) = \mathrm{supp}(f) \cup M \setminus \{\alpha^{j_1}, \ldots, \alpha^{j_r}\}$ has maximum AI

Corollary 2 states that singleswap can be used for identifying some of the coefficients of u_{j_s} in Theorem 4 (for $k = E + 1$ all the coefficients of u_{j_s} are determined). Thus, by appropriately combining Theorem 4 and Corollary 2, we get Algorithm modifyCF - which utilizes singleswap- in order to efficiently modify a Carlet–Feng function in many positions so as to ensure maximum AI.

Theorem 6. *The Algorithm* modifyCF *provides functions with maximum AI, whilst its worst–case computational complexity is* $\mathcal{O}(rkL)$, *for* $L = \max\{k, r \log_2 k\}$.

Proof. The fact that any function obtained from modifyCF has maximum AI is straightforward from Theorem 4 and Corollary 2. Note that each execution of singleswap (line 2) is of computational complexity $\mathcal{O}(k^2)$, whilst there are r executions of this algorithm. Moreover, the procedure in line 6 of the algorithm rests with searching for specific elements within ordered arrays of numbers with length at most k; hence, for each such element of $S^{(i)}$, we apply binary search on at most $r - 1$ arrays (sets). At the worst case, $k(r - 1)$ searches are needed for choosing j_i from $S^{(i)}$, thus the overall complexity for all i is $\mathcal{O}(kr^2 \log_2 k)$ for the worst case, leading to the desired result.   □

Algorithm modifyCF is not deterministic, since in general there are many choices for selecting j_i from $S^{(i)}$ - hence, the initial choice of j_i could be random, with subsequent checking whether it satisfies the desired property.

Proposition 6. *For any odd* n, *there always exists a Boolean function* g *constructed via Theorem 4 such that* $\deg(g) = n - 1$.

Proof. According to (4), it holds $\deg(g) = n - 1$ if and only $A_{N-1} \neq 0$ or, equivalently, if and only if $\sum_{x \in \mathrm{supp}(g)} x \neq 0$. Assume that a function g obtained by Theorem 4 has degree less than $n - 1$, i.e. $\sum_{x \in \mathrm{supp}(g)} x = 0$. Then, with the notation of Theorem 4, replacing α^{j_r} with any element $\alpha^{j_r'} \in \mathrm{supp}(g+1)$ so that the properties stated therein are satisfied, we get that the function g' with

Table 1. Application of singleswap to $f : \text{supp}(f) = \{1, \alpha, \ldots, \alpha^E\}$ with $n = 7$

m_i	Set $S^{(i)}$ of all possible j_i
80	0 3 6–9 11–15 17 18 21–24 28 29 33 36 38–41 43 45–47 53 54 56 58 61 63
81	0–2 4–7 11 13 14 18 19 21 22 25 26 29 31–33 38–45 49 51 53–55 57 58–61 63
90	0 2 3 7 10 15–17 19 22 24 27 29 32 33 38–40 45 46 48 50 51 53–56 58 60 61 63
91	0–6 9 10 12 15 17 18 20 21 24–26 28 31 32 37–41 43 45 48 52–60 63

$\text{supp}(g') = (\text{supp}(g) \setminus \{\alpha^{j_r}\}) \cup \{\alpha^{j'_r}\}$ is also derived from Theorem 4 and clearly has maximum degree $n - 1$. If such $\alpha^{j'_r}$ does not exist, then we may consider the function $\tilde{g}$ with $\text{supp}(\tilde{g}) = (\text{supp}(g) \setminus \{\alpha^{j_r}\}) \cup \{\alpha^{i_r}\}$, which clearly satisfies $\deg(\tilde{g}) = n - 1$.   □

Proposition 7. *With the notation of Theorem 4, it holds* $\text{nl}(g) > 2^{n-1} - \left(\frac{\ln 2}{\pi} n + 0.74\right) 2^{n/2} - 2r - 1.$

Proof. Since g is obtained from the Carlet–Feng function f by swapping r elements between $\text{supp}(f)$ and $\text{supp}(f + 1)$, it holds $\text{nl}(g) \geq \text{nl}(f) - 2r$. The best known lower bound of $\text{nl}(f)$ is $2^{n-1} - \left(\frac{\ln 2}{\pi} n + 0.74\right) 2^{n/2} - 1$ as proved in [28, Theorem 7] and the claim follows.   □

Proposition 7 states that the nonlinearity of g is strongly contingent on the nonlinearity of f. Hence, since the actual nonlinearity of f seems to be much higher than the aforementioned lower bound [4,31], it is expected that Algorithm modifyCF can lead to functions with high nonlinearities. This is also shown in the subsequent example, where much higher nonlinearities than the above bound are achieved.

Example 7. Table 1 illustrates, for each $m_i \in \{80, 81, 90, 91\}$, all possible j_i such that the function $g \in \mathbb{B}_7$ with $\text{supp}(g) = \text{supp}(f) \setminus \{\alpha^{j_i}\} \cup \{\alpha^{m_i}\}$ has maximum AI, with f a Carlet–Feng function on 7 variables. In other words, Table 1 is obtained by executing singleswap (in line 2 of modifyCF) for $M = \{\alpha^{80}, \alpha^{81}, \alpha^{90}, \alpha^{91}\}$ and $k = 64$ (the maximum possible). Then, a possible output of Algorithm modifyCF is the set $S = \{47, 49, 50, 52\}$ (for instance, Line 6 of Algorithm modifyCF may return $j_1 = 47$, since 47 is the largest integer which lies in $S^{(1)}$ - the first row of Table 1 - and is not present in any $S^{(j)}$, $j = 2, 3, 4$). Hence the function $g \in \mathbb{B}_7$ defined as follows has maximum AI, equal to 4

$$\text{supp}(g) = \text{supp}(f) \cup M \setminus \{\alpha^{47}, \alpha^{49}, \alpha^{50}, \alpha^{52}\}$$

whereas $\deg(g) = 6$ and $\text{nl}(g) = 52$ (while $\text{nl}(f) = 54$). This output could also be obtained even if singleswap at line 2 was executed for $k = 17$.

Note that any $\{s_1, s_2, s_3, s_4\}$ with $s_1 \in \{8, 23, 36, 47\}$, $s_2 \in \{42, 44, 49\}$, $s_3 \in \{16, 27, 50\}$ and $s_4 \in \{20, 37, 52\}$ can be also derived from modifyCF, giving 108 different functions. The number of possible output functions further increases if we allow ourselves to compute functions that differ in less than 8 places from f. The vast majority of all these functions have nonlinearity 52, that is very close to the nonlinearity of f (i.e. the nonlinearity is decreased, with respect to the Carlet–Feng function f, by 2 and not by $2r = 8$). It is expected though that, in general, values equal to or higher than the nonlinearity of f may be also achieved; for instance, $\tilde{g} \in \mathbb{B}_7$ with $\mathrm{supp}(\tilde{g}) \setminus \{\alpha^{50}\} \cup \{\alpha^{90}\}$ has nonlinearity 54.

Finally, computer experiments show that g behaves the same way as the Carlet–Feng function f with respect to fast algebraic attacks; namely, g does not admit any pair (e, d) with $e = 1$ and $e + d \leq n - 1$, whilst for $e > 1$ there is no any pair (e, d) satisfying $e + d < n - 1$. $\qquad\Box$

6 Conclusions

A general approach to appropriately modify any function with maximum AI in odd number of variables without reducing this maximum value is provided. This approach, when applied to the Carlet–Feng construction, leads to an efficient algorithm to construct new functions with maximum AI. Since Carlet–Feng functions have good cryptographic properties, it is expected that the proposed approach leads to functions that also behave well with respect to other cryptographic criteria. This was confirmed by experimental results, and it constitutes subject of ongoing research.

Acknowledgment. The authors would like to thank the anonymous reviewers for the helpful comments and suggestions.

References

1. Canteaut, A.: Open problems related to algebraic attacks on stream ciphers. In: Ytrehus, Ø. (ed.) WCC 2005. LNCS, vol. 3969, pp. 120–134. Springer, Heidelberg (2006)
2. Carlet, C., Dalai, D.K., Gupta, K.C., Maitra, S.: Algebraic immunity for cryptographically significant Boolean functions: analysis and construction. IEEE Trans. Inform. Theory **52**, 3105–3121 (2006)
3. Carlet, C.: Constructing balanced functions with optimum algebraic immunity. In: Proceedings of IEEE International Symposium on Information Theory (ISIT), pp. 451–455 (2007)
4. Carlet, C., Feng, K.: An infinite class of balanced functions with optimal algebraic immunity, good immunity to fast algebraic attacks and good nonlinearity. In: Pieprzyk, J. (ed.) ASIACRYPT 2008. LNCS, vol. 5350, pp. 425–440. Springer, Heidelberg (2008)
5. Carlet, C., Gaborit, P.: On the construction of balanced Boolean functions with a good algebraic immunity. In: Proceedings of IEEE International Symposium on Information Theory (ISIT), pp. 1101–1105 (2005)
6. Carlet, C., Zeng, X., Li, C., Hu, L.: Further properties of several classes of Boolean functions with optimum algebraic immunity. Des. Codes Cryptogr. **52**, 303–338 (2009)

7. Carlet, C.: Comments on "constructions of cryptographically significant Boolean functions using primitive polynomials". IEEE Trans. Inform. Theor. **57**, 4852–4853 (2011)
8. Chen, Y., Lu, P.: Two classes of symmetric Boolean functions with optimum algebraic immunity: construction and analysis. IEEE Trans. Inform. Theor. **57**, 2522–2538 (2011)
9. Courtois, N.T., Meier, W.: Algebraic attacks on stream ciphers with linear feedback. In: Biham, Eli (ed.) EUROCRYPT 2003. LNCS, vol. 2656, pp. 345–359. Springer, Heidelberg (2003)
10. Courtois, N.T.: Fast algebraic attacks on stream ciphers with linear feedback. In: Boneh, D. (ed.) CRYPTO 2003. LNCS, vol. 2729, pp. 176–194. Springer, Heidelberg (2003)
11. Dalai, D.K., Maitra, S., Sarkar, S.: Basic theory in construction of Boolean functions with maximum possible annihilator immunity. Des. Codes Cryptogr. **40**, 41–58 (2006)
12. Li, N., Qi, W.: Construction and analysis of boolean functions of $2t+1$ variables with maximum algebraic immunity. In: Lai, X., Chen, K. (eds.) ASIACRYPT 2006. LNCS, vol. 4284, pp. 84–98. Springer, Heidelberg (2006)
13. Li, J., Carlet, C., Zeng, X., Li, C., Hu, L., Shan, J.: Two constructions of balanced Boolean functions with optimal algebraic immunity, high nonlinearity and good behavior against fast algebraic attacks. Des. Codes Cryptogr. **76**, 279–305 (2015)
14. Limniotis, K., Kolokotronis, N., and Kalouptsidis, N.: Constructing Boolean functions in odd number of variables with maximum algebraic immunity. In: IEEE International Symposium on Information Theory (ISIT), pp. 2686–2690 (2011)
15. Limniotis, K., Kolokotronis, N., Kalouptsidis, N.: Secondary constructions of Boolean functions with maximum algebraic immunity. Cryptogr. Comm. **5**, 179–199 (2013)
16. Liu, M., Zhang, Y., Lin, D.: Perfect algebraic immune functions. In: Wang, X., Sako, K. (eds.) ASIACRYPT 2012. LNCS, vol. 7658, pp. 172–189. Springer, Heidelberg (2012)
17. Liu, M., Lin, D.: Fast algebraic attacks and decomposition of symmetric Boolean functions. IEEE Trans. Inform. Theory **57**, 4817–4821 (2011)
18. MacWilliams, F.N., Sloane, N.: The Theory of Error Correcting Codes. North-Holland Publishing Company, Amsterdam (1977)
19. Meier, W., Pasalic, E., Carlet, C.: Algebraic attacks and decomposition of boolean functions. In: Cachin, C., Camenisch, J.L. (eds.) EUROCRYPT 2004. LNCS, vol. 3027, pp. 474–491. Springer, Heidelberg (2004)
20. Mesnager, S.: Bent and hyper-bent functions in polynomial form and their link with some exponential sums and dickson polynomials. IEEE Trans. Inform. Theory **57**, 5996–6009 (2011)
21. Lidl, R., Niederreiter, H.: Finite Fields. Encyclopedia of Mathematics and its Applications, vol. 20. Cambridge University Press, Cambridge (1996)
22. Pasalic, E.: Almost fully optimized infinite classes of Boolean functions resistant to (fast) algebraic cryptanalysis. In: Lee, P.J., Cheon, J.H. (eds.) ICISC 2008. LNCS, vol. 5461, pp. 399–414. Springer, Heidelberg (2009)
23. Qu, L., Feng, K., Liu, F., Wang, L.: Constructing symmetric Boolean functions with maximum algebraic immunity. IEEE Trans. Inform. Theory **55**, 2406–2412 (2009)
24. Rizomiliotis, P.: On the resistance of Boolean functions against algebraic attacks using univariate polynomial representation. IEEE Trans. Inform. Theory **56**, 4014–4024 (2010)

25. Sarkar, S., Maitra, S.: Construction of rotation symmetric Boolean functions on odd number of variables with maximum algebraic immunity. In: Boztaş, S., Lu, H.-F.F. (eds.) AAECC 2007. LNCS, vol. 4851, pp. 271–280. Springer, Heidelberg (2007)
26. Su, S., Tang, X., Zeng, X.: A systematic method of constructing Boolean functions with optimal algebraic immunity based on the generator matrix of the Reed-Muller code. Des. Codes Cryptogr. **72**, 653–673 (2014)
27. Su, S., Tang, X.: Construction of rotation symmetric Boolean functions with optimal algebraic immunity and high nonlinearity. Des. Codes Cryptogr. **71**, 183–199 (2014)
28. Tang, D., Carlet, C., Tang, X.: Highly nonlinear Boolean functions with optimal algebraic immunity and good behavior against fast algebraic attacks. IEEE Trans. Inform. Theory **59**, 653–664 (2013)
29. Tu, Z., Deng, Y.: A conjecture on binary string and its applications on constructing Boolean functions of optimal algebraic immunity. Des. Codes Cryptogr. **60**, 1–14 (2011)
30. Wang, Q., Peng, J., Kan, H.: Constructions of cryptographically significant Boolean functions using primitive polynomials. IEEE Trans. Inform. Theory **56**, 3048–3053 (2010)
31. Zeng, X., Carlet, C., Shan, J., Hu, L.: More balanced Boolean functions with optimal algebraic immunity and good nonlinearity and resistance to fast algebraic attacks. IEEE Trans. Inform. Theory **57**, 6310–6320 (2011)

Results on Characterizations of Plateaued Functions in Arbitrary Characteristic

Sihem Mesnager[1,2,3], Ferruh Özbudak[4,5], and Ahmet Sınak[5,6]([✉])

[1] Department of Mathematics, University of Paris VIII, Saint-Denis, France
smesnager@univ-paris8.fr
[2] LAGA, UMR 7539, CNRS, University of Paris XIII, Villetaneuse, France
[3] Telecom ParisTech, Paris, France
[4] Department of Mathematics, Middle East Technical University, Ankara, Turkey
[5] Institute of Applied Mathematics, Middle East Technical University,
Ankara, Turkey
{ozbudak,ahmet.sinak}@metu.edu.tr
[6] Department of Mathematics and Computer Sciences,
Necmettin Erbakan University, Konya, Turkey

Abstract. Bent and plateaued functions play a significant role in cryptography since they can have various desirable cryptographic properties. In this work, we first provide the characterizations of plateaued functions in terms of the moments of their Walsh transforms. Next, we generalize the characterizations of Boolean bent and plateaued functions in terms of their second-order derivatives to arbitrary characteristic. Moreover, we present a new characterization of plateaued functions in terms of fourth power moments of their Walsh transforms. Furthermore, we give a new proof of the characterization of vectorial bent functions. Finally, we present the characterizations of vectorial s-plateaued functions in terms of moments of their Walsh transforms and the zeros of their second-order derivatives.

Keywords: Bent functions · Plateaued functions · Vectorial functions

1 Introduction

The functions over a binary field are called *Boolean* functions. Boolean bent functions are a special type of Boolean functions. These functions were introduced by Rothaus in [26], generalized to p-ary bent functions by Kumar et al. in [19] and further studied in [14,15,17,27]. Plateaued functions over a binary field are a generalization of Boolean bent functions. They were introduced and initially studied by Zheng and Zhang in [28]. The Walsh-Hadamard spectrum is an important tool to define and design plateaued functions. Some plateaued functions have low Hadamard transform, which provides protection against fast correlation attacks and linear cryptanalysis. In addition to the useful properties of bent functions such as high nonlinearity, resiliency, low additive autocorrelation, high algebraic degree and satisfy propagation criteria, some plateaued

© Springer International Publishing Switzerland 2016
E. Pasalic and L.R. Knudsen (Eds.): BalkanCryptSec 2015, LNCS 9540, pp. 17–30, 2016.
DOI: 10.1007/978-3-319-29172-7_2

functions may have the other desirable cryptographic properties such as balancedness and correlation immunity. On the other hand, plateaued functions include three significant classes of Boolean functions: the well-known bent functions (called 0-plateaued functions), the near-bent functions (called 1-plateaued functions) and the semi-bent functions (called 2-plateaued functions). Boolean plateaued functions have been widely studied (for example, see in [1,6–8,18,20–22,29]) due to their cryptographic properties. A complete survey on Boolean plateaued functions was given by Mesnager in [24].

In characteristic 2, 0-plateaued functions and 2-plateaued functions exist when n is even, while 1-plateaued functions exist when n is odd. Therefore, Boolean plateaued functions were generalized to p-ary plateaued functions (for example, see in [11]). Recently, Mesnager [23] characterized p-ary plateaued functions in terms of the moments of their Walsh transforms. Moreover, in characteristic p, she established a link between the fourth power moment and the derivative. More recently, interesting characterizations of plateaued functions in characteristic 2 (different from those exhibited (in characteristic p) in [23]) have been provided (without proofs) by Carlet in [3].

In this paper, we are motivated by [7,23] and our results are valid in arbitrary characteristic. After presenting the basic tools in Sect. 2, we give in Sect. 3 the characterizations of plateaued functions in terms of the moments of their Walsh transforms. In Sect. 4, we generalize the characterizations of bent and plateaued functions in characteristic 2 given in [7] to arbitrary characteristic. Moreover, we present a new characterization of plateaued functions in terms of the fourth power moments of their Walsh transforms. In Sect. 5, we furthermore provide a link between the balancedness of the first-order derivatives of vectorial bent functions and the number of zeros of their second-order derivatives. Finally, Sect. 6 gives the characterizations of vectorial s-plateaued functions in terms of the moments of their Walsh transforms and the number of zeros of their second-order derivatives.

2   Preliminaries

We denote the finite field with p^n elements by $\mathbb{F}_{p^n}$ where p is a prime number and n is a positive integer. The set of nonzero elements of $\mathbb{F}_{p^n}$ is denoted by $\mathbb{F}_{p^n}^\star$. Notice that the finite field $\mathbb{F}_{p^n}$ can be seen as an n-dimensional vector space over $\mathbb{F}_p$ and denoted by $\mathbb{F}_p^n$. The *trace* function of $\alpha \in \mathbb{F}_{p^n}$ over $\mathbb{F}_p$ is defined as $\mathrm{Tr}_{\mathbb{F}_{p^n}/\mathbb{F}_p}(\alpha) = \alpha + \alpha^p + \cdots + \alpha^{p^{n-1}}$. In this paper, the *absolute trace* of α over $\mathbb{F}_p$ is denoted by $\mathrm{Tr}_p^n(\alpha)$. Let f be a function from $\mathbb{F}_{p^n}$ to $\mathbb{F}_p$ and ϵ_p be a *primitive p-th root of unity* in $\mathbb{C}$. The *sign* function of f from $\mathbb{F}_p^n$ to $\mathbb{C}$ is denoted by χ_f defined as $\chi_f(x) = \epsilon_p^{f(x)}$ for all $x \in \mathbb{F}_p^n$. The Fourier transform $\widehat{\chi_f}$ of the function χ_f is defined as

$$\widehat{\chi_f} : \mathbb{F}_p^n \to \mathbb{C}$$
$$\omega \longmapsto \widehat{\chi_f}(\omega) = \sum_{x \in \mathbb{F}_p^n} \chi_f(x) \epsilon_p^{-\omega \cdot x},$$

called the *Walsh transform* of f at $w \in \mathbb{F}_p^n$, where "$\cdot$" is any scalar product in $\mathbb{F}_p^n$. As the notion of Walsh transform concerns a scalar product, it is suitable to take the isomorphism between the scalar product "$\cdot$" in $\mathbb{F}_p^n$ and the trace of the product $w \cdot x = \mathrm{Tr}_p^{p^n}(wx)$ in $\mathbb{F}_{p^n}$. Thus, the Walsh transform of f at $w \in \mathbb{F}_{p^n}$ can be given as

$$\widehat{\chi}_f(w) = \sum_{x \in \mathbb{F}_{p^n}} \epsilon_p^{f(x) - \mathrm{Tr}_p^{p^n}(wx)}.$$

A function f is called *bent* if $|\widehat{\chi}_f(w)| = p^{\frac{n}{2}}$ for all $w \in \mathbb{F}_{p^n}$, and f is called *s-plateaued* if $|\widehat{\chi}_f(w)| \in \left\{0, p^{\frac{n+s}{2}}\right\}$ for all $w \in \mathbb{F}_{p^n}$ and a fixed integer $0 \le s \le n$. It is obvious that bent functions are 0-plateaued functions. The following equation is known as the *Parseval identity*:

$$\sum_{w \in \mathbb{F}_{p^n}} |\widehat{\chi}_f(w)|^2 = p^{2n}. \tag{1}$$

The following tools were previously introduced in the literature (for example, see in [4] and [23]). The below Lemma is useful to prove some results in the next sections.

Lemma 1. *Let f be an s-plateaued function from $\mathbb{F}_{p^n}$ to $\mathbb{F}_p$. Then for $w \in \mathbb{F}_{p^n}$, $|\widehat{\chi}_f(w)|$ takes p^{n-s} times the value $p^{\frac{n+s}{2}}$ and $p^n - p^{n-s}$ times the value 0.*

For a non-negative integer i, the moment of Walsh transforms of f is defined as

$$S_i(f) = \sum_{w \in \mathbb{F}_{p^n}} |\widehat{\chi}_f(w)|^{2i}.$$

It is obvious that $S_0(f) = p^n$ and $S_1(f) = p^{2n}$ by (1). For every integer A and every non-negative integer i, the following equation holds

$$\sum_{w \in \mathbb{F}_{p^n}} \left(|\widehat{\chi}_f(w)|^2 - A\right)^2 |\widehat{\chi}_f(w)|^{2i} = S_{i+2}(f) - 2AS_{i+1}(f) + A^2 S_i(f). \tag{2}$$

The derivative of f at $a \in \mathbb{F}_{p^n}$ is the map $\mathcal{D}_a f$ from $\mathbb{F}_{p^n}$ to $\mathbb{F}_p$ defined as

$$\mathcal{D}_a f(x) = f(x + a) - f(x), \quad \forall x \in \mathbb{F}_{p^n}.$$

Let F be a vectorial function from $\mathbb{F}_{p^n}$ to $\mathbb{F}_{p^m}$. The derivative of F at $a \in \mathbb{F}_{p^n}$ is the map $\mathcal{D}_a F$ from $\mathbb{F}_{p^n}$ to $\mathbb{F}_{p^m}$ defined as

$$\mathcal{D}_a F(x) = F(x + a) - F(x), \quad \forall x \in \mathbb{F}_{p^n}.$$

3   Characterizations of Plateaued Functions

In this section, our results are originated from [23]. We give the characterizations of s-plateaued functions via the sequence of even moments of their Walsh transforms. The following seems to be more practical than [23, Theorem 1] in some applications.

Theorem 1. *Let f be a function from $\mathbb{F}_{p^n}$ to $\mathbb{F}_p$. Let s be an integer with $0 \leq s \leq n$ and $i, j \in \mathbb{Z}^+$. Then the followings are equivalent:*

1. f is s-plateaued for $s > 0$.

2. $S_i(f)S_j(f) = S_{i+1}(f)S_{j-1}(f)$ for all $i \geq 1$ and $j \geq 2$.

Moreover, f is bent if and only if (2) holds for all $i, j \in \mathbb{Z}^+$.

Proof. Suppose that f is s-plateaued for $s > 0$. By Lemma 1, it is easily seen that

$$S_i(f)S_j(f) = S_{i+1}(f)S_{j-1}(f), \quad \forall i \geq 1, j \geq 2.$$

Conversely, for $j = i + 2$ and $A = \frac{S_{i+1}(f)}{S_i(f)}$ in (2), the proof is the same as the proof of [23, Theorem 1]. $\qquad\square$

In fact, Theorem 1 is equivalent to [23, Theorem 1], which can be shown as follows.

Corollary 1. *Let f be a function from $\mathbb{F}_{p^n}$ to $\mathbb{F}_p$. Then the followings are equivalent:*

1. $S_i(f)S_i(f) = S_{i+1}(f)S_{i-1}(f)$ for all $i \geq 2$.
2. $S_i(f)S_j(f) = S_{i+1}(f)S_{j-1}(f)$ for all $i, j \geq 2$.

Proof. Suppose that (1) holds. Without loss of generality, we may assume $i < j$ and fix $i \geq 2$. We proceed by induction on j. For $j = i + 1$ and $j = i + 2$, then (2) trivial holds. Let $j = i + 3$. From (1), we get

$$S_{i+1}(f)S_{i+1}(f) = S_{i+2}(f)S_i(f),$$
$$S_{i+2}(f)S_{i+2}(f) = S_{i+3}(f)S_{i+1}(f).$$

It follows that $S_i(f)S_{i+3}(f) = S_{i+1}(f)S_{i+2}(f)$. Then, (2) holds for $j = i + 3$. For $j = i + k$, assume that (2) holds. We then have

$$S_i(f)S_{i+k}(f) \qquad = S_{i+1}(f)S_{i+k-1}(f),$$
$$S_{i+k-1}(f)S_{i+k+1}(f) = S_{i+k}(f)S_{i+k}(f).$$

It follows that $S_i(f)S_{i+k+1}(f) = S_{i+1}(f)S_{i+k}(f)$. Therefore, (2) holds for $j = i + k + 1$. The converse is obvious for $j = i$. $\qquad\square$

For a function f from $\mathbb{F}_{p^n}$ to $\mathbb{F}_p$, Mesnager in [23] showed that $S_2(f) \geq p^{3n}$ and also

$$S_2(f) = p^{3n} \text{ if and only if } f \text{ is bent.} \qquad (3)$$

We deduce that, for a bent function f, the sequence $S_i(f)$ is a simple geometric sequence.

Corollary 2. *Let f be a function from $\mathbb{F}_{p^n}$ to $\mathbb{F}_p$. If f is a bent function, then for all $i \in \mathbb{N}$*

$$S_i(f) = p^{(i+1)n}. \qquad (4)$$

Proof. By (1) and (3), $S_1(f) = p^{2n}$ and $S_2(f) = p^{3n}$, respectively. By Theorem 1, we get $S_i(f) = \frac{S_{i-1}(f)^2}{S_{i-2}(f)} = p^{(i+1)n}$ for all $i \geq 3$, recursively. Thus, (4) holds for all $i \in \mathbb{N}$. □

We also deduce from (3) the following characterization of s-plateaued functions via the moments of their Walsh transforms.

Theorem 2. *Let f be a function from $\mathbb{F}_{p^n}$ to $\mathbb{F}_p$ and s be an integer with $1 \leq s \leq n$. Then*

$$f \text{ is } s\text{-plateaued if and only if } S_2(f) = p^{3n+s} \text{ and } S_3(f) = p^{4n+2s}.$$

Proof. Assume that f is s-plateaued. By (2) with $A = p^{n+s}$ and $i = 0$,

$$\sum_{\omega \in \mathbb{F}_{p^n}} \left(|\widehat{\chi}_f(\omega)|^2 - p^{n+s} \right)^2 = S_2(f) - 2p^{n+s}S_1(f) + p^{2n+2s}S_0(f)$$

$$= (p^n - p^{n-s})(-p^{n+s})^2 \tag{5}$$

where the last equality of (5) follows from Lemma 1. Therefore, $S_2(f) = p^{3n+s}$ from (5) and $S_3(f) = \frac{S_2(f)^2}{S_1(f)} = p^{4n+2s}$ by Theorem 1.

Conversely, suppose that $S_2(f) = p^{3n+s}$ and $S_3(f) = p^{4n+2s}$. By (2) with $A = p^{n+s}$ and $i = 1$, we get the following:

$$\sum_{\omega \in \mathbb{F}_{p^n}} \left(|\widehat{\chi}_f(\omega)|^2 - p^{n+s} \right)^2 |\widehat{\chi}_f(\omega)|^2 = S_3(f) - 2p^{n+s}S_2(f) + p^{2n+2s}S_1(f) = 0.$$

Therefore, $|\widehat{\chi}_f(\omega)| \in \left\{ 0, p^{\frac{n+s}{2}} \right\}$ for all $\omega \in \mathbb{F}_{p^n}$, which implies that f is s-plateaued. □

We deduce that, for an s-plateaued function f, the sequence $S_i(f)$ is also a simple geometric sequence.

Corollary 3. *Let f be a function from $\mathbb{F}_{p^n}$ to $\mathbb{F}_p$ and s be an integer with $1 \leq s \leq n$. If f is an s-plateaued function, then for all $i \in \mathbb{Z}^+$*

$$S_i(f) = p^{(i+1)n+(i-1)s}. \tag{6}$$

Proof. By Theorem 2, $S_2(f) = p^{3n+s}$ and $S_3(f) = p^{4n+2s}$. By Theorem 1, we get

$$S_i(f) = \frac{S_{i-1}(f)^2}{S_{i-2}(f)} = p^{(i+1)n+(i-1)s}$$

for all $i \geq 4$, recursively. Thus, (6) holds for all $i \in \mathbb{Z}^+$. □

4   Characterizations of Bent and Plateaued Functions

The characterizations of bent and plateaued functions in characteristic 2 in terms of the second-order derivatives were firstly given by Carlet and Prouff in [7]. We provide the generalization of their characterizations for any characteristic p as the following.

Theorem 3. *Let f be a function from $\mathbb{F}_{p^n}$ to $\mathbb{F}_p$ and s be an integer with $0 \leq s \leq n$. Then, f is s-plateaued if and only if*

$$\sum_{a,b\in\mathbb{F}_{p^n}} \epsilon_p^{D_b D_a f(x)} = \theta, \quad \forall x \in \mathbb{F}_{p^n} \tag{7}$$

with $\theta = p^{n+s}$. In particular, f is bent if and only if $\theta = p^n$ for $s = 0$.

Proof. For a function f,

$$\sum_{a,b\in\mathbb{F}_{p^n}} \epsilon_p^{D_b D_a f(x)} = \sum_{a,b\in\mathbb{F}_{p^n}} \epsilon_p^{f(x+a+b)-f(x+a)-f(x+b)+f(x)} = \theta, \quad \forall x \in \mathbb{F}_{p^n}$$

if and only if

$$\sum_{a,b\in\mathbb{F}_{p^n}} \epsilon_p^{f(x+a+b)-f(x+a)-f(x+b)} = \theta\epsilon_p^{-f(x)}, \quad \forall x \in \mathbb{F}_{p^n}. \tag{8}$$

Let $a_1 = x + a$ and $b_1 = x + b$ for $a_1, b_1 \in \mathbb{F}_{p^n}$. Thus, (8) is equivalent to

$$\sum_{a_1,b_1\in\mathbb{F}_{p^n}} \epsilon_p^{f(a_1+b_1-x)-f(a_1)-f(b_1)} = \theta\epsilon_p^{-f(x)}, \quad \forall x \in \mathbb{F}_{p^n}. \tag{9}$$

Let the left-hand side of (9) be $G_1(x)$ and its right-hand side be $G_2(x)$ for all $x \in \mathbb{F}_{p^n}$, i.e., $G_1(x) = G_2(x)$ for all $x \in \mathbb{F}_{p^n}$. We recall the following well-known property of the Fourier transform: for a function G from $\mathbb{F}_{p^n}$ to $\mathbb{C}$,

$$G(x) = 0 \quad \forall x \in \mathbb{F}_{p^n} \quad \text{if and only if} \quad \widehat{G}(\omega) = \sum_{x\in\mathbb{F}_{p^n}} G(x)\epsilon_p^{-\text{Tr}_p^{p^n}(\omega x)} = 0, \quad \forall \omega \in \mathbb{F}_{p^n}$$

where $\widehat{G}$ is the Fourier transform of G. Then, for all $\omega \in \mathbb{F}_{p^n}$ the Fourier transforms of G_1 and G_2 are equal:

$$\widehat{G}_1(\omega) = \sum_{x\in\mathbb{F}_{p^n}} G_1(x)\epsilon_p^{-\text{Tr}_p^{p^n}(\omega x)} = \sum_{x\in\mathbb{F}_{p^n}} G_2(x)\epsilon_p^{-\text{Tr}_p^{p^n}(\omega x)} = \widehat{G}_2(\omega).$$

The Fourier transform $\widehat{G}_1$ of G_1 at $\omega \in \mathbb{F}_{p^n}$ can be computed in terms of $\widehat{\chi}_f$ as the following:

$$\widehat{G}_1(\omega) = \sum_{x\in\mathbb{F}_{p^n}} G_1(x)\epsilon_p^{-\text{Tr}_p^{p^n}(\omega x)} = \sum_{x\in\mathbb{F}_{p^n}}\sum_{a_1,b_1\in\mathbb{F}_{p^n}} \epsilon_p^{f(a_1+b_1-x)-f(a_1)-f(b_1)}\epsilon_p^{-\text{Tr}_p^{p^n}(\omega x)}$$

$$= \sum_{a_1\in\mathbb{F}_{p^n}} \epsilon_p^{-f(a_1)-\text{Tr}_p^{p^n}(\omega a_1)}\sum_{b_1\in\mathbb{F}_{p^n}} \epsilon_p^{-f(b_1)-\text{Tr}_p^{p^n}(\omega b_1)}\sum_{x\in\mathbb{F}_{p^n}} \epsilon_p^{f(a_1+b_1-x)-\text{Tr}_p^{p^n}(-\omega(a_1+b_1-x))}$$

$$= (-\widehat{\chi}_f)(\omega)(-\widehat{\chi}_f)(\omega)\widehat{\chi}_f(-\omega).$$

Similarly, for all $\omega \in \mathbb{F}_{p^n}$

$$\widehat{G}_2(\omega) = \sum_{x\in\mathbb{F}_{p^n}} G_2(x)\epsilon_p^{-\text{Tr}_p^{p^n}(\omega x)} = \sum_{x\in\mathbb{F}_{p^n}} \theta\epsilon_p^{-f(x)-\text{Tr}_p^{p^n}(\omega x)} = \theta(-\widehat{\chi}_f)(\omega).$$

Recall that for all $\omega \in \mathbb{F}_{p^n}$

$$(-\widehat{\chi}_f)(\omega) = \sum_{x \in \mathbb{F}_{p^n}} \epsilon_p^{-f(x)-\mathrm{Tr}_p^n(\omega x)} = \overline{\sum_{x \in \mathbb{F}_{p^n}} \epsilon_p^{f(x)+\mathrm{Tr}_p^n(\omega x)}} = \overline{\sum_{x \in \mathbb{F}_{p^n}} \epsilon_p^{f(x)-\mathrm{Tr}_p^n(-\omega x)}} = \overline{\widehat{\chi}_f(-\omega)}.$$

Then for all $\omega \in \mathbb{F}_{p^n}$

$$\widehat{\chi}_f(-\omega)\overline{\widehat{\chi}_f(-\omega)}\widehat{\chi}_f(-\omega) = \theta\widehat{\chi}_f(-\omega).$$

Therefore, (7) holds if and only if $|\widehat{\chi}_f(\omega)|^2 \in \{0, \theta\}$ for all $\omega \in \mathbb{F}_{p^n}$ where $\theta = p^{n+s}$. In particular, for $s = 0$, (7) holds if and only if $|\widehat{\chi}_f(\omega)|^2 = p^n$ for all $\omega \in \mathbb{F}_{p^n}$. □

Theorem 3 can be rewritten as the following.

Corollary 4. *Let f be a function from $\mathbb{F}_{p^n}$ to $\mathbb{F}_p$ and s be an integer with $0 \le s \le n$. Then, f is s-plateaued if and only if*

$$\sum_{a,b,x \in \mathbb{F}_{p^n}} \epsilon_p^{\mathcal{D}_b \mathcal{D}_a f(x)} = p^{2n+s}.$$

We remember a link between the second-order derivatives and the fourth power moments of the Walsh transforms in characteristic p in the following Proposition (see [23, Proposition 1], [16, Theorem 10] and in [13]).

Proposition 1. *Let f be a function from $\mathbb{F}_{p^n}$ to $\mathbb{F}_p$. Then*

$$S_2(f) = \sum_{\omega \in \mathbb{F}_{p^n}} |\widehat{\chi}_f(\omega)|^4 = p^n \sum_{a,b,x \in \mathbb{F}_{p^n}} \epsilon_p^{\mathcal{D}_b \mathcal{D}_a f(x)}.$$

We deduce a new characterization of s-plateaued functions in terms of the fourth power moments of their Walsh transforms.

Theorem 4. *Let f be a function from $\mathbb{F}_{p^n}$ to $\mathbb{F}_p$ and s be an integer with $0 \le s \le n$. Then, f is s-plateaued if and only if*

$$S_2(f) = \sum_{\omega \in \mathbb{F}_{p^n}} |\widehat{\chi}_f(\omega)|^4 = p^{3n+s}.$$

In particular, f is bent if and only if $S_2(f) = p^{3n}$.

Proof. By Corollary 4 and Proposition 1, f is s-plateaued if and only if

$$S_2(f) = \sum_{\omega \in \mathbb{F}_{p^n}} |\widehat{\chi}_f(\omega)|^4 = p^n \sum_{a,b,x \in \mathbb{F}_{p^n}} \epsilon_p^{\mathcal{D}_b \mathcal{D}_a f(x)} = p^{3n+s}.$$

□

Notice that Theorem 2 is also a direct corollary of Theorem 4. Let us introduce an example of quadratic s-plateaued functions.

Example 1. Let p be an odd prime and $n \geq 2$ be an integer. Let f be an arbitrary $\mathbb{F}_p$-quadratic form from $\mathbb{F}_{p^n}$ to $\mathbb{F}_p$ defined as

$$f(x) = \text{Tr}_p^{p^n}\left(a_0 x^2 + a_1 x^{p+1} + a_2 x^{p^2+1} + \cdots + a_{\lfloor \frac{n}{2} \rfloor} x^{p^{\lfloor \frac{n}{2} \rfloor}+1}\right).$$

The radical of f given by

$$W = \{x \in \mathbb{F}_{p^n} : f(x+y) = f(x) + f(y), \forall y \in \mathbb{F}_{p^n}\}$$

is an $\mathbb{F}_p$-linear subspace of $\mathbb{F}_{p^n}$. Let $\dim_{\mathbb{F}_p} W = s$. It follows from [9, the proof of Theorem 4.1] that for all $\omega \in \mathbb{F}_{p^n}$

$$|\widehat{\chi}_f(\omega)|^2 = 0 \quad \text{or} \quad p^{2s} \sum_{y_1,\ldots,y_{n-s} \in \mathbb{F}_p} \sum_{z_1,\ldots,z_{n-s} \in \mathbb{F}_p} \epsilon_p^{H(y_1,\ldots,y_{n-s}) - H(z_1,\ldots,z_{n-s})}$$

where $H(x_1,\ldots,x_{n-s}) = \frac{1}{2}(x_1^2 + \cdots + x_{n-s-1}^2 + dx_{n-s}^2)$ and $d \in \mathbb{F}_p^\star$. For each pair y_i and z_i where $i = 1,\ldots,n-s$, it is easy to see that

$$\sum_{y_i,z_i \in \mathbb{F}_p} \epsilon_p^{\frac{1}{2}(y_i^2 - z_i^2)} = \sum_{t_{i1},t_{i2} \in \mathbb{F}_p} \epsilon_p^{\frac{1}{2}(t_{i1}t_{i2})} = \sum_{t_{i2} \in \mathbb{F}_p} \left(\sum_{t_{i1} \in \mathbb{F}_p} \epsilon_p^{\frac{1}{2}t_{i1}} \right) = p.$$

Therefore, we conclude that $|\widehat{\chi}_f(\omega)|^2 \in \{0, p^{n+s}\}$ for all $\omega \in \mathbb{F}_{p^n}$. Moreover, [10, Proposition 5.8] gives an algorithm to construct a such quadratic form f with radical W of dimension s with $0 \leq s \leq n-1$. In fact, this algorithm holds for any finite field $\mathbb{F}_q$ where q is a prime power. Hence, for each odd prime p, integers $n \geq 2$ and s with $0 \leq s \leq n-1$, there exists a quadratic p-ary s-plateaued function f from $\mathbb{F}_{p^n}$ to $\mathbb{F}_p$. For example, for $p = 3$ and $n = 5$, we provide the following s-plateaued functions:

- $f_1(x) = \text{Tr}_3^{3^5}(x^2 + x^4 + 2x^{10})$ is the quadratic 0-plateaued function,
- $f_2(x) = \text{Tr}_3^{3^5}(x^2 + x^4 + x^{10})$ is the quadratic 1-plateaued function,
- $f_3(x) = \text{Tr}_3^{3^5}(\xi x^2 + x^4 + 2x^{10})$ is the quadratic 2-plateaued function,
- $f_4(x) = \text{Tr}_3^{3^5}(\xi^2 x^2 + 2x^4 + \xi^{28} x^{10})$ is the quadratic 3-plateaued function and
- $f_5(x) = \text{Tr}_3^{3^5}(x^2 + 2x^4 + 2x^{10})$ is the quadratic 4-plateaued function

where ξ is a primitive element of $\mathbb{F}_{3^5}$ with $\xi^5 + 2\xi + 1 = 0$.

5   Characterization of Vectorial Bent Functions

The present section provides a new proof of characterization of vectorial bent functions given in [23]. The vectorial bent function is defined as the following.

Definition 1. Let F be a vectorial function from $\mathbb{F}_{p^n}$ to $\mathbb{F}_{p^m}$. For every $\lambda \in \mathbb{F}_{p^m}^\star$, the component function f_λ from $\mathbb{F}_{p^n}$ to $\mathbb{F}_p$ is defined as $f_\lambda(x) = \text{Tr}_p^{p^m}(\lambda F(x))$ for all $x \in \mathbb{F}_{p^n}$. Then, F is called *vectorial bent* if f_λ is bent for all $\lambda \in \mathbb{F}_{p^m}^\star$.

In [25, Theorem 2.3], vectorial bent functions were characterized by using their derivatives: A vectorial function F is bent if and only if $\mathcal{D}_a F$ is balanced for all $a \in \mathbb{F}_{p^n}^\star$. Recently, Mesnager characterized the vectorial bent functions in [23, Theorem 6] by using the number of zeros of second-order derivatives: A vectorial function F is bent if and only if

$$\mathfrak{N}(F) = |\{(a, b, x) \in \mathbb{F}_{p^n}^3 : \mathcal{D}_b \mathcal{D}_a F(x) = 0\}| = p^{3n-m} + p^{2n} - p^{2n-m}.$$

It would be interesting to prove directly that $\mathcal{D}_a F$ is balanced for all $a \in \mathbb{F}_{p^n}^\star$ if and only if $\mathfrak{N}(F) = p^{3n-m} + p^{2n} - p^{2n-m}$ without using the bentness of vectorial function F. Before proving it, we start with a well-known result.

Lemma 2. *Let $x_1, x_2, \ldots, x_m$ be positive real numbers such that $x_1 + x_2 + \cdots + x_m = n$. We then have*

$$x_1^2 + x_2^2 + \cdots + x_m^2 \geq \frac{n^2}{m} \tag{10}$$

and the equality in (10) holds if and only if $x_1 = x_2 = \cdots = x_m$.

The following Lemma is similar to Proposition 1, items (1) and (2) in [5], but it is valid in arbitrary characteristic.

Lemma 3. *Let G be a vectorial function from $\mathbb{F}_{p^n}$ to $\mathbb{F}_{p^m}$. Then*

$$|\{(x_1, x_2) \in \mathbb{F}_{p^n}^2 : G(x_1) = G(x_2)\}| \geq p^{2n-m} \tag{11}$$

and the equality in (11) holds if and only if G is balanced.

Proof. Let $A_j = \{x \in \mathbb{F}_{p^n} : G(x) = y_j \in \mathbb{F}_{p^m}\}$ and $z_j = |A_j|$ for $j \in \{1, \ldots, p^m\}$. Then we have

$$|\{(x_1, x_2) \in \mathbb{F}_{p^n}^2 : G(x_1) = G(x_2)\}| = \left| \bigcup_{j=1}^{p^m} \{(x_1, x_2) \in \mathbb{F}_{p^n}^2 : x_1, x_2 \in A_j\} \right| = \sum_{j=1}^{p^m} |A_j|^2 = \sum_{j=1}^{p^m} z_j^2.$$

By Lemma 2, for $\sum_{j=1}^{p^m} z_j = p^n$ and $z_j \geq 0$, we get $\sum_{j=1}^{p^m} z_j^2 \geq p^{2n-m}$. Thus, (11) holds. Notice that G is balanced if and only if $z_1 = z_2 = \cdots = z_{p^m}$. The final assertion also follows from Lemma 2. $\qquad\square$

Proposition 2. *Let F be a vectorial function from $\mathbb{F}_{p^n}$ to $\mathbb{F}_{p^m}$. Then*

$$\mathcal{D}_a F \text{ is balanced for all } a \in \mathbb{F}_{p^n}^\star \iff \mathfrak{N}(F) = p^{3n-m} + p^{2n} - p^{2n-m} \tag{12}$$

where $\mathfrak{N}(F) = |\{(a, b, x) \in \mathbb{F}_{p^n}^3 : \mathcal{D}_b \mathcal{D}_a F(x) = 0\}|$.

Proof. The second-order derivative of F at $(a, b) \in \mathbb{F}_{p^n}^2$ is

$$\mathcal{D}_b \mathcal{D}_a F(x) = F(x + a + b) + F(x) - F(x + b) - F(x + a).$$

Notice that for $(a, b, x) \in \mathbb{F}_{p^n}^3$, $\mathcal{D}_b \mathcal{D}_a F(x) = 0$ if and only if

$$\mathcal{D}_a F(x) = \mathcal{D}_a F(x + b). \tag{13}$$

First, for $n = m$, let us prove that $\mathcal{D}_a F$ is balanced for all $a \in \mathbb{F}_{p^n}^\star$ if and only if $\mathfrak{N}(F) = 2p^{2n} - p^n$. For $a = 0$, it is easy to see that (13) holds for all $b, x \in \mathbb{F}_{p^n}$ since $\mathcal{D}_a F$ is zero map. Then, $|\{(0, b, x) \in \mathbb{F}_{p^n}^3 : \mathcal{D}_b \mathcal{D}_a F(x) = 0\}| = p^{2n}$. For $a \neq 0$, by Lemma 3, the number of pairs $(b, x) \in \mathbb{F}_{p^n}^2$ satisfying (13) is equal to p^n if and only if $\mathcal{D}_a F$ is balanced. Then, $|\{(a, b, x) \in \mathbb{F}_{p^n}^3 : a \neq 0, \mathcal{D}_b \mathcal{D}_a F(x) = 0\}| = p^{2n} - p^n$. Therefore, $\mathcal{D}_a F$ is balanced for all $a \in \mathbb{F}_{p^n}^\star$ if and only if $\mathfrak{N}(F) = 2p^{2n} - p^n$.

Now, let $n \neq m$. For $a = 0$, we get $|\{(0, b, x) \in \mathbb{F}_{p^n}^3 : \mathcal{D}_b \mathcal{D}_a F(x) = 0\}| = p^{2n}$. For $a \neq 0$, by Lemma 3, the number of pairs $(b, x) \in \mathbb{F}_{p^n}^2$ satisfying (13) is equal to p^{2n-m} if and only if $\mathcal{D}_a F$ is balanced. Then, $|\{(a, b, x) \in \mathbb{F}_{p^n}^3 : a \neq 0, \mathcal{D}_b \mathcal{D}_a F(x) = 0\}| = (p^n - 1)p^{2n-m}$. Thus, (12) holds. $\square$

In [23, Corollary 1], F is vectorial bent if and only if $\mathfrak{N}^\star(F) = (p^n - 1)(p^{2n-m} - p^n)$ where
$$\mathfrak{N}^\star(F) = |\{(a, b, x) \in \mathbb{F}_{p^n}^\star \times \mathbb{F}_{p^n}^\star \times \mathbb{F}_{p^n} : \mathcal{D}_b \mathcal{D}_a F(x) = 0\}|.$$

Then, $\mathcal{D}_a F$ is balanced for all $a \in \mathbb{F}_{p^n}^\star$ if and only if $\mathfrak{N}^\star(F) = (p^n - 1)(p^{2n-m} - p^n)$. This can be easily seen by Lemma 3.

6   Characterizations of Vectorial s-Plateaued Functions

In this section, we are interested in a special class of vectorial plateaued functions, which are called *vectorial s-plateaued* functions where $s \in \mathbb{N}$. We provide their characterizations in terms of the moments of their Walsh transforms and the number of zeros of their second-order derivatives.

The notion of vectorial plateaued functions in characteristic 2 were defined by Carlet in [2]. This can be given in arbitrary characteristic.

Definition 2. Let F be a vectorial function from $\mathbb{F}_{p^n}$ to $\mathbb{F}_{p^m}$. For every $\lambda \in \mathbb{F}_{p^m}^\star$, the component function f_λ from $\mathbb{F}_{p^n}$ to $\mathbb{F}_p$ is defined as $f_\lambda(x) = \mathrm{Tr}_p^{p^m}(\lambda F(x))$ for all $x \in \mathbb{F}_{p^n}$. Then, F is called *vectorial plateaued* if f_λ is plateaued for all $\lambda \in \mathbb{F}_{p^m}^\star$.

The notion of vectorial s-plateaued functions in arbitrary characteristic can be given as the following (for example, see in [12]).

Definition 3. Let F be a vectorial function from $\mathbb{F}_{p^n}$ to $\mathbb{F}_{p^m}$ and s be an integer with $0 \leq s \leq n$. For every $\lambda \in \mathbb{F}_{p^m}^\star$, the component function f_λ from $\mathbb{F}_{p^n}$ to $\mathbb{F}_p$ is defined as $f_\lambda(x) = \mathrm{Tr}_p^{p^m}(\lambda F(x))$ for all $x \in \mathbb{F}_{p^n}$. Then, F is called *vectorial s-plateaued* if f_λ is s-plateaued with the same amplitude s for all $\lambda \in \mathbb{F}_{p^m}^\star$.

Notice that F is said to be *vectorial s-plateaued* if and only if f_λ is s-plateaued with the same amplitude s for all $\lambda \in \mathbb{F}_{p^m}^\star$.

We can extract from Theorem 2 the following characterization of vectorial s-plateaued functions.

Theorem 5. *Let F be a vectorial function from $\mathbb{F}_{p^n}$ to $\mathbb{F}_{p^m}$. Then, F is a vectorial s-plateaued function if and only if*

$$\sum_{\lambda \in \mathbb{F}_{p^m}^\star} S_2(f_\lambda) = p^{3n+s}(p^m - 1) \quad and \quad \sum_{\lambda \in \mathbb{F}_{p^m}^\star} S_3(f_\lambda) = p^{4n+2s}(p^m - 1). \quad (14)$$

Proof. Suppose that F is vectorial s-plateaued. By Theorem 2 for all $\lambda \in \mathbb{F}_{p^m}^\star$, f_λ is s-plateaued if and only if $S_2(f_\lambda) = p^{3n+s}$ and $S_3(f_\lambda) = p^{4n+2s}$. Thus, (14) holds.

Conversely, suppose that (14) holds. By (2) with $A = p^{n+s}$ and $i = 1$, for all $\lambda \in \mathbb{F}_{p^m}^\star$

$$D_\lambda = \sum_{\omega \in \mathbb{F}_{p^n}} (|\widehat{\chi}_{f_\lambda}(\omega)|^2 - p^{n+s})^2 |\widehat{\chi}_{f_\lambda}(\omega)|^2 = S_3(f_\lambda) - 2p^{n+s} S_2(f_\lambda) + p^{2(n+s)} S_1(f_\lambda).$$

Then by (1) and (14),

$$\sum_{\lambda \in \mathbb{F}_{p^m}^\star} D_\lambda = p^{4n+2s}(p^m - 1) - 2p^{n+s} p^{3n+s}(p^m - 1) + p^{2n+2s} p^{2n}(p^m - 1) = 0.$$

Since $D_\lambda \geq 0$ and $\sum_{\lambda \in \mathbb{F}_{p^m}^\star} D_\lambda = 0$, we get $D_\lambda = 0$ for every $\lambda \in \mathbb{F}_{p^m}^\star$. Then, for every $\lambda \in \mathbb{F}_{p^m}^\star$, $|\widehat{\chi}_{f_\lambda}(\omega)| \in \left\{0, p^{\frac{n+s}{2}}\right\}$ for all $\omega \in \mathbb{F}_{p^n}$. Therefore, F is vectorial s-plateaued function. □

For a vectorial function F, the relation between the sum of $S_2(f_\lambda)$ for all $\lambda \in \mathbb{F}_{p^m}^\star$ and $\mathfrak{N}(F)$ was given by Mesnager in [23] as follows.

Proposition 3. *Let F be a vectorial function from $\mathbb{F}_{p^n}$ to $\mathbb{F}_{p^m}$. Then*

$$\sum_{\lambda \in \mathbb{F}_{p^m}^\star} S_2(f_\lambda) = p^{n+m} \mathfrak{N}(F) - p^{4n}$$

where $\mathfrak{N}(F) = |\{(a, b, x) \in \mathbb{F}_{p^n}^3 : \mathcal{D}_b \mathcal{D}_a F(x) = 0\}|$.

We conclude the following characterization of vectorial s-plateaued functions.

Theorem 6. *Let F be a vectorial function from $\mathbb{F}_{p^n}$ to $\mathbb{F}_{p^m}$. Then, F is vectorial s-plateaued if and only if $S_3(f_\lambda) = p^{4n+2s}$ for all $\lambda \in \mathbb{F}_{p^m}^\star$ and*

$$\mathfrak{N}(F) = p^{3n-m} + p^{2n+s} - p^{2n+s-m}$$

where $\mathfrak{N}(F) = |\{(a, b, x) \in \mathbb{F}_{p^n}^3 : \mathcal{D}_b \mathcal{D}_a F(x) = 0\}|$.

Proof. By Proposition 3 and Theorem 5, we get $p^{3n+s}(p^m - 1) = p^{n+m} \mathfrak{N}(F) - p^{4n}$. Thus, we obtain

$$\mathfrak{N}(F) = p^{3n-m} + p^{2n+s} - p^{2n+s-m}.$$

Conversely, by Proposition 3, we get

$$\sum_{\lambda \in \mathbb{F}_{p^m}^*} S_2(f_\lambda) = p^{n+m}(p^{3n-m} + p^{2n+s} - p^{2n+s-m}) - p^{4n} = p^{3n+s}(p^m - 1).$$

By assumption, $\sum_{\lambda \in \mathbb{F}_{p^m}^*} S_3(f_\lambda) = p^{4n+2s}(p^m - 1)$. Therefore, by Theorem 5, F is vectorial s-plateaued functions.   □

Let us give an example of vectorial quadratic s-plateaued functions.

Example 2. Let p be an odd prime, $m \geq 2$ and $r \geq 2$ be integers and $q = p^m$. Let f be an arbitrary $\mathbb{F}_q$-quadratic form from $\mathbb{F}_{q^r}$ to $\mathbb{F}_q$ given by

$$f(x) = \mathrm{Tr}_q^{q^r}(a_0 x^2 + a_1 x^{q+1} + a_2 x^{q^2+1} + \cdots + a_{\lfloor \frac{r}{2} \rfloor} x^{q^{\lfloor \frac{r}{2} \rfloor}+1}).$$

As in Example 1, by [9,10], we have an algorithm to construct f with radical

$$W = \{x \in \mathbb{F}_{q^r} : f(x+y) = f(x) + f(y), \forall y \in \mathbb{F}_{q^r}\} \tag{15}$$

of prescribed dimension s over $\mathbb{F}_q$ for each given integer s with $0 \leq s \leq r - 1$. For $\lambda \in \mathbb{F}_{p^m}^*$, the component function g_λ from $\mathbb{F}_{p^n}$ to $\mathbb{F}_p$ given by $g_\lambda(x) = \mathrm{Tr}_p^{p^m}(\lambda f(x))$ is an $\mathbb{F}_p$-quadratic form with radical

$$W_\lambda = \{x \in \mathbb{F}_{p^n} : g_\lambda(x+y) = g_\lambda(x) + g_\lambda(y), \forall y \in \mathbb{F}_{p^n}\} \tag{16}$$

where $n = mr$. For a $\mathbb{F}_q$-quadratic form f on $\mathbb{F}_{q^r}$ and $\lambda \in \mathbb{F}_q^*$, the radical W in (15) is the set of the roots of the equation

$$a_0 x + a_1 x^q + (a_1 x)^{q^{-1}} + a_2 x^{q^2} + (a_2 x)^{q^{-2}} + \cdots + a_{\lfloor \frac{r}{2} \rfloor} x^{q^{\lfloor \frac{r}{2} \rfloor}} + \left(a_{\lfloor \frac{r}{2} \rfloor} x\right)^{q^{-\lfloor \frac{r}{2} \rfloor}} \tag{17}$$

in $\mathbb{F}_{q^r}$ and W_λ in (16) is the set of the roots of the equation

$$\lambda a_0 x + \lambda a_1 x^q + (\lambda a_1 x)^{q^{-1}} + \lambda a_2 x^{q^2} + (\lambda a_2 x)^{q^{-2}} + \cdots + \lambda a_{\lfloor \frac{r}{2} \rfloor} x^{q^{\lfloor \frac{r}{2} \rfloor}} + \left(\lambda a_{\lfloor \frac{r}{2} \rfloor} x\right)^{q^{-\lfloor \frac{r}{2} \rfloor}} \tag{18}$$

(for example, see [10, Lemma 2.1]). As $\lambda \in \mathbb{F}_q^*$, it is easy to observe from (17) and (18) that $W = W_\lambda$. Therefore, we obtain vectorial s-plateaued function F from $\mathbb{F}_{p^n}$ to $\mathbb{F}_{p^m}$ (notice that $F(x) = f(x)$ for all $x \in \mathbb{F}_{p^n}$). This shows existence of an algorithm to construct vectorial s-plateaued functions F for any integer s with $0 \leq s \leq r - 1$. For example, if $p = 3$, $m = 2$ and $n = 6$, then

- $f_1(x) = \mathrm{Tr}_{3^2}^{3^6}(x^2 + x^{10})$ is the vectorial 0-plateaued function and
- $f_2(x) = \mathrm{Tr}_{3^2}^{3^6}(x^2 + 2x^{10})$ is the vectorial 1-plateaued function.

Example 3. Let p be an odd prime and n be a positive even integer. Let f_1 and f_2 be the quadratic p-ary s_1-plateaued and s_2-plateaued functions from $\mathbb{F}_{p^n}$ to $\mathbb{F}_p$ with $s_1 \neq s_2$, respectively. For any $\theta \in \mathbb{F}_{p^2} \setminus \mathbb{F}_p$, a function F given as

$$F(x) = f_1(x) + \theta f_2(x)$$

is the vectorial plateaued function from $\mathbb{F}_{p^n}$ to $\mathbb{F}_{p^2}$, but it is not the vectorial s-plateaued function for any integer s. This shows that the vectorial plateaued functions are strictly more general than the vectorial s-plateaued function for any s.

7 Conclusion

This paper studies the characterizations of (vectorial) bent and plateaued functions in arbitrary characteristic. First, we provide the results on characterizations of bent and plateaued functions. Next, we generalize their characterizations in characteristic 2 in terms of the second-order derivatives given in [7] to arbitrary characteristic. Moreover, we present a new characterization of plateaued functions in terms of fourth power moments of their Wash transforms. Furthermore, we give a direct proof between the balancedness of the first-order derivatives of vectorial bent functions and the number of zeros of their second-order derivatives. Lastly, we present the characterizations of vectorial s-plateaued functions.

Acknowledgment. The third author is partially supported by the Scientific and Technological Research Council of Turkey (TÜBİTAK)-BİDEB 2211 program.

References

1. Cao, X., Chen, H., Mesnager, S.: Further results on semi-bent functions in polynomial form. J. Adv. Math. Commun. (AMC) (To appear)
2. Carlet, C.: Vectorial boolean functions for cryptography. Boolean Models Methods Math. Comput. Sci. Eng. **134**, 398–469 (2010)
3. Carlet, C.: On the properties of vectorial functions with plateaued components and their consequences on APN functions. In: El Hajji, S., Nitaj, A., Carlet, C., Souidi, E.M. (eds.) Codes, Cryptology, and Information Security. LNCS, vol. 9084, pp. 63–73. Springer, Heidelberg (2015)
4. Carlet, C., Ding, C.: Highly nonlinear mappings. Spec. Issue Complex. Issues Coding Crypt. J. Complex. **20**(2–3), 205–244 (2004)
5. Carlet, C., Ding, C.: Nonlinearities of S-boxes. Finite Fields Appl. **13**(1), 121–135 (2007)
6. Carlet, C., Mesnager, S.: On semi-bent boolean functions. IEEE Trans. Inf. Theory **58**(5), 3287–3292 (2012)
7. Carlet, C., Prouff, E.: On plateaued functions and their constructions. In: Johansson, T. (ed.) FSE 2003. LNCS, vol. 2887, pp. 54–73. Springer, Heidelberg (2003)
8. Cohen, G., Mesnager, S.: On constructions of semi-bent functions from bent functions. J. Contemp. Math. **625**, 141–154 (2014). Discrete Geometry and Algebraic Combinatorics, American Mathematical Society
9. Çakçak, E., Özbudak, F.: Curves related to coulter's maximal curves. Finite Fields Appl. **14**(1), 209–220 (2008)
10. Çakçak, E., Özbudak, F.: Some Artin-Schreier type function fields over finite fields with prescribed genus and number of rational places. J. Pure Appl. Algebra **210**(1), 113–135 (2007)

11. Çeşmelioğlu, A., Meidl, W.: A construction of bent functions from plateaued functions. Des. Codes Crypt. **66**(1–3), 231–242 (2013)
12. Çeşmelioğlu, A., Meidl, W.: Non weakly regular bent polynomials from vectorial quadratic functions. In: Topics in Finite Fields-Proceedings of Fq11, Contemporary Mathematics, AMS, vol. 632, pp. 83–94 (2015)
13. Dobbertin, H., Helleseth, T., Kumar, P.V., Martinsen, H.M.: Ternary m-sequences with three-valued cross-correlation function: new decimations of Welch and Niho type. IEEE Trans. Inf. Theory **47**(4), 1473–1481 (2001)
14. Helleseth, T., Kholosha, K.: Monomial and quadratic bent functions over the finite filed of odd characteristic. IEEE Trans. Inf. Theory **52**(5), 2018–2032 (2006)
15. Helleseth, T., Kholosha, A.: On the dual of monomial quadratic p-ary bent functions. In: Golomb, S.W., Gong, G., Helleseth, T., Song, H.-Y. (eds.) SSC 2007. LNCS, vol. 4893, pp. 50–61. Springer, Heidelberg (2007)
16. Helleseth, T., Rong, C., Sandberg, D.: New families of almost perfect nonlinear power mappings. IEEE Trans. Inf. Theory **45**(2), 475–485 (1999)
17. Hou, X.-D.: p-ary and q-ary versions of certain results about bent functions and resilient functions. Finite Fields Appl. **10**(4), 566–582 (2004)
18. Khoo, G.: A new characterization of semi-bent and bent functions on finite fields. Des. Codes Crypt. **38**(2), 279–295 (2006)
19. Kumar, P.V., Scholtz, R.A., Welch, L.R.: Generalized bent functions and their properties. J. Comb. Theory Ser. A **40**(1), 90–107 (1985)
20. Mesnager, S.: Semi-bent functions from Dillon and Niho exponents, Kloosterman sums and Dickson polynomials. IEEE Trans. Inf. Theory **57**(11), 7443–7458 (2011)
21. Mesnager, S.: Semi-bent functions with multiple trace terms and hyperelliptic curves. In: Hevia, A., Neven, G. (eds.) LatinCrypt 2012. LNCS, vol. 7533, pp. 18–36. Springer, Heidelberg (2012)
22. Mesnager, S.: Semi-bent functions from oval polynomials. In: Stam, M. (ed.) IMACC 2013. LNCS, vol. 8308, pp. 1–15. Springer, Heidelberg (2013)
23. Mesnager, S.: Characterizations of plateaued and bent functions in characteristic p. In: Schmidt, K.-U., Winterhof, A. (eds.) SETA 2014. LNCS, vol. 8865, pp. 72–82. Springer, Heidelberg (2014)
24. Mesnager, S.: On semi-bent functions and related plateaued functions over the Galois field F_{2^n}. In: Koç, Ç.K. (ed.) Open Problems in Mathematics and Computational Science, pp. 243–273. Springer International Publishing, Switzerland (2014)
25. Nyberg, K.: Perfect nonlinear S-boxes. In: Davies, D.W. (ed.) EUROCRYPT 1991. LNCS, vol. 547, pp. 378–386. Springer, Heidelberg (1991)
26. Rothaus, O.S.: On bent functions. J. Comb. Theory Ser. A **20**(3), 300–305 (1976)
27. Tan, Y., Yang, J., Zhang, X.: A recursive construction of p-ary bent functions which are not weakly regular. In: IEEE International Conference on Information Theory and Information Security (ICITIS), pp. 156–159 (2010)
28. Zheng, Y., Zhang, X.-M.: Plateaued functions. In: Varadharajan, V., Mu, Y. (eds.) ICICS 1999. LNCS, vol. 1726, pp. 284–300. Springer, Heidelberg (1999)
29. Zheng, Y., Zhang, X.-M.: Relationships between bent functions and complementary plateaued functions. In: Song, J.S. (ed.) ICISC 1999. LNCS, vol. 1787, pp. 60–75. Springer, Heidelberg (2000)

Cryptographically Strong S-Boxes Generated by Modified Immune Algorithm

Georgi Ivanov[1], Nikolay Nikolov[1], and Svetla Nikova[2(✉)]

[1] Institute of Mathematics and Informatics, Bulgarian Academy of Sciences,
Sofia, Bulgaria
[2] Department of ESAT/COSIC and iMinds, KU Leuven, Leuven, Belgium
svetla.nikova@esat.kuleuven.be

Abstract. S-boxes play an important role in ensuring the resistance of block ciphers against cryptanalysis as often they are their only non-linear components. The cryptographic properties of S-boxes and a variety of constructions have been studied extensively over the past years. Techniques for S-box generation include algebraic constructions, pseudo-random generation and heuristic approaches. The family of artificial immune algorithms is a particular example of a heuristic approach. In this paper we propose an S-box generation technique using a special kind of artificial immune algorithm, namely the clonal selection algorithm, combined with a slightly modified hill climbing method for S-boxes. Using this special algorithm we generate large sets of highly nonlinear bijective S-boxes of low differential uniformity in a reasonable search time.

Keywords: Immune algorithms · S-boxes · Nonlinearity · Differential uniformity

1 Introduction and Motivation

Most block ciphers in modern cryptography contain one or more non-linear components that have the ability to provide the effect of confusion [26], which is of vital importance for the strength of the cipher. Often these components are n to m Boolean mappings, the so called S-boxes. Among the whole set of S-boxes the bijective ones are particularly interesting.

In order to improve the resistance of a block cipher to *linear* and *differential cryptanalysis* [2,3,17], two main approaches are used - either by increasing the number of active S-boxes or by using S-boxes with strong cryptographic properties. The most important cryptographic properties an S-box should possess are *regularity*, high *nonlinearity*, high *algebraic degree*, low *differential uniformity* and low *autocorrelation*. The known techniques for the construction of S-boxes

---

The research is done as a part of the project "Finite geometries, coding theory and cryptography" between the Research Foundation - Flanders (FWO) and the Bulgarian Academy of Sciences.

E. Pasalic and L.R. Knudsen (Eds.): BalkanCryptSec 2015, LNCS 9540, pp. 31–42, 2016.
DOI: 10.1007/978-3-319-29172-7_3

can be divided into three main streams: *algebraic constructions, pseudo-random generation* and *heuristic techniques*.

The first approach is the most popular one, where the S-boxes are designed according to some proven mathematical relations and principles. The most famous representatives of this approach are the bijective $(n \times n)$ S-boxes based on inversion in the finite field $GF(2^n)$. They are the best S-boxes found and are simultaneously optimal with respect to most of the desired criteria. The best values achieved for nonlinearity and differential uniformity using algebraic constructions are $N_{inv} = 2^{n-1} - 2^{\frac{n}{2}}$ and $\delta_{inv} = 4$, [21]. The (8×8) S-box of AES [10] is such an S-box, which has high algebraic degree - 7, high nonlinearity - 112, low autocorrelation - 32 and low differential uniformity - 4. Although these S-boxes are often preferred because of their excellent cryptographic properties, there are some concerns related to their simple algebraic structure and possible future vulnerability to algebraic attacks [9]. Furthermore, the number of these S-boxes is small and all of them are affine equivalent.

The *pseudo-random* S-box generation technique consists of constructing the S-box from a table of random numbers followed by its conformity testing. This approach is doomed to failure from the very beginning as most of the desired cryptographic criteria are often contradictory to each other, which greatly reduces the number of S-boxes that are good with respect to all criteria and diminishes the probability of picking up a good S-box.

Heuristic algorithms are used for S-box generation in a process of iteratively improving an S-box or a whole set of S-boxes with respect to one or more properties. In contrast to the algebraic constructions, heuristic techniques are able to produce big sets of S-boxes as they use direct search methods. Most commonly the cryptographic properties of S-boxes obtained by heuristic algorithms are not as good as the ones of the algebraically constructed S-boxes. However, in recent years the difference between these properties is getting more and more indistinguishable. The latter is achieved by using some specific heuristic techniques like the hill climbing method, the simulated annealing method, the genetic algorithms or different combinations of these. With respect to nonlinearity, the highest value achieved in the case of (8×8) bijective S-boxes by: the hill climbing method is 100 [18]; the *simulated annealing method* is 102 [8]; and by a special genetic algorithm is 104 [27]. Recently, in [16], values of 104 for nonlinearity were achieved by a method, referred to as the *modified gradient descent*, based on swapping certain number of values in a permutation. In [15], values of 112, equal to the ones of the S-box of AES, for nonlinearity were achieved by a method, referred to as the *reversed genetic algorithm*, starting from initial population full of S-boxes based on inversion in the finite field and obtaining large sets of *non-equivalent* S-boxes. As regards to differential uniformity, the lowest value achieved in the case of (8×8) *bijective* S-boxes is 4, [15,22,23]. Although most of the methods described give good results for constructing bijective S-boxes with respect to only one of the main criteria, it becomes much more challenging when both nonlinearity and differential uniformity should be considered simultaneously. In [8,18,27] differential uniformity is not considered at all. In [16] the

S-box reported has nonlinearity 104 and differential uniformity 8. In [22,23] the best value obtained for differential uniformity is 4, while the respective nonlinearity value is 98. In [15] combinations $(112, 6)$ and $(110, 4)$ for nonlinearity and differential uniformity are reported.

1.1 Contribution

In this paper we propose a new *heuristic method* for generation of big sets of $(n \times n)$ *bijective* S-boxes possessing a good combination of the target properties like: high nonlinearity, high algebraic degree, low differential uniformity and low autocorrelation. The method, referred to as the *SpImmAlg*, is based on using a specific *artificial immune algorithm* (Sect. 7.2 of [4]) combined with a modification of the *hill climbing method* for S-boxes [18]. The input of *SpImmAlg* is an $(n \times n)$ bijective S-box, which can either be pseudo-randomly generated or some other S-box possessing specific properties. In the case of random input and $n = 8$, the output of the algorithm after 10 days work on a cluster with 32 cores is a large set of thousands of (8×8) bijective S-boxes with nonlinearity 104 and differential uniformity 6. Compared to the finite field inversion-based S-boxes and the ones obtained in [13,15], these S-boxes seem to be worse, but after considering the fact that the former either are affine equivalent to the finite field inversion-based S-boxes or at least share to a certain extent their algebraic structure, then the latter S-boxes appear to be much more attractive due to their random origin and the expected better resistance to algebraic attacks [9].

2 Preliminaries

In this section we recall some basic definitions and properties of Boolean functions. We refer to [5,6] for a comprehensive survey on Boolean functions.

Let $S : \mathbb{B}^n \rightarrow \mathbb{B}^m$ be an n-binary input m-binary output mapping, referred to as an $(n \times m)$ S-box. Then, to each $x = (x_1, x_2, \ldots, x_n) \in \mathbb{B}^n$ some $y = (y_1, y_2, \ldots, y_m) \in \mathbb{B}^m$ is assigned by $S(x) = y$, where $\mathbb{B} = \{0, 1\}$ is the 1-dimensional Boolean space. The $(n \times m)$ S-box S can be considered as a vectorial Boolean function comprising m individual Boolean functions $f_1, f_2, \ldots, f_m : \mathbb{B}^n \rightarrow \mathbb{B}$, where $f_i(x) = y_i$ for $i = 1, 2, \ldots, m$. These functions are referred to as the *coordinate* Boolean functions of the S-box. It is well known that most of desirable cryptographic properties of the S-box can be defined also in terms of all non-trivial linear combinations of the coordinate functions, referred to as the S-box *component* Boolean functions: $g_c : \mathbb{B}^n \rightarrow \mathbb{B}$, where $g_c = c_1 f_1 \oplus c_2 f_2 \oplus \ldots \oplus c_m f_m$ and $c = (c_1, c_2, \ldots, c_m) \in \mathbb{B}^m \setminus \{0\}$.

2.1 Boolean Functions

A Boolean function $f : \mathbb{B}^n \rightarrow \mathbb{B}$ can be represented by its binary output vector containing 2^n elements, referred to as the *truth table*. The function can also be represented by its polarity truth table, where instead of f the signed function $\widehat{f} = (-1)^f$ is considered.

Another way of representing f is by its *algebraic normal form*, denoted by ANF_f:

$$ANF_f = a_0 \oplus a_1 x_1 \oplus a_2 x_2 \oplus \ldots \oplus a_n x_n \oplus a_{1,2} x_1 x_2 \oplus \ldots \oplus a_{1,2,\ldots,n} x_1 x_2 \ldots x_n,$$

where $a_I \in \mathbb{B}, I \subseteq \{1, 2, \ldots, n\}$. The *algebraic degree* of f, denoted by $deg(f)$, is the number of variables of the largest product term of ANF_f having a non-zero coefficient.

The *Walsh-Hadamard transform (WHT)* of an n-variable Boolean function f, represented by its polarity form $\widehat{f}$, is denoted by $\widehat{F}_f(w)$ and defined as:

$$\widehat{F}_f(w) = \sum_{x \in \mathbb{B}^n} \widehat{f}(x)(-1)^{<w,x>} = \sum_{x \in \mathbb{B}^n} (-1)^{f(x) \oplus <w,x>} = \sum_{x \in \mathbb{B}^n} \widehat{f}(x)\widehat{l}_w(x),$$

where $\widehat{l}_w(x)$ is the signed function of the linear function $l_w(x) = <w, x>$.

$\widehat{F}_f(w) \in [-2^n, 2^n], \forall w \in \mathbb{B}^n$, and $\widehat{F}_f(w)$ is known as a *spectral Walsh coefficient*, while the real-valued vector of all 2^n spectral coefficients is referred to as the WHT Spectrum. The maximum absolute value, taken by $\widehat{F}_f$, is given by: $WHT_{max}(f) = max_{(w \in \mathbb{B}^n)} |\widehat{F}_f(w)|$.

The *autocorrelation transform (ACT)*, taken with respect to $\alpha \in \mathbb{B}^n$, of an n-variable Boolean function f, represented by its polarity form $\widehat{f}$, is denoted by $\widehat{r}_f(\alpha)$ and defined as:

$$\widehat{r}_f(\alpha) = \sum_{x \in \mathbb{B}^n} (-1)^{f(x) \oplus f(x \oplus \alpha)} = \sum_{x \in \mathbb{B}^n} \widehat{f}(x)\widehat{f}(x \oplus \alpha)$$

Thus, $\widehat{r}_f(\alpha) \in [-2^n, 2^n], \forall \alpha \in \mathbb{B}^n$, and $\widehat{r}_f(0) = 2^n$. $\widehat{r}_f(\alpha)$ is known as a *spectral autocorrelation coefficient* of the function, while the real-valued vector of all 2^n autocorrelation coefficients is referred to as its *ACT Spectrum*.

Three of the important cryptographic properties that any n-variable Boolean function f should possess are *balance*, high *nonlinearity* and low *autocorrelation*.

f is balanced if $w_H(f) = 2^{n-1}$, where $w_H(f)$ denotes the Hamming weight of f.

The nonlinearity of f, denoted by N_f, is the Hamming distance between f and the set $A(n)$ containing all n-variable affine Boolean functions. It is given by:

$$N_f = 2^{n-1} - \frac{1}{2}WHT_{max}(f) = 2^{n-1} - \frac{1}{2}max_{(w \in \mathbb{B}^n)}|\widehat{F}_f(w)|$$

The *absolute indicator* of f, denoted by $AC(f)_{max}$, is defined as the maximal non-trivial absolute autocorrelation value. It is given by: $AC(f)_{max} = max_{(\alpha \in \mathbb{B}^n \setminus \{0\})} |\widehat{r}_f(\alpha)|$.

Two n-variable Boolean functions f and g are *affine equivalent* if and only if there exist some invertible $(n \times n)$ binary matrix A, vectors $b, c \in \mathbb{B}^n$ and a scalar $d \in \mathbb{B}$, such that $g(x) = f(Ax \oplus b) \oplus <c, x> \oplus d$.

2.2   Vectorial Boolean Functions

All Boolean function properties discussed so far can be extended to the case of vectorial Boolean functions (S-boxes). The important difference in the manner the S-box properties are derived consists in that it is necessary the properties of the S-box component Boolean functions to be considered rather than the coordinate Boolean functions only.

Any good S-box should be *regular* (balanced) in order to avoid trivial statistical attacks. An $(n \times m)$ S-box S with $n \geq m$ is said to be regular if, for each its output $y \in \mathbb{B}^m$, there are exactly 2^{n-m} inputs that are mapped to y. Clearly, each *bijective* $(n \times n)$ S-box S is always regular since it represents a *permutation*. It is well known that an $(n \times m)$ S-box with $n \geq m$ is regular if and only if all its component Boolean functions are balanced [25].

In order to improve the cipher immunity against linear cryptanalysis, [17], any $(n \times m)$ S-box S should have small magnitude entries in its *linear approximation table* LAT_S, which is shown to be equivalent in [24] to the statement that the *nonlinearity* of each component Boolean function of S should be high. Thus, the nonlinearity of S, denoted by N_S, is given by the minimal nonlinearity among the nonlinearities of the component Boolean functions:

$$N_S = min_{(c \in \mathbb{B}^m \setminus \{0\})} \, g_c = min_{(c=(c_1,c_2,\dots,c_m) \in \mathbb{B}^m \setminus \{0\})} \, N_{c_1 f_1 \oplus c_2 f_2 \oplus \dots \oplus c_m f_m}$$

In order to resist *low order approximation* attacks each $(n \times m)$ S-box S should have an algebraic degree as high as possible, [14,20]. The *(minimal) algebraic degree* of S, denoted by $deg(S)$, is defined as the minimal algebraic degree among the degrees of the component Boolean functions. It can be expressed as follows:

$$deg(S) = min_{(c \in \mathbb{B}^m \setminus \{0\})} \, deg(g_c) = min_{(c=(c_1,c_2,\dots,c_m) \in \mathbb{B}^m \setminus \{0\})} \, deg(c_1 f_1 \oplus c_2 f_2 \oplus \dots \oplus c_m f_m)$$

In order to improve the cipher immunity against *differential cryptanalysis*, [2], any $(n \times m)$ S-box S with $n \geq m$ should have small entries in its *difference distribution table* DDT_S, not counting the first entry in the first row [1,7,11]. That is, S should have as low *differential uniformity* as possible, where differential or δ-uniformity, denoted by δ, is defined by:

$$\delta = max_{(\alpha \in \mathbb{B}^n \setminus \{0\})} \, max_{(\beta \in \mathbb{B}^m)} \, |\{x \in \mathbb{B}^n | S(x) \oplus S(x \oplus \alpha) = \beta\}|$$

It is well known that δ takes always only even values in $[2^{n-m}, 2^n]$. Then, the smallest possible value of δ in the case of bijective S-boxes ($n = m$) is 2. Such S-boxes are referred to as the *almost perfect nonlinear* (*APN*) permutations.

In order to improve the *avalanche effect* of the cipher, [12], any $(n \times m)$ S-box S should have low autocorrelation, that is, the *absolute indicators* of the component Boolean functions of the S-box should be as small as possible. In other words, the maximal absolute indicator among all the absolute indicators, denoted by $AC(S)_{max}$, should be as small as possible.

Thus, we are looking in this paper for $(n \times n)$ bijective S-boxes possessing high nonlinearity and high algebraic degree as well as low differential uniformity and low autocorrelation.

Both $(n \times n)$ *bijective* S-boxes S_1 and S_2 are said to be affine equivalent if there exist invertible affine permutations $A(x)$ and $B(x)$, such that $S_1 = B \circ S_2 \circ A$.

3   Heuristic Techniques

There are different types of heuristic methods suitable for solving computational problems. Some of them are inspired by a physical process (simulated annealing), some - by the process of biological evolution (genetic algorithms), while other methods are inspired by the process and mechanisms of the biological immune system (immune algorithms). Related to S-box generation, all types of heuristic techniques share the same approach. It involves a process, where given S-box or a set of S-boxes are iteratively improved with respect to one or more of their properties until either some reasonable number of iterations is reached or some chosen in advance specific threshold values for these properties are achieved.

Hill climbing method consists in applying some small modifications of a certain number of distinct elements of a function in order one or more its cryptographic properties iteratively to be improved. Simulated annealing method involves a sort of extension to the hill climbing technique, allowing the searching process to move out of a local optimum in order to continue. Genetic algorithms work with populations of candidate solutions. Being iteratively subject to the three main operations inspired by the natural evolution - crossover, mutation and selection, these populations transform into better ones, possessing all the properties desired. Each new generation is formed by those individuals from the previous one that have passed the fitness test. The fitness test is based on using a fitness or a cost function, responsible for taking the decision whether the evaluated individuals will survive to the next generation or not. Only the fittest individuals (those of maximal fitness or of low cost respectively) survive. In contrast to genetic algorithms, immune algorithms work only with one candidate solution, corresponding to the most appropriate type of general immune cells (lymphocytes) that will fight a specific pathogen. Once the initial solution is selected, it starts proliferating. During the proliferation process the initial solution is subject to some small copying errors, referred to as the somatic hypermutation. The main goal of the combined process is by this duplication and variation the adaptation and the fighting power of the initial solution to be improved or in other words, the genetic variation preventing from falling into a local optimum to be present. Then, the process is iterated by replacing the initial solution with a new one, which is selected as the fittest solution from the new generation by a fitness or a cost function like in the case of genetic algorithms. At the end, the fittest solution (the one of maximal fitness or respectively of the lowest cost) of the final generation is the best solution.

4   New Method

The proposed new method is based on a heuristic algorithm, denoted by *SpImmAlg*, which combines a modified algorithm from the *artificial immune algorithms* family, referred to as *clonal selection algorithm* (Sect. 7.2 of [4]), with a modification of the known *hill climbing method* for S-boxes [18]. The basic idea is to start from an S-box and iteratively to improve its cryptographic properties. The main goal of the algorithm is rapidly to be constructed a variety of strong $(n \times n)$ *bijective* S-boxes, which possess target cryptographic properties such as: high *nonlinearity*, high algebraic degree, low differential uniformity and low autocorrelation.

4.1 Algorithm Description

SpImmAlg has as input an $(n \times n)$ bijective S-box S_0. The initial S-box S_0 can be of any type - either a pseudo-randomly generated S-box or a specific one possessing certain cryptographic properties. The modified hill climbing method is applied to S_0. It consists of repeatedly swapping any two elements of S_0 and calculating the *cost* of the newly obtained S-box S by a *cost* function $cost(\cdot)$. If $cost(S) < cost(S_0)$, the process iteratively continues form S on. Otherwise, a new S-box S is obtained and so on. The output S of the modified hill climbing method, possessing the lowest cost, is then forwarded as an input to the *modified clonal selection algorithm*. By means of two different *somatic mutation* functions - $mutation_1(\cdot)$ and $mutation_2(\cdot)$ it produces 4 new S-boxes S_1, S_2, S_3 and S_4. We use 4 S-boxes in order to speed up the execution, however any other number of "children" is also possible. Each of these S-boxes is then transformed into a better new one by the modified hill climbing method. The best S-box of the four with respect to the respective cost function is then forwarded to the input of the modified clonal selection algorithm and the process starts all over. The algorithm makes use of 5 main functions, all having as an input argument any $(n \times n)$ *bijective* S-box S. These are the three distinct cost functions - $cost_1(\cdot)$, $cost_2(\cdot)$ and $cost_3(\cdot)$, forming as a product the final *cost* function $cost(\cdot)$ that has to be minimized, and both *mutation* functions - $mutation_1(\cdot)$ and $mutation_2(\cdot)$ used in order to guarantee the wide variety of the new generations:

1. The first *cost* function $cost_1(\cdot)$ calculates the cost of S by the rule:

$$cost_1(S) = \sum_{c<d\in\mathbb{B}^n\setminus\{0\}} \sum_{w\in\mathbb{B}^n} \left| \, |\widehat{F}_{c_1f_1\oplus c_2f_2\oplus...\oplus c_nf_n}(\omega)|^3 - |\widehat{F}_{d_1f_1\oplus d_2f_2\oplus...\oplus d_nf_n}(\omega)|^3 \, \right|^7.$$

The goal of this cost function is to increase the S-box nonlinearity by making the absolute WHT spectrum as flat as possible.

2. The second *cost* function $cost_2(\cdot)$ calculates the cost of S by the rule:

$$cost_2(S) = \sum_{c=(c_1,c_2,...,c_n)\in\mathbb{B}^n\setminus\{0\}} \sum_{w\in\mathbb{B}^n} |\widehat{F}_{c_1f_1\oplus c_2f_2\oplus...\oplus c_nf_n}(\omega) - 21|^7.$$

The cost function $\sum_{c=(c_1,c_2,...,c_n)\in\mathbb{B}^n\setminus\{0\}} \sum_{w\in\mathbb{B}^n} |\widehat{F}_{c_1f_1\oplus c_2f_2\oplus...\oplus c_nf_n}(\omega) - X|^R$ for X, R real was first proposed in [8]. Later in [27] many pairs of parameters have been investigated for (8×8) S-boxes and the pair $X = 21, R = 7$ was shown to achieve the best results.

3. The third *cost* function $cost_3(\cdot)$ calculates the cost of S by the rule:

$$cost_3(S) = \sum_{\delta_{11} \neq \delta_{ij} \in DDT_S} (\delta_{ij} - 1)^2.(\delta_{ij} - 2)^2.(\delta_{ij} - 4)^2, \text{ where}$$

δ_{ij} $(i, j = 1, 2, \ldots, 2^n)$ are the elements of the difference distribution table DDT_S of S. Naturally this cost function achieves its minimum when the δ-uniformity is 2 or 4.

4. The final cost function $cost(\cdot)$ calculates the overall cost of S by the rule:

$$cost(S) = cost_1(S).cost_2(S).cost_3(S),$$

i.e. by combining (and minimizing) the 3 cost functions.

5. The first mutation function $mutation_1(\cdot)$ transforms S into S' by the rule:

$$S' = mutation_1(S), \text{ where}$$

S' is obtained from S by swapping two its neighboring elements. The positions p and $p-1$ of the elements that are going to be swapped depend on the number p in the range from 2 to 2^n, which is chosen at random at each execution of the function. The latter serves as a guarantee that whenever the mutation function $mutation_1(\cdot)$ is being executed, the resulting S-box will be different from the previous ones.

6. The second *mutation* function $mutation_2(\cdot)$ transforms S into S'' by the rule:

$$S'' = mutation_2(S), \text{ where}$$

S'' is obtained from S in the following manner: a block of an arbitrary length q in the range from 2 to 8 of neighboring elements is modified in S. If q is an even number, then the elements that are symmetric with respect to the position p, which splits the block into two parts of equal length, are swapped. Otherwise, the element in the middle of the block stays in place, while all the other elements that are symmetric with respect to this element are swapped. In both cases, due to the random choice of q and p, the resulting S-box again will differ all the previous ones at each execution of the function. It should be noted that $mutation_2$ is an extension of $mutation_1$ (case $q = 2$). In general different values of q can be used, our experiments for (8×8) S-boxes show that the best results can be expected when q is upper bounded by 8.

4.2 Algorithm Pseudo-code

STEP 1 (Initialization)
- Define an integer n, representing the dimensions of desired $(n \times n)$ *bijective* S-boxes.
- Generate a random $(n \times n)$ *bijective* S-box S_0.

STEP 2 (Initial selection)
- Start the modified hill climbing method (MHCM) with S_0 as an input.

– In result, obtain the $(n \times n)$ bijective S-box S, which has the lowest cost: $cost(S) = cost_1(S).cost_2(S).cost_3(S)$, $S = MHCM(S_0)$.

STEP 3 (Somatic hypermutation)

– Twice apply the *mutation* function $mutation_1(\cdot)$ with S as an input: $S_1 = mutation_1(S)$ and $S_2 = mutation_1(S)$.

– Twice apply the *mutation* function $mutation_2(\cdot)$ with S as an input: $S_3 = mutation_2(S)$ and $S_4 = mutation_2(S)$.

– Obtain 4 different $(n \times n)$ bijective S-boxes S_1, S_2, S_3 and S_4.

STEP 4 (Selection)

– Start the modified hill climbing method for each of S_1, S_2, S_3 or S_4 as an input.

– In result, obtain four low-cost $(n \times n)$ bijective S-boxes S_1', S_2', S_3' and S_4' : $S_1' = MHCM(S_1)$, $S_2' = MHCM(S_2)$, $S_3' = MHCM(S_3)$ and $S_4' = MHCM(S_4)$.

– Compare the overall cost, $cost(\cdot)$, of each of the four S-boxes S_1', S_2', S_3', S_4' and set S' to be the one with the lowest cost.

STEP 5 (Stopping criterion)

– If some chosen in advance threshold number of iterations or execution time e.g. 10 days is reached, then STOP.

– Otherwise, set S to S' and go to step 3.

5 Experimental Results

In this section the results obtained by *SpImmAlg* are provided. The goal was to produce a variety of (8×8) *bijective* S-boxes with main cryptographic properties as close as possible to the finite field inversion-based S-boxes starting from a random S-box. For the sake of simplicity, we chose as a criterion to stop the algorithm after it runs for 10-days (instead of some threshold number of iterations).

5.1 Results Obtained by *SpImmAlg* in the Case of (8×8) *Bijective* S-boxes

We ran *SpImmAlg* with a randomly generated (8×8) bijective S-box S_0. As a result, in 10 days neither APN permutations nor S-boxes better than the finite field inversion-based ones were found. The majority (35 000) of the obtained (8×8) bijective S-boxes have nonlinearity 104 and differential uniformity 6. As far as we know, such variety of S-boxes, possessing such a good combination of both properties, has not been obtained yet by any other heuristic method, when starting from a random S-box. We compare our results with all other generation methods we know in Table 1. The comparison is with respect to the target properties: nonlinearity, algebraic degree, autocorrelation and differential uniformity. Whenever the value for one of these properties was not reported, we assumed that it had not been considered and we put "-" in the table. Most of the previous works do not consider differential uniformity but only nonlinearity as a target criterion. Therefore, it is hard to compare with their results. From one side it is to be expected that if one more property is targeted that property will possess better values than if neglected. However, the other properties usually get worse since there are vast connections between those parameters and they cannot be independently optimized. Since most of the previous works do not publish the best S-boxes they have found it is impossible to compare the results. In Appendix A we provide one of the best (8×8) S-boxes obtained by *SpImmAlg*.

Table 1. Known methods for generation of (8×8) *bijective* S-boxes

Generation methods/properties	N_S	deg(S)	$AC(S)_{max}$	δ-uniformity
Pseudo-random generation [18,19]	98	-	-	-
Finite field inversion [21]	112	7	32	4
Hill climbing method [18]	100	-	-	-
Genetic algorithm/hill climbing [19]	100	-	-	-
Simulated annealing method [8]	102	-	80	-
Special genetic algorithm [27]	104	-	-	-
Tweaking method [13]	106	7	56	6
Gradient descent method [16]	104	7	80	8
4-uniform permutations method [22,23]	98	-	-	4
Reversed genetic algorithm [15]	110	7	40	4
Reversed genetic algorithm [15]	112	7	32	6
SpImmAlg [this paper]	104	7	88	6

6   Conclusions

The proposed new method produces repeatedly and reasonably fast thousands of *bijective* S-boxes, possessing a very good combination for *nonlinearity* and *differential uniformity* - $(104, 6)$. Such values have only been achieved by finite field inversion-based S-boxes and the methods described in [13,15]. However, these methods either belong to *algebraic constructions*, meaning a limited number of solutions and possible vulnerability to algebraic attacks [9], or by *heuristic algorithms* working in a reverse way, i.e., "skiing-down" from finite field inversion-based S-boxes and obtaining new ones possessing similar or worse properties. The algorithm presented in this paper follows the classical "climbing-up" approach starting from random S-boxes and improving their properties. The results obtained are the best known compared to all previously published works that consider the properties *nonlinearity* and *differential uniformity* and use the same or similar approach [8,18,19,27].

The work presented in this paper can be extended in several directions. The most promising one is to apply some changes in the number of the *mutation* functions and in the functions themselves aiming at producing S-boxes with $N > 104$ and $\delta = 4$ that are different from the finite field inversion-based ones. At least, from [15] we know that such S-boxes exist.

A   Appendix

Here we present in hex notations the generated by the *SpImmAlg* (8×8) *bijective* S-box *S*. It was described in Table 1 and has *nonlinearity* 104, *algebraic degree* 7, maximal *autocorrelation* 88 and *differential uniformity* 6:

```
70  C6 7C D9 97 5D C2  23 D8 CF E7  6E BA D5 88 F2
68  47  25 6C 2B  5B 7A AB 69 B5 C1 8D A6  57 A2 C9
7F  FA 67 5C A7 FF 81  8E  09 A4 80  28  14 FE  56 F7
15  13  91 AA AC 3B FC DA 9B 37 D2 46 C3  00 45 AF
10  90 6D B1  D0 5E C7 A1 61 E4  12  F0 F4  38 76 FD
BE E1 59 EB  3F 87 4A 4B E9  54 DB 2A AD D3 29 83
CD 3D 4D DF B0 4E 0E 22 75 F9  03  27  19  8C 3A 1F
B2  66  73 0C  7E 1E 85 8F E2 E8  39  16  94 E0 1C DE
5F  58  7B  44 DD 24 60  95 C5 6A 7D  40 2E EA  64 21
92  F5  26  48  08 B4 01 4C  34 93  79  8B CC 0A B3 98
ED  B6 CE 77 63 B8 9D 51  05 F1  11 2C  72 E5 C8 DC
F3  78  4F E3 2D E6 02 9F  18  8A CA CB 82 62  31 2F
41  17  1A BF EC 1B 04 0B  99 32  3E 71 AE  33 A3 53
42  49  D6 BC D4 30 6B A9 FB EE BB 07  EF A5 96 74
5A D1  50  84  43 6F  36 D7 89 A0  65 BD B9 06 C4 9A
A8 3C  B7 F8  9E 1D 0F 0D 52 F6  35 86  C0  9C 20 55
```

References

1. Biham, E.: On Matsui's linear cryptanalysis. In: De Santis, A. (ed.) EUROCRYPT 1994. LNCS, vol. 950, pp. 341–355. Springer, Heidelberg (1995)
2. Biham, E., Shamir, A.: Differential cryptanalysis of DES-like cryptosystems. In: Menezes, A., Vanstone, S.A. (eds.) CRYPTO 1990. LNCS, vol. 537, pp. 2–21. Springer, Heidelberg (1991)
3. Biham, E., Shamir, A.: Differential cryptanalysis of DES-like cryptosystems. J. Cryptol. **4**, 3–72 (1991)
4. Brownlee, J.: Clever Algorithms: Nature-Inspired Programming Recipes, 1st edn. LuLu, January 2011
5. Carlet, C.: Boolean functions for cryptography and error correcting codes. In: Boolean Models and Methods in Mathematics, Computer Science, and Engineering, pp. 257–397. Cambridge University Press (2010)
6. Carlet, C.: Vectorial Boolean Functions for Cryptography. In: Boolean Models and Methods in Mathematics, Computer Science, and Engineering, pp. 257–397. Cambridge University Press (2010)
7. Chabaud, F., Vaudenay, S.: Links between differential and linear cryptanalysis. In: De Santis, A. (ed.) EUROCRYPT 1994. LNCS, vol. 950, pp. 356–365. Springer, Heidelberg (1995)
8. Clark, J.A., Jacob, J.L., Stepney, S.: The design of s-boxes by simulated annealing. New Gener. Comput. Arch. **23**(3), 219–231 (2005)
9. Courtois, N.T., Pieprzyk, J.: Cryptanalysis of block ciphers with overdefined systems of equations. In: Zheng, Y. (ed.) ASIACRYPT 2002. LNCS, vol. 2501, pp. 267–287. Springer, Heidelberg (2002)

10. Daeman, J., Rijmen, V.: The Design of Rijndael: AES - The Advanced Encryption Standard. Springer, Heidelberg (2002)
11. Daemen, J., Govaerts, R., Vandewalle, J.: Correlation matrices. In: Preneel, B. (ed.) FSE 1994. LNCS, vol. 1008, pp. 275–285. Springer, Heidelberg (1995)
12. Feistel, H.: Cryptography and computer privacy. Sci. Am. **228**(5), 15–23 (1973)
13. Fuller, J., Millan, W.L.: Linear redundancy in S-boxes. In: Johansson, T. (ed.) FSE 2003. LNCS, vol. 2887, pp. 74–86. Springer, Heidelberg (2003)
14. Golić, J.D.: Fast low order approximation of cryptographic functions. In: Maurer, U.M. (ed.) EUROCRYPT 1996. LNCS, vol. 1070, pp. 268–282. Springer, Heidelberg (1996)
15. Ivanov, G., Nikolov, N., Nikova, S.: Reversed genetic algorithms for generation of bijective s-boxes with good cryptographic properties. Special Issue of CCDS on Boolean Functions and Their Applications. IACR Cryptology ePrint Archive, Report 2014/801 (2014, to appear). http://eprint.iacr.org/2014/801.pdf
16. Kazymyrov, O., Kazymyrova, V., Oliynykov, R.: A method for generation of high-nonlinear s-boxes based on gradient descent. IACR Cryptology ePrint Archive (2013)
17. Matsui, M.: Linear cryptanalysis method for DES cipher. In: Helleseth, T. (ed.) EUROCRYPT 1993. LNCS, vol. 765, pp. 386–397. Springer, Heidelberg (1994)
18. Millan, W.L.: How to improve the nonlinearity of bijective S-boxes. In: Boyd, C., Dawson, E. (eds.) ACISP 1998. LNCS, vol. 1438, pp. 181–192. Springer, Heidelberg (1998)
19. Millan, W.L., Burnett, L., Carter, G., Clark, A., Dawson, E.: Evolutionary heuristics for finding cryptographically strong S-boxes. In: Varadharajan, V., Mu, Y. (eds.) ICICS 1999. LNCS, vol. 1726, pp. 263–274. Springer, Heidelberg (1999)
20. Millan, W.L.: Low order approximation of cipher functions. In: Dawson, E.P., Golić, J.D. (eds.) Cryptography: Policy and Algorithms 1995. LNCS, vol. 1029, pp. 144–155. Springer, Heidelberg (1996)
21. Nyberg, K.: Differentially uniform mappings for cryptography. In: Helleseth, T. (ed.) EUROCRYPT 1993. LNCS, vol. 765, pp. 55–64. Springer, Heidelberg (1994)
22. Qu, L., Tan, Y., Li, C., Gong, G.: More constructions of differentially 4-uniform permutations on $\mathbb{F}_{2^{2k}}$. arxiv.org/pdf/1309.7423 (2013)
23. Qu, L., Tan, Y., Tan, C., Li, C.: Constructing differentially 4-uniform permutations over $\mathbb{F}_{2^{2k}}$ via the switching method. IEEE Trans. Inform. Theory **59**(7), 4675–4686 (2013)
24. Seberry, J., Zhang, X.M., Zheng, Y.: Systematic generation of cryptographically robust s-boxes. In: Proceedings of the First ACM Conference on Computer and Communications Security, pp. 171–182. The Association for Computing Machinery, Fairfax (1993)
25. Seberry, J., Zhang, X.-M., Zheng, Y.: Relationships among nonlinearity criteria. In: De Santis, A. (ed.) EUROCRYPT 1994. LNCS, vol. 950, pp. 376–388. Springer, Heidelberg (1995)
26. Shannon, C.E.: Communication theory of secrecy systems. Bell Syst. Tech. J. **28**, 656–715 (1949)
27. Tesař, P.: A new method for generating high non-linearity s-boxes. Radioengineering **19**(1), 23–26 (2010)

Cryptanalysis

Analysis of the Authenticated Cipher MORUS (v1)

Aleksandra Mileva[1]([envelope]), Vesna Dimitrova[2], and Vesselin Velichkov[3]

[1] Faculty of Computer Science, University "Goce Delčev",
Štip, Republic of Macedonia
aleksandra.mileva@ugd.edu.mk
[2] Faculty of Computer Science and Engineering,
University "Ss Cyril and Methodius", Skopje, Republic of Macedonia
vesna.dimitrova@finki.edu.mk
[3] Laboratory of Algorithmics, Cryptology and Security (LACS),
Université du Luxembourg, SnT/FSTC, Luxembourg, Luxembourg
vesselin.velichkov@uni.lu

Abstract. We present several new observations on the CAESAR candidate MORUS (v1). First, we report a collision on its StateUpdate(S, M) function. Second, we describe a distinguisher in a nonce-reuse scenario with probability 1. Finally, we observe that the differences in some words of the state after the initialization have probabilities significantly higher than the random case. We note that the presented results do not threaten the security of the scheme. This is the first external analysis of the authenticated cipher MORUS.

Keywords: Symmetric-key · Cryptanalysis · Authenticated encryption · CAESAR · MORUS

1 Introduction

In 2013 the Competition for Authenticated Encryption: Security, Applicability, and Robustness (CAESAR) was announced [2]. It is initiated by the University of Illinois at Chicago, USA and is supported by the US National Institute of Standards and Technology (NIST). CAESAR is similar in nature to widely successful previous competitions such as AES [3] and SHA-3 [4]. While the latter were about standardizing dedicated algorithms for confidentiality [5] and integrity [6] respectively, the goal of CAESAR is to select algorithm/s that can ensure both confidentiality and integrity within a single primitive. It is very likely that these algorithms will end up in standardization and will be implemented and used by the industry worldwide. In total 56 candidates have been submitted to CAESAR and as of March 15, 2014, the competition has entered its public evaluation phase.

In this paper we present the first public analysis of one of the algorithms submitted to CAESAR – the authenticated cipher MORUS [1]. The latter is

© Springer International Publishing Switzerland 2016
E. Pasalic and L.R. Knudsen (Eds.): BalkanCryptSec 2015, LNCS 9540, pp. 45–59, 2016.
DOI: 10.1007/978-3-319-29172-7_4

a very promising design – both efficient and secure – on which no weaknesses have been reported so far. We describe several new observations on MORUS as summarized below:

1. Distinguisher with probability 1 in a nonce-reuse scenario.
2. Differential biases in some words of the state after the initialization.
3. Collision on the StateUpdate(S, M) function of MORUS.

We note that the presented results do not threaten the security of MORUS.

The rest of the paper is organized as follows. We begin with a brief description of MORUS in Sect. 2. A distinguisher on MORUS is presented in Sect. 3, followed by a description of differential biases in some words of the state after the initialization (Sect. 4). In Sect. 5 we describe a collision on the StateUpdate function and we briefly comment on the possibility of using it for a tag forgery attack (Sect. 6). Section 7 concludes the paper. Theorem proofs and equation derivations are provided in Appendix A and Appendix B. Notation is given in Table 1.

Table 1. Notation.

Symbol	Meaning
$\oplus$	Bit-wise exclusive OR
$\wedge$	Bit-wise AND
$\|\|$	Concatenation
$\lll$	Bit rotation to the left
$\ggg$	Bit rotation to the right
$b^{(n)}$	A sequence of n binary digits $b \in \{0, 1\}$
$\|X\|$	Length of the bit string X (in bits)
$\overline{x}$	Negation of all bits of x i.e. $\overline{x} = x \oplus 1^{(n)}$
Rotl_xxx_yy(x, b)	Divide the xxx-bit block x into 4 yy-bit words and rotate each word left by b bits. Example: Rotl_128_32(x, b) is used in MORUS-640 and Rotl_256_64(x, b) is used in MORUS-1280
Rotr_xxx_yy(x, b)	Analogous to Rotl_xxx_yy(x, b) with a right rotation
LSB, MSB	Least Significant Bit, Most Significant Bit
IV	Initialization Vector (Nonce)

2 Description of MORUS

MORUS is a very efficient family of authenticated encryption schemes using only bitwise operations: bit shift, AND and XOR. The size of the internal state is 640 or 1280 bits resp. for MORUS-640 and MORUS-1280 and is represented as five 128 or 256 bit registers respectively. MORUS supports 128 and 256 bit keys which are loaded into the input state together with a public 128 bit IV and three specified constants.

The main building block of MORUS is the state update function StateUpdate (S, M), where S is the state, and M is a message block with length $|S|/5$. This function consists of 5 rounds with similar operations that update the state S. In each round, only two state elements are modified: one with left rotation with coefficients w_i, and other with Rotl_xxx_yy operation with coefficients b_i, where $i \in \{0, 1, 2, 3, 4\}$. The StateUpdate function is shown in Fig. 1.

MORUS operates in four phases: (1) Initialization, (2) Processing of associated data, (3) Encryption and (4) Finalization. In the initialization phase of MORUS-640, five state elements are initialized with an initialization vector IV, a key K, a 128 bit string of ones $1^{(128)}$, and two constants $const_0$ and $const_1$. Next the state is updated by 16 applications of the round function StateUpdate and the result is XOR-ed with the key K.

In the second phase the associated data AD is processed using again the StateUpdate function. In the third phase the plaintext P is encrypted in blocks of 128 bits. In the final phase the authentication tag is generated by 8 applications of StateUpdate using the length of associated data `adlen` and the length of the message `msglen` as additional inputs. The output of the full process in encryption mode is a ciphertext together with an authentication tag of size at most 128 bits.

For the detailed specification of MORUS we refer the reader to the original proposal [1].

3   Distinguisher

In this section we describe a distinguisher on MORUS-640 in a nonce-reuse scenario. An analogous distinguisher also exists for MORUS-1280. We begin with a more formal description of the four phases of MORUS: initialization, processing of associated data, encryption and finalization.

Let $S^0 = (s_0, s_1, s_2, s_3, s_4)$ be the output of the initialization phase. Let the size of the associate data (AD) be 128 bits: $|AD| = 128$ and let the plaintext P consist of a single 128-bit block M. Then the output after the second phase is expressed as:

$$S^1 = (x_0, x_1, x_2, x_3, x_4) = \text{StateUpdate}(S^0, \text{AD}), \tag{1}$$

and the output of the third phase is the ciphertext C and the state S^2:

$$C = M \oplus x_0 \oplus (x_1 \lll 96) \oplus (x_2 \wedge x_3), \tag{2}$$

$$S^2 = (z_0, z_1, z_2, z_3, z_4) = \text{StateUpdate}(S^1, M). \tag{3}$$

In the final (fourth) phase the authentication tag T is obtained through the following steps:

1. $\text{tmp} = z_3 \oplus (\text{adlen} \parallel \text{msglen})$
2. $z_4 = z_4 \oplus z_0$
3. For $i = 2$ to 9 do $S^{i+1} = \text{StateUpdate}(S^i, \text{tmp})$
4. $T = \oplus_{i=1}^4 S_i^{10}$

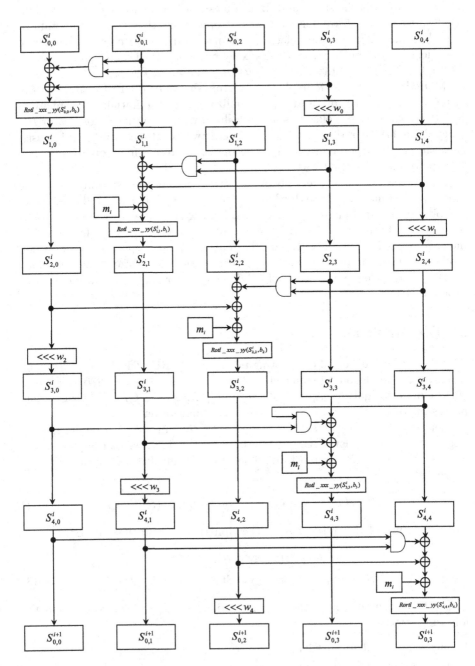

Fig. 1. The StateUpdate(S, M) function of MORUS.

The following theorem is instrumental in the construction of the distinguisher:

Theorem 1. *Let $S^0 = (s_0, s_1, s_2, s_3, s_4)$ be the state of MORUS-640 after initialization under 128 bit secret key K and 128 bit public IV. Let $\mathrm{AD}_1 = 0^{(128)}$ and $\mathrm{AD}_2 = 0^{(127)}||1$ be two 128 bit blocks of associated data that differ only in their least significant bit. Finally, let X and Y be the internal states of MORUS after the second phase (processing of associated data) under AD_1 and AD_2 respectively:*

$$X = (x_0, x_1, x_2, x_3, x_4) = \mathrm{StateUpdate}(S^0, \mathrm{AD}_1), \tag{4}$$

$$Y = (y_0, y_1, y_2, y_3, y_4) = \mathrm{StateUpdate}(S^0, \mathrm{AD}_2). \tag{5}$$

Then the following statements are true:

1. *$x_0 = y_0$.*
2. *x_1 and y_1 differ only in the 33-th bit.*
3. *x_2 and y_2 differ only in the 89-th bit.*
4. *x_3 and y_3 differ only in the 106-th and 107-th bit.*
5. *x_4 and y_4 differ only in the 108-th and 115-th bit (with probability 1) and in the 33-th bit with probability 1/2.*

Note: all bits within the 128 bit words X and Y are counted starting from MSB (bit 1) down to LSB (bit 128).

Proof. Appendix A.

Next we describe the construction of the distinguisher. Let $\mathrm{AD}_1, \mathrm{AD}_2, X = (x_0, x_1, x_2, x_3, x_4)$ and $Y = (y_0, y_1, y_2, y_3, y_4)$ be as in Theorem 1 and denote $x_j = (x_{j0}, x_{j1}, x_{j2}, x_{j3})$ and $y_j = (y_{j0}, y_{j1}, y_{j2}, y_{j3})$, where $|x_{ji}| = |y_{ji}| = 32$ bits and $0 \le j \le 4$, $1 \le i \le 3$. Further let M be a 128 bit message block. Then, according to the encryption function of MORUS (see Eq. (2)) the two ciphertexts C_1 and C_2 resp. under AD_1 and AD_2 are expressed as:

$$C_1 = M \oplus x_0 \oplus (x_1 \lll 96) \oplus (x_2 \wedge x_3), \tag{6}$$

$$C_2 = M \oplus y_0 \oplus (y_1 \lll 96) \oplus (y_2 \wedge y_3). \tag{7}$$

Note that

$$(x_1 \lll 96) = ((x_{10}, x_{11}, x_{12}, x_{13}) \lll 96) = (x_{13}, x_{10}, x_{11}, x_{12}). \tag{8}$$

Due to Statement 2 of Theorem 1 (see also Eq. (44) in Appendix A) it holds that:

$$y_1 = (y_{10}, y_{11}, y_{12}, y_{13}) = (x_{10}, x_{11} \oplus (1||0^{(31)}), x_{12}, x_{13}). \tag{9}$$

Therefore

$$(y_1 \lll 96) = ((x_{10}, x_{11} \oplus (1||0^{(31)}), x_{12}, x_{13}) \lll 96)$$
$$= (x_{13}, x_{10}, x_{11} \oplus (1||0^{(31)}), x_{12}). \tag{10}$$

It follows that $(x_1 \lll 96)$ and $(y_1 \lll 96)$ differ only in the 65-th bit. Further, in (6) note that

$$(x_2 \wedge x_3) = (x_{20} \wedge x_{30}, x_{21} \wedge x_{31}, x_{22} \wedge x_{32}, x_{23} \wedge x_{33}). \tag{11}$$

Due to Statement 3 of Theorem 1 (see also Eq. (57) in Appendix A) it holds that:

$$y_2 = (y_{20}, y_{21}, y_{22}, y_{23}) = (x_{20}, x_{21}, x_{22} \oplus (0^{(24)}||1||0^{(7)}), x_{23}), \tag{12}$$

and due to Statement 4 of Theorem 1 (see also Eq. (67) in Appendix A) it holds that:

$$y_3 = (y_{30}, y_{31}, y_{32}, y_{33}) = (x_{30}, x_{31}, x_{32}, x_{33} \oplus (0^{(9)}||11||0^{(21)})). \tag{13}$$

From the last two equations it follows that

$$(y_2 \wedge y_3) = ((x_{20}, x_{21}, x_{22} \oplus (0^{(24)}||1||0^{(7)}), x_{23}) \wedge$$
$$(x_{30}, x_{31}, x_{32}, x_{33} \oplus (0^{(9)}||11||0^{(21)}))) \tag{14}$$
$$= (x_{20} \wedge x_{30}, \ x_{21} \wedge x_{31}, \ ((x_{22} \oplus (0^{(24)}||1||0^{(7)})) \wedge x_{32}),$$
$$(x_{23} \wedge (x_{33} \oplus (0^{(9)}||11||0^{(21)})))). \tag{15}$$

From Eqs. (11) and (15) it follows that $(x_2 \wedge x_3)$ and $(y_2 \wedge y_3)$ differ at most in the 89-th, 106-th and 107-th bit (counting from MSB to LSB), each with probability $1/2$.

From the above analysis it follows that C_1 and C_2 differ in 4 bits in total. Namely, they differ in the 65-th bit with probability 1 and in the 89-th, 106-th and 107-th bit with probability $1/2$ (for each of the three bits). Therefore given the ciphertext C_1 under message (AD_1, M), an attacker can predict 125 bits of an (unknown) ciphertext C_2 under a different message (AD_2, M) with probability 1. The same probability for a random oracle is 2^{-125} and can therefore clearly be used as a distinguisher.

The same technique can also trivially be extended to distinguish pairs of plaintexts (AD_1, M_1) and (AD_2, M_2) that contain also differences in the message words, i.e., $AD_1 \neq AD_2$ and $M_1 \neq M_2$ and such that the messages M_1 and M_2 have the same length as a single block: $|M_1| = |M_2| = 128$. In this case a difference in any k bits of M_1 and M_2 (other than bits 89, 106 and 107) results in a difference in the corresponding k bits of the ciphertexts C_1 and C_2 with probability 1.

In conclusion, we would like to stress that the described distinguisher relies on the re-use of the same IV under the same message M. We note that this scenario is explicitly forbidden in the design document, where it is stated: *In MORUS, each key and IV pair should be used to protect only one message* [1, Sect. 3]. Therefore the results in this section do not directly harm the security of the algorithm. Nevertheless they remain of high importance in scenarios in which the *IV* is involuntarily re-used e.g. due to an implementation or human error.

4   Differential Biases After Initialization

In this section we describe differential biases in the words of the state after initialization in reduced word versions of MORUS.

We analyze versions of MORUS with 8 bit and 10 bit words (resp. 160 bit and 200 bit state), denoted resp. MORUS-160 and MORUS-200. In the latter, the rotation constants are the same as in the original version modulo the word size. For both small versions we initialize the input state to a fixed random value. Next we try all differences in one word of the IV and we measure the probabilities with which differences in the words of the state after the initialization appear.

For MORUS-160 the best observed probability is $2^{-4.19}$ (see Example 1 below), while for MORUS-200 it is 2^{-6}. These values are higher than what is expected in the random case resp. 2^{-8} and 2^{-10}. Due to the bitwise nature of the cipher, these results also suggest that for the original 32 and 64 bit versions of MORUS resp. MORUS-640 and MORUS-1280 we can expect probabilities significantly higher than resp. 2^{-32} and 2^{-64}.

Example 1 (Differential bias in MORUS-160). Let X be an input state initialized to the following random values (in hexadecimal) for MORUS-160:

$$X = (3B, 77, E3, DE, F0, EC, D9, DD, 2F, D0, F5, C7, DF, 7E, C8, DD, E7, 1D, 3A, 73),   (16)$$

where the first (i.e. leftmost) four entries correspond to the IV and the next four entries correspond to the key K i.e. IV = 3B77E3DE and K = F0ECD9DD. Let $X' = X \oplus \Delta X$ be a second input state that differs from X only in the first (i.e. leftmost) word of the IV by the difference:

$$\Delta X = (AB, 0, 0, 0, 0, 0, 0, 0, 0, 0, 0, 0, 0, 0, 0, 0, 0, 0, 0, 0).   (17)$$

Then the sixth word of the output difference ΔY between the corresponding output states Y and Y' after initialization is expected to be 4 with probability $2^{-4.19}$. The latter can be expressed as the following truncated differential:

$$P(\Delta X = (AB, 0, 0, 0, 0, 0, 0, 0, 0, 0, 0, 0, 0, 0, 0, 0, 0, 0, 0, 0) \xrightarrow{\text{Init.}}$$
$$\Delta Y = (*, *, *, *, *, 4, *, *, *, *, *, *, *, *, *, *, *, *, *, *)) = 2^{-4.19},$$

where $*$ denotes an unknown difference.   □

We note that the above analysis is different than the analysis described by the designers in [1, Sect. 4.1]. There, for a given difference in the IV, the designers estimate the probability of a full state after the initialization as opposed to a state truncated to a single word. Finally, we stress that the described observation does not directly threaten the security of MORUS. Nevertheless its full security implications should further be investigated.

5 Collisions in the StateUpdate(S, M) Function

In this section we present a collision on the internal StateUpdate(S, M) function. We begin by describing an alternative representation of the state update function.

Proposition 1. *Let M, $x_i \in \mathbb{Z}_2^n$, $i \geq 0$ and $n \in \{128, 256\}$, and let $w_i \leq n$ and $b_i \leq n/4$ be some rotation constants. Then the following function $F_M : (\mathbb{Z}_2^n)^5 \to (\mathbb{Z}_2^n)^5$ is a permutation on $(\mathbb{Z}_2^n)^5$:*

$$F_M(x_i, x_{i+1}, x_{i+2}, x_{i+3}, x_{i+4})$$
$$= (\text{Rotl\_xxx\_yy}(x_i \oplus (x_{i+1} \wedge x_{i+2}) \oplus x_{i+3} \oplus M, b_i),$$
$$x_{i+1}, \ x_{i+2}, \ (x_{i+3} \lll w_i), \ x_{i+4}). \tag{18}$$

Each round of StateUpdate(S, M) can be represented as five applications of the function F_{m_i}, where $m_i = M$ for $i = \{1, 2, 3, 4\}$ and $m_i = 0^{(n)}$ for $i = 0$:

$$(s_i, s_{(i+1)}, s_{(i+2)}, s_{(i+3)}, s_{(i+4)}) = F_{m_i}(s_i, s_{(i+1)}, s_{(i+2)}, s_{(i+3)}, s_{(i+4)}), \tag{19}$$

and the additions $(i+1), \ldots, (i+4)$ in the indices of s are performed modulo 5. From the fact that StateUpdate(S, M) is a composition of permutations on $(\mathbb{Z}_2^n)^5$ it follows that for fixed $M \in \mathbb{Z}_2^n$, the function is a permutation on $(\mathbb{Z}_2^n)^5$. Next, we describe a collision on the F_M function.

Proposition 2. *Let $w_i \leq n$ and $b_i \leq n/4$, where $i \geq 0$ and $n = \{128, 256\}$, be some rotation constants. For all $M_1, M_2 \in \mathbb{Z}_2^n$ and each vector $(x_0, x_1, x_2, x_3, x_4) \in (\mathbb{Z}_2^n)^5$, the following holds:*

$$F_{M_1}(x_0, x_1, x_2, x_3, x_4) = F_{M_2}(M_1 \oplus M_2 \oplus x_0, x_1, x_2, x_3, x_4). \tag{20}$$

Proof.

$$F_{M_2}(M_1 \oplus M_2 \oplus x_0, x_1, x_2, x_3, x_4)$$
$$= (\text{Rotl\_xxx\_yy}(M_1 \oplus M_2 \oplus x_0 \oplus (x_1 \wedge x_2) \oplus x_3 \oplus M_2, b_i),$$
$$x_1, x_2, (x_3 \lll w_i), x_4) \tag{21}$$
$$= (\text{Rotl\_xxx\_yy}(M_1 \oplus x_0 \oplus (x_1 \wedge x_2) \oplus x_3, b_i), x_1, x_2, (x_3 \lll w_i), x_4) \tag{22}$$
$$= F_{M_1}(x_0, x_1, x_2, x_3, x_4). \tag{23}$$

$\square$

Proposition 2 is extended to a collision on the state update function due to the following corollary:

Corollary 1. *For all $M_1, M_2 \in \mathbb{Z}_2^n, n = \{128, 256\}$ and each vector $(x_0, x_1, x_2, x_3, x_4) \in (\mathbb{Z}_2^n)^5$, the following holds:*

$$\text{StateUpdate}((x_0, x_1, x_2, x_3, x_4), M_1) =$$
$$\text{StateUpdate}((x_0, \ M_1 \oplus M_2 \oplus x_1, M_1 \oplus M_2 \oplus x_2, \ M_1 \oplus M_2 \oplus x_3,$$
$$M_1 \oplus M_2 \oplus x_4), \ M_2). \tag{24}$$

In the following section we briefly comment on the possibility of using the collision (24) to construct a tag forgery attack in a nonce-reuse scenario.

6 On Producing a Tag Forgery

Let (M_1, AD_1) be a pair of a 128 bit message block and a 128 bit associated data block encrypted by MORUS under key K and IV. Let $S^0 = (s_0, s_1, s_2, s_3, s_4)$ be the output of the initialization phase and let the output of the next phase (processing of associated data) be $S^1 = (x_0, x_1, x_2, x_3, x_4) =$ StateUpdate(S^0, AD_1). We want to find a 128 bit block ΔM and a 128 bit associated data block $AD_2 \neq AD_1$ that will relate StateUpdate(S^0, AD_1) to StateUpdate(S^0, AD_2) as follow:

$$\text{StateUpdate}(S^0, AD_2) = (x_0, x_1 \oplus \Delta M, x_2 \oplus \Delta M, x_3 \oplus \Delta M, x_4 \oplus \Delta M) \quad (25)$$

$$= (x_0, x_1, x_2, x_3, x_4) \oplus (0^{(n)}, \Delta M, \Delta M, \Delta M, \Delta M) \quad (26)$$

$$= \text{StateUpdate}(S^0, AD_1) \oplus$$
$$(0^{(n)}, \Delta M, \Delta M, \Delta M, \Delta M). \quad (27)$$

If such AD_2 and ΔM exist, then using Corollary 1 (Eq. (24)) we can construct the message $M_2 = M_1 \oplus \Delta M$ that will produce a collision in the internal state after the encryption phase:

$$\text{StateUpdate}(\text{StateUpdate}(S^0, AD_1), M_1) \quad (28)$$

$$= \text{StateUpdate}((x_0, x_1, x_2, x_3, x_4), M_1) \quad (29)$$

$$= \text{StateUpdate}((x_0, M_1 \oplus M_2 \oplus x_1, M_1 \oplus M_2 \oplus x_2, M_1 \oplus M_2 \oplus x_3,$$
$$M_1 \oplus M_2 \oplus x_4), M_2) \quad (30)$$

$$= \text{StateUpdate}((x_0, \Delta M \oplus x_1, \Delta M \oplus x_2, \Delta M \oplus x_3, \Delta M \oplus x_4), M_2) \quad (31)$$

$$= \text{StateUpdate}(\text{StateUpdate}(S^0, AD_2), M_2) \quad (32)$$

Therefore, under the same IV the two messages M_1 and $M_2 = M_1 \oplus \Delta M$ produce the same internal state after the encryption phase. Furthermore, since both pairs (AD_1, M_1) and (AD_2, M_2) have the same adlen and msglen, the above collision ultimately results in the same tag for the messages M_1 and M_2.

As to finding the required blocks ΔM and AD_2, in Appendix B we show that this is equivalent to solving the following system of equations for $(x_0, x_1, \Delta A, \Delta M)$, where $\Delta A = AD_1 \oplus AD_2$:

$$\begin{cases} \text{Rotr\_xxx\_yy}(\Delta M \ggg w_3, b_1) = \Delta A \\ \text{Rotr\_xxx\_yy}(\Delta M \ggg w_4, b_2) = \Delta A \\ \text{Rotr\_xxx\_yy}(\Delta M, b_3) = (\Delta M \ggg w_3) \oplus \Delta A \\ \text{Rotr\_xxx\_yy}(\Delta M, b_4) = (x_0 \wedge x_1) \oplus (x_0 \wedge (x_1 \oplus \Delta M)) \oplus (\Delta M \ggg w_4) \end{cases} \quad (33)$$

We exhaustively searched for a solution to a reduced version of the system (33) composed of the first three equations with 8 bit variables and rotation constants equal to the original ones modulo 8. No solution was found apart from the trivial one: $(\Delta M, \Delta A) = (0, 0)$.

7   Conclusions

In this paper we presented the first external analysis of the authenticated cipher MORUS. In particular we reported the following new observations: (1) distinguisher with probability 1 in a nonce-reuse scenario, (2) differential biases in the words of the state after initialization and (3) collision on the StateUpdate function of MORUS. Our results do not threaten the security of the scheme and indicate that MORUS is a well-designed cipher and a good candidate for the second round of the CAESAR competition.

Acknowledgments. We would like to thank the anonymous reviewers for their time and valuable comments. In particular, we thank Reviewer 2 for pointing out the natural extension of our technique to the case where differences in the message blocks are allowed. Finally, we extend our thanks to the organizers of WG4 Meeting on Authenticated Encryption, COST CryptoAction IC1306, co-located with Eurocrypt 2015, for giving us the opportunity to work on this topic.

A   Proof of Theorem 1

Proof. The state update function of MORUS-640 under AD_1 is expressed as follow:

$$(x_0, x_1, x_2, x_3, x_4) = \text{StateUpdate}((s_0, s_1, s_2, s_3, s_4), AD_1), \quad (34)$$

where

$$x_0 = \text{Rotl\_xxx\_yy}(s_0 \oplus (s_1 \wedge s_2) \oplus s_3, 5) \lll 96, \quad (35)$$

$$x_1 = \text{Rotl\_xxx\_yy}(s_1 \oplus (s_2 \wedge (s_3 \lll 32)) \oplus s_4 \oplus AD_1, 31) \lll 64, \quad (36)$$

$$x_2 = \text{Rotl\_xxx\_yy}(s_2 \oplus ((s_3 \lll 32) \wedge (s_4 \lll 64)) \oplus$$
$$(x_0 \ggg 96) \oplus AD_1, 7) \lll 32, \quad (37)$$

$$x_3 = \text{Rotl\_xxx\_yy}((s_3 \lll 32) \oplus ((s_4 \lll 64) \wedge x_0) \oplus$$
$$(x_1 \ggg 64) \oplus AD_1, 22), \quad (38)$$

$$x_4 = \text{Rotl\_xxx\_yy}((s_4 \lll 64) \oplus (x_0 \wedge x_1) \oplus (x_2 \ggg 32) \oplus AD_1, 13). \quad (39)$$

We recall that each element x_j and y_j of the states $X = (x_0, x_1, x_2, x_3, x_4)$ and $Y = (y_0, y_1, y_2, y_3, y_4)$ is of size 128 bits organized in an array of four 32 bit words. Denote these words as $x_j = (x_{j0}, x_{j1}, x_{j2}, x_{j3})$ and $y_j = (y_{j0}, y_{j1}, y_{j2}, y_{j3})$, where $|x_{ji}| = |y_{ji}| = 32$ bits for $0 \le j \le 4, 1 \le i \le 3$.

Proof of Statement 1: $x_0 = y_0$. Since Eq. (35) does not depend on the associated data block, it will be the same for both AD_1 and AD_2. It follows that $x_0 = y_0$.

Proof of Statement 2: Difference Between Words x_1 and y_1. In Eq. (36) denote

$$a_1 = s_1 \oplus (s_2 \wedge (s_3 \lll 32)) \oplus s_4 , \tag{40}$$

$$\begin{aligned} b_1 &= (b_{10}, b_{11}, b_{12}, b_{13}) \\ &= \text{Rotl\_xxx\_yy}(a_1 \oplus \text{AD}_1, 31) \\ &= \text{Rotl\_xxx\_yy}(a_1, 31) . \end{aligned} \tag{41}$$

After rotation by 64 (see Eq. (36)) we have

$$x_1 = (x_{10}, x_{11}, x_{12}, x_{13}) = (b_{12}, b_{13}, b_{10}, b_{11}) . \tag{42}$$

For the second associated data block $\text{AD}_2 = (0^{(127)}||1)$ denote

$$\begin{aligned} c_1 &= (c_{10}, c_{11}, c_{12}, c_{13}) \\ &= \text{Rotl\_xxx\_yy}(a_1 \oplus \text{AD}_2, 31) \\ &= \text{Rotl\_xxx\_yy}(a_1 \oplus (0^{(127)}||1), 31) . \end{aligned} \tag{43}$$

Analogously to AD_1, after rotation by 64 (see Eq. (36)) we get

$$y_1 = (y_{10}, y_{11}, y_{12}, y_{13}) = (x_{10}, x_{11} \oplus (1||0^{(31)}), x_{12}, x_{13}) . \tag{44}$$

For the words of b_1 and c_1, the following equalities hold:

$$c_{10} = b_{10} = x_{12} , \tag{45}$$

$$c_{11} = b_{11} = x_{13} , \tag{46}$$

$$c_{12} = b_{12} = x_{10} , \tag{47}$$

$$c_{13} = b_{13} \oplus (1||0^{(31)}) = x_{11} \oplus (1||0^{(31)}) . \tag{48}$$

Therefore x_1 and y_1 differ only in the 33-th bit (counting from MSB to LSB).

Proof of Statement 3: Difference Between Words x_2 and y_2. In Eq. (37) denote

$$a_2 = s_2 \oplus ((s_3 \lll 32) \wedge (s_4 \lll 64)) \oplus (x_0 \ggg 96) , \tag{49}$$

$$\begin{aligned} b_2 &= (b_{20}, b_{21}, b_{22}, b_{23}) \\ &= \text{Rotl\_xxx\_yy}(a_2 \oplus \text{AD}_1, 7) \\ &= \text{Rotl\_xxx\_yy}(a_2, 7) . \end{aligned} \tag{50}$$

After rotation by 32 (see Eq. (36)) we have

$$x_2 = (x_{20}, x_{21}, x_{22}, x_{23}) = (b_{21}, b_{22}, b_{23}, b_{20}) . \tag{51}$$

For the second associated data block $\text{AD}_2 = (0^{(127)}||1)$ denote

$$c_2 = (c_{20}, c_{21}, c_{22}, c_{23})$$
$$= \text{Rotl\_xxx\_yy}(a_2 \oplus AD_2, 7)$$
$$= \text{Rotl\_xxx\_yy}(a_2 \oplus (0^{(127)}||1), 7). \tag{52}$$

For the words of b_2 and c_2, the following equalities hold:

$$c_{20} = b_{20} = x_{23}, \tag{53}$$
$$c_{21} = b_{21} = x_{20}, \tag{54}$$
$$c_{22} = b_{22} = x_{21}, \tag{55}$$
$$c_{23} = b_{23} \oplus (0^{(24)}||1||0^{(7)}) = x_{22} \oplus (0^{(24)}||1||0^{(7)}), \tag{56}$$

and so

$$y_2 = (y_{20}, y_{21}, y_{22}, y_{23}) = (x_{20}, x_{21}, x_{22} \oplus (0^{(24)}||1||0^{(7)}), x_{23}). \tag{57}$$

Therefore x_2 and y_2 differ only in the 89-th bit (counting from MSB to LSB).

Proof of Statement 4: Difference Between Words x_3 and y_3. In Eq. (38) denote

$$a_3 = (s_3 \lll 32) \oplus ((s_4 \lll 64) \wedge x_0). \tag{58}$$

For x_3 we have

$$x_3 = \text{Rotl\_xxx\_yy}(a_3 \oplus (x_1 \ggg 64) \oplus AD_1, 22) \tag{59}$$
$$= \text{Rotl\_xxx\_yy}(a_3 \oplus (x_{12}, x_{13}, x_{10}, x_{11}), 22) \tag{60}$$
$$= ((a_{30} \oplus x_{12}) \lll 22, \ (a_{31} \oplus x_{13}) \lll 22, \ (a_{32} \oplus x_{10}) \lll 22,$$
$$(a_{33} \oplus x_{11}) \lll 22) \tag{61}$$
$$= (x_{30}, x_{31}, x_{32}, x_{33}). \tag{62}$$

For y_3 we have

$$y_3 = \text{Rotl\_xxx\_yy}(a_3 \oplus (y_1 \ggg 64) \oplus AD_2, 22) \tag{63}$$
$$= \text{Rotl\_xxx\_yy}(a_3 \oplus (x_{12}, x_{13}, x_{10}, x_{11} \oplus (1||0^{(31)})) \oplus (0^{(127)}||1), 22) \tag{64}$$
$$= \text{Rotl\_xxx\_yy}(a_3 \oplus (x_{12}, x_{13}, x_{10}, x_{11} \oplus (1||0^{(31)}) \oplus (0^{(31)}||1)), 22) \tag{65}$$
$$= ((a_{30} \oplus x_{12}) \lll 22, (a_{31} \oplus x_{13}) \lll 22, (a_{32} \oplus x_{10}) \lll 22,$$
$$(a_{33} \oplus x_{11} \oplus (1||0^{(31)}) \oplus (0^{(31)}||1)) \lll 22) \tag{66}$$
$$= (x_{30}, x_{31}, x_{32}, x_{33} \oplus (0^{(9)}||11||0^{(21)})). \tag{67}$$

Therefore x_3 and y_3 differ only in the 106-th and 107-th bit (counting from MSB to LSB).

Proof of Statement 5: Difference Between Words x_4 and y_4. In Eq. (39) denote

$$a_4 = s_4 \lll w_1. \tag{68}$$

Then x_4 can be expressed as:

$$x_4 = \text{Rotl\_xxx\_yy}(a_4 \oplus (x_0 \wedge x_1) \oplus (x_2 \ggg 32) \oplus AD_1, 13) \tag{69}$$

$$= \text{Rotl\_xxx\_yy}(a_4 \oplus (x_0 \wedge x_1) \oplus (x_{23}, x_{20}, x_{21}, x_{22}), 13) \tag{70}$$

$$= ((a_{40} \oplus (x_{00} \wedge x_{10}) \oplus x_{23}) \lll 13,\ (a_{41} \oplus (x_{01} \wedge x_{11}) \oplus x_{20}) \lll 13,$$
$$(a_{42} \oplus (x_{02} \wedge x_{12}) \oplus x_{21}) \lll 13,\ (a_{43} \oplus (x_{04} \wedge x_{14}) \oplus x_{22}) \lll 13) \tag{71}$$

$$= (x_{40}, x_{41}, x_{42}, x_{43}), \tag{72}$$

and y_4 is expressed as:

$$y_4 = \text{Rotl\_xxx\_yy}(a_4 \oplus (y_0 \wedge y_1) \oplus (y_2 \ggg 32) \oplus AD_2, 13) \tag{73}$$

$$= \text{Rotl\_xxx\_yy}(a_4 \oplus (x_0 \wedge y_1) \oplus$$
$$(x_{23}, x_{20}, x_{21}, x_{22} \oplus (0^{(24)}||1||0^{(7)})) \oplus (0^{(127)}||1), 13) \tag{74}$$

$$= ((a_{40} \oplus (x_{00} \wedge x_{10}) \oplus x_{23}) \lll 13,$$
$$(a_{41} \oplus (x_{01} \wedge (x_{11} \oplus (1||0^{(31)}))) \oplus x_{20}) \lll 13,$$
$$(a_{42} \oplus (x_{02} \wedge x_{12}) \oplus x_{21}) \lll 13,$$
$$(a_{43} \oplus (x_{04} \wedge x_{14}) \oplus x_{22} \oplus (0^{(24)}||1||0^{(6)}||1)) \lll 13) \tag{75}$$

$$= ((a_{40} \oplus (x_{00} \wedge x_{10}) \oplus x_{23}) \lll 13,$$
$$(a_{41} \oplus (x_{01} \wedge (x_{11} \oplus (1||0^{(31)}))) \oplus x_{20}) \lll 13,$$
$$(a_{42} \oplus (x_{02} \wedge x_{12}) \oplus x_{21}) \lll 13,$$
$$(a_{43} \oplus (x_{04} \wedge x_{14}) \oplus x_{22}) \lll 13 \oplus (0^{(11)}||1||0^{(6)}||1||0^{(13)})) \tag{76}$$

$$= (x_{40}, x'_{41}, x_{42}, x_{43} \oplus (0^{(11)}||1||0^{(6)}||1||0^{(13)})), \tag{77}$$

where x'_{41} differ from x_{41} at most in the first (i.e. most significant) bit with probability 1/2. Therefore x_4 and y_4 differ only in the 108-th and 115-th bit, and the 33-th bit is different with probability 1/2.   □

B   Derivation of the System of Equations (33) in Sect. 6

Let $X = (x_0, x_1, x_2, x_3, x_4) = \text{StateUpdate}(S^0, AD_1)$, and $Y = (y_0, y_1, y_2, y_3, y_4) = \text{StateUpdate}(S^0, AD_2)$. Let $x_1 \oplus y_1 = x_2 \oplus y_2 = x_3 \oplus y_3 = x_4 \oplus y_4 = \Delta M$. Clearly $x_0 = y_0$.

For $x_1 \oplus y_1$ we derive:

$$x_1 \oplus y_1 = \text{Rotl\_xxx\_yy}(s_1 \oplus (s_2 \wedge (s_3 \lll w_0)) \oplus s_4 \oplus AD_1, b_1) \lll w_3 \oplus$$
$$\text{Rotl\_xxx\_yy}(s_1 \oplus (s_2 \wedge (s_3 \lll w_0)) \oplus s_4 \oplus AD_2, b_1) \lll w_3 \tag{78}$$

$$\text{Rotr\_xxx\_yy}((x_1 \oplus y_1) \ggg w_3, b_1) = s_1 \oplus (s_2 \wedge (s_3 \lll w_0)) \oplus$$
$$s_4 \oplus AD_1 \oplus s_1 \oplus (s_2 \wedge (s_3 \lll w_0)) \oplus s_4 \oplus AD_2 \tag{79}$$

$$\text{Rotr\_xxx\_yy}((x_1 \oplus y_1) \ggg w_3, b_1) = AD_1 \oplus AD_2 \tag{80}$$

For $x_2 \oplus y_2$ we derive:

$$\begin{aligned}
x_2 \oplus y_2 = {}&\text{Rotl\_xxx\_yy}(s_2 \oplus ((s_3 \lll w_0) \wedge (s_4 \lll w_1)) \oplus \\
&(x_0 \ggg w_2) \oplus \text{AD}_1, b_2) \lll w_4 \oplus \\
&\text{Rotl\_xxx\_yy}(s_2 \oplus ((s_3 \lll w_0) \wedge (s_4 \lll w_1)) \oplus \\
&(y_0 \ggg w_2) \oplus \text{AD}_2, b_2) \lll w_4
\end{aligned} \tag{81}$$

$$\begin{aligned}
\text{Rotr\_xxx\_yy}((x_2 \oplus y_2) \ggg w_4, b_2) = {}&s_2 \oplus ((s_3 \lll w_0) \wedge (s_4 \lll w_1)) \oplus \\
&(x_0 \ggg w_2) \oplus \text{AD}_1 \oplus s_2 \oplus ((s_3 \lll w_0) \wedge (s_4 \lll w_1)) \oplus \\
&(y_0 \ggg w_2) \oplus \text{AD}_2
\end{aligned} \tag{82}$$

$$\text{Rotr\_xxx\_yy}((x_2 \oplus y_2) \ggg w_4, b_2) = \text{AD}_1 \oplus \text{AD}_2 \tag{83}$$

For $x_3 \oplus y_3$ we derive:

$$\begin{aligned}
x_3 \oplus y_3 = {}&\text{Rotl\_xxx\_yy}((s_3 \lll w_0) \oplus ((s_4 \lll w_1) \wedge x_0) \oplus (x_1 \ggg w_3) \oplus \\
&\text{AD}_1, b_3) \oplus \text{Rotl\_xxx\_yy}((s_3 \lll w_0) \oplus ((s_4 \lll w_1) \wedge y_0) \oplus \\
&(y_1 \ggg w_3) \oplus \text{AD}_2, b_3)
\end{aligned} \tag{84}$$

$$\begin{aligned}
\text{Rotr\_xxx\_yy}(x_3 \oplus y_3, b_3) = {}&\\
&(s_3 \lll w_0) \oplus ((s_4 \lll w_1) \wedge x_0) \oplus (x_1 \ggg w_3) \oplus \\
&\text{AD}_1 \oplus (s_3 \lll w_0) \oplus ((s_4 \lll w_1) \wedge y_0) \oplus (y_1 \ggg w_3) \oplus \text{AD}_2
\end{aligned} \tag{85}$$

$$\text{Rotr\_xxx\_yy}(x_3 \oplus y_3, b_3) = (x_1 \ggg w_3) \oplus (y_1 \ggg w_3) \oplus \text{AD}_1 \oplus \text{AD}_2 \tag{86}$$

For $x_4 \oplus y_4$ we derive:

$$\begin{aligned}
x_4 \oplus y_4 = {}&\text{Rotl\_xxx\_yy}((s_4 \lll w_1) \oplus (x_0 \wedge x_1) \oplus (x_2 \ggg w_4) \oplus \\
&\text{AD}_1, b_4) \oplus \text{Rotl\_xxx\_yy}((s_4 \lll w_1) \oplus (y_0 \wedge y_1) \oplus \\
&(y_2 \ggg w_4) \oplus \text{AD}_2, b_4)
\end{aligned} \tag{87}$$

$$\begin{aligned}
\text{Rotr\_xxx\_yy}(x_4 \oplus y_4, b_4) = {}&(s_4 \lll w_1) \oplus (x_0 \wedge x_1) \oplus (x_2 \ggg w_4) \oplus \\
&\text{AD}_1 \oplus (s_4 \lll w_1) \oplus (y_0 \wedge y_1) \oplus (y_2 \ggg w_4) \oplus \text{AD}_2
\end{aligned} \tag{88}$$

$$\begin{aligned}
\text{Rotr\_xxx\_yy}(x_4 \oplus y_4, b_4) = {}&(x_0 \wedge x_1) \oplus (y_0 \wedge y_1) \oplus (x_2 \ggg w_4) \oplus \\
&(y_2 \ggg w_4) \oplus \text{AD}_1 \oplus \text{AD}_2
\end{aligned} \tag{89}$$

From Eqs. (80), (83), (86) and (89) we obtain the following system that is equivalent to the system (33) from Sect. 6:

$$\left\{ \begin{aligned}
&\text{Rotr\_xxx\_yy}((x_1 \oplus y_1) \ggg w_3, b_1) = \text{AD}_1 \oplus \text{AD}_2 \\
&\text{Rotr\_xxx\_yy}((x_2 \oplus y_2) \ggg w_4, b_2) = \text{AD}_1 \oplus \text{AD}_2 \\
&\text{Rotr\_xxx\_yy}(x_3 \oplus y_3, b_3) = (x_1 \ggg w_3) \oplus (y_1 \ggg w_3) \oplus \text{AD}_1 \oplus \text{AD}_2 \\
&\text{Rotr\_xxx\_yy}(x_4 \oplus y_4, b_4) = (x_0 \wedge x_1) \oplus (y_0 \wedge y_1) \oplus (x_2 \ggg w_4) \oplus \\
&\qquad\qquad\qquad\qquad\qquad (y_2 \ggg w_4) \oplus \text{AD}_1 \oplus \text{AD}_2
\end{aligned} \right. \tag{90}$$

References

1. Wu, H., Huang, T.: The authenticated cipher MORUS (v1), CAESAR candidate, 15 March 2014

2. CAESAR - Competition for Authenticated Encryption: Security, Applicability, and Robustness (2014). http://competitions.cr.yp.to/caesar.html
3. National Institute of Standards and Technology, Announcing Request for Candidate Algorithm Nominations for a the Advanced Encryption Standard (AES), Federal Register, vol. 62, pp. 48051–48058, September 1997. http://csrc.nist.gov/archive/aes/pre-round1/aes_9709.htm
4. National Institute of Standards and Technology, Announcing Request for Candidate Algorithm Nominations for a New Cryptographic Hash Algorithm (SHA-3) Family, Federal Register, vol. 27, pp. 62212–62220, November 2007. http://csrc.nist.gov/groups/ST/hash/documents/FR_Notice_Nov07.pdf
5. Daemen, J., Rijmen, V.: AES and the wide trail design strategy. In: Knudsen, L.R. (ed.) EUROCRYPT 2002. LNCS, vol. 2332, pp. 108–109. Springer, Heidelberg (2002)
6. Bertoni, G., Daemen, J., Peeters, M., Van Assche, G.: Keccak. In: Johansson, T., Nguyen, P.Q. (eds.) EUROCRYPT 2013. LNCS, vol. 7881, pp. 313–314. Springer, Heidelberg (2013)

Linear Cryptanalysis and Modified DES with Embedded Parity Check in the S-boxes

Yuri Borissov$^{(\boxtimes)}$, Peter Boyvalenkov, and Robert Tsenkov

Institute of Mathematics and Informatics, Bulgarian Academy of Sciences,
8 G. Bonchev str., 1113 Sofia, Bulgaria
youri@math.bas.bg

Abstract. It is a common belief that the presence of linear relations in the S-boxes of some block cipher algorithm facilitates its linear cryptanalysis and related attacks towards. In the present work, we clarify that claim in respect to a linear cryptanalysis (in the very spirit of Matsui's classic one) applied to modified DES algorithm with S-boxes having parity check bits. The results of our investigations show that embedding parity checks in the outputs of these S-boxes does not generally guarantee more suitable for that kind of cryptanalysis best multi-round linear characteristics. Their structure, the corresponding bias and the number of effective bits depend crucially on the parity position chosen, and may lead not only to reduction but as well to growth in complexity of successful linear cryptanalysis compared to that towards the original DES.

1 Introduction

Around 1993 two general techniques to mount attacks against the modern symmetric block ciphers have appeared in the public domain: the so-called differential and linear cryptanalysis [2,11]. Both of them were applied to the Data Encryption Standard (DES) and showed that the standard is breakable faster than an exhaustive key search in corresponding attack scenarios. Although the primary target of these attacks was the DES, the wide applicability of them to numerous other block ciphers is out of any doubt. Moreover, today, one of the first questions which the members of cryptographic community pose to each new proposal for block cipher algorithm is whether it outstands those kind of cryptanalysis [8,17]. Another recent contribution [4] concerns both kinds of cryptanalysis with respect to affine equivalence of the employed S-boxes.

Roughly speaking, the idea of linear cryptanalysis of block ciphers, is to employ linear probabilistic relations of the following type:

$$\mathbf{P}[\chi_P] + \mathbf{C}[\chi_C] = \mathbf{K}[\chi_K],$$

where $\mathbf{P}, \mathbf{C}$ and $\mathbf{K}$ denote the plaintext, the corresponding ciphertext and the secret key, respectively, while $\mathbf{B}[\chi_B]$ stands for $B_{b_1} \oplus B_{b_2} \oplus \cdots \oplus B_{b_m}$ with $\chi_B = \{b_1, b_2, \ldots, b_m\}$ a subset (or mask) of bit positions in $\mathbf{B}$. Among these relations (also called characteristics), the most valuable for cryptanalysis are those, effective ones, that hold true with probability deviating significantly from $1/2$. In practice, for the iterative block ciphers based on S-boxes, e.g. Feistel or SP

© Springer International Publishing Switzerland 2016
E. Pasalic and L.R. Knudsen (Eds.): BalkanCryptSec 2015, LNCS 9540, pp. 60–78, 2016.
DOI: 10.1007/978-3-319-29172-7_5

networks, effective characteristics can be obtained by fixing, at first, the generic firmed correlations between the inputs and outputs of the individual boxes, and then concatenating these local 1-round linear dependencies through the involved round F-functions in multi-round ones valid for the global cipher structure.

The experience gained in carrying out that method has enabled the development of its modifications and extensions, and improving of the respective encryption algorithms in order to be more resistant against it (see, e.g. [1,7,12,14] and definitely this list of references is not exhaustive).

In this paper, we are focused on linear cryptanalysis towards one of the possible modifications of DES. Our aim is to clarify more comprehensively the intuition behind the claim that introducing some strict linear relation in the S-boxes of this algorithm will weaken the cipher facilitating significantly a cryptanalysis of that kind. Though there are other possibilities for inserting such relations which deserved to be explored in respect to the aforementioned claim (e.g. setting an output bit to be equal to a linear function of the input bits of an S-box), we elaborate only on a modification for which chosen in advance position of output of the original S-boxes is changed to the parity check of the other three positions that are kept unchanged. The reason for studying this particular variant of the algorithm is twofold. On the one hand, an S-box obtained in the described way preserves the nonlinearity between the input and output, and simultaneously meets the requirements of other desirable criteria, see e.g. [10, p. 301]. (In particular, such S-box satisfies automatically the criteria concerning spectrum of Hamming distances between its outputs, relevant in case of differential cryptanalysis [5].) On the other hand, in regard to the kind of cryptanalysis we are interested, it turns out that this modification does not worsen half of the local characteristics and even improves upon the bias of the maximum effective one with nonempty input mask. But of course, by all means it is not clear whether the change of these local characteristics leads to global ones that do spoil the resistance of cipher.

The outline of the present paper is as follows. In Sect. 2, we introduce the needed notations and definitions, recall some of Matsui's results and describe briefly the settings of our experiment. Section 3 is devoted to study of the properties of the new linear approximation tables and some consequences. In Sect. 4, we prove that effectiveness of the optimal 3-round characteristic decreases. In Sect. 5, we describe in more detail our algorithm for construction of best characteristics including the case when a parity check has been embedded. We see that the presence of parity increases the number of the possible combinations between 1-round characteristics in consecutive rounds. The final results, their analysis and conclusions are presented in Sects. 6 and 7.

2 Preliminaries

2.1 Notations and Definitions

For easier comparison of the results we use in our work the Matsui conventions for bit indexing and S-boxes [11–13]. Each S-box is represented as one-dimensional array with input of the S-box as index. The index of the S-boxes themselves remains the same as in the standard. Everywhere the less significant bit is the right most bit and its index is 0.

Let us consider a family of Feistel type cryptographic algorithms with n rounds and denote:

P, C – the plaintext and the ciphertext, both $2b$ bits long;
K, K_j – the secret key and the corresponding j-th round subkey;
X_j, F_j – the j-th round transformation data input/output;
$f_j(X_j, K_j)$ – the j-th round transformation;
S_k – the k-th S-box; $S(j)$ – the active S-box in the j-th round, when there is at most one such S-box; $S(j) = \phi$ means no active S-box is chosen;
$I_X(j), I_K(j), I_F(j)$ – sets of indices of all bits of X_j, K_j and F_j respectively, that take part in the j-th round linear approximation;
$I_X(S_k, j), I_X(S(j)), I_K(S_k, j), I_K(S(j)), I_F(S_k, j), I_F(S(j))$ – sets of indices of all bits of X_j, K_j and F_j respectively, that are part of the input and the output of $S_k/S(j)$ respectively in the j-th round;
$A[i]$ – the i-th bit of the vector A; $A[i, j, \ldots, k] = A[i] \oplus A[j] \oplus \cdots \oplus A[k]$;
$A[B]$ – the XOR-sum of all bits of A with indices in the set B.

Definition 1. *An 1-round linear characteristic for the round j of a Feistel cipher is a pair $(I_X(j), I_F(j))$ of sets of bit indices from the input and the output of this round, respectively. An n-round linear characteristic for rounds $1, \ldots, n$, $n \geq 3$, is an n-tuple $((I_X(1), I_F(1)), \ldots, (I_X(n), I_F(n)))$ of 1-round linear characteristics with the property*

$$I_F(j + 1) = (I_F(j - 1) \cup I_X(j)) \setminus (I_F(j - 1) \cap I_X(j)) \tag{1}$$

for all $2 \leq j \leq n - 1$ (i.e. if $I_F(j + 1)$ is the symmetric difference of $I_F(j - 1)$ and $I_X(j)$).

Every characteristic is associated with a given pair of chosen subsets of indices of input/output bits and the corresponding probability of coincidence of their respective sums.

Definition 2. *For given S-box S_k with a-bit input and c-bit output and given numbers α and β, such that $0 \leq \alpha \leq 2^a - 1$ and $0 \leq \beta \leq 2^c - 1$, we define $NS_k(\alpha, \beta)$ as the number of times out of 2^a input patterns of S_k, such that an XOR-ed value of the input bits masked by α coincides with an XOR-ed value of the output bits masked by β. In other words $NS_k(\alpha, \beta) = \#\{x | 0 \leq x \leq 2^a - 1 \text{ and } \oplus_s(x[s] \circ \alpha[s]) = \oplus_t(S_k(x)[t] \circ \beta[t])\}$, where the symbol $\circ$ denotes bitwise AND operator. The table, where the vertical and the horizontal axes indicate α and β respectively, and each entry contains the value*

$$NS_k^*(\alpha, \beta) = NS_k(\alpha, \beta) - 2^{a-1}$$

is referred to as linear approximation table *(LAT) for S_k.*

For the purpose of comparing different characteristics we consider approximations of type

$$P[i_1, \ldots, i_p] \oplus C[j_1, \ldots, j_q] \oplus f_1(P, K_1)[u_1, \ldots, u_s] \oplus$$
$$\oplus f_n(C, K_n)[v_1, \ldots, v_t] = K[k_1, \ldots, k_r], \tag{2}$$

that can be drawn from an $(n-2)$-round characteristic combined with the structural dependencies in the first and final round, respectively. (In fact, that kind of approximations are the main used in Algorithm 2, the second out of the two cryptanalytic algorithms suggested in [12], which requires a lower amount of plaintext/ciphertext pairs and is more efficient than the first Algorithm 1.)

Definition 3. *If a linear approximation holds with probability $p \neq 1/2$ for randomly given plaintext P and the corresponding ciphertext C, the absolute value of the* bias $p - 1/2$ *represents the* effectiveness *of that approximation.*

Definition 4. *A linear characteristic is called* best characteristic *when the effectiveness of corresponding linear approximation is maximal. Respectively, its probability will be called* best probability.

Example 1. There is an unique best 1-round characteristic for DES (see, e.g., [16]), namely corresponding to the global minimum $NS_5^*(16, 15) = -20$ with effectiveness 0.31.

Definition 5. *All key bits and text (plaintext and ciphertext) bits, that affect the left side of the Eq. (2) are referred to as* effective bits.

2.2   A Brief Overview of Matsui's Work

In his corner-stone papers, Matsui [11,13] has analyzed LATs, found best characteristics for 3 to 20 rounds and studied some approaches for mounting attacks against different rounds of DES cipher.

The main properties of LATs are given in the next proposition that is stated as lemma in [11].

Proposition 1. (i) $NS_k(\alpha, \beta)$ *is even.*
(ii) *If $\alpha = 1, 32$ or 33, then $NS_k(\alpha, \beta) = 32$ for all S_k and β.*

The effectiveness of an 1-round approximation is deduced directly from the LATs, while for multi-round approximation the so-called Piling-up Lemma [11] is applied.

The first experimental cryptanalytic attack on DES, carried out by Matsui [13], is based on approximations of type (2) derived from best 14-round characteristics. He has found two such characteristics, that are symmetric to each other but can be considered as statistically independent, and possess effectiveness of 1.19×2^{-21}. Each of the exploited linear approximations has also two active S-boxes and can recover 13 effective key bits. After fixing the values of these key bits (and consequently a total of 26 secret key bits) using a maximum likelihood method, the remaining 30 unknown key bits are found by an exhaustive search.

Matsui has shown [13] that the complexity of a linear attack, based on approximation of type (2), practically depends only on the effectiveness e of that approximation and the output bits $u_1, \ldots, u_s, v_1, \ldots, v_t$. The latter bits themselves depend on the effective text and key bits. The number of plaintext/ciphertext pairs needed for an attack to be successful with high probability is proportional to e^{-2}. As a result, by that approach the DES becomes breakable with complexity 2^{43} at success rate of 85 % if 2^{43} known plaintexts are available.

2.3 Our Experiment

During the experiment we carry out the following steps:

1. Embedding parity check bit in all S-boxes of the original DES cipher and analyzing the newly obtained LATs.
2. Finding best characteristics for 3 to 20 rounds of the modified cipher when the parity bit position is the same in all S-boxes.
3. Comparing the results obtained to that for the original cipher.
4. Studying in details the 16-round linear approximations based on the best 14-round characteristics found for modified DES.

Without loss of generality we assume embedding of odd parity. We associate the index of the parity bit in S-box S_k with its mask π_k. Parity bit masks can take values 0, 1, 2, 4 and 8 or their 4-bit representations. A mask with value 0 will mean no parity is embedded. When all S-boxes have a parity bit at the same position, we will call this "case". For example "case 1000" means all S-boxes have a parity bit at left-most position in their outputs. In addition, we will use the following notation: $S_{k(\pi)}$ for the S-box, obtained from S_k by embedding a parity bit with mask π, and $NS_k(\pi; \alpha, \beta)$ and $NS_k^*(\pi; \alpha, \beta)$ for the corresponding values in the LATs.

Example 2. The result from embedding the parity check with mask 0100 on the output of S_7 in hexadecimal format is given in Table 1. For reader's convenience, we remind that the chosen parity embedding is odd.

Table 1. S_7 and $S_{7(0100)}$ (first 16 elements)

index	00	01	02	03	04	05	06	07	08	09	10	11	12	13	14	15
S_7	4	d	b	0	2	b	e	7	f	4	0	9	8	1	d	a
$S_{7(0100)}$	4	d	b	4	2	b	e	7	b	4	4	d	8	1	d	e

3 Properties of LATs of S-boxes with Embedded Parity Check

In this section, we describe the relations between elements of the LATS of newly obtained S-boxes that are due to parity check embedded.

For the sake of clarity, we study separately the case of simultaneously non-zero input and output mask and the remaining case, i.e. when at least one of these masks equals 0.

3.1 The Part of LATs with Non-zero Input and Output Masks

In this subsection, we assume that both input mask α and output mask β are $\neq 0$. The properties of corresponding part of the new LATs are summarized in the next proposition.

Proposition 2. *Let S_k be an S-box of DES. Let $\pi \neq 0$ be an odd parity bit mask on the output of S_k and & denotes tuple-wise AND operator. Then with small abuse in notations:*

(i) $NS_k^*(\pi; \alpha, 15) = 0$ *for all α;*
(ii) $NS_k^*(\pi; \alpha, \beta) = NS_k^*(\alpha, \beta)$ *for all α and β such that $\beta \& \pi = 0$;*
(iii) $NS_k^*(\pi; \alpha, \beta) = -NS_k^*(\alpha, 15 - \beta)$ *for all α and $\beta < 15$ such that $\beta \& \pi \neq 0$.*

Proof. We use the expressions in Definition 2 introducing the following notations: $g_\alpha[x] = \oplus_s(x[s] \circ \alpha[s])$ and $h_\beta^\pi[x] = \oplus_t(S_{k(\pi)}(x)[t] \circ \beta[t])$. When π is fixed then $h_\beta^\pi[x]$ is well defined. Due to the odd parity relation, we have: $h_{15}^\pi[x] = 1$ for any x when $\pi \neq 0$.

(i) According to Definition 2, for $\alpha \neq 0$, we have:

$$NS_k(\pi; \alpha, 15) = \#\{x | 0 \leq x \leq 63, g_\alpha[x] = h_{15}^\pi[x]\}$$
$$= \#\{x | 0 \leq x \leq 63, g_\alpha[x] = 1\} = 32$$

and therefore $NS_k^*(\pi; \alpha, 15) = NS_k(\pi; \alpha, 15) - 32 = 0$.

(ii) The only difference between $h_\beta^0[x]$ and $h_\beta^\pi[x]$ is in the component with the index of the parity bit, say t_π. Hence, if $\beta \& \pi = 0$, then $\beta[t_\pi] = 0$ and $h_\beta[x] = h_\beta^\pi[x]$. Thus $NS_k(\pi; \alpha, \beta) = NS_k(\alpha, \beta)$ and $NS_k^*(\pi; \alpha, \beta) = NS^*(\alpha, \beta)$.

(iii) Let us denote $\overline{\beta} = 15 - \beta$. It holds that $\beta[t] \oplus \overline{\beta}[t] = 1$ for any t. Since by assumption $\beta \& \pi \neq 0$, it follows that $\overline{\beta} \& \pi = 0$ and the assertion (ii) is applicable to $\overline{\beta}$. Using the parity identity we can derive the following relation:

$$1 = \oplus_t S_{k(\pi)}(x)[t] = \oplus_t(S_{k(\pi)}(x)[t] \circ (\beta[t] \oplus \overline{\beta}[t]))$$
$$= \oplus_t(S_{k(\pi)}(x)[t] \circ \beta[t]) \oplus \oplus_t(S_{k(\pi)}(x)[t] \circ \overline{\beta}[t]) = h_\beta^\pi[x] \oplus h_{\overline{\beta}}^\pi[x].$$

This means that for every x the sum $g_\alpha[x]$ coincides with exactly one of the sums $h_\beta^\pi[x]$ and $h_{\overline{\beta}}^\pi[x]$. Hence

$$\#\{x | 0 \leq x \leq 63, g_\alpha[x] = h_\beta^\pi[x]\} + \#\{x | 0 \leq x \leq 63, g_\alpha[x] = h_{\overline{\beta}}^\pi[x]\} = 64$$

Table 2. $NS^*_{7(0100)}$ part

β/α	01	02	03	04	05	06	07	08	09	10	11	12	13	14	15
01	0	0	0	0	0	0	0	0	0	0	0	0	0	0	0
02	0	2	-6	0	0	-2	-2	2	2	0	0	6	-2	0	0
03	0	-2	6	4	4	-2	-2	2	2	-4	-4	-6	2	0	0
04	0	2	2	-2	-10	-4	-4	4	4	10	2	-2	-2	0	0
05	0	2	10	2	-6	8	0	0	-8	6	-2	-10	-2	0	0
06	4	0	-4	-2	2	6	2	-2	-6	-2	2	4	0	-4	0

and thus $NS_k(\pi; \alpha, \beta) - 32 = -(NS_k(\pi; \alpha, \overline{\beta}) - 32)$, so $NS^*_k(\pi; \alpha, \beta) = -NS^*_k(\pi; \alpha, \overline{\beta})$ and finally $NS^*_k(\pi; \alpha, \beta) = -NS^*_k(\alpha, \overline{\beta})$. □

Example 3. Table 2 represents partially that part of LAT with non-zero input/output masks when the parity bit mask 0100 is applied to the output of S_7.

3.2   The Part of LATs Containing Zero Masks

The properties of particular interest in this case are given by the following proposition.

Proposition 3. *For any S-box S_k of DES and an odd parity bit mask $\pi \neq 0$ applied to its output, we have:*

(i) $NS^*_k(\pi; 0, \beta) = 0$ *for all $\beta : 15 > \beta > 0$;*
(ii) $NS^*_k(\pi; 0, 15) = -32$ *while $NS^*_k(\pi; 0, 0) = 32$;*
(iii) $NS^*_k(\pi; \alpha, 0) = 0$ *for all $\alpha \neq 0$.*

Sketch of Proof. In case of (i) the proof follows from the fact that three amongst the coordinate functions of the modified S-box coincide with coordinate functions of the original box and the remaining fourth function is a negation of the sum of those three. Therefore the nontrivial linear combinations of all coordinate functions, except their sum, are balanced functions like in DES itself. The first part of (ii) follows by the generic feature of modified S-box, namely because the sum of bits in each output equals to 1. The rest follows by the usual assumption that the S-box input is generated uniformly at random. □

Remark 1. We would like to emphasize that by contrast to the original DES for every modified S-box there exists an 1-round linear characteristic with zero input mask and non-zero (namely, 15) output mask having non-zero bias (in fact it has probability 1). But that characteristic is useless within the framework of linear cryptanalysis with "at most one active S-box per each round" because it does not contribute anything more to the multi-round approximate expression compared to the trivial zero-to-zero characteristic except an additive constant.

Based on the above reasoning, we exclude from further consideration the 1-round linear characteristics with zero masks, like Matsui has done this for the original DES (of course, in his case all such characteristics are unbiased). However, we have to admit that for linear cryptanalysis which exploits more than one active S-box at some rounds, the issue whether such kind of characteristics are useful is an entirely different matter explored in ongoing research whose first results are briefly reported in Appendix D.

4 The Decreasing Effectiveness for Small Number of Rounds

First, for the sake of completeness, we recall that trivial linear expressions used in linear cryptanalysis of Feistel ciphers are those obtained by exploiting the shift of the right half of input into the left half of output at given round (see, e.g. [6, Ch. 6.3]). Let us stress again that non-trivial characteristics considered here have non-zero masks.

Next, we state and briefly sketch some arguments in support of a proposition whose first claim will be referred further on as modified Knudsen observation (see, [9]).

Proposition 4. (i) *The number of non-trivial 1-round characteristics needed to create a multi-round characteristic for the considered Feistel ciphers is (at least) two for every three rounds;*

(ii) *One can construct best 3-round characteristic making use two times of best 1-round non-trivial characteristic.*

Sketch of Proof. To show (i), we remark that the chains "$L--$", "$-L-$", "$--L$" and "$---$" where L stands for non-trivial 1-round characteristic while "$-$" for subset of trivial expressions, cannot cancel the intermediate variables.

To prove (ii) notice that due to the special Feistel structure of the considered ciphers, "$L-L$" is a 3-round characteristic for any 1-round non-trivial characteristic L. Now, taking into account (i) and using the Piling-up Lemma, one deduce that characteristic "$A-A$" for any A being best 1-round non-trivial characteristic, becomes best 3-round characteristic with effectiveness $e_3 = 2(e_1)^2$ where e_1 is the effectiveness of A. □

Finally, we are in position to prove the following theorem.

Theorem 1. *Any non-zero parity mask applied to the S-boxes of DES leads to a reduction of the highest effectiveness of the 1-round and 3-round linear characteristics obtained within the framework of linear cryptanalysis with "at most one active S-box per round".*

Proof. By Proposition 2(i), the global extremum of all entries of the LATs of DES (see, *Example 1*) is replaced in the modified S_5 by 0 regardless of the non-zero parity mask applied. Thus the non-zero absolute values of all entries in the interesting part of new LATs form a proper subset (not including that extremum) of those from the original cipher. Hence for any box $S_k, k \neq 5$, it holds the following:

$$\max_{(\alpha,\beta)} |NS_k^*(\pi; \alpha, \beta)| \leq \max_{(\alpha,\beta)} |NS_k^*(\alpha, \beta)| < \max_{(\alpha,\beta)} |NS_5^*(\alpha, \beta)| = |NS_5^*(16, 15)|,$$

that together with the decreased effectiveness on S_5 completes the proof with respect to 1-round characteristics. Finally, the overall proof follows by using Proposition 4(ii).   □

Remark 2. An additional fact of interest concerning DES is that we can eliminate the second maximal value of the LATs in case of applying the parity mask $\pi = 0100$.

5   Construction of Best Characteristics

For constructing best characteristics in case of the considered ciphers, one could use the original algorithm proposed by Matsui in [14, Sect. 4] because the technique described there can be applied also to various block ciphers having S-box-like tables. However, for the purpose announced, we develop our own version which incorporates the modified Knudsen observation and will be referred as Basic Search Algorithm.

5.1   Basic Search Algorithm (BSA)

5.1.1   Approach for Construction
The aim of the BSA is to construct all n-round ($n \geq 3$) characteristics with non-zero linear bias. The algorithm includes two main phases: (1) Initialization and (2) Round chaining with finalization in the last round.

5.1.2   Construction Phases

Initialization.

Input: Empty sequence.

Output: Completely constructed $I_F(1)$, $I_X(1)$ and $I_F(2)$ and partially constructed $I_X(2)$.

Round chaining (one step; consecutively executed for $j = 2, 3, \ldots, n - 1$).

Input: Completely constructed $I_F(j - 1)$ and $I_F(j)$ and partially constructed $I_X(j)$.

Output: Completely constructed $I_X(j)$ and $I_F(j + 1)$, partially constructed $I_X(j + 1)$ if $j + 1 < n$ and completely constructed $I_X(j + 1)$ if $j + 1 = n$.

5.1.3   Construction Logic

The main care at joining consecutive 1-round characteristics is to decide whether the relation (1) between F_{j-1}, X_j and F_{j+1} holds true (see Fig. 1). Another compact representation of the relation (1) is by so-called masks [14], but we use sets of indices for more convenient description of the BSA. In our case the modified Knudsen observation means that at least two of the sets $I_F(j-1)$, $I_X(j)$ and $I_F(j+1)$ are nonempty for every j. This property can be easily derived from the relation (1). Making use of the last and taking into account that we consider only characteristics, based on at most one active S-box per round, we can deduce a few useful internal relations (intensively exploited in the algorithm) and summarized as follows.

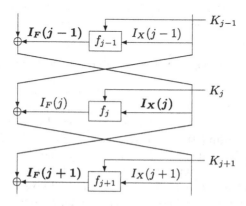

Fig. 1. Round j and its neighbor rounds

Proposition 5. *Any multi-round characteristic, based on at most one active S-box per round, has the following properties (for all relevant indices):*

(i)   *If $S(j) = \phi$ then $S(j-2) \neq \phi$, $S(j-1) \neq \phi$, $S(j+1) \neq \phi$ and $S(j+2) \neq \phi$.*
(ii) *If $S(j) = \phi$ then $S(j+1) = S(j-1)$ and $I_F(j+1) = I_F(j-1)$.*
(iii) *If $S(j-1) \neq S(j+1)$ then $I_X(j) = I_F(j-1) + I_F(j+1)$.*

Proof. (i) Follows from the modified Knudsen observation, applied to $(j-2)$-th till $(j+2)$-th round.

(ii) Using Eq. (1), we see that $I_X(j) = \phi$ implies $I_F(j+1) = I_F(j-1)$ whence $S(j+1) = S(j-1)$.

(iii) The condition $S(j-1) \neq S(j+1)$ implies $I_F(j-1) \cap I_F(j+1) = \phi$. Using this and applying again (1), we consecutively get $I_F(j-1) \cap I_X(j) = I_F(j-1)$, $I_F(j-1) \subseteq I_X(j)$, $I_F(j-1) \cup I_X(j) = I_X(j)$, $I_F(j+1) = I_X(j) \backslash I_F(j-1)$ and finally $I_X(j) = I_F(j-1) + I_F(j+1)$. □

Detailed description of the BSA logic is given in Appendix A. This algorithm could be applied to a wide family of ciphers that we call "Generalized Cipher" and describe in Appendix B. Also, it can be easily adapted and optimized in specific settings as we point out bellow.

5.2   Application to the DES Cipher

Searching best characteristics in case of the DES cipher we make two additional changes in the BSA. First, when choose $I_X(1)$ and $I_X(n)$, we optimize the choice by selecting only optimal configurations, i.e. configurations with maximal bias. Second, after finding a new full-round characteristic, we calculate its bias and if it is the maximum one till now, we save the characteristic and the bias as currently best found.

For the purposes of our experiment we implement the search algorithm in C++. It turns out that implementation takes about 2^{17} recursive calls to find the best 14-rounds characteristics for the original DES cipher.

5.3   Adaptation in Case of S-boxes with Embedded Parity Check

The idea behind relation (1) is to assure a presence only of bits of P, C and K in the final sum of all bits participating in the characteristic. If there are some additional internal bit dependencies, they could lead to new cases, when the requirement regarding the final sum is fulfilled. Embedding parity check in the S-boxes is exactly such a case. Therefore we need to modify the search algorithm to take into account the parity. First, because of the symmetry of LATs we can restrict the choices of $I_F(j)$ to half of all possibilities (for instance, excluding only those combinations with parity bit). Second, when checking the intermediate value of $I_F(j+1)$ in point 2.2 of "round chaining" phase of BSA, we must check not only for $I_F(j+1) \neq \phi$, but also for

$$I_F(j+1) \neq I_F(S(j+1)).$$

This new condition relaxes restrictions to the structure of the "valid" characteristics, taking into account the presence of parity. In the general case $I_F(j+1) = \phi$ is the only condition which assures that there is no intermediate bit remaining to "compensate" in the current local sum. When parity is embedded, there exists a second possibility to have such a situation, namely when the condition $I_F(j+1) = I_F(S(j+1))$ holds true. In both cases the current local sum takes a constant value, 0 or 1 respectively, and this is the only necessary condition that must be checked regarding the logic of the algorithm at this stage.

Remark 3. In our investigation, including the search algorithm, we restrict the search for best characteristics only to the first found optimal configurations for $I_X(1)$ and $I_X(n)$ when $I_F(1)$ and $I_F(n)$ are already fixed. There may exist another optimal choices for $I_X(1)$ and $I_X(n)$, which we do not examine, because the active S-boxes remain the same. The reason for doing this is that our goal is mainly to compare the best probabilities and the best characteristics structure.

6 Results and Their Analysis

6.1 Effects of Embedding Parity Check

When parity check is embedded in the S-boxes, it influences the linear approximations in two main aspects – their structure and their probabilities. Some of the non-zero biases of 1-round approximations become zero and these approximations can not participate in a multi-round characteristic anymore. Next, some zero biases become non-zero and give a possibility to construct a completely new multi-round characteristics. Third, some non-zero biases change their absolute values and consequently their contribution to the bias of multi-round characteristics is changed. In addition the presence of parity check increases the internal possibilities for chaining consecutive 1-round approximations and gives an opportunity to get more multi-round approximation with non-zero bias.

6.2 Best Probabilities

The probability biases corresponding to best characteristics are given in Table 3.

Table 3. Probability biases corresponding to best characteristics

$n \downarrow$	0000	0001	0010	0100	1000
3	$+0.781 \cdot 2^{-2}$	$+0.632 \cdot 2^{-2}$	$+0.632 \cdot 2^{-2}$	$+0.5 \cdot 2^{-2}$	$+0.632 \cdot 2^{-2}$
4	$-0.976 \cdot 2^{-4}$	$-0.562 \cdot 2^{-4}$	$-0.820 \cdot 2^{-5}$	$-0.984 \cdot 2^{-5}$	$-0.957 \cdot 2^{-5}$
5	$+0.610 \cdot 2^{-5}$	$+0.562 \cdot 2^{-5}$	$+0.878 \cdot 2^{-7}$	$+0.861 \cdot 2^{-6}$	$+0.598 \cdot 2^{-6}$
6	$-0.976 \cdot 2^{-8}$	$-0.703 \cdot 2^{-8}$	$-0.562 \cdot 2^{-10}$	$-0.656 \cdot 2^{-8}$	$-0.527 \cdot 2^{-10}$
7	$+0.976 \cdot 2^{-9}$	$+0.527 \cdot 2^{-9}$	$-0.820 \cdot 2^{-13}$	$+0.820 \cdot 2^{-10}$	$-0.615 \cdot 2^{-12}$
8	$-0.610 \cdot 2^{-10}$	$+0.703 \cdot 2^{-11}$	$-0.738 \cdot 2^{-15}$	$-0.75 \cdot 2^{-12}$	$+0.769 \cdot 2^{-14}$
9	$-0.953 \cdot 2^{-13}$	$+0.878 \cdot 2^{-13}$	$+0.562 \cdot 2^{-17}$	$+0.656 \cdot 2^{-13}$	$+0.692 \cdot 2^{-16}$
10	$-0.762 \cdot 2^{-14}$	$-0.659 \cdot 2^{-14}$	$+0.562 \cdot 2^{-20}$	$-0.984 \cdot 2^{-15}$	$+0.703 \cdot 2^{-19}$
11	$+0.953 \cdot 2^{-15}$	$+0.988 \cdot 2^{-16}$	$+0.861 \cdot 2^{-22}$	$+0.861 \cdot 2^{-16}$	$+0.968 \cdot 2^{-21}$
12	$-0.596 \cdot 2^{-16}$	$+0.659 \cdot 2^{-17}$	$-0.562 \cdot 2^{-24}$	$-0.656 \cdot 2^{-18}$	$-0.605 \cdot 2^{-22}$
13	$+0.745 \cdot 2^{-18}$	$+0.878 \cdot 2^{-19}$	$-0.711 \cdot 2^{-27}$	$+0.820 \cdot 2^{-20}$	$+0.757 \cdot 2^{-24}$
14	$-0.596 \cdot 2^{-20}$	$-0.617 \cdot 2^{-20}$	$-0.830 \cdot 2^{-30}$	$-0.75 \cdot 2^{-22}$	$-0.527 \cdot 2^{-27}$
15	$+0.596 \cdot 2^{-21}$	$+0.926 \cdot 2^{-22}$	$+0.562 \cdot 2^{-31}$	$+0.656 \cdot 2^{-23}$	$-0.527 \cdot 2^{-29}$
16	$-0.745 \cdot 2^{-23}$	$+0.617 \cdot 2^{-23}$	$-0.830 \cdot 2^{-34}$	$-0.984 \cdot 2^{-25}$	$+0.527 \cdot 2^{-31}$
17	$-0.582 \cdot 2^{-25}$	$+0.772 \cdot 2^{-25}$	$+0.968 \cdot 2^{-37}$	$+0.861 \cdot 2^{-26}$	$-0.988 \cdot 2^{-34}$
18	$-0.931 \cdot 2^{-27}$	$-0.579 \cdot 2^{-26}$	$-0.562 \cdot 2^{-38}$	$-0.656 \cdot 2^{-28}$	$+0.791 \cdot 2^{-36}$
19	$+0.582 \cdot 2^{-27}$	$+0.869 \cdot 2^{-28}$	$+0.968 \cdot 2^{-41}$	$+0.820 \cdot 2^{-30}$	$+0.988 \cdot 2^{-38}$
20	$-0.727 \cdot 2^{-29}$	$+0.579 \cdot 2^{-29}$	$+0.889 \cdot 2^{-44}$	$-0.75 \cdot 2^{-32}$	$+0.988 \cdot 2^{-40}$

It can be seen from Table 3 that, despite of decreasing the effectiveness of best 1-round approximations, the effectiveness associated with best multi-round

Table 4. Number and type of the best characteristics

$n \to$	3	4	5	6	7	8	9	10	11	12	13	14	15	16	17	18	19	20
0000	1	2	1	2	2	2	2	2	1	2	1	2	2	2	2	2	1	2
0001	1	2	1	22	2	2	11	22	11	2	1	22	2	2	11	22	11	2
0010	1	2	11	2	2	22	11	2	1	2	211	22	11	22	2	2	1	22
0100	11	2	1	2	2	2	2	2	1	2	2	2	2	2	1	2	2	2
1000	1	2	1	2	22	2	2	2	1	2	1	2	22	2	2	2	1	2

Table 5. 16-round and 19-round best linear approximations details

π	16-round approximations			19-round approximations		
	Effectiveness	appr	S-boxes	Effectiveness	appr	S-boxes
0000	$0.596 \cdot 2^{-20}$	$appr_1, appr_2$	2	$0.582 \cdot 2^{-25}$	$appr_{15}, appr_{16}$	10
0001	$0.617 \cdot 2^{-20}$	$appr_3, appr_4$	7	$0.772 \cdot 2^{-25}$	$appr_{17}$	2
		$appr_5, appr_6$	3		$appr_{18}$	2
0010	$0.830 \cdot 2^{-30}$	$appr_7, appr_8$	9	$0.968 \cdot 2^{-37}$	$appr_{19}, appr_{20}$	9
		$appr_9, appr_{10}$	8			
0100	$0.75 \cdot 2^{-22}$	$appr_{11}, appr_{12}$	2	$0.861 \cdot 2^{-26}$	$appr_{21}$	12
1000	$0.527 \cdot 2^{-27}$	$appr_{13}, appr_{14}$	3	$0.988 \cdot 2^{-34}$	$appr_{22}, appr_{23}$	10

characteristics can grow ($\pi = 0001$ and $n = 14$, 17 and 18) or diminish (the remaining cases), depending on the parity bit position.

6.3 Best Characteristics: Number and Type

The number and structure of the best characteristics are given in Table 4. The notations used are: '1' – for one symmetric characteristic, '2' – for a pair different and symmetric to each other characteristics. For example "211" means "one pair symmetric to each other characteristics and two individual symmetric characteristics".

Table 4 clearly shows that the number and the structure of the best characteristics strongly depend on the presence and the place of the parity bit. In almost all cases in our experiment the number of best characteristics in the modified cipher is at least equal to that in the original one. However, there exists also an exception in case 0100, $n = 17$.

6.4 Comparison of Best Multi-round Approximate Expressions

We summarize some details concerning best 16-round and 19-round linear approximate expressions of type (2) in Table 5. The table includes notation of approximations, their effectiveness and the number of the active S-boxes for the expressions.

This table shows that there is no clear rule for dependence of complexity of a potential attack from the presence of parity. When parity is embedded there are cases of lower or higher effectiveness combined with more or less active S-boxes comparing with the original cipher. Some more details and comments about best 16-round linear approximate expressions are given in Appendix C.

7   Conclusions

In this work, from the linear cryptanalysis perspective, we have examined the effect of inserting a bit of additional linearity in the round's output of DES by embedding parity check in the outputs of its S-boxes. Similar to [11,13], our research is focused on best characteristics obtained on the base of "at most one active S-box per each round", since its primary goal is to compare the results with those for the original cipher.

We prove that such embedding reduces the effectiveness of optimal 1-round and 3-round characteristics. However, as shown by experiments based on our search algorithm, this is not true for greater number of rounds. So, in general, a modification of this type does not necessarily mean a reduction or growth in the effectiveness of interest. Also, the number of yielded best characteristics varies depending on the choice of the parity position. So does the number of active S-boxes in the respective to them linear approximations with highest probability that in turn implies differences in the number of resultant effective key and text bits.

Therefore, we could conclude that successful attacks based on this approach have varying magnitude of complexity and at the same time they are not inevitably more efficient than the corresponding primary attacks towards the original cipher.

Acknowledgments. This work was partially supported under the Bulgarian NSF contract I01/0003. The authors would like to thank the anonymous reviewers for helpful comments which substantially improved the manuscript. The second author is also with South-Western University (Faculty of Mathematics and Natural Sciences), Blagoevgrad, Bulgaria.

Appendix

A   Basic Search Algorithm

1. Notations and Definitions. For description of the BSA we make use of the following additional notations and definitions.

Definition 6. *The set of indices* $I_{com}(j) = I_F(S(j)) \cap I_X(S(j + 1))$, *where* $S(j) \neq \phi$ *and* $S(j + 1) \neq \phi$, *is called* compatibility set *regarding the j-th round. The set of indices* $I_{rev}(j) = I_F(S(j)) \cap I_X(S(j - 1))$, *where* $S(j) \neq \phi$ *and* $S(j - 1) \neq \phi$, *is called* reverse compatibility set *regarding the j-th round.*

Definition 7. Let $S(j) \neq \phi$ and $S(j+1) \neq \phi$. If $I_{com}(j) \neq \phi$, then we say that $S(j)$ and $S(j+1)$ are compatible. If $I_{rev}(j+1) \neq \phi$, the $S(j)$ and $S(j+1)$ are reversely compatible.

Remark 4. Applying the BSA to the DES we always have $|I_{com}(j)| \leq 1$ and $|I_{rev}(j)| \leq 1$.

We use $NS(I_X(j), I_F(j))$ to denote $NS_k^*(\alpha, \beta)$, where $S_k = S(j)$ and α and β are masks on the input and the output of S_k, corresponding to $I_X(j)$ and $I_F(j)$.

2. Algorithm Description

Initialization.

1) Set $S(1)$ and $S(2)$.
   1.1) Choose $S(1)$: $S(1) \neq \phi$ or $S(1) = \phi$.
   1.2) If $S(1) = \phi$, then choose $S(2)$: $S(2) \neq \phi$.
   1.3) Else (i.e. $S(1) \neq \phi$) choose $S(2)$: $S(2) = \phi$ or $S(2) \neq \phi$.
2) Construct $I_F(1)$, $I_X(1)$ and $I_F(2)$ and partially construct $I_X(2)$:
   2.1) If $S(1) = \phi$:
      2.1.1) Set $I_F(1) \leftarrow \phi$, $I_X(1) \leftarrow \phi$.
      2.1.2) Set $I_X(2) \leftarrow \phi$.
      2.1.3) Choose $I_F(2)$: $I_F(2) \subseteq I_F(S(2))$, $I_F(2) \neq \phi$.
   2.2) Else (i.e. $S(1) \neq \phi$):
      2.2.1) If $S(2) = \phi$:
         2.2.1.1) Set $I_F(2) \leftarrow \phi$, $I_X(2) \leftarrow \phi$.
         2.2.1.2) Choose $I_F(1)$: $I_F(1) \subseteq I_F(S(1))$, $I_F(1) \neq \phi$.
      2.2.2) Else (i.e. $S(2) \neq \phi$):
         2.2.2.1) Check for compatibility:
            2.2.2.1.1) If $I_{com}(1) = \phi$, then return.
            2.2.2.1.2) Choose $I_X(2)$: $I_X(2) \subseteq I_{com}(1)$, $I_X(2) \neq \phi$.
         2.2.2.2) Choose $I_F(2)$: $I_F(2) \subseteq I_F(S(2))$, $I_F(2) \neq \phi$.
         2.2.2.3) Check for reverse compatibility:
            2.2.2.3.1) If $I_{rev}(2) = \phi$, then set $I_F(1) \leftarrow I_X(2)$.
            2.2.2.3.2) Else (i.e. $I_{rev}(2) \neq \phi$)
               choose $I_F(1)$: $I_F(1) \subseteq I_F(S(1))$, $I_F(1) \neq \phi$.
      2.2.3) Choose $I_X(1)$: $NS(I_X(1), I_F(1)) \neq 0$.

Round chaining.

1) Set $j \leftarrow 2$.
2) Finalize $I_X(j)$ and construct $I_F(j+1)$:
   2.1) Calculate $I_F(j+1)$: $I_F(j+1) \leftarrow (I_F(j-1) \cup I_X(j)) \setminus (I_F(j-1) \cap I_X(j))$.
   2.2) If $I_F(j+1) \neq \phi$:
      2.2.1) If $I_X(j) \neq \phi$ and $NS(I_X(j), I_F(j)) = 0$, then return.
      2.2.2) Set $S(j+1) \leftarrow S(j-1)$.
   2.3) Else (i.e. $I_F(j+1) = \phi$):
      2.3.1) If $I_X(j) = \phi$:
         2.3.1.1) Choose $S(j+1)$: $S(j+1) \neq \phi$, $I_{rev}(j+1) \neq \phi$.
         2.3.1.2) Choose $I_X(j)$: $I_X(j) \subseteq I_{rev}(j+1)$, $I_X(j) \neq \phi$.

2.3.1.3) If $NS_{S(j)}(I_X(j), I_F(j)) = 0$, than return.

2.3.2) Else (i.e. $I_X(j) \neq \phi$):

2.3.2.1) Set $S(j+1) \leftarrow \phi$ or choose
$S(j+1)$: $S(j+1) \neq \phi$, $S(j+1) \neq S(j-1)$, $I_{rev}(j+1) \neq \phi$.

2.3.2.2) If $S(j+1) \neq \phi$:

2.3.2.2.1) Choose I_X: $I_X \neq \phi$, $I_X \subseteq I_{rev}(j+1)$.

2.3.2.2.2) If $NS_{S(j)}(I_X(j) \cup I_X, I_F(j)) = 0$, than return.

2.3.2.2.3) Recalculate $I_X(j)$: $I_X(j) \leftarrow I_X(j) \cup I_X$.

2.3.3) Recalculate $I_F(j+1)$:
$I_F(j+1) \leftarrow (I_F(j-1) \cup I_X(j)) \backslash (I_F(j-1) \cap I_X(j))$.

3) Process $I_X(j+1)$:

3.1) If $(j+1) < n$, partially construct $I_X(j+1)$:

3.1.1) If $S(j) = \phi$ or $S(j+1) = \phi$, then Set $I_X(j) \leftarrow \phi$.

3.1.2) Else (i.e. $S(j) \neq \phi$ and $S(j+1) \neq \phi$) check for compatibility:

3.1.2.1) If $I_{com}(j) = \phi$, then return.

3.1.2.2) Else (i.e. $I_{com}(j) \neq \phi$) choose
$I_X(j+1)$: $I_X(j+1) \subseteq I_{com}(j)$, $I_X(j+1) \neq \phi$.

3.1.3) Increment j: $j \leftarrow j+1$.

3.1.4) Go to 2).

3.2) Else (i.e. $(j+1) = n$)
if $S(n) \neq \phi$, then choose $I_X(n)$: $NS(I_X(n), I_F(n)) \neq 0$.

Initialization completely constructs a linear characteristic for the first round and partially constructs one for the second round. Round chaining consists of repetition of a group of operations in each step until final round is reached. Each execution of this group of operations creates a characteristic for the current round and partially constructs a characteristic for next round. When the next round is the last, its characteristic is constructed completely. During the search each return is to the point of the last choice made and requires another choice to be made. For finding all characteristics, all possible choices must be exhaustively checked in every point of choice in the algorithm.

B   Generalized Cipher

Generalized Cipher is a family of Feistel type ciphers with block length of $2b$ and j-th round function

$$f_j(X_j, K_j) = Prm(Sub(Exp(X_j) \oplus K_j)),$$

where:

- Exp is an expansion function from b bits to e bits, i.e. for every s $Exp(X)[s] = X[i]$ for some i;
- Sub is a substitution function, $Sub(X) = S_1(X)\|S_2(X)\|\ldots\|S_m(X)$, as S_k is an S-box from (e/m) bits to (b/m) bits, $1 \leq k \leq m$, and $\|$ is concatenation of binary vectors;
- Prm is a permutation of b bits.

In order the BSA to be applicable to such a cipher, we assume that it possess LATs with no valuable biases with zero input masks and non-zero output masks.

C   More Details About 16-round Best Approximations

Table 5 from Sect. 6.4 contains some details concerning best 16-round linear approximate expressions of type (2). In Example 1, two of the underlying best characteristics are described thoroughly. X', F' and K' denote the input data, output data and the round key for an individual round.

Example 1 (The best characteristics used in $appr_5$ and $appr_{11}$).

$appr_5$: -ABC-CBA-ABC-D,
A: $X'[29] \oplus F'[1,15] = K'[44]$, B: $X'[15] \oplus F'[29] = K'[22]$, C: $X'[29] \oplus F'[1] = K'[44]$, D: $X'[0,30] \oplus F'[1] = K'[45,47]$.

$appr_{11}$: -EG-GE-EG-GE-H,
E: $X'[22] \oplus F'[16] = K'[33]$, G: $X'[16] \oplus F'[22] = K'[25]$, H: $X'[23] \oplus F'[16] = K'[34]$.

It can be seen from Table 5 that in three out of all four cases the complexity is higher than for the original cipher. So, there is a case, namely of parity mask (0001), when the complexity is lower. It can be seen as well that the number of active S-boxes varies from 2 till 9. Also, in the case of parity mask (0100) the number of active S-boxes equals to, while in the remaining three cases it prevails over that of the original cipher. In general, more active S-boxes mean more effective bits and consequently this complicates the maximum likelihood method applied, simplifying at the same time the subsequent exhaustive search.

The number of best approximations varies as well providing different possibilities for combining them in an attack. Indeed, a suitable combination of such approximations may result in a significant reduction in the cost of the attack. For instance, one possible approach is firstly to apply the maximum likelihood method with those approximations having fewer effective bits and then to employ the fixed bits in another approximation to reduce its number of remaining effective bits. This approach is applicable in the case (0001), as follows. After analyzing the dependencies, we see that both approximations $appr_5$ and $appr_6$ have 16 effective key bits and 19 effective text bits. For $appr_3$ the relevant facts are as follows: 39 effective key bits and 35 effective text bits, while for $appr_4$ they are 38 and 35, respectively. Following the general technique described above, we can apply the maximum likelihood method at first with $appr_5$ and $appr_6$ and subsequently with $appr_3$ and $appr_4$. Thus, we can get the remaining effective bits: for $appr_3$ – 17 key and 21 text bits, and for $appr_4$ – 15 key and 21 text bits, respectively. This greatly simplifies the use of $appr_3$ and $appr_4$, and represents a way of exploiting multiple linear relations to extract several bits of information about the key (see, e.g., [3,15]).

D   Two-Round Iterative Characteristics Based on Two or More Active S-boxes Per Round

In case of the DES cipher there are 1-round approximations containing no input variables and having valuable probability that could be found taking into account two S-boxes approximations in a single round. Using such an approximation a 2-round iterative characteristic can be constructed, where every second round is a trivial expression. Matsui has shown such approximations (based on the pairs of adjacent S-boxes) in [12, Ch. 5.4] giving a warning that resultant global probability is worse than in the case of at most one active S-box per round. When parity bit is embedded the same type of approximations exist, too. S-boxes approximations, whose combination give best 1-round approximations of the type considered, are given in Table 6 with their corresponding values in the LATs. From this table one can see that in the cases of proper embedded parity bits these characteristics have lower effectiveness compared to the original cipher.

Table 6. Best combinations for getting a characteristic with zero input mask

Parity	0000	0001	0010	0100	1000
LAT Values	$NS_7^*(3,15) = 8$ $NS_8^*(48,13) = -12$ (Matsui [12])	$NS_2^*(3,5) = 8$ $NS_3^*(48,2) = -6$	$NS_7^*(3,3) = 6$ $NS_8^*(48,2) = 12$	$NS_6^*(3,6) = 6$ $NS_7^*(48,6) = -8$	$NS_4^*(3,3) = 8$ $NS_5^*(48,5) = -6$
Bias	-0.0469	-0.0234	0.0352	-0.0234	-0.0234

In addition, we observed that embedding of parity bits gives rise to yet another class 1-round approximations of that particular interest which then could be used for constructing 2-round iterative approximations. Roughly speaking, their corresponding characteristics involve as input all four output bits of some S-boxes applied in the previous round and transposed by the round permutation. However, the effectiveness of these characteristics can be bounded from above by 0.0352, which is again worse. We will consider the details elsewhere.

References

1. Baignères, T., Junod, P., Vaudenay, S.: How far can we go beyond linear cryptanalysis? In: Lee, P.J. (ed.) ASIACRYPT 2004. LNCS, vol. 3329, pp. 432–450. Springer, Heidelberg (2004)
2. Biham, E., Shamir, A.: Differential Cryptanalysis of the Data Encryption Standard. Springer, New York (1993)
3. Biryukov, A., De Cannière, C., Quisquater, M.: On multiple linear approximations. In: Franklin, M. (ed.) CRYPTO 2004. LNCS, vol. 3152, pp. 1–22. Springer, Heidelberg (2004)
4. Canteaut, A., Roué, J.: On the behaviors of affine equivalent S-boxes regarding differential and linear attacks. In: Oswald, E., Fischlin, M. (eds.) EUROCRYPT 2015. LNCS, vol. 9056, pp. 45–74. Springer, Heidelberg (2015)

5. Coppersmith, D.: The Data Encryption Standard (DES) and its strength against attacks. IBM J. Res. Dev. **30**, 243–250 (1993)
6. Daemen, J., Rijmen, V.: The Design of Rijndael: AES the Advanced Encryption Standard. Springer, New York (2002)
7. Hermelin, M., Cho, J.Y., Nyberg, K.: Multidimensional extension of Matsui's algorithm 2. In: Dunkelman, O. (ed.) FSE 2009. LNCS, vol. 5665, pp. 209–227. Springer, Heidelberg (2009)
8. Heys, H.M.: A tutorial on linear and differential cryptanalysis. Cryptologia **26**, 189–221 (2002)
9. Knudsen, L.R.: Practically secure Feistel ciphers. In: Anderson, R. (ed.) FSE 1993. LNCS, vol. 809, pp. 211–221. Springer, Heidelberg (1993)
10. Konheim, A.G.: Computer Security and Cryptography. Wiley, New Jersey (2007)
11. Matsui, M.: Linear cryptanalysis method of DES cipher. In: Helleseth, T. (ed.) EUROCRYPT 1993. LNCS, vol. 765, pp. 386–397. Springer, Heidelberg (1993)
12. Matsui, M.: Linear cryptanalysis of DES cipher (I), version 1.03. http://www.cs.bilkent.edu.tr/~selcuk/teaching/cs519/Matsui-LC.pdf
13. Matsui, M.: The first experimental cryptanalysis of the Data Encryption Standard. In: Desmedt, Y.G. (ed.) CRYPTO 1994. LNCS, vol. 839, pp. 1–11. Springer, Heidelberg (1994)
14. Matsui, M.: On correlation between the order of S-boxes and the strength of DES. In: De Santis, A. (ed.) EUROCRYPT 1994. LNCS, vol. 950, pp. 366–375. Springer, Heidelberg (1995)
15. Semaev, I.: New results in the linear cryptanalysis of DES. IACR Cryptology ePrint Archive 2014: #361 (2014)
16. Shamir, A.: On the security of DES. In: Williams, H.C. (ed.) CRYPTO 1985. LNCS, vol. 218, pp. 280–281. Springer, Heidelberg (1986)
17. National Institute of Standards and Technology, Advanced Encryption Standard (AES). http://www.nist.gov/aes

Time-Advantage Ratios Under Simple Transformations: Applications in Cryptography

Maciej Skórski[(✉)]

Cryptology and Data Security Group, University of Warsaw, Warsaw, Poland
`maciej.skorski@mimuw.edu.pl`

Abstract. Security of cryptographic primitives is quantified by bounding the probability ϵ that an adversary with certain resources t win the security game. We derive a clear formula showing how the security measured as the worst *time-to-success ratio* changes under a broad class of reductions. Applications include comparisons of (a) bounds for pseudoentropy chain rules, (b) leakage resilient stream ciphers security, and (c) security of weak pseudorandom functions fed with weak keys.

Keywords: Reduction-based proofs · Time-to-advantage ratio · Time-to-succcess ratio · Leakage-resilient cryptography

1 Introduction

1.1 Reduction-Based Security Proofs

In cryptography one typically constructs more complicated object P (a scheme, protocol) from a more standard and better understood primitive P'. A standard way to argue about security in such a case is to proceed by a reduction argument: assume that an adversary with certain time resources t (which may be running time, circuit complexity, or number of oracle queries...) can break a scheme/protocol P with probability ϵ, and then construct another adversary who using t' resources can break a building primitive P' with probability ϵ'. Turning this statement around, we obtain that the security of P against adversaries with bounded time or success probability is implied by the security of P' against *somewhat stronger* adversaries. Assume, for the sake of this discussion, that the security of P reduces to the security of P' in the following quantitative way:

Security Reduction: If P can be broken by an adversary running in time t with success probability ϵ, then P' can be broken by an adversary running in time t' with success probability ϵ' where

$$\begin{aligned} t' &= p(t, \epsilon), \\ \epsilon' &= q(t, \epsilon) \end{aligned} \tag{1}$$

for some functions $p(\cdot), q(\cdot)$.

M. Skórski—This work was partly supported by the WELCOME/2010-4/2 grant founded within the framework of the EU Innovative Economy Operational Programme.

E. Pasalic and L.R. Knudsen (Eds.): BalkanCryptSec 2015, LNCS 9540, pp. 79–91, 2016.
DOI: 10.1007/978-3-319-29172-7_6

In the simplest case, the functions $p(\cdot)$ and $q(\cdot)$ are algebraic functions of original parameters, like $\epsilon' = \epsilon^2$ or $t' = t\epsilon^{-2}$ (the latter case appears particularly often as a result of the Chernoff Bound applied). In leakage-resilient cryptography these formulas are more complicated and typically involve some additional parameters, like the leakage length or the number of queries.

1.2 Quantifying Security for a Given Adversary

Time-to-Success Ratio. Intuitively, the security of a primitive measures the computational resources needed by any adversary to break it. There are two natural resources to consider here: the time resources t and the success probability ϵ and the standard tool for evaluating security is the simple time-success ratio $\frac{t}{\epsilon}$, introduced by Luby. Since the adversary may want to trade time for success probability, one takes here the minimum over the pairs (t, ϵ).

Example. For example, the strongest block ciphers like AES are believed to satisfy $t/\epsilon \geqslant 2^k$ for any adversary with running time t and success probability ϵ, where $k = 256$ is the length of the key. If such an inequality holds for a primitive P and some number k, we say that P is 2^k-secure or that is has k bits of security (see Definition 6).

1.3 Quantifying Security Losses in Reductions

How Much Security do We Lose in Reductions? The natural question here is how the security, understood as the time-success ratios $\frac{t}{\epsilon}$ and $\frac{t'}{\epsilon'}$, of P and P' are related to each other. Suppose that we know that (for instance by Eq. (1))

$$\frac{t'}{\epsilon'} = O\left(\left(\frac{t}{\epsilon}\right)^c\right)$$

holds for every pair (t, ϵ) such that $t/\epsilon \leqslant 2^k$ and some constant $c \geqslant 1$[1]. Then we have $\frac{t'}{\epsilon'} \leqslant 2^{k'}$ where $k' = ck$. Turning this statement around we obtain $k = \frac{1}{c} \cdot k'$. Such a reduction is called poly-preserving if $c > 1$ or linear if $c = 1$ [LM94]. All the reductions considered in this paper will be poly-preserving. Note that the smaller c is, the more of the original security in P' is transferred to the security of P; more concretely, the security level measured in bits decreases by the factor c. In general, determining the relation between k and k' is not so simple, as $\frac{t}{\epsilon'}$ is not necessary a function of $\frac{t}{\epsilon}$.

1.4 Problem Statement

The discussion above motivates the following question.

---

[1] The constant is at least 1 because one cannot increase the security level by black-box reductions.

Question: Consider the reduction in Eq. (1). Suppose that P' has k' bits of security. How much secure is P, if we know the concrete form of $p(\cdot)$ and $q(\cdot)$?

We would like to obtain a clear formula which allows us to compute k such that P is 2^k-secure, given k', $p(\cdot)$ and $q(\cdot)$. Of course, no general formula can exists if we do not assume anything specific about $p(\cdot)$ and $q(\cdot)$. Our goal is therefore to abstract a possibly wide class of functions and obtain a possibly clear bound within this class.

2 Our Results and Techniques

Summary of Our Results. We obtain a clear formula showing how the time-success ratio changes, valid for reasonably large class of functions $p(\cdot), q(\cdot)$. The result is elementary, yet very useful as shown in the following concrete applications:

(a) A comprehensive analysis of security for pseudoentropy chain rules, by the time-success ratio analysis.
(b) A comprehensive analysis of provable security for leakage-resilient stream ciphers, by the time-success ratio analysis.
(c) A comparison of known bounds for security of weak pseudorandom functions on weak keys.

2.1 The Time-Success Ratio Under Reductions

We need the following result, which is a direct consequence of definitions and is stated without a proof.

Theorem 1 (Time-Success Ratio Under Reductions). *Let P and P' be related as in Eq. (1). Suppose that K, K' satisfy*

$$K' = \max_{t,\epsilon} \frac{p(t,\epsilon)}{q(t,\epsilon)} \tag{2}$$

where the maximum is over the set of pairs (t, ϵ) satisfying the constraints

$$1 \leqslant t,\ 0 < \epsilon \leqslant 1,\ \frac{t}{\epsilon} \leqslant K. \tag{3}$$

Then the fact that P' is K'-secure implies that P is K-secure.

In general, when the functions $p(\cdot), q(\cdot)$ are arbitrary, we cannot say much more. However, the most typical case is when they are polynomial in t, ϵ, possibly with some extra parameters.

Theorem 2 (Time-Success Ratio Under Simple Reductions). *Suppose that the following holds: if P can be broken with running time t and success probability ϵ then P' can be broken with running time t' and success probability ϵ' where*

$$t' = c_1 t^{\alpha_1} \epsilon^{-\beta_1} + c_3 \epsilon^{-\beta_3}$$
$$\epsilon' = c_2 t^{-\alpha_2} \epsilon^{\beta_2}. \tag{4}$$

and $\alpha_1, \alpha_2, c_1, c_2, c_3, \beta_1, \beta_2, \beta_3$ are positive constants. Then the following holds: if P' is K'-secure then P is K-secure where K' and K satisfy

$$K' = (1 + \psi) \cdot \max\left(\frac{c_1}{c_2} \cdot K^{\max(\alpha_1 + \alpha_2, \beta_1 + \beta_2)}, \frac{c_3}{c_2} \cdot K^{\max(\alpha_2, \beta_2 + \beta_3)} \right) \tag{5}$$

for some parameter $0 \leqslant \psi \leqslant 1$.

2.2 Application to Pseudoentropy Chain Rules

Introduction. Information-theoretic entropy notions take into account unbounded parties. For example, Shannon entropy gives a tight bound (over all algorithms) on the compression rate of a given distribution for every algorithm, and min-entropy gives a tight bound (over all algorithms) on the probability of predicting a sample from a given distribution. Most entropy notions satisfy a property called chain rule, which roughly capture the fact that when additionally conditioning on a variable Z, the entropy $H(\cdot)$ of X goes down at most by the length of Z

$$H(X|Z) \geqslant H(X) - |Z|.$$

In modern cryptography, one considers computational generalizations of the classical entropy notions. These so called pseudoentropy notions capture the fact that a given distribution only appears to have high entropy for computationally bounded parties. For pseudoentropy notions not only *quantity* matters but also its *quality* is important. The quality measures how close is the given distribution to a high-entropy distribution. Pseudoentropy found a lot of applications, including leakage-resilient cryptography [DP08, Pie09, YSPY10, FPS12, YS13], deterministic encryption [FOR15], memory delegation [CKLR11], computational complexity [RTTV08, Sko15b], hardness amplification [Sko15a] and foundations of cryptography [VZ13]. The most important pseudoentropy notion is HILL entropy. Informally, we say that X given Z has n bits of HILL pseudoentropy of quality (t, ϵ) if X is indistinguishable from a distribution Y of n-bits of *min-entropy*, given Z (for a formal definition see Definition 2). Chain rules for HILL pseudoentropy are central tools in security proofs, in particular in leakage-resilient stream ciphers [DP08, Pie09, YSPY10, FPS12, YS13]. They are similar to chain rules for information-theoretic entropies except one detail: they involve a loss in quality, as stated below.

Pseudoentropy chain rules. If X has n bits of pseudoentropy of quality (t', ϵ') then X given $Z \in \{0,1\}^\lambda$ has $n - \lambda$ bits of pseudoentropy of quality (t, ϵ) provided that $t' = \text{poly}\left(t, \epsilon^{-1}, 2^\lambda\right)$ and $\epsilon' = \text{poly}(\epsilon, 2^{-\lambda})$.

Our Result: A Time-Success Ratio Analysis of the Known Chain Rules. Proving chain rules is a challenging task and many techniques were proposed. This resulted in a different quality tradeoffs between (t, ϵ) and (t', ϵ'). Different quantitative bounds, known in the literature, are summarized in Table 1. In addition, based on Theorem 2, we compare them in the important setting where the ratio t/ϵ of quality parameters is constant for any choice of t. This is, for example, the case of AES256 when $t/\epsilon \approx 2^{256}$ for all adversaries (t, ϵ), or more generally any weak PRF with a k-bit key[2]; in particular this is how the chain rules are often used.

Table 1. Qualitative bounds on chain rules for HILL entropy. To compare different chain rules, we consider a (t', ϵ')-secure weak PRF where $t'/\epsilon' = 2^{k'}$ (for any choice of t'), then after λ bits of leakage on the key, the PRF is $t/\epsilon = 2^k$ secure (for any choice of t), where depending on the chain rule used, k can take the values as indicated in the table.

Reference	Technique	$t' =$	$\epsilon' =$	Security Loss our contribution
(a) [DP08]	Worst-Case Metric Entropy	$O\left(t \cdot 2^{-2\lambda}\epsilon^{-2}\right)$	$\Omega(2^{-\lambda}\epsilon^2)$	$k \approx \frac{k'}{4} - \frac{3}{4}\lambda$
(b) [RTTV08]	Dense Model Theorem	$O\left(t \cdot \text{poly}(\frac{1}{\epsilon}, \frac{1}{\min_z(\Pr[Z=z])})\right)$	$\Omega(2^{-\lambda}\epsilon)$	worse than in (c)
(c) [FOR15]	Worst-Case Metric Entropy	$O\left(t \cdot 2^{-2\lambda}\epsilon^{-2}\right)$	$\Omega(2^{-\lambda}\epsilon)$	$k \approx \frac{k'}{3} - \frac{\lambda}{3}$
(d) [JP14a]	Simulating Auxiliary Inputs	$O\left(t \cdot 2^{3\lambda}\epsilon^{-2} + 2^{4\lambda}\epsilon^{-2}\right)$	$\Omega(\epsilon)$	$k \approx \frac{k'}{3} - \lambda$
(e) [VZ13]	Simulating Auxiliary Inputs	$\Omega\left(s \cdot 2^{\lambda}\epsilon^{-2} + 2^{\lambda}\epsilon^{-4}\right)$	$\Omega(\epsilon)$	$k \approx \frac{k'}{5} - \frac{2}{5}\lambda$
(f) [GW11]	Relaxed HILL Entropy	$O\left(s \cdot 2^{\lambda}\epsilon^{-2} - 2^{2\lambda}\epsilon^{-2}\right)$	$\Omega(\epsilon)$	$k \approx \frac{k'}{3} - \frac{2}{3}\lambda$
(g) [PS15]	Average Metric Entropy	$O\left(s \cdot 2^{\lambda}\epsilon^{-2} - 2^{2\lambda}\right)$	$\Omega(\epsilon)$	$k \approx \frac{k'}{3} - \frac{\lambda}{3}$

From this comparison we obtain the following corollaries:

Corollary 1 (How Tight Are Chain Rules?). *For the all known chain rules, the reduction is polynomial of degree 3, with some extra loss of a factor depending (exponentially) on the leakage length λ.*

Unfortunately, this loss is really big in practice. Consider for example the AES as weak PRF. It has roughly 2^{256} security. But with leakage of just one bit, we cannot prove more security than $2^{\frac{256}{3}} \approx 2^{85}$!

Corollary 2 (Which Chain Rule Is Best?). *The best chain rule is (g) when we want to keep ϵ possibly small (comparing to ϵ) and (c) when we want to keep s possibly big (with respect to s'). The gain, comparing to other chain rules, is by a factor exponential in λ.*

This clear analysis may be useful for authors interesting in chain rules (for example, those working in leakage-resilient crypto), as different and complicated bounds for chain rules are considered confusing in folklore.

---

[2] We consider the security of AES256 as a weak PRF, and not a standard PRF, because of non-uniform attacks which show that no PRF with a k bit key can have $s/\epsilon \approx 2^k$ security [DTT09], at least unless we additionally require $\epsilon \gg 2^{-k/2}$.

2.3   Application to Leakage-Resilient Stream Ciphers

Introduction. Traditional security notions in cryptography consider adversaries who can interact with a primitive only in a black-box manner, observing its input/output behavior. Unfortunately, this assumption is unrealistic in practice. In fact, information might leak from cryptograms at the *physical implementation* layer. The attacks that capture information this way are called *side-channel attacks*, and include power consumption analysis [KJJ99], timing attacks [Koc96], fault injection attacks [BBKN12] or memory attacks [HSH+08]. Searching for countermeasures against side-channel attacks, one can try to prevent them modifying software or further secure hardware. However, these techniques are more ad-hoc than generic. A completely different viewpoint is to provide primitives which are *provably secure against leakage*. The research field following this paradigm is called *leakage-resilient cryptography*, and has become very popular in recent years. A lot of work and progress has been done in this topic so far, since the breakthrough paper on resilient stream ciphers [DP08], much more than we could mention here. We refer the reader to [ADW10, Mol10] for good surveys, and focus now on leakage-resilient stream ciphers. Intuitively, leakage-resilient stream ciphers generate a bitstream to encrypt data bit by bit, similarly to standard stream ciphers, but need to tolerate some information leakage in every round.

Design Based on Weak PRFs. On Fig. 1 below we present a simplified version of the first leakage-resilient stream cipher [DP08], which is due to [Pie09]. The construction is based on a weak pseudorandom function (wPRF), which "looks" like a random function when queried on random inputs (see Definition 3). Leakage is modeled in the so called *continuous bounded leakage model*, where the overal execution of a cryptographic protocol is divided into time frames, and in every round leakage comes only from the parts of the internal state which are touched by computations. This way the amount of leakage is bounded in every round but unbounded overall. This is perhaps the most popular line of research restricting the leakage type, based on the *only computation leaks information* axiom introduced by Micali and Reyzin [MR04]. A drawback of this modeling approach is the fact that it allows for working only with relatively short leakage. However, no good alternative has been found so far. More general models, like "security against auxiliary inputs", are very hard to work with. Here one should mention the follow-up works [YSPY10, FPS12, YS13] which use essentially the same design with some changes, trying to reduce the randomness in secret keys at the cost of using public randomness [YSPY10, FPS12], or further reduce the length of the public key [YS13].

Our Contribution: An Analysis of Security Bounds. We provide a time-success ratio analysis of security bounds for leakage-resilient stream ciphers (in the standard model, that is without random-oracle based assumptions). We compare the security of the underlying weak PRF (quantified by (t', ϵ')) and the security of the cipher (quantified by (t, ϵ)); the exact security loss is obtained by putting reduction parameters from related works (columns t', ϵ') into Theorem 2. In addition,

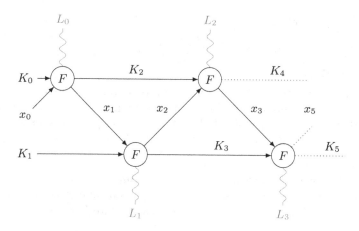

Fig. 1. The EUROCRYPT'09 stream cipher (adaptive leakage). F denotes a weak PRF. By K_i and x_i we denote, respectively, values of the secret state and keystream bits. Leakages are denotted in gray with L_i.

we discuss the limitations of best known proof techniques. From this comparison we obtain the following corollaries.

Corollary 3 (How Good Are Security Bounds for Leakage-Resilient Stream Ciphers?). *For the all known constructions, the reduction from the cipher to the underyling weak PRF is polynomial of a degree varying from 4 to 6 (depending on the technique), with some extra loss of a factor depending (exponentially) on the leakage length λ.*

Unfortunately, all these bounds are not practical. Consider for example the cipher where the weak PRF is instantiated with AES. It has roughly 2^{256} security. But with leakage of just one bit, we cannot guarantee more security for the cipher than $2^{\frac{256}{5}} \approx 2^{51}$ (the cipher (3) provides $2^{\frac{256}{4}} \approx 2^{64}$ security but under non-standard assumptions)!

Table 2. Different bounds for wPRF-based leakage-resilient stream ciphers. The underlying weak PRF(s) has k' bits of security, and the cipher has k bits of security, understood in terms of the time-success ratio. The numbers denote: (1) The EUROCRYPT'09 cipher, (2) The CSS'10/CHESS'12 cipher, (3) The CT-RSA'13 cipher. The dream bound refers to better bounds claimed in [JP14b] which remain unproven because of a subtle flaw [Pie].

Cipher	Analysis	Proof techniques	$t' =$	$\epsilon' =$	Security Level our contribution	Comments/Restrictions
(1)	[Pie09]	Pseudoentropy chain rules	$t \cdot \mathrm{poly}(\epsilon^{-1}, 2^\lambda)$	$\mathrm{poly}(\epsilon, 2^{-\lambda})$	$k \ll \frac{1}{5}k'$	large number of blocks
(1)	[JP14b]	Aux. Inputs Simulator	$O\left(t \cdot 2^{4\lambda}\epsilon^{-4}\right)$	$\Omega\left(2^{-2\lambda}\epsilon\right)$	$k \approx \frac{k'}{5} - \frac{8}{5}\lambda$	
(1)	[VZ13]	Aux. Inputs Simulator	$O\left(t \cdot 2^{\lambda}\epsilon^{-2} + \epsilon^{-4}\right)$	$\Omega\left(2^{-2\lambda}\epsilon\right)$	$k \approx \frac{k'}{4} - \frac{1}{2}\lambda$	
(1)	Dream bound	Aux. Inputs Simulator	$O\left(t \cdot 2^{3\lambda}\epsilon^{-2}\right)$	$\Omega\left(2^{-2\lambda}\epsilon\right)$	$k \approx \frac{k'}{4} - \lambda$	unproven (a flaw in [JP14b])
(2)	[FPS12]	Pseudoentropy chain rules	$O\left(t \cdot 2^{4\lambda}\epsilon^{-4}\right)$	$\Omega\left(2^{-2\lambda}\epsilon\right)$	$k \approx \frac{k'}{5} - \frac{6}{5}\lambda$	large public seed
(3)	[YS13]	Square-friendly apps.	$O\left(t \cdot \epsilon^{-2}\right)$	$\Omega\left(2^{-3\lambda}\epsilon^2\right)$	$k \approx \frac{k'}{4} - \frac{3}{4}\lambda$	only in minicrypt

Corollary 4 (Which Technique Is Best?). *The most promising proof technique is the so called "auxiliary inputs simulator" introduced in [JP14b]. If we proved the dream bound in Table 2, it would offer a significant increase in the (provable) security level.*

The analysis we provide may be useful for authors interesting in leakage-resilient stream ciphers, and important for future research as we identify promising research directions (the proposed dream bound conjecture offers a massive improvement in security bounds). For the sake of completeness we state this conjecture below.

Conjecture 1 (Dream Bounds for Simulating Auxiliary Inputs). Let $X \in \{0,1\}^n$, $Z \in \{0,1\}^m$ be random variables. Then there exists a simulator h of complexity $O(t \cdot \text{poly}(2^m) \cdot \epsilon^{-2})$ such that (X, Z) and $(X, h(X))$ are (t, ϵ)-indistinguishable.

This tool can be directly applied to prove security of the cipher (1). Unfortunately, for now we only know how to construct this simulator with complexity $O(t \cdot \text{poly}(2^m) \cdot \epsilon^{-4})$ or $O(t \cdot \text{poly}(2^m) \cdot \epsilon^{-2} + \text{poly}(2^m) \cdot \epsilon^{-4})$ which yield comparably bad bounds (see Table 2). The dream bound would improve massively the security of the cipher, as shown in the table.

2.4 Applications to Weak Pseudorandom Functions

Weak pseudorandom functions are key components of the leakage-resilient design we discussed in the previous section. The following fact, which states that weak PRFs are secure not only with uniform but also high-entropy keys, is the main technical ingredient in these proofs.

Lemma 1 (Weak PRFs with High-Entropy Keys). *Let $F : \{0,1\}^k \times \{0,1\}^n \to \{0,1\}^m$ be a (t', ϵ', q)-secure weak PRF. Then for K and auxiliary information Z such that $\tilde{\mathbf{H}}_\infty(K|Z) \geq n - \lambda$ we have that F is (t, ϵ)-secure with the key K given Z, if either of the following holds*

(a) $q = \lambda \cdot (\epsilon')^{-2}$, $t = t' \cdot (\epsilon)^2$, $\epsilon = 2^\lambda \epsilon'$ [Pie09].
(b) $q = 2$, $t \approx t'$, $\epsilon = \sqrt{2^\lambda \epsilon'}$ [DY13].

Below in Table 3 we give a comparison of these two bounds, arguing by Theorem 2 that the second bound is better and quantifying the gain.

Corollary 5. *The bound (b) is better, as it guarantees roughly $\frac{1}{2}$ of the original security, whereas (a) gives only $\frac{1}{3}$ of the original security.*

Table 3. Different bounds for wPRFs with weak keys. A weak PRF which has k' bits of security with the uniform keys, has k bits of security for keys with entropy deficiency λ.

Bound	Analysis	Proof techniques	$t' =$	$\epsilon' =$	Security Loss our contribution	Comments/Restrictions
(a)	[Pie09]	Pseudoentropy chain rules	$O\left(t \cdot \epsilon^{-2}\right)$	$\Omega\left(2^{-\lambda}\epsilon\right)$	$k \approx \frac{k'}{3} - \frac{1}{3}\lambda$	large number of queries
(b)	[DY13]	Square-security	$O(t)$	$\Omega\left(2^{-\lambda}\epsilon^2\right)$	$k' \approx \frac{k}{2} - \frac{1}{2}\lambda$	

3   Preliminaries

3.1   Min-Entropy

We say that X has k bits of min-entropy given Z if the value of X cannot be guessed with probability better than 2^{-k}.

Definition 1 (Conditional Min-Entropy). *X has k bits of min-entropy given Z, denoted by $\tilde{\mathbf{H}}_\infty(X|Z) \geq k$, when $\mathbb{E}_{z \leftarrow Z} \max_x \Pr[X = x|Z = z] \leqslant 2^{-k}$.*

3.2   Computational Distance and Computational Entropy

We say that two distributions X, Y are (s, ϵ)-close and denote by $X \approx^{(s,\epsilon)} Y$ if for every circuit D of size s we have $|\Pr[D(X) = 1] - \Pr[D(Y) = 1]| \leqslant \epsilon$. We also say that X and Y are (s, ϵ)-indistinguishable (note that with $s = \infty$ we recover the standard notion of the statistical distance). Based on the concept of computational indistinguishability, we define pseudoentropy

Definition 2 (HILL Pseudoentropy [HLR07]). *Let (X, Z) be a joint distribution of random variables. Then X has **conditional HILL** entropy k conditioned on Z, denoted by $\mathbf{H}^{\text{HILL}}_{\epsilon,s}(X|Z) \geq k$, if there exists a joint distribution (Y, Z) such that $\tilde{\mathbf{H}}_\infty(Y|Z) \geqslant k$, and $(X, Z) \sim_{s,\epsilon} (Y, Z)$.*[3]

3.3   Leakage-Resilient Stream Ciphers

The notion of weak pseudorandom function capture the idea of a function which looks randomly on random inputs.

Definition 3 (Weak Pseudorandom Functions). *A function $\mathsf{F} : \{0,1\}^k \times \{0,1\}^n \to \{0,1\}^m$ is an (s, ϵ, q)-secure weak PRF if its outputs on q random inputs are indistinguishable from random by any distinguisher of size s, that is*

$$|\Pr\left[\mathrm{D}\left((X_i)^q_{i=1}, \mathsf{F}((K, X_i)^q_{i=1}) = 1\right] - \Pr\left[\mathrm{D}\left((X_i)^q_{i=1}, (R_i)^q_{i=1}\right) = 1\right]| \leqslant \epsilon$$

where the probability is over the choice of the random $X_i \leftarrow \{0,1\}^n$, the choice of a random key $K \leftarrow \{0,1\}^k$ and $R_i \leftarrow \{0,1\}^m$ conditioned on $R_i = R_j$ if $X_i = X_j$ for some $j < i$.

Stream ciphers generate a keystream in a recursive manner. The security requires the output stream should be indistinguishable from uniform[4].

---

[3] Let us stress that using the same letter Z for the 2nd term in (X, Z) and (Y, Z) means that we require that the marginal distribution Z of (X, Z) and (Y, Z) is the same.

[4] We note that in a more standard notion the entire stream $X_1, \ldots, X_q$ is indistinguishable from random. This is implied by the notion above by a standard hybrid argument, with a loss of a multiplicative factor of q in the distinguishing advantage.

Definition 4 (Stream Ciphers). *A stream-cipher* $\mathsf{SC} : \{0,1\}^k \rightarrow \{0,1\}^k \times \{0,1\}^n$ *is a function that need to be initialized with a secret state* $S_0 \in \{0,1\}^k$ *and produces a sequence of output blocks* $X_1, X_2, \ldots$ *computed as*

$$(S_i, X_i) := \mathsf{SC}(S_{i-1}).$$

A stream cipher SC *is* (ϵ, s, q)-*secure if for all* $1 \leqslant i \leqslant q$, *the random variable* X_i *is* (s, ϵ)-*pseudorandom given* $X_1, \ldots, X_{i-1}$ *(the probability is also over the choice of the initial random key* S_0).

Now we define the security of leakage resilient stream ciphers, which follow the "only computation leaks" assumption.

Definition 5 (Leakage-Resilient Stream Ciphers). *A leakage-resilient stream-cipher is* $(\epsilon, s, q, \lambda)$-*secure if it is* (ϵ, s, q)-*secure as defined above, but where the distinguisher in the* j-*th round gets* λ *bits of arbitrary deceptively chosen leakage about the secret state accessed during this round. More precisely, before* $(S_j, X_j) := \mathsf{SC}(S_{j-1})$ *is computed, the distinguisher can choose any leakage function* f_j *with range* $\{0,1\}^\lambda$, *and then not only get* X_j, *but also* $\Lambda_j := f_j(\hat{S}_{j-1})$, *where* $\hat{S}_{j1}$ *denotes the part of the secret state that was modified (i.e., read and/or overwritten) in the computation* $\mathsf{SC}(S_{j-1})$.

3.4 Time-Success Ratio

The running time (circuit size) t and success probability ϵ of attacks (practical and theoretical) aggainst a particular primitive or protocol may vary. For this reason Luby [LM94] introduced the worst case time-success ratio $\frac{t}{\epsilon}$ as a universal measure of security. This model is widely used to analyze provable security, cf. [BS04,BN10,BL13] and related works.

Definition 6 (Security by Time-Success Ratio [LM94]). *A primitive* P *is said to be* 2^k-*secure if for every adversary with time resources (circuit size in the nonuniform model)* t, *the success probability in breaking* P *(advantage) is at most* $\epsilon < t \cdot 2^{-k}$. *We also say that the time-success ratio of* P *is* 2^k, *or that is has* k *bits of security.*

For example, AES with a 256-bit random key is believed to have almost 256 bits of security as a *weak* PRF[5].

4   Proof of Theorem 2

For shortness, denote by $\mathcal{S}$ the set of pairs (t, ϵ) satisfying (3). According to Theorem 1 we want to find the maximum of

$$\frac{t'}{\epsilon'} = \frac{c_1 t^{\alpha_1} \epsilon^{-\beta_1} + c_3 \epsilon^{-\beta_3}}{c_2 t^{-\alpha_2} \epsilon^{\beta_2}}$$

$$= \frac{c_1}{c_2} t^{\alpha_1 + \alpha_2} \epsilon^{-\beta_1 - \beta_2} + \frac{c_3}{c_2} t^{\alpha_2} \epsilon^{-\beta_3 - \beta_2}$$

---

[5] We consider the security of AES256 as a weak PRF, and not a standard PRF, because of non-uniform attacks which show that no PRF with a k bit key can have $s/\epsilon \approx 2^k$ security [DTT09], at least unless we additionally require $\epsilon \gg 2^{-k/2}$.

where $t/\epsilon \leqslant K$, $0 < \epsilon \leqslant 1$ and $1 \leqslant t$. Consider first the term $t^{\alpha_1 + \alpha_2} \epsilon^{-\beta_1 - \beta_2}$. Note that

$$t^{\alpha_1 + \alpha_2} \epsilon^{-\beta_1 - \beta_2} = (t/\epsilon)^{\alpha_1 + \alpha_2} \cdot \epsilon^{\alpha_1 + \alpha_2 - \beta_1 - \beta_2} = (t/\epsilon)^{\beta_1 + \beta_2} \cdot t^{\alpha_1 + \alpha_2 - \beta_1 - \beta_2}.$$

From this we can see that the maximum over $\mathcal{S}$ equals $K^{\alpha_1 + \alpha_2}$ when $\alpha_1 + \alpha_2 > \beta_1 + \beta_2$ (achieved at $t = K, \epsilon = 1$), and equals $K^{\beta_1 + \beta_2}$ otherwise (achieved at $t = 1, \epsilon = \frac{1}{K}$). Equivalently, this is simply $K^{\max(\alpha_1 + \alpha_2, \beta_1 + \beta_2)}$. Similarly, we write

$$t^{\alpha_2} \epsilon^{-\beta_2 - \beta_3} = (t/\epsilon)^{\alpha_2} \cdot \epsilon^{\alpha_2 - \beta_2 - \beta_3} = (t/\epsilon)^{\beta_2 + \beta_3} \cdot t^{\alpha_2 - \beta_1 - \beta_2}.$$

and see that the maximum over $\mathcal{S}$ equals K^{α_2} when $\alpha_2 > \beta_2 + \beta_3$ (achieved at $t = K, \epsilon = 1$ and equals $K^{\beta_2 + \beta_3}$ otherwise, which is simply $K^{\max(\alpha_2, \beta_2 + \beta_3)}$. Therefore we have

$$\max_{(t,\epsilon) \in \mathcal{S}} \left[\frac{c_1}{c_2} \cdot \frac{t^{\alpha_1 + \alpha_2}}{\epsilon^{\beta_1 + \beta_2}} + \frac{c_3}{c_2} \cdot \frac{t^{\alpha_2}}{\epsilon^{\beta_2 + \beta_3}} \right] \leqslant \frac{c_1}{c_2} \max_{(t,\epsilon) \in \mathcal{S}} \frac{t^{\alpha_1 + \alpha_2}}{\epsilon^{\beta_1 + \beta_2}} + \max_{(t,\epsilon) \in \mathcal{S}} \frac{c_3}{c_2} \cdot \frac{t^{\alpha_2}}{\epsilon^{\beta_2 + \beta_3}}$$
$$\leqslant \frac{c_1}{c_2} \cdot K^{\max(\alpha_1 + \alpha_2, \beta_1 + \beta_2)} + \frac{c_3}{c_2} \cdot K^{\max(\alpha_2, \beta_2 + \beta_3)}$$

and clearly

$$\max_{(t,\epsilon) \in \mathcal{S}} \left[\frac{c_1}{c_2} \cdot \frac{t^{\alpha_1 + \alpha_2}}{\epsilon^{\beta_1 + \beta_2}} + \frac{c_3}{c_2} \cdot \frac{t^{\alpha_2}}{\epsilon^{\beta_2 + \beta_3}} \right] \geqslant \max \left(\frac{c_1}{c_2} \cdot K^{\max(\alpha_1 + \alpha_2, \beta_1 + \beta_2)}, \frac{c_3}{c_2} \cdot K^{\max(\alpha_2, \beta_2 + \beta_3)} \right).$$

and the proof follows.

5   Conclusion

The formula for the security loss in reductions we derived is simple, yet useful in applications. We will provide some additional applications in the full version of this paper, available online.

References

[ADW10] Dodis, Y., Alwen, J., Wichs, D.: Survey: leakage resilience and the bounded retrieval model. In: Kurosawa, K. (ed.) ICITS 2009. LNCS, vol. 5973, pp. 1–18. Springer, Heidelberg (2010)

[BBKN12] Barenghi, A., Breveglieri, L., Koren, I., Naccache, D.: Fault injection attacks on cryptographic devices: theory, practice, and countermeasures. Proc. IEEE **100**, 3056–3076 (2012)

[BL13] Laanoja, R., Buldas, A.: Security proofs for hash tree time-stamping using hash functions with small output size. In: Boyd, C., Simpson, L. (eds.) ACISP 2013. LNCS, vol. 7959, pp. 235–250. Springer, Heidelberg (2013)

[BN10] Buldas, A., Niitsoo, M.: Optimally tight security proofs for hash-then-publish time-stamping. In: Steinfeld, R., Hawkes, P. (eds.) ACISP 2010. LNCS, vol. 6168, pp. 318–335. Springer, Heidelberg (2010)

[BS04] Buldas, A., Saarepera, M.: On provably secure time-stamping schemes. In: Lee, P.J. (ed.) ASIACRYPT 2004. LNCS, vol. 3329, pp. 500–514. Springer, Heidelberg (2004)

[CKLR11] Kalai, Y.T., Chung, K.-M., Raz, R., Liu, F.-H.: Memory delegation. In: Rogaway, P. (ed.) CRYPTO 2011. LNCS, vol. 6841, pp. 151–168. Springer, Heidelberg (2011)

[DP08] Dziembowski, S., Pietrzak, K.: Leakage-resilient cryptography. In: Proceedings of the 2008 49th Annual IEEE Symposium on Foundations of Computer Science, FOCS 2008, pp. 293–302. IEEE Computer Society, Washington, DC (2008)

[DTT09] De, A., Trevisan, L., Tulsiani, M.: Non-uniform attacks against one-way functions and PRGs. Electron. Colloquium Comput. Complex. (ECCC) 16, 113 (2009)

[DY13] Dodis, Y., Yu, Y.: Overcoming weak expectations. In: Sahai, A. (ed.) TCC 2013. LNCS, vol. 7785, pp. 1–22. Springer, Heidelberg (2013)

[FOR15] Fuller, B., O'Neill, A., Reyzin, L.: A unified approach to deterministic encryption: new constructions and a connection to computational entropy. J. Cryptology 28(3), 671–717 (2015)

[FPS12] Faust, S., Pietrzak, K., Schipper, J.: Practical leakage-resilient symmetric cryptography. In: Prouff, E., Schaumont, P. (eds.) CHES 2012. LNCS, vol. 7428, pp. 213–232. Springer, Heidelberg (2012)

[GW11] Gentry, C., Wichs, D.: Separating succinct non-interactive arguments from all falsifiable assumptions. In: Proceedings of the Forty-Third Annual ACM Symposium on Theory of Computing, STOC 2011, pp. 99–108. ACM, New York (2011)

[HLR07] Reyzin, L., Lu, C.-J., Hsiao, C.-Y.: Conditional computational entropy, or toward separating pseudoentropy from compressibility. In: Naor, M. (ed.) EUROCRYPT 2007. LNCS, vol. 4515, pp. 169–186. Springer, Heidelberg (2007)

[HSH+08] Alex Halderman, J., Schoen, S.D., Heninger, N., Clarkson, W., Paul, W., Cal, J.A., Feldman, A.J., Felten, E.W.: Least we remember: cold boot attacks on encryption keys. In: USENIX Security Symposium (2008)

[JP14a] Pietrzak, K., Jetchev, D.: How to fake auxiliary input. In: Lindell, Y. (ed.) TCC 2014. LNCS, vol. 8349, pp. 566–590. Springer, Heidelberg (2014)

[JP14b] Jetchev, D., Pietrzak, K.: How to fake auxiliary input. In: Lindell, Y. (ed.) TCC 2014. LNCS, vol. 8349, pp. 566–590. Springer, Heidelberg (2014)

[KJJ99] Kocher, P.C., Jaffe, J., Jun, B.: Differential power analysis. In: Wiener, M. (ed.) CRYPTO 1999. LNCS, vol. 1666, pp. 388–397. Springer, Heidelberg (1999)

[Koc96] Kocher, P.C.: Timing attacks on implementations of Diffie-Hellman, RSA, DSS, and other systems. In: Koblitz, N. (ed.) CRYPTO 1996. LNCS, vol. 1109, pp. 104–113. Springer, Heidelberg (1996)

[LM94] Luby, M.G., Michael, L.: Pseudorandomness and Cryptographic Applications. Princeton University Press, Princeton (1994)

[Mol10] Mol, P.: Leakage-resilient cryptography: a survey of recent advances (2010). http://cseweb.ucsd.edu/pmol/Documents/RE.pdf

[MR04] Micali, S., Reyzin, L.: Physically observable cryptography. In: Naor, M. (ed.) TCC 2004. LNCS, vol. 2951, pp. 278–296. Springer, Heidelberg (2004)

[Pie] Pietrzak, K.: Private communication, May

[Pie09] Pietrzak, K.: A leakage-resilient mode of operation. In: Joux, A. (ed.) EUROCRYPT 2009. LNCS, vol. 5479, pp. 462–482. Springer, Heidelberg (2009)

[PS15] Pietrzak, K., Skórski, M.: The chain rule for HILL pseudoentropy, revisited. In: Lauter, K., Rodríguez-Henríquez, F. (eds.) LatinCrypt 2015. LNCS, vol. 9230, pp. 81–98. Springer, Heidelberg (2015)

[RTTV08] Reingold, O., Trevisan, L., Tulsiani, M., Vadhan, S.: Dense subsets of pseudorandom sets. In: Proceedings of the 2008 49th Annual IEEE Symposium on Foundations of Computer Science, FOCS 2008, pp. 76–85. IEEE Computer Society, Washington, DC (2008)

[Sko15a] Skorski, M.: Metric pseudoentropy: characterizations, transformations and applications. In: Lehmann, A., Wolf, S. (eds.) ICITS 2015. LNCS, vol. 9063, pp. 105–122. Springer, Heidelberg (2015)

[Sko15b] Skorski, M.: Nonuniform indistinguishability and unpredictability hardcore lemmas: new proofs and applications to pseudoentropy. In: Lehmann, A., Wolf, S. (eds.) ICITS 2015. LNCS, vol. 9063, pp. 123–140. Springer, Heidelberg (2015)

[VZ13] Zheng, C.J., Vadhan, S.: A uniform min-max theorem with applications in cryptography. In: Canetti, R., Garay, J.A. (eds.) CRYPTO 2013, Part I. LNCS, vol. 8042, pp. 93–110. Springer, Heidelberg (2013)

[YS13] Standaert, F.-X., Yu, Y.: Practical leakage-resilient pseudorandom objects with minimum public randomness. In: Dawson, E. (ed.) CT-RSA 2013. LNCS, vol. 7779, pp. 223–238. Springer, Heidelberg (2013)

[YSPY10] Yu, Y., Standaert, F.-X., Pereira, O., Yung, M.: Practical leakage-resilient pseudorandom generators. In: Proceedings of the 17th ACM Conference on Computer and Communications Security, CCS 2010, pp. 141–151. ACM, New York (2010)

Security and Protocols

Synchronous Universally Composable Computer Networks

Dirk Achenbach[1]([✉]), Jörn Müller-Quade[1], and Jochen Rill[2]

[1] Karlsruhe Institute of Technology (KIT), Karlsruhe, Germany
{dirk.achenbach,joern.mueller-quade}@kit.edu
[2] FZI Forschungszentrum Informatik, Karlsruhe, Germany
rill@fzi.de

Abstract. Designers of modern IT networks face tremendous security challenges. As systems grow ever more complex and connected it is essential that they resist even previously-*unknown* attacks. Using formal models to analyse the security of cryptographic protocols is a well-established practice. However, the security of complex networks is often still evaluated in an ad-hoc fashion. We analyse the applicability of formal security models for complex networks and narrow the gap between security proofs for abstract cryptographic protocols and real-world systems. Specifically we use the Universal Composability framework together with Katz et al.'s extensions for synchronous computation and bounded-delay channels [15]. This allows us to model availability guarantees. We propose a 5-phase paradigm for specifying protocols in a clear representation. To capture redundant formalisms and simplify defining network topologies, we introduce two functionalities $\mathcal{F}_{\mathsf{wrap}}$ and $\mathcal{F}_{\mathsf{net}}$. Demonstrating the applicability of our approach, we re-prove Lamport et al.'s well-known solution to the Byzantine Generals Problem [16] with four parties. We further complete a result of Achenbach et al. [1], proving that a "firewall combiner" for three network firewalls is available.

Keywords: Network firewalls · Universal composability · Security architectures · Formal models

1 Introduction

Information Technology (IT) systems are at the heart of most automated systems today. Not only cars and airplanes rely on networked computer systems, but also factories, water supply plants, and nuclear facilities. At the same time, IT systems have never faced more serious threats—national and foreign secret services, criminal organisations, and even corporate hacker groups threaten the integrity and availability of services society relies on.

The aim of research in provable security is to construct IT systems that are invulnerable to attack. Because one faces an intelligent adversary when constructing IT systems it is not sufficient to test for known vulnerabilities before shipping a security solution. One needs a method for defending against previously-unknown attacks. To achieve this goal, formal security models are used. However, since

© Springer International Publishing Switzerland 2016
E. Pasalic and L.R. Knudsen (Eds.): BalkanCryptSec 2015, LNCS 9540, pp. 95–111, 2016.
DOI: 10.1007/978-3-319-29172-7_7

proofs in these models are naturally very technical, they only exist for individual system components like secure channels [8] or simple protocols such as fair coin tosses [2]. However, since modern IT networks are very complex, they are usually not proven secure in a formal security model but only empirically tested for known security weaknesses. This constitutes a significant gap between systems which are proven to be secure and those which are actually in use.

This gap can be somewhat narrowed by security notions that offer *composability*: When the cryptographic framework ensures that the composition of secure components yields a secure system, security analysis can be broken down into analysing components with manageable complexity. Specifically, when one analyses computer network components, the secure composability property allows to focus on one sub-network without specifying the rest of the network. (One essentially proves the security of the component *for any* surrounding network.)

Achenbach et al. [1] use the Universal Composition (UC) framework introduced by Canetti [3] to analyse and rigorously prove the security of a combination of multiple—possibly untrusted—network firewalls. As a setup assumption they use a trusted hardware "packet comparator" that compares incoming network packets from several sources and blocks them if they don't match. Using this assumption, they show how to combine multiple untrusted firewalls to yield a provably secure firewall "combiner". Their result does not provide a formal availability guarantee, however.

In this work, we address the research question whether established formal security models can be used to analyse real computer networks. We specifically focus on the Universal Composability framework and provide a "recipe" for modeling and analysing networks. Our model covers availability. It is our belief that this work demonstrates the actual usability of the UC framework and formal security models for computer networks.

1.1 Our Contribution

In this paper we investigate the analysis of computer networks in the UC framework. We show how to obtain rigorous proofs of security for real network systems and narrow the gap between provably secure functionalities and real systems. We propose a methodology consisting of two generalized functionalities $\mathcal{F}_{wrap}$ and $\mathcal{F}_{net}$ for modeling network functions and a 5-step paradigm to model protocols. By abstracting various technical details of the framework, our methodology allows protocol designers to give a natural description of the network and its functionality and thus greatly simplifies its analysis. By incorporating a result of Katz et al. [15] our model also covers availability. Using our methodology, we restate a well known result from Lamport et al. [16] and complete the work of Achenbach et al. [1] by modeling availability.

1.2 Related Work

Universally Composing Security. There are various approaches to secure protocol composition. One of the best known is Canetti's Universal Composability

(UC) framework [3,4]. Other models are Hofheinz' and Shoup's GNUC [10], Pfitzmann's and Waidner's Reactive Simulatability framework [21], Maurer's and Renner's Abstract Cryptography [18], and Maurer's Constructive Cryptography [17]. Among these models, the UC framework has received the most attention. Many protocols for cryptographic building blocks are proven as UC secure. As we base our work on the UC framework as well, these protocols are compatible with our results.

Synchronous Universal Composition. The UC framework is asynchronous— exactly one machine is running at any given moment. This convention greatly simplifies analysis but at the same time makes modeling the progression of time difficult. More concretely, one cannot simultaneously prove input completeness (the inputs of all honest parties are considered) and guaranteed termination (the protocol does not "hang"). There have been various approaches to modeling synchrony in the UC framework [9,13,19]. They, however, either lack in expressiveness or modify the foundations of the framework. The recently proposed approach by Katz, Maurer, Tackmann, and Zikas [15] generalises previous results. It hinges on two ideal hybrid functionalities $\mathcal{F}_{BD}$ and $\mathcal{F}_{clock}$ that do not change the framework.

UC Proofs for Practical Protocols. The UC framework is the quasi state-of-the-art framework for proving the security of cryptographic *building block* protocols like Commitments [5] or Oblivious Transfer [20]. Because it has a composition theorem, it is argued that more complex protocols can then be composed of these components. However, the UC framework has also been used to prove the security of more complex schemes, such as TLS [8], OAuth [6], disk encryption [7], and robust combinations of network firewalls [1]. Our contribution falls in line with this work. We investigate composing large computer networks.

Formal Analysis of Computer Networks. While network security is considered a practical field, formal methods have also been applied to computer networks. Research generally concentrates on modeling attacks and vulnerabilities [12] and on generating verififation policies [11] While such approaches help in configuring specific network components and in mitigating threats, they do not have the advantages of cryptographic security models.

2   Universally Composable Computer Networks

In this section we introduce our methodology for modeling computer networks with the Universal Composability framework. We first give a brief introduction to Universal Composability and its extension for synchronous computation. We then describe the tools we developed and show how to use them by giving a concrete example.

2.1 Universal Composability

Due to space constraints, we only give a brief review of the Universal Composability (UC) framework. For details, we refer the reader to Canetti's original work [3] and the updated version [4]. Using the framework, one proves the security of multi-party protocols by comparing their execution with an idealised version of the protocol. If there is no efficient means of distinguishing the real protocol from its idealised version, we say the protocol securely realises the ideal protocol.

All machines are modeled as Interactive Turing Machines (ITMs). A protocol is a number of interacting ITMs. The execution of a protocol π in the UC framework is in the context of two additional ITMs: the adversary $\mathcal{A}$ and the environment $\mathcal{Z}$. (The environment represents the "surrounding network".) There may be other ITMs realising *ideal hybrid-functionalities* $\mathcal{F}$.

The execution of the protocol is turn-based. If an ITM is activated, it can perform computations and write to tapes of other ITMs. Then its turn ends. If an ITM receives input on one of its tapes, it is the next to be activated. The first ITM to be activated is the environment machine $\mathcal{Z}$.

The output of the whole protocol is the output of $\mathcal{Z}$ and we assume, without loss of generality, that it consists of one bit. The distribution of all outputs of $\mathcal{Z}$ is a random ensemble based on the two parameters z (the input) and k (the security parameter), denoted by $\mathsf{EXEC}_{\pi,\mathcal{A},\mathcal{Z}}$.

The security of a protocol execution in the UC framework is based on a comparison with an execution of an idealised version of the protocol. In the ideal protocol, the *ideal functionality* $\mathcal{F}_{\mathsf{ideal}}$ completely realises the desired properties of the analysed protocol. There, all parties only act as dummies which directly hand their input to the ideal functionality and receive back their output without performing any computation themselves. The ideal functionality may communicate with the adversary in order to model the influence $\mathcal{A}$ is allowed to have. We call this adversary the "adversary simulator" $\mathcal{S}$. Note that this does not model an absolute security guarantee but a guarantee relative to the defined ideal functionality. We denote the output of $\mathcal{Z}$ interacting with the ideal protocol $\mathsf{IDEAL}_{\mathcal{F}}$ and simulator $\mathcal{S}$ as $\mathsf{EXEC}_{\mathsf{IDEAL}_{\mathcal{F}},\mathcal{S},\mathcal{Z}}$.

Informally, a protocol π is UC secure if, for every adversary $\mathcal{A}$ there is an adversary simulator $\mathcal{S}$ such that no environment $\mathcal{Z}$ can distinguish if it is interacting with π or with the ideal protocol implementing π:

$$\forall \mathcal{A} \exists \mathcal{S} \forall \mathcal{Z} : \mathsf{EXEC}_{\pi,\mathcal{A},\mathcal{Z}} \approx \mathsf{EXEC}_{\mathsf{IDEAL}_{\mathcal{F}},\mathcal{S},\mathcal{Z}}$$

where $\approx$ denotes computational indistinguishability.

The composition theorem states that if π securely realises an ideal functionality $\mathcal{F}_{\mathsf{ideal}}$, one can use π instead of $\mathcal{F}_{\mathsf{ideal}}$ in hybrid protocols without losing the security guarantee.

Universally Composable Synchronous Computation. The Universal Composability framework is inherently asynchronous. Exactly one machine can run at any given moment. This simplification guarantees that the result of an execution is non-ambiguous. We perceive reality to be concurrent, however. Specifically, time passes and can be measured independently of the actions of any network component. To model a synchronised network with bounded latency we make use of the results of Katz, Maurer, Tackmann, and Zikas [15]. Specifically, we use their $\mathcal{F}_{\text{clock}}$ functionality (Fig. 1) as a synchronisation primitive. $\mathcal{F}_{\text{clock}}$ allows the parties to wait for each other at synchronisation points. A party can signal when its round is complete. When all parties have completed their round, the round counter is reset.

Further, we use Katz et al.'s bounded-delay channels to model our network function $\mathcal{F}_{\text{net}}$ (Fig. 2). Each channel has an incoming queue. The idea is that the adversary may increase the channel delay up to a predefined limit. When a party polls the incoming queue for a channel, the counter is decreased. When it reaches zero, the party receives the next element from the channel queue.

$\mathcal{F}_{\text{clock}}$ together with bounded-delay channels are sufficient to prove *guaranteed termination* for multi-party protocols [15], i.e. the protocol does not "hang" indefinitely. We express the availability of networks using this property.

The clock function $\mathcal{F}_{\text{clock}}$

Initialise for each party p_i a bit $d_i := 0$.

- Upon receiving message (RoundOK) from party p_i set $d_i = 1$. If for all honest parties $d_i = 1$, then reset all d_i to 0. In any case, send (switch, p_i) to $\mathcal{A}$.
- Upon receiving message (RequestRound) from p_i, send d_i to p_i.

Fig. 1. The ideal $\mathcal{F}_{\text{clock}}$ functionality by Katz et al. [15]. Parties can signal that they are done for the current round. When all honest parties have signalled RoundOK the round counter is reset. Further, parties can request the status of the round counter, learning whether the round has changed.

2.2 How to Model a Computer Network

We use the notion of computer networks in a very general way: a computer network consists of multiple machines performing packet based communication with each other. We therefore abstract from concrete network layers, but point out that our results hold for any networking layers in the protocol stack. We focus on sub-networks of larger networks, i.e. a network has connections to outside components. We connect these connections to the environment machine $\mathcal{Z}$. The environment in the model represents "any surrounding network". Machines on the network are modeled as protocol parties in the UC framework. Their channels for communication are hybrid functionalities.

Corruption and Communication Model. We assume the communication channel between two parties to be authenticated (e.g. a party will always know from which other party it received a message) but not secure (e.g. the adversary can eavesdrop on the communication). This model represents the scenario where one is communicating with known partners over an insecure line—for example over a network cable. Networks can also have connections to the "outside world"—e.g. the Internet. According to our communication model, we assume an adversarial entity might compromise hosts on the network but not physically control the communication channels or insert messages without compromising the corresponding host first. How machines are connected in a network can be expressed by a directed graph. Nodes of the graph represent physical machines and edges represent physical links. In our (hybrid) model, we provide an ideal network functionality $\mathcal{F}_{\mathsf{net}}^G$ which routes packets according to a predefined network graph $G = (V, E)$.

To simplify the exposition, we do not use the adaptive corruption messages of the UC framework. Instead we assume a static corruption model i.e. the adversary chooses which parties to corrupt before the start of the protocol execution.

The Basic Tools for Modeling a Computer Network. Ideally, modeling and analysing a network would require four steps: (1) Specify what the wanted functionality of the network is, (2) draw a graph of the network layout, (3) specify the protocol the machines in the network adhere to, and (4) prove that the protocol does achieve what the wanted functionality does.

We designed tools that capture various technical details of the UC framework and allow to use it in a way that is close to the intuitive approach. Specifically,

1. By defining $\mathcal{F}_{\mathsf{wrap}}$, we simplify the specification of an ideal network functionality.
2. We provide an ideal network functionality $\mathcal{F}_{\mathsf{net}}^G$ that routes messages according to a given network topology induced by a network graph G.
3. We propose a 5-phase paradigm which allows for an easy and structured modeling of the behaviour of machines in the network.

The Ideal Network Functionality. We model the network as a directed graph $G = (V, E)$, while V is the set of machines in the network and $E \subseteq V^2$ is a relation on V. (We model the network as a directed graph to account for unidirectional links [14].) To model bidirectional links, one requires that $(v, v') \in E$ iff $(v', v) \in E$. There is a delivery queue for each edge in the graph. Nodes can send messages for each outgoing edge and can poll incoming messages from each incoming edge. To send a packet, a party *src* can call the network functionality $\mathcal{F}_{\mathsf{net}}^G$ with a (finite) set of packets with corresponding recipients $\{(dest_1, msg_1), (dest_2, msg_2), \dots\}$. Each packet in the set will then be appended to the queue associated with the edge between nodes *src* and $dest_i$, if it exists. Further, modeling Katz et al.'s bounded delay channels [15], we associate two counters with each edge in the graph—one for the total delay and one for the accumulated delay of the channel. The adversary can increase the delay of a channel up to a fixed maximum amount. When a machine polls a queue the delay counter is decreased. When the delay has reached 0, a message is taken from the queue and handed to the machine. This allows for explicit modeling of different network latencies across different communication channels and allows the adversary to take advantage of that. This functionality makes it easy to define the communication channels for a network since one provides a graph of the network and the corresponding channel topology for the UC framework is generated automatically. We point out that we implicitly use Katz et al.'s "multisend" functionality where parties send multiple packets in one atomic call to the network. Because we do not consider adaptive corruption, the adversary cannot preempt parties during a send operation.

The 5-Phase Paradigm. We propose a 5-phase paradigm for modeling network protocols. We require each honest party to follow this paradigm. An honest party will need exactly five explicit activations by the environment machine to finish its round. During its first activation ("input phase"), the party will accept input by the environment. Upon the second activation ("fetch phase"), it will issue a

---

The ideal parameterised network function $\mathcal{F}_{net}^{G,\delta}$

Interpret $G = (V, E)$ with $E \subseteq V^2$ as a directed graph. For each edge $e \in E$, initialise a queue Q_e and two variables d_e and d'_e which represent the current and the accumulated delay for the queue.

- Upon receiving a message (send, M) with $M = \{(dest_1, msg_1), (dest_2, msg_2), \dots\}$ from party src, for each tuple $(dest, msg) \in M$ do:
  - Check if $src, dest \in V$ and $(src, dest) \in E$. If so, continue. Else, ignore this tuple and start processing the next message.
  - Append msg to queue $Q_{(src,dest)}$. Hand msg to the adversary.
- Upon receiving message (delay, e, T) from $\mathcal{A}$: Let (d_e, d'_e) be the delay variables for the queue of edge e. If $d'_e + T \leq \delta$, set $d_e = d_e + T$ and $d'_e = d'_e + T$ and return (delay-set) to the adversary. Else halt.
- Upon receiving message (fetch, Q) from party P and if $Q \subseteq V$:
  - Initialise a set of responses $r := \emptyset$ and for every party $P' \in Q \subseteq V$ with $(P', P) \in E$:
    * Let $(d_{(P',P)}, d'_{(P',P)})$ be the delay variables for edge (P', P).
    * Set $d_{(P',P)} = d_{(P',P)} - 1$. If $d_{(P',P)} = 0$, remove the first message msg from $Q_{(P',P)}$, set $d'_{(P',P)} = 0$, and set $r = r \cup (msg, (P', P))$.
  - If $r \neq \emptyset$, send r to P. Else halt.

Fig. 2. The generalised ideal network function. It is parameterised with a graph that features protocol participants as nodes and expresses links as edges. We model the network as a directed graph to accommodate for specialised connection types as for example optical fibres or data diodes [14]. We also implemented Katz et al.'s bounded delay-channel [15] to model links with a delay.

fetch request to the network to get its input which it will process and possibly send to other parties in one single call during the third activation ("send phase"). The fourth activation ("output phase") is the only activation in which a party will produce output to the environment. The fifth activation is used to signal "RoundOK" to $\mathcal{F}_{\text{clock}}$: all work is done for this round.

Upon further activations the party will wait for the next round to begin. We stress that an honest party will poll the network exactly once per round while a compromised party might poll the network more often. We assume that every party will initialise and update a round counter and further maintain state for the number of activations per round and whether (RoundOK) has already been signaled. This requires sending $\mathcal{F}_{\text{clock}}$ a (RequestRound) request on activation and accordingly updating state information, but imposes no limitations for the party.

The Wrapper Functionality. To simplify the definition of ideal functionalities, we introduce an ideal "wrapper" functionality $\mathcal{F}_{\text{wrap}}$ (see Fig. 3 (a)). It "wraps around" the ideal functionality and moderates its communication with the dummy parties in the ideal world. Its main task is to count activations of dummy parties. Since honest parties adhere to the 5-phase paradigm, it will only notify the ideal functionality if the environment gives input to a party (during the first activation), if a party could create output in the real model (during its fourth activation), and when a round is complete. It also ensures that the adversary is activated at least as often as in the real model.

Specifying Ideal Functionalities. The tools introduced above allow for a natural description of ideal functionalities. $\mathcal{F}_{\text{wrap}}$ will send a notification for important events (e.g. inputs, outputs and round changes) and the ideal functionality reacts to them appropriately. Specifically, the ideal functionality will not be required to count activations itself or activate the adversary sufficiently often. Since the network functionality provides a bound for the maximum delay a channel can have, it is also easily possible to model availability. The ideal functionality only has to maintain a counter corresponding to the delay δ of the channel for each packet and reduce this counter by one every time a round is complete. When the counter reaches zero, the packet can be output immediately when output is requested by $\mathcal{F}_{\text{wrap}}$. Since all honest parties will poll for new packets once per round the adversary can delay a packet delivery for a maximum of δ rounds per channel.

Note that we only specify the behaviour for input by honest parties. We implicitly assume that messages from the adversary to corrupted parties or vice versa are delivered immediately.

2.3   Example: Byzantine Generals

As an example, we will use the presented methodology to model a popular example from the literature: the Byzantine Generals problem. We will then restate a popular result concerning this problem by giving a proof in our framework.

The wrapping function for ideal functionalities $\mathcal{F}_{\mathsf{wrap}}$

Maintain an activation counter c_p for each of the honest dummy parties. Relay all communication from $\mathcal{F}_{\mathsf{ideal}}$ directly to the environment. Upon activation by the environment, i.e. upon receiving input m through a dummy party p:

- If $c_p < 5$ increase the activation counter of the party.
- If $c_p = 1$ send message (input, m, p) to $\mathcal{F}_{\mathsf{ideal}}$.
- If $c_p = 2$ or $c_p = 3$, send message (activated, p) to the adversary.
- If $c_p = 4$ send message (output, p) to $\mathcal{F}_{\mathsf{ideal}}$.
- If $\forall p' : c_{p'} = 5$ reset all activation counters and send (RoundComplete) to $\mathcal{F}_{\mathsf{ideal}}$.

(a)

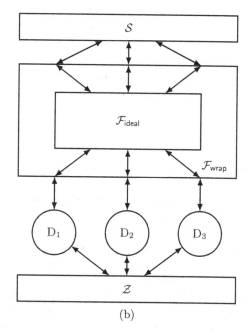

(b)

Fig. 3. The ideal "wrapper" functionality $\mathcal{F}_{\mathsf{wrap}}$ acts as a relay between the dummy parties and the ideal functionality. It counts activations of parties and notifies the ideal functionality of important events like round changes, thus simplifying the formulation of ideal functionalities.

The Byzantine Generals Problem. The Byzantine Generals problem was first introduced by Lamport, Shostak, and Pease [16]. The motivation is as follows: suppose that a commanding general wants to give orders (for the sake of simplicity he will only use "attack" or "retreat") to his lieutenants but he does not know which of them are trustworthy. Also, the lieutenants do not know whether the general himself is trustworthy. Now suppose that each of the participants can communicate with each other participant via "oral" messages. The Byzantine Generals problem is to find an algorithm that, given a number of parties n (one of them is the general), ensures that:

1. All loyal lieutenants obey the same order, and
2. If the general is loyal, then every loyal lieutenant obeys the order he sends.

Note that a disloyal (corrupted) lieutenant can arbitrarily lie about messages he received and try to deceive other lieutenants. He can also refuse to send any messages. However, it is assumed that loyal parties will notice when messages

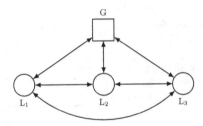

Fig. 4. The network graph byz $= (V, E)$ for the Byzantine Generals problem with $V = \{G, L_1, L_2, L_3\}$ and $E = V^2$. It is fully connected—each party can communicate with every other party.

are missing. Lamport et al. [16] show that there can not be a generic solution to the problem for three parties, but there is a solution for four parties. We will now model the Byzantine Generals problem with four parties according to our methodology and give a formal security proof for a specific solution to the problem.

Modeling the Byzantine Generals Problem. The network in this example is fully connected. Every party can transmit messages to every other party. There is a maximum latency of 2δ until a packet is output by one of the parties: a possible delay of δ from the general to the lieutenants and another possible delay of δ for a packet from one lieutenant to reach the others.

The Byzantine Generals problem statement implies that a party notices if it will not receive any message from another party anymore so that it will not wait indefinitely. In reality this is usually realised by timeouts—we will use the same mechanism here.

Figure 5 shows the protocol which implements a solution to the generals problem. Figure 6 shows the corresponding ideal functionality. This functionality fulfills the requirements for a solution to the Generals problem given earlier.

We will now show that this protocol realises the ideal functionality.

Theorem 1. π_{byz} *realises* $\mathcal{F}_{\mathsf{byz\text{-}ideal}}$ *in the* $\mathcal{F}_{\mathsf{net}}^{\mathsf{byz},\delta}$*-hybrid model.*

Proof. We prove the theorem by giving a step-wise transformation from the real model to the ideal model. We argue that the individual transformation steps are indistinguishable for the environment, and thus, by the transitivity of indistinguishability, the real model is indistinguishable from the ideal model. Start with the real protocol.

Regroup all parties into a new machine $\mathcal{S}$. The adversary simulator $\mathcal{S}$ will simulate the real network in all transformation steps. Introduce dummy parties $D_G, D_{L_1}, D_{L_2}, D_{L_3}$ for all protocol parties and relay messages from and to $\mathcal{Z}$ appropriately. Introduce a new machine $\mathcal{F}_{\mathsf{byz\text{-}ideal}}$. Route all communication from the dummies to $\mathcal{S}$ and vice versa through $\mathcal{F}_{\mathsf{byz\text{-}ideal}}$. The regrouping of parties is indistinguishable for the environment. In the upcoming transformation steps, we will gradually expand $\mathcal{F}_{\mathsf{byz\text{-}ideal}}$'s functionality:

A solution to the Byzantine Generals problem with four parties π_{byz}
Each party maintains a local round counter r.

- Party G:
  - "Input": Upon first activation this round and input m by $\mathcal{Z}$, save m and ignore further inputs.
  - "Send": Upon third activation, call $\mathcal{F}_{\mathsf{net}}^{\mathsf{byz}}(\mathsf{send}, (\mathrm{L}_1, m), (\mathrm{L}_2, m), (\mathrm{L}_3, m))$ if m was saved.
  - "RoundOK": Upon fifth activation, send (RoundOK) to $\mathcal{F}_{\mathsf{clock}}$.
- Party L_n:
  - "Fetch": Upon second activation,
    * call $\mathcal{F}_{\mathsf{net}}^{\mathsf{byz}}(\mathsf{fetch}, \{\mathrm{G}, \mathrm{L}_k, \mathrm{L}_j\})$ for $k \neq j \neq n$. If the call was successful, save the messages for the corresponding parties.
  - "Send": Upon third activation,
    * if there is a message m by party G which has not been broadcast yet, broadcast it: call $\mathcal{F}_{\mathsf{net}}^{\mathsf{byz}}(\mathsf{send}, (\mathrm{L}_k, m), (\mathrm{L}_j, m))$ with $k, j \neq n$.
  - "Output": Upon fourth activation,
    * if $r < 2\delta$ and there are two identical messages m from two different parties (other than G), output m. If there are three different messages from the different parties, output the message from party 1;
    * if $r = 2\delta$ output retreat.
  - "RoundOK": Upon fifth activation, send (RoundOK) to $\mathcal{F}_{\mathsf{clock}}$.

Fig. 5. The protocol for the Byzantine Generals problem with four parties. The ideal network functionality allows for a maximum delay of δ for each message and messages have to be sent from the general first and from the lieutenants afterwards. Thus a party will assume a timeout after 2δ rounds.

1. Initialise variables m_{L_1}, m_{L_2}, and m_{L_3}. When receiving a message m from dummy party G, set $m_{L_1} := m$, $m_{L_2} := m$ and $m_{L_3} := m$. Also initialise and save a round counter $d := 2\delta$. This modification is indistinguishable, since it only stores information and does not alter the communication.
2. If G is corrupted, accept a message $(\mathsf{set}, m_1, m_2, m_3)$ from $\mathcal{S}$. Check if there are $i \neq j$ such that $m_i = m_j$. If so, set $m_{L_1}, m_{L_2}, m_{L_3}$ to m_i. Else set $m_{L_1} = m_1, m_{L_2} = m_2, m_{L_3} = m_3$. This modification again only stores information.
3. When $\mathcal{S}$ attempts to pass output m from an uncorrupted party p in the simulation back to the dummy party, only allow it to pass through $\mathcal{F}_{\mathsf{byz\text{-}ideal}}$ if either
   (a) m has been stored as m_p in $\mathcal{F}_{\mathsf{byz\text{-}ideal}}$, or
   (b) the message is retreat.
   We have to argue the indistinguishability of this modification. A real protocol party will only output a message other than retreat when it has received two identical messages. This will only happen if
   (a) G is honest—then, m will have been provided by $\mathcal{Z}$ through dummy party G and thus saved for every party in the ideal functionality, or

---

The ideal functionality of the Byzantine Generals problem with four parties $\mathcal{F}^{\delta}_{\text{byz-ideal}}$.

Upon initialisation store a delay value $d := (2\delta)$ and initialise three variables $m_{L_1} := \bot, m_{L_2} := \bot, m_{L_3} := \bot$.

- Upon receiving message (input, m, G) from $\mathcal{F}_{\text{wrap}}$ and if G is honest: store $m_{L_p} := m$ for $p \in \{1, 2, 3\}$ and send (input, m, G) to the adversary.
- Upon receiving message (set, m_1, m_2, m_3) from the adversary and if G is corrupted: if $m_{L_1} = \bot, m_{L_2} = \bot, m_{L_3} = \bot$, and there are two identical messages m_i, m_j with $i \neq j$, set $m_{L_1}, m_{L_2}, m_{L_3} := m_i$, else set $m_{L_1}, m_{L_2}, m_{L_3} := m_j$ where j is the smallest index for which $m_j \neq \bot$.
- Upon receiving message (output, p_1, p_2, p_3) from the adversary: mark messages $m_{p_1}, m_{p_2}, m_{p_3}$ as ready for output.
- Upon receiving message (output, p) from $\mathcal{F}_{\text{wrap}}$:
  - If $d = 0$: output retreat to p.
  - if $d \neq 0$ and if m_p is marked as ready for output, output m_p to p.
- Upon receiving message (RoundComplete) from $\mathcal{F}_{\text{wrap}}$, decrease d by 1 and send (RoundComplete) to the adversary.

Fig. 6. The ideal functionality of the three generals problem. If the general is honest, all honest parties will obey his order. If he is corrupted, all parties will obey the same order. As in the real protocol the adversary can not delay the output for more than 2δ rounds.

(b) G is corrupted and sent two identical messages. In this case, $\mathcal{S}$ will have used the set-message to provide these messages and they will also have been saved for every party.

4. Introduce $\mathcal{F}_{\text{wrap}}$ as a wrapper around $\mathcal{F}_{\text{byz-ideal}}$. For each notification that a round is complete from $\mathcal{F}_{\text{wrap}}$ decrease the delay value d and notify $\mathcal{S}$ that the round is complete. $\mathcal{F}_{\text{wrap}}$ will not notify $\mathcal{S}$ about activations in phase 4 ("output"), but $\mathcal{F}_{\text{byz-ideal}}$ instead. The simulator is thus not able to accurately simulate the exact order of outputs. However, the simulator is still able to determine the set of messages to output for each party in each round: he still is notified about the input to the protocol, when a party sends a message, and when a round is complete. We alter the strategy of $\mathcal{S}$ to make the modification indistinguishable: in each round, observe which parties will output a message and notify the ideal functionality that these parties are ready for output. Now, when $\mathcal{Z}$ activates a party and expects output, the ideal functionality will output possible messages for that specific party. This allows for all messages other than retreat to be output correctly. So, if $d = 0$ after the fourth activation of a party, $\mathcal{F}_{\text{byz-ideal}}$ just outputs retreat, mimicking the behaviour in the real model. $\mathcal{F}_{\text{byz-ideal}}$ and $\mathcal{S}$ now behave as specified in the ideal model, perfectly emulating the real model.

This concludes the proof.   □

3   Firewalls Revisited

In this section, we improve upon the result of Achenbach, Müller-Quade, and Rill [1]. They show that a quorum of three firewalls realises a secure firewall under the condition that at most one firewall is corrupted. Their analysis lacks an availability guarantee though. We prove this guarantee for their construction in our improved model. First, we briefly restate their construction. We refer to the original publication by Achenbach et al. [1] for details.

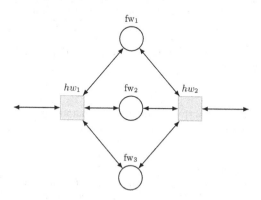

Fig. 7. The three-firewall network of Achenbach et al. [1]. The graph directly serves as the network model for $\mathcal{F}_{net}^G$: $G = (V, E)$ with $V = \{hw_1, hw_2, fw_1, fw_2, fw_3\}$ and $E' = \{(hw_1, fw_1), (hw_1, fw_2), (hw_1, fw_3), (hw_2, fw_1), (hw_2, fw_2), (hw_2, fw_3)\}, E = E' \cup \{(v, u) \mid (u, v) \in E'\}$.

A firewall network connects an "outside" network (e.g. the Internet) to an "inside" network (e.g. a Local-Area Network). The model completely abstracts from defining what kind of network traffic is harmful. It follows the idea that uncompromised firewalls will behave identical with exception of the order of packets. Further, there is a trusted hardware device that "distributes" network traffic in one direction and merges it in the other, realising a quorum (majority) decision. Then, assuming only one firewall is compromised, a quorum of three firewalls behaves like the compromised firewall was not present.

In a two-firewall quorum a single non-compliant firewall can completely shut down the network. Intuitively, a three-firewall quorum does not suffer this weakness. Achenbach, Müller-Quade, and Rill introduce a combination of three firewalls shown in Fig. 7 in an effort to improve the availability of the network. Because the plain UC model cannot represent synchrony, they cannot prove their intuition. We give a proof using our methodology.

Definition 1 (The functionality of an ideal firewall F_{fw_j}).

$$F_{fw_j} : P \times V \times S \to (P \cup \bot) \times (V \cup \bot) \times S$$

The protocol π_{fw}

party hw$_k$:

- "Input": Upon first activation by message (input, m) from $\mathcal{Z}$, save m.
- "Fetch": Upon second activation by message (output) from $\mathcal{Z}$,
  - call $\mathcal{F}_{\text{fw-net}}$(fetch, $\{\text{fw}_1, \text{fw}_2, \text{fw}_3\}$), save the message m corresponding to fw$_i$ as (m, i);
  - if there are two entries (m, i) and $(-m, i)$ on the tape, delete both.
- "Send": Upon third activation by message (output) from $\mathcal{Z}$, call $\mathcal{F}_{\text{fw-net}}$(send, $(\text{fw}_1, m), (\text{fw}_2, m), (\text{fw}_3, m)$) if m was saved previously. Delete m.
- "Output": Upon fourth activation by message (output) from $\mathcal{Z}$, if there are two saved entries (m, i) and (m', i') with $m \equiv m'$ and $i \neq i'$: delete both messages and output m. If $i, i' \neq 1$, save $(-m, 1)$, else if $i, i' \neq 2$, save $(-m, 2)$, else if $i, i' \neq 3$, save $(-m, 3)$.
- "RoundOK": Upon fifth activation by message (output) from $\mathcal{Z}$, send (RoundOK) to $\mathcal{F}_{\text{clock}}$.

party fw$_k$:

- "Fetch": Upon second activation by message (output) from $\mathcal{Z}$,
  - call $\mathcal{F}_{\text{fw-net}}$(fetch, hw$_1$, hw$_2$) and save the message m corresponding to hw$_i$ as (m, i);
  - for all saved messages (m, i): compute $F_{\text{fw}_k}(m, i, s) = (m', i', s')$ and replace that (m, i) with (m', i').
- "Output": Upon fourth activation by message (output) from $\mathcal{Z}$, if there are two messages (m, i) and (m', i'), call $\mathcal{F}_{\text{fw-net}}$(send, $(\text{hw}_i, m), (\text{hw}_{i'}, m')$).
- "RoundOK": Upon fifth activation, send (RoundOK) to $\mathcal{F}_{\text{clock}}$.

The ideal functionality of the firewall architecture $\mathcal{F}^{\delta}_{\text{fw-ideal}}$

Maintain a list of scheduled packets for each direction: $\mathbf{Q}_1, \mathbf{Q}_2$. Let w.l.o.g fw$_3$ be the corrupted party. In each case, if there are multiple entries to choose from, pick the first.

- Upon receiving (input, m, hw$_k$) from $\mathcal{F}_{\text{wrap}}$: Compute the firewall functions and update the internal states. Let the outputs of F_{fw_1} and F_{fw_2} be p' and p''. Store (in, $1, p', 2\delta$) and (in, $2, p'', 2\delta$) in $\mathbf{Q}_k$ if there is no entry (missing, $1, p', 0$) or (missing, $2, p'', 0$) respectively. Send (input, m, hw$_k$) to the adversary.
- Upon receiving (output, hw$_k$) from $\mathcal{F}_{\text{wrap}}$:
  - If there are two entries (in, $1, p', 0$) and (in, $2, p', 0$) in $\mathbf{Q}_k$, erase the corresponding entries from the queue and output p' to hw$_k$.
  - Else: if there is an entry (deliver, i, p, d) in $\mathbf{Q}_k$ remove it. Check if there is another entry (in, i', p, d') in $\mathbf{Q}_k$ with $i \neq i'$. If so, remove that entry too, if not, add an entry (missing, $|i - 3|, p, 0$) to $\mathbf{Q}_k$.
- Upon receiving (RoundComplete) from $\mathcal{F}_{\text{wrap}}$: Replace each entry (in, i, p, d) (or deliver, i, p, d) with $d > 0$ in $\mathbf{Q}$ with (in, $i, p, d - 1$) (or (deliver, i, p, d) and send (RoundComplete) to the adversary.
- Upon receiving (output, p, hw$_k$) from the adversary: if there is an entry (in, i, p, d) in $\mathbf{Q}_k$, replace it by (deliver, i, p, d).

Fig. 8. The parallel network protocol of Achenbach et al. [1] and their ideal functionality, expressed using our tools (see Sect. 2.2). Parties hw are responsible for distributing incoming and merging outgoing packets. They will output a packet to the environment not more than once per round.

$$F_{\text{fw}_j}(p, v, s) = \begin{cases} (p', v', s') & \text{if output is generated,} \\ (\perp, \perp, s') & \text{else.} \end{cases}$$

Definition 1 provides a modified definition of the firewall function used by Achenbach et al. [1], adapted to work with our graph based network model (Fig. 2). The function accepts a packet p from the set of all packets P, a node from the network graph $v \in V$ and a state $s \in S$ and outputs another packet, another node (the receiver of that packet) and a new state.

Figure 8 shows the protocol of the three firewall solution as expressed using our tools as well as the corresponding ideal functionality.

Theorem 2 π_{parallel} *realises* $\mathcal{F}_{\text{fw-ideal}}$ *in the* $\mathcal{F}_{\text{net}}^{\text{fw},\delta}$-*hybrid model.*

Due to space constraints, we omit the proof here. See Appendix A for the full proof.

4   Conclusion and Directions for Future Research

In this work we investigate the application of a formal security model to real network systems. More concretely, we use the Universal Composability framework to analyse a protocol for the Byzantine Generals problem and a combiner for network firewalls. We define two ideal functionalities $\mathcal{F}_{\text{wrap}}$ and $\mathcal{F}_{\text{net}}$ that capture redundant formalisms and facilitate an easier modeling. Further, we propose a 5-phase paradigm to allow for a clear presentation of network protocols. We conclude that analysing computer networks in the UC framework is indeed feasible.

In future work, our methodology should be improved to ease the handling of adaptive corruptions. Another important direction for future research is to simplify the representation of protocols and guarantees further. Enclosing technicalities in the framework instead of the protocol description facilitates a simpler exposition of core ideas while still yielding a formally sound security analysis. It is our belief that an intuitive access to formal security notions increases their acceptance in practice and thus helps improve the security of systems in use.

A   Firewalls Revisited

We give the full proof for Theorem 2 here.

Theorem 2 π_{parallel} *realises* $\mathcal{F}_{\text{fw-ideal}}$ *in the* $\mathcal{F}_{\text{net}}^{\text{fw},\delta}$-*hybrid model.*

Proof We prove the lemma via game hopping, starting from the real model. In each step we will modify the ideal functionality and argue that the modification is indistinguishable. We will w.l.o.g. assume that fw_3 is corrupted. Encapsulate the network in a new machine $\mathcal{S}$, introduce dummies for all fw_i and hw_i, and construct a new machine $\mathcal{F}_{\text{fw-ideal}}$ which connects the dummy machines with their counterparts in the (now simulated) real network. Modify $\mathcal{F}_{\text{fw-ideal}}$ step-wise:

1. Introduce variables to keep state for the firewalls. When receiving (input, m) through hw_k, evaluate the firewall functionalities F_{fw_1} and F_{fw_2}, update the respective firewall states and save the output packets p_1 and p_2 in a list Q_k as $(\text{in}, 1, p_1, 2\delta)$ and $(\text{in}, 2, p_2, 2\delta)$. This modification stores additional information but does not alter the communication and is thus indistinguishable.

2. When being advised to output a message p for a party hw_k by the simulator, only do so if there is an entry (in, i, p, d) in Q_k and delete that entry. Every message scheduled by the simulator in this manner was output by one of the firewalls in its simulation. Consequently, this message is also stored in Q_k. The real protocol party fw_k will internally delete all messages it outputs. Thus, this modification is indistinguishable.

3. When a packet p is output based on any entry $(\dots, i, p, d)$ in Q_k, check if there is another entry $(\dots, j, p, d)$ with $i \neq j$. If so, delete that entry as well. If not, add an entry $(\text{missing}, |i - 3|, p, d)$ to Q_k. Further, when receiving (input, m) through hw_k and evaluating the firewall functionalities, before saving the resulting packets p_1 and p_2, check if there is an entry $(\text{missing}, 1, p_1, 2\delta)$ or $(\text{missing}, 2, p_2, 2\delta)$ in Q_k. If there is, remove that entry and do not save the resulting packet. This modification is indistinguishable as $\mathcal{F}_{\text{fw-ideal}}$ now implements the exact behaviour of hw_1 and hw_2.

4. Add $\mathcal{F}_{\text{wrap}}$ as a wrapper around $\mathcal{F}_{\text{fw-ideal}}$. When receiving (RoundComplete) from $\mathcal{F}_{\text{wrap}}$, decrease the delay value d of each entry in Q_1 and Q_2 by 1. Send (RoundComplete) to the simulator. When being advised to output a packet p for party hw_k by the simulator, instead of outputting the packet immediately, replace the corresponding entry in Q_k by $(\text{deliver}, i, p, d)$. When being asked to provide output for party hw_j by $\mathcal{F}_{\text{wrap}}$, check if there is an entry in Q_j with $d = 0$. If so, output that packet. If not, check if there is an entry marked for delivery. If so, output the corresponding packet. Always perform the output according to the mechanism described in Step 3.

The simulator's simulation of the real network is not perfect after transformation step 4. Concretely, $\mathcal{S}$ is not notified of the fourth activation ("output") of honest protocol parties. However, as we argued in the proof of Theorem 1, the output *decision* is made during prior activations. Hence, by $\mathcal{S}$ announcing output early to $\mathcal{F}_{\text{fw-ideal}}$, $\mathcal{S}$ and $\mathcal{F}_{\text{fw-ideal}}$ perfectly emulate the real protocol. ($\mathcal{F}_{\text{wrap}}$ delivers output after the fourth activation only.)   □

References

1. Müller-Quade, J., Rill, J., Achenbach, D.: Universally Composable Firewall Architectures Using Trusted Hardware. In: Ors, B., Preneel, B. (eds.) BalkanCryptSec 2014. LNCS, vol. 9024, pp. 57–74. Springer, Heidelberg (2015). http://eprint.iacr.org/2015/099.pdf
2. Blum, M.: Coin flipping by telephone a protocol for solving impossible problems. ACM SIGACT News **15**(1), 23–27 (1983)
3. Canetti, R.: Universally composable security: a new paradigm for cryptographic protocols. In: 42nd IEEE Symposium on Foundations of Computer Science, Proceedings, October 2001

4. Canetti, R.: Universally composable security: a new paradigm for cryptographic protocols. Cryptology ePrint Archive, Report 2000/067. http://eprint.iacr.org/ (2013)

5. Canetti, R., Fischlin, M.: Universally composable commitments. In: Kilian, J. (ed.) CRYPTO 2001. LNCS, vol. 2139, pp. 19–40. Springer, Heidelberg (2001). doi:10. 1007/3-540-44647-8_2

6. Chari, S., Jutla, C.S., Roy, A.: Universally composable security analysis of oauth v2. 0. IACR Cryptology ePrint Archive 2011, vol. 526 (2011)

7. Damgård, I., Dupont, K.: Universally composable disk encryption schemes. Cryptology ePrint Archive, Report 2005/333. http://eprint.iacr.org/2005/333 (2005)

8. Schwenk, J., Pereira, O., Sadeghi, A.-R., Manulis, M., Gajek, S.: Universally composable security analysis of TLS. In: Baek, J., Bao, F., Chen, K., Lai, X. (eds.) ProvSec 2008. LNCS, vol. 5324, pp. 313–327. Springer, Heidelberg (2008)

9. Hofheinz, D., Müller-Quade, J.: A synchronous model for multi-party computation and the incompleteness of oblivious transfer. FCS'04 p. 117 (2004)

10. Hofheinz, D., Shoup, V.: Gnuc: A new universal composability framework. IACR Cryptology ePrint Archive **2011**, 303 (2011)

11. Huang, H., Kirchner, H.: Formal specification and verification of modular security policy based on colored petri nets. IEEE Trans. Dependable Secure Comput. **8**(6), 852–865 (2011)

12. Ingols, K., Chu, M., Lippmann, R., Webster, S., Boyer, S.: Modeling modern network attacks and countermeasures using attack graphs. In: Computer Security Applications Conference, 2009, Annual, ACSAC 2009, pp. 117–126. IEEE (2009)

13. Kalai, Y.T., Lindell, Y., Prabhakaran, M.: Concurrent general composition of secure protocols in the timing model. In: Proceedings of the Thirty-Seventh Annual ACM Symposium on Theory of Computing, pp. 644–653. ACM (2005)

14. Kang, M.H., Moskowitz, I.S., Chincheck, S.: The pump: a decade of covert fun. In: 21st Annual Computer Security Applications Conference, p. 7. IEEE (2005)

15. Katz, J., Zikas, V., Maurer, U., Tackmann, B.: Universally composable synchronous computation. In: Sahai, A. (ed.) TCC 2013. LNCS, vol. 7785, pp. 477–498. Springer, Heidelberg (2013)

16. Lamport, L., Shostak, R., Pease, M.: The byzantine generals problem. ACM Trans. Program. Lang. Syst. **4**(3), 382–401. http://doi.acm.org/10.1145/357172.357176 (1982)

17. Maurer, U.: Constructive cryptography – a new paradigm for security definitions and proofs. In: Mödersheim, S., Palamidessi, C. (eds.) TOSCA 2011. LNCS, vol. 6993, pp. 33–56. Springer, Heidelberg (2012)

18. Maurer, U., Renner, R.: Abstract cryptography. In: Chazelle, B. (ed.) The Second Symposium in Innovations in Computer Science, ICS 2011, pp. 1–21. Tsinghua University Press, January 2011

19. Nielsen, J.B.: On protocol security in the cryptographic model. Ph.D. thesis, BRICS, Computer Science Department, University of Aarhus (2003)

20. Peikert, C., Vaikuntanathan, V., Waters, B.: A framework for efficient and composable oblivious transfer. In: Wagner, D. (ed.) CRYPTO 2008. LNCS, vol. 5157, pp. 554–571. Springer, Heidelberg (2008)

21. Pfitzmann, B., Waidner, M.: A model for asynchronous reactive systems and its application to secure message transmission. In: 2001 IEEE Symposium on Security and Privacy, S&P 2001, Proceedings, pp. 184–200. IEEE (2001)

Key-Policy Attribute-Based Encryption for General Boolean Circuits from Secret Sharing and Multi-linear Maps

Constantin Cătălin Drăgan[1] and Ferucio Laurenţiu Ţiplea[2(✉)]

[1] CNRS, LORIA, 54506 Nancy, Vandoeuvre-lès-Nancy Cedex, France
catalin.dragan@loria.fr
[2] Department of Computer Science, Alexandru Ioan Cuza University of Iaşi,
700506 Iaşi, Romania
fltiplea@info.uaic.ro

Abstract. We propose a Key-policy Attribute-based Encryption (KP-ABE) scheme for general Boolean circuits, based on secret sharing and on a very particular and simple form of leveled multi-linear maps, called *chained multi-linear maps*. The number of decryption key components is substantially reduced in comparison with the scheme in [7], and the size of the multi-linear map (in terms of bilinear map components) is less than the Boolean circuit depth, while it is quadratic in the Boolean circuit depth for the scheme in [7]. Moreover, the multiplication depth of the chained multi-linear map in our scheme can be significantly less than the multiplication depth of the leveled multi-linear map in the scheme in [7]. Selective security of the proposed scheme in the standard model is proved, under the decisional multi-linear Diffie-Hellman assumption.

Keywords: Attribute-based encryption · Multi-linear map · Boolean circuit

1 Introduction

Attribute-based encryption (ABE) was introduced in [11] as a generalization of *identity-based encryption* [12]. There are two forms of ABE: *key-policy ABE* (KP-ABE) and *ciphertext-policy ABE* (CP-ABE) [2,9]. A KP-ABE scheme encrypts messages taking into consideration specific sets of attributes; decryption keys are distributed for an entire access structure build over the set of attributes so that correct decryption is allowed only to authorized sets of attributes (defined by the access structure). A CP-ABE scheme proceeds somehow vice-versa than a KP-ABE scheme: messages are encrypted together with access structures while decryption keys are given for specific sets of attributes. In all these cases, the access structures are defined by Boolean circuits [13].

This paper focuses on KP-ABE. The first KP-ABE scheme was proposed in [9], where the access structures were specified by monotone Boolean formulas (Boolean circuits of fan-out one with no negation gates). An extension to

© Springer International Publishing Switzerland 2016
E. Pasalic and L.R. Knudsen (Eds.): BalkanCryptSec 2015, LNCS 9540, pp. 112–133, 2016.
DOI: 10.1007/978-3-319-29172-7_8

non-monotonic Boolean formulas has later been proposed [10]. A direct extension of these schemes to the general case (access structures defined by general Boolean circuits) faces the backtracking attack [5,7]. The first KP-ABE scheme for general Boolean circuits was proposed [7], based on leveled multi-linear maps. Later soon, another KP-ABE scheme for general Boolean circuits has been proposed [8]; its construction is based on lattices and on the Learning With Errors (LWE) problem. Inspired by [8], Boneh et.al. [3] have proposed a KP-ABE scheme for functions that can be represented as (polynomial-size) arithmetic circuits. The scheme is based on the LWE problem as well. Its decryption key size is quadratic in the circuit depth, while for the schemes proposed in [7,8] it is linear in the number of Boolean gates or wires in the circuit. On the other side, the size of its public parameters is quadratic, while for the schemes in [7,8] is linear, in the number of input wires.

Contribution. In this paper we propose a new KP-ABE scheme for general Boolean circuits based on secret sharing and a very particular and simple form of leveled multi-linear maps, called *chained multi-linear maps*. We can think of our approach as a bridge between the simple and elegant approach in [9] based on secret sharing and just one bilinear map (but limited to Boolean formulas), and the more complex one in [7] based only on leveled multi-linear maps (which works for general Boolean circuits). This novel approach leads to a scheme more efficient than the one in [7], both in terms of the decryption key size and of the multi-linear map size and graded encoding multiplication depth. The size of the chained multi-linear maps we use is less than the circuit depth, while the leveled multi-linear maps used in [7] have a quadratic size in the circuit depth. To define a chained multi-linear map one has just to define k bilinear maps from $G_i \times G_1$ into G_{i+1}, $1 \leq i \leq k$, and a generator of the group G_1. In the case of leveled multi-linear maps, supplementary constraints regarding the groups generators, are needed.

Our construction works for general Boolean circuits. For a clear understanding of the construction, the logic gates of fan-out two or more are split into logics gates of fan-out one and fanout-gates (FO-gates) whose role is to multiply the output of the logic gates (we emphasize that this splitting is just for the easiness of the presentation and has no technical reasons). Then, a secret sharing procedure works top-down to share some secret, and a bottom-up procedure reconstructs a "hidden" form of the secret by using chained multi-linear maps. The generator of the chained multi-linear map is changed each time a FO-level (level that contains FO-gates) is reached. Decryption key components are assigned to input wires, FO-gates, and circuit FO-levels. The size of the decryption key is at most a third of the size of the decryption key in the construction in [7]. Using graded encoding systems [6] to define multi-linear maps as in [7], the multiplication depth of the chained multi-linear maps in our scheme is exactly the number of FO-levels (and does not depend on the circuit depth). As the number of FO-levels can be significantly less than or equal to the circuit depth minus three, we conclude that the multiplication depth of the chained multi-linear maps in our scheme can be significantly less than the multiplication depth of the leveled multi-linear maps in [7] (where it is given by the circuit depth). In other words, a chained multi-linear map of multiplication depth r can be used with any Boolean circuit with r FO-levels, no matter its depth. This is not possible for the construction in [7].

The selective security of our KP-ABE scheme is proved in the standard model under the decisional multi-linear Diffie-Hellman assumption.

Paper Organization. The paper is organized into eight sections. The next section fixes the basic terminology and notation used throughout the paper. The third section discusses the scheme in [7] and how it thwarts the backtracking attack, and gives an informal overview of our solution. Our construction is presented in the fourth section, its security is discussed in the fifth one, while the sixth section presents some comparisons between our scheme and the one in [7]. Section seven proposes some extensions of our scheme, and the last one concludes the paper.

2   Preliminaries

Access Structures. It is customary to represent access structures [13] by Boolean circuits [1]. A Boolean circuit consists of a number of input wires (which are not gate output wires), a number of output wires (which are not gate input wires), and a number of OR-, AND-, and NOT-gates. The OR- and AND-gates have two input wires, while NOT-gate has one input wire. All of them may have more than one output wire. That is, the fan-in of the circuit is at most two, while the fan-out may be arbitrarily large but at least one. A Boolean circuit is *monotone* if it does not have NOT-gates, and it is of *fan-out one* if all gates have fan-out one. In this paper all Boolean circuits are monotone and have exactly one output wire. Boolean circuits of fan-out one correspond to *Boolean formulas*.

If the input wires of a Boolean circuit $\mathcal{C}$ are in a one-to-one correspondence with the elements of a set $\mathcal{U}$ (whose elements will be called *attributes*) we will say that $\mathcal{C}$ is a Boolean circuit over $\mathcal{U}$. Each $A \subseteq \mathcal{U}$ evaluates the circuit $\mathcal{C}$ to one of the Boolean values 0 or 1 by simply assigning 1 to all input wires associated to elements in A, and 0 otherwise. We will write $\mathcal{C}(A)$ for the value obtained by evaluating $\mathcal{C}$ for A. The access structure defined by $\mathcal{C}$ is the set of all A that evaluates $\mathcal{C}$ to 1.

Attribute-Based Encryption. A KP-ABE scheme consists of four probabilistic polynomial-time (PPT) algorithms [9]:

$Setup(\lambda)$: this is a PPT algorithm that takes as input the security parameter λ and outputs a set of public parameters PP and a master key MSK;

$Enc(m, A, PP)$: this is a PPT algorithm that takes as input a message m, a non-empty set of attributes $A \subseteq \mathcal{U}$, and the public parameters, and outputs a ciphertext E;

$KeyGen(\mathcal{C}, MSK)$: this is a PPT algorithm that takes a Boolean circuit $\mathcal{C}$ and the master key MSK, and outputs a decryption key D (for the entire Boolean circuit $\mathcal{C}$);

$Dec(E, D)$: this is a deterministic polynomial-time algorithm that takes as input a ciphertext E and decryption key D, and outputs a message m or the special symbol $\perp$.

The following correctness property is required to be satisfied by any KP-ABE scheme: for any $(PP, MSK) \leftarrow Setup(\lambda)$, any Boolean circuit $\mathcal{C}$ over a set $\mathcal{U}$ of attributes, any message m, any $A \subseteq \mathcal{U}$, and any $E \leftarrow Enc(m, A, PP)$, if $\mathcal{C}(A) = 1$ then $m = Dec(E, D)$, for any $D \leftarrow KeyGen(\mathcal{C}, MSK)$.

Security Models. We consider the standard notion of selective security [9]. Specifically, in the *Init* phase the *adversary* (PPT algorithm) announces the set A of attributes that he wishes to be challenged upon, then in the *Setup* phase he receives the public parameters PP of the scheme, and in *Phase 1* oracle access to the decryption key generation oracle is granted for the adversary. In this phase, the adversary issues queries for decryption keys for access structures defined by Boolean circuits $\mathcal{C}$, provided that $\mathcal{C}(A) = 0$. In the *Challenge* phase the adversary submits two equally length messages m_0 and m_1 and receives the ciphertext associated to A and one of the two messages, say m_b, where $b \leftarrow \{0,1\}$. The adversary may receive again oracle access to the decryption key generation oracle (with the same constraint as above); this is *Phase 2*. Eventually, the adversary outputs a guess $b' \leftarrow \{0,1\}$ in the *Guess* phase.

The *advantage* of the adversary in this game is $P(b' = b) - 1/2$. The KP-ABE scheme is *secure* (in the selective model) if any adversary has only a negligible advantage in the selective game above.

Leveled Multi-linear Maps [7]. Given G_1, G_2, and G_T three multiplicative cyclic groups of prime order p, a map $e : G_1 \times G_2 \to G_T$ is called *bilinear* if it satisfies:

- $e(x^a, y^b) = e(x, y)^{ab}$, for any $x \in G_1$, $y \in G_2$, and $a, b \in \mathbb{Z}_p$;
- $e(g_1, g_2)$ is a generator of G_T, for any generator g_1 (g_2) of G_1 (G_2).

Given k multiplicative groups $G_1, \ldots, G_k$ of prime order p with generators $g_1, \ldots, g_k$, resp., a set $\mathbf{e} = \{e_{i,j} : G_i \times G_j \to G_{i+j} | i, j \geq 1, i + j \leq k\}$ of bilinear maps is called a *leveled multi-linear map* if $e_{i,j}(g_i^a, g_j^b) = g_{i+j}^{ab}$, for all $i, j \geq 1$ with $i + j \leq k$ and all $a, b \in \mathbb{Z}_p$.

Leveled multi-linear maps defined as above should be viewed generically. Practical constructions have also been obtained: [6] proposes a construction based on ideal lattices, while [4] proposes a construction based on integers. Both of them are developed inside the formalism called *graded encoding systems*.

The Decisional MDH Assumption [7]. The *decisional Multi-linear Diffie-Hellman* (MDH) problem for a leveled multi-linear map $\mathbf{e}$ as given above is the problem to distinguish between $g_k^{sc_1 \cdots c_k}$ and a random element in G_k given $g_1, g_1^s, g_1^{c_1}, \ldots, g_1^{c_k}$, where $s, c_1, \ldots, c_k$ are randomly chosen from $\mathbb{Z}_p$. The *decisional MDH assumption* for $\mathbf{e}$ states that no PPT algorithm $\mathcal{A}$ can solve the decisional MDH problem for $\mathbf{e}$ with more than a negligible advantage.

3   An Informal View of Our Construction

Our approach to construct a KP-ABE scheme uses both secret sharing as in [9] and multi-linear maps as in [7]. To clearly understand how these two techniques are combined, let us briefly recall them. The approach in [9] works only for Boolean formulas. The main idea is quite simple and elegant:

- choose a bilinear map $e : G_1 \times G_1 \rightarrow G_2$ and a generator g of G_1;
- to encrypt a message m by a set A of attributes, just multiply m by $e(g,g)^{ys}$, where y and s are random integers chosen in the setup and encryption, respectively, phases. Moreover, an attribute dependent quantity is also computed for each $i \in A$;
- the integer y is then top-down shared on the Boolean circuit, and the shares associated to attributes are used to compute the decryption key (which consists of a key component for each attribute);
- in order to decrypt $me(g,g)^{ys}$, one has to compute $e(g,g)^{ys}$. This can be done only if A is an authorized set of attributes. The computation of $e(g,g)^{ys}$ is bottom-up on the Boolean circuit, starting from the key components associated to the attributes in A.

It was pointed out in [7] that the construction in [9] cannot directly be used to design KP-ABE schemes for general Boolean circuits. The reason is the *backtracking attack* [7]. In case of OR-gates, any value computed at an input wire should be the same with the value computed at the other input wire (this is because of the way secrets are shared at OR-gates). Therefore, knowing the value at one of the input wires of an OR-gate implicitly leads to the knowledge of the value at the other input wire (although these values are computed by different workflows), and this value can further "migrate" to other gates if the gate fan-out is two or more. This aspect leads to the possibility of computing the value at the output wire of the circuit starting from values associated to some unauthorized set of attributes. The backtracking attack cannot occur when access structures are defined by Boolean formulas as in [9] because, in such cases, the input wires of OR-gates are not used by any other gates.

To thwart the backtracking attack, [7] uses a "one-way" construction in evaluating general Boolean circuits (the encryption technique is almost the same as the one in [9]):

- consider a leveled multi-linear map (as the one in the previous section);
- the decryption key components are associated to the input wires of the circuit and to each gate output wire (in [7], each gate has one output wire which may further be used by more than one gate);
- the circuit is evaluated bottom-up and the values associated to output wires of gates on level j are powers of g_{j+1};
- as the mappings $e_{i,j}$ work only in the "forward" direction, it is not feasible to invert values on the level $j+1$ in order to obtain values on the level j, defeating thus the backtracking attack.

Our approach combines secret sharing and a simpler form of leveled multi-linear maps. To clearly understand the secret sharing procedure, we split each logic gate of fan-out two or more into a logic gate of fan-out one and a *fanout-gate* (FO-gate) which multiplies the output of the logic gate. We emphasize that this splitting is just for the sake of clearness and has no other technical reasons. Then, the secret sharing procedure works top-down and:

1. the shares associated to the output wires of a FO-gate are processed via a random value associated to the input wire of the gate, and this random value is passed down to the logic gate for sharing;
2. the share associated to the output wire of a logic gate is shared to its input wires by taking into consideration the input wire level of the gate.

When all input wires of the circuit get their shares, a "reconstruction" procedure evaluates the circuit bottom-up by computing values to each wire. Each value is the power of some group generator, and the generator is changed only when a FO-level (level that contains FO-gates) is reached. Due to the way secrets are shared, the multi-linear map we need consists of just $r + 1$ bilinear maps $e_i : G_i \times G_1 \to G_{i+1}$ ($1 \leq i \leq r + 1$) with no other constraints (r is the number of FO-levels). As the maps e_i work only in the forward direction, our scheme defeats the backtracking attack.

4   Our Construction and Its Security

We begin the description of our scheme by fixing first the terminology and notation regarding the way Boolean circuits are used in our construction:

1. each Boolean circuit has a number of *circuit input gates*, but at least one. Each input gate has no input wire and exactly one output wire (called a *circuit input wire*);
2. each Boolean circuit has exactly one *circuit output gate*, which has one input wire (called the *circuit output wire*) and no output wire;
3. each Boolean circuit has a number of *logic gates* of two types: OR-gates and AND-gates. Each of them has exactly two input wires and exactly one output wire;
4. each Boolean circuit may have a number of *FO-gates*. Each FO-gate has exactly one input wire and at least two output wires. Their role is to propagate (multiply) the logic gate outputs;
5. no two FO-gates are directly connected (no output wire of a FO-gate is the input wire of another FO-gate).

The restriction to monotone Boolean circuits does not constitute a loss of generality (see page 7 in [7]). Figure 1 pictorially represents a Boolean circuit under our conventions.

Assuming that the wires are labeled, we may write the gates as tuples (w_1, w_2, OR, w), (w_1, w_2, AND, w), and $(w, FO, w_1, \ldots, w_j)$, by specifying the input wires, the gate name, and then the output wires. The output wire of a

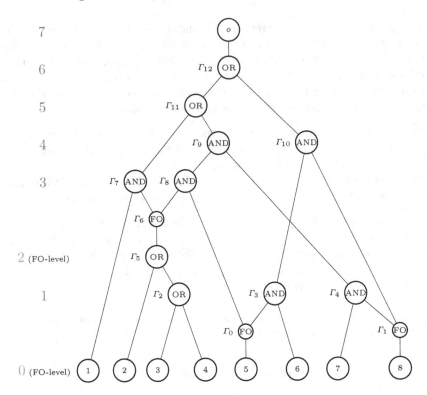

Fig. 1. Boolean circuit with FO-gates

Boolean circuit will always be denoted by o, and the input wires by $1, \ldots, n$ (assuming that the circuit has n input wires).

All gates of a Boolean circuit are distributed on *levels*:

1. the $0th$ *level*, also called the *input level*, consists of all circuit input gates together with all FO-gates directly connected to them;
2. if the $(i-1)$st level has been defined and there are logic gates whose input gates are on the first $(i-1)$ levels but at least one input gate on the $(i-1)$st level, then the ith level consists of all such logic gates together with all FO-gates directly connected to them;
3. if the $(i-1)$st level has been defined and there is no logic gates as above, then the ith level consists only of the output gate (this is also called the *output level* of the circuit).

Figure 1 illustrates the way levels are counted in our Boolean circuits.

By $level(\Gamma)$ we denote the level of the gate Γ. The *depth* of a Boolean circuit $\mathcal{C}$, denoted $depth(\mathcal{C})$, is the number of $\mathcal{C}$'s output level. A level is called an *FO-level* if it contains FO-gates. Remark that the input level may be an FO-level, but the output level as well as its direct predecessor cannot be FO-levels (in fact, assuming that no logic gate has an FO-gate as input gate for both its inputs, each FO-level i satisfies $i \leq depth(\mathcal{C}) - 3$).

Let Γ be a logic gate and Γ' be a gate such that Γ and Γ' are directly connected and $i = Level(\Gamma) > Level(\Gamma') = j$ (that is, Γ' is an input gate of Γ). The *FO-level sequence* from Γ to Γ' is a sequence, possible empty, of FO-level indexes defined as follows:

1. if Γ' is an input or logic gate, then the FO-level sequence from Γ to Γ' is the sequence of all FO-level numbers taken in decreasing order from $i - 1$ to j;
2. if Γ' is a FO-gate, then the FO-level sequence from Γ to Γ' is the sequence of all FO-level numbers taken in decreasing order from $i - 1$ to $j + 1$.

As an example, in the Boolean circuit in Fig. 1, (2,0) is the FO-level sequence from Γ_7 to the input gate 1, and (2) is the FO-level sequence from Γ_8 to Γ_0.

To each logic gate Γ, two FO-level sequences are associated: the *left* one, from Γ to its left input gate, and the *right* one, from Γ to its right input gate. It is clear that both of them can be empty and one of them is a prefix of the other one. These two sequences will play an important role in the sharing procedure described below.

Now, we need to fix the terminology on multi-linear maps.

Definition 1. *A* chained multi-linear map *is a sequence of bilinear maps* $(e_i : G_i \times G_1 \rightarrow G_{i+1} | 1 \leq i \leq k)$, *where* $G_1, \ldots, G_{k+1}$ *are multiplicative groups of the same prime order.*

Remark 1. Let $(e_i | 1 \leq i \leq k)$ be a chained multi-linear map as above. If $g_1 \in G_1$ is a generator of G_1, then $g_{i+1} = e_i(g_i, g_1)$ is a generator of G_{i+1}, for all $1 \leq i \leq k$ (because e_i is a bilinear map). Therefore, $(e_i | 1 \leq i \leq k)$ can be regarded as a special form of leveled multi-linear map.

Chained multi-linear maps will be used in our construction as follows. Assume that r is the number of FO-levels in the Boolean circuits we consider, and $(e_i | 1 \leq i \leq r + 1)$ is a chained multi-linear map as above. A message $m \in G_{r+2}$ will be encrypted by mg_{r+2}^{ys}, where y is a random integer chosen in the setup phase and s is a random integer chosen in the encryption phase. To decrypt this message, one needs to compute g_{r+2}^{ys}, and this will be done by using a secret sharing procedure and a secret reconstruction procedure.

The secret sharing procedure $Share(y, C)$ below inputs a Boolean circuit C and a value $y \in \mathbb{Z}_p$, and outputs three functions S, P, and L with the following meaning:

1. S assigns to each wire of C an element in $\mathbb{Z}_p$;
2. P assigns to each output wire of a FO-gate an *FO-key* in G_1;
3. L assigns to each FO-level an *FO-level-key* in G_1.

Share(y, C)

1. Initially, all gates of C are unmarked and $S(o) := y$;
2. For each FO-level i, $0 \leq i < depth(C) - 2$, choose uniformly at random $a_i \in \mathbb{Z}_p$ and assign $L(i) := g_1^{a_i}$;

3. If $\Gamma = (w_1, w_2, OR, w)$ is an unmarked OR-gate and $S(w) = x$, then mark Γ and assign $S(w_1) := xa_{i_1}^{-1} \cdots a_{i_u}^{-1} \bmod p$ and $S(w_2) := xa_{j_1}^{-1} \cdots a_{j_v}^{-1} \bmod p$, where $i_1 \cdots i_u$ and $j_1 \cdots j_v$ are the left and right FO-level sequences of Γ, respectively (if the left FO-level sequence is empty, then $S(w_1) := x$, and similarly for the other case);

4. If $\Gamma = (w_1, w_2, AND, w)$ is an unmarked AND-gate and $S(w) = x$, then mark Γ and do the followings:
   (a) choose x_1 uniformly at random from $\mathbb{Z}_p$ and compute x_2 such that $x = (x_1 a_{i_1} \cdots a_{i_u} + x_2 a_{j_1} \cdots a_{j_v}) \bmod p$, where $i_1 \cdots i_u$ and $j_1 \cdots j_v$ are the left and right FO-level sequences of Γ, respectively (if $i_1 \cdots i_u$ is the empty sequence then $a_{i_1} \cdots a_{i_u} = 1$, and similarly for the other case);
   (b) assign $S(w_1) := x_1$ and $S(w_2) := x_2$;

5. If $\Gamma = (w, FO, w_1, \ldots, w_j)$ is an unmarked FO-gate and $S(w_i) = x_i$ for all $1 \le i \le j$, then mark Γ and do the followings:
   (a) choose uniformly at random $x \in \mathbb{Z}_p$ and compute b_i such that $x_i = xb_i \bmod p$, for all $1 \le i \le j$;
   (b) assign $S(w) := x$ and $P(w_i) := g_1^{b_i}$, for all $1 \le i \le j$;

6. repeat the last three steps above until all gates get marked.

We will write $(S, P, L) \leftarrow Share(y, \mathcal{C})$ to denote that (S, P, L) is an output of the probabilistic algorithm $Share$ on input $(y, \mathcal{C})$. $S(i)$ will be called the *share* of the input wire i associated to the secret y, for all $1 \le i \le n$, where n is the number of input wires of $\mathcal{C}$. The procedure $Share$ is illustrated in Fig. 2 in Appendix A.

The secret reconstruction procedure $Recon(\mathcal{C}, P, L, A, V_A)$ reconstructs a "hidden form" of the secret y starting from "hidden forms" of shares associated to some set A of attributes. This procedure is deterministic and outputs an evaluation function R which assigns to each wire either a value in some group $G_1, \ldots, G_{r+2}$ or the undefined value $\perp$, where r is the number of FO-levels of $\mathcal{C}$. The notation and conventions here are:

- $\mathcal{C}$ is a Boolean circuit with n input wires and $A \subseteq \{1, \ldots, n\}$;
- (S, P, L) is an output of $Share(y, \mathcal{C})$, for some secret y;
- $V_A = (V_A(i) | 1 \le i \le n)$, where $V_A(i) = g_2^{\alpha_i}$ for all $i \in A$ and some $\alpha_i \in \mathbb{Z}_p$, and $V_A(i) = \perp$ for all $i \notin A$;
- $\perp$ is an *undefined value* for which the following conventions are adopted: $\perp \notin \cup_{i=1}^{r+2} G_i$, $\perp < x$, $\perp \cdot z = \perp$, $z/\perp = \perp$, and $\perp^z = \perp$, for all $x \in \cup_{i=1}^{r+2} G_i$ and $z \in (\cup_{i=1}^{r+2} G_i) \cup \{\perp\}$, where r is the number of FO-levels of $\mathcal{C}$.

Before describing the procedure $Recon$, we need one more notation. Given $g_i^\alpha \in G_i$ for some i and α, an FO-level sequence $i_1 \cdots i_u$, and an output L of the $Share$ procedure, denote by $Shift(g_i^\alpha, i_1 \cdots i_u, L)$ the element $g_{i+u}^{\alpha a_{i_1} \cdots a_{i_u}} \in G_{i+u}$ obtained as follows:

$$g_{i+u}^{\alpha a_{i_1} \cdots a_{i_u}} := \begin{cases} g_i^\alpha, & \text{if } i_1 \cdots i_u \text{ is empty} \\ e_{i+u-1}(\cdots e_i(g_i^\alpha, L(i_u)) \cdots, L(i_1)), & \text{otherwise} \end{cases}$$

(recall that $i_u < \cdots < i_1$). Moreover, define $Shift(\perp, i_1 \cdots i_u, L) = \perp$.

$Recon(\mathcal{C}, P, L, A, V_A)$

1. Initially, all gates of $\mathcal{C}$ are unmarked and $R(i) := V_A(i)$, for each input wire i of $\mathcal{C}$;
2. If $\Gamma = (w_1, w_2, OR, w)$ is an unmarked OR-gate and both $R(w_1)$ and $R(w_2)$ were defined, then mark Γ and assign $R(w)$ by

$$R(w) := sup\{Shift(R(w_1), i_1 \cdots i_u, L), Shift(R(w_2), j_1 \cdots j_v, L)\},$$

where $i_1 \cdots i_u$ and $j_1 \cdots j_v$ are the left and right FO-level sequences of Γ, respectively.
Remark: either $Shift(R(w_1), i_1 \cdots i_u, L)$ or $Shift(R(w_2), j_1 \cdots j_v, L)$ is $\perp$ in case that $Shift(R(w_1), i_1 \cdots i_u, L) \neq Shift(R(w_2), j_1 \cdots j_v, L)$;
3. If $\Gamma = (w_1, w_2, AND, w)$ is an unmarked AND-gate and both $R(w_1)$ and $R(w_2)$ were defined, then mark Γ and assign $R(w)$ by

$$R(w) := Shift(R(w_1), i_1 \cdots i_u, L) \cdot Shift(R(w_2), j_1 \cdots j_v, L),$$

where $i_1 \cdots i_u$ and $j_1 \cdots j_v$ are the left and right FO-level sequences of Γ, respectively.
Remark: there exists i such that both $Shift(R(w_1), i_1 \cdots i_u, L)$ and $Shift(R(w_2), j_1 \cdots j_v, L)$ are powers of g_i;
4. If $\Gamma = (w, FO, w_1, \ldots, w_j)$ is an unmarked FO-gate and $R(w)$ was defined, then mark Γ and assign $R(w_i) = e_u(R(w), P(w_i))$ for all $1 \leq i \leq j$, where $R(w)$ is of the form g_u^α for some u and α.
Remark: $P(w_i)$ is of the form $g_1^{b_i}$ for all i and some b_i. Therefore, $R(w_i)$ is of the form $g_{u+1}^{\alpha b_i}$, for all i;
5. repeat the last three steps above until all gates get marked.

The procedure $Recon$ is illustrated in Fig. 3 in Appendix A.
We are now in a position to define our KP-ABE scheme.

KP-ABE Scheme

$Setup(\lambda, n, r)$: the setup algorithm uses the security parameter λ and the parameter r to choose a prime p, $r + 2$ multiplicative groups $G_1, \ldots, G_{r+2}$ of prime order p, a generator $g_1 \in G_1$, and a sequence of bilinear maps $(e_i : G_i \times G_1 \rightarrow G_{i+1} | 1 \leq i \leq r + 1)$. Let $g_{i+1} = e_i(g_i, g_1)$, for all i. Then, it defines the set of attributes $\mathcal{U} = \{1, \ldots, n\}$, chooses $y \in \mathbb{Z}_p$ and, for each attribute $i \in \mathcal{U}$, chooses $t_i \in \mathbb{Z}_p$. Finally, the algorithm outputs the public parameters

$$PP = (n, r, p, G_1, \ldots, G_{r+2}, g_1, e_1, \ldots, e_{r+1}, Y = g_{r+2}^y, (T_i = g_1^{t_i} | i \in \mathcal{U}))$$

and the master key $MSK = (y, t_1, \ldots, t_n)$;
$Encrypt(m, A, PP)$: the encryption algorithm encrypts a message $m \in G_{r+2}$ by a non-empty set $A \subseteq \mathcal{U}$ of attributes as follows:
- $s \leftarrow \mathbb{Z}_p$;
- output $E = (A, E' = mY^s, (E_i = T_i^s = g_1^{t_i s} | i \in A))$;

$KeyGen(\mathcal{C}, MSK)$: the decryption key generation algorithm generates a decryption key D for a Boolean circuit $\mathcal{C}$ with n input wires and r FO-levels, as follows:

- $(S, P, L) \leftarrow Share(y, \mathcal{C})$;
- output $D = ((D(i)|i \in \mathcal{U}), P, L)$, where $D(i) = g_1^{S(i)/t_i}$, for all i;

$Decrypt(E, D)$: given E and D as above, the decryption works as follows:

- compute $V_A = (V_A(i)|i \in \mathcal{U})$, where

$$V_A(i) = e_1(E_i, D(i)) = e_1(g_1^{t_i s}, g_1^{S(i)/t_i}) = g_2^{S(i)s}$$

  for all $i \in A$, and $V_A(i) = \bot$ for all $i \in \mathcal{U} - A$;
- $R := Recon(\mathcal{C}, P, L, A, V_A)$;
- compute $m := E'/R(o)$.

It is straightforward to prove the correctness of our KP-ABE_Scheme.

Theorem 1. *The KP-ABE_Scheme above satisfies the correctness property. That is, using the notation above, for any $E = (A, mY^s, (E_i|i \in A))$, any circuit $\mathcal{C}$ with n inputs wires and r FO-levels and $\mathcal{C}(A) = 1$, and any $(S, P, L) \leftarrow Share(y, \mathcal{C})$, the valuation R returned by $Recon(\mathcal{C}, P, L, A, V_A)$ satisfies $R(o) = Y^s$.*

Proof. By an inspection of the *Share* and *Recon* procedures. □

Translation to Graded Encoding Systems. Our KP-ABE_Scheme can be translated into the graded encoding system formalism [4,6] exactly as in [7] and, therefore, the details are omitted. We only emphasize that:

1. the *Share* procedure is unchanged except for the following aspects:
   (a) for the P and L functions it returns level-1 encodings (similarly computed as in [7]);
   (b) for each input wire i it returns an integer $S(i)$. The sampling procedure (in the graded encoding system) outputs a level-0 encoding for such integers;
2. the *Recon* procedure, as well as the *KP_ABE_Scheme*, are adapted to graded encoding systems in a similar way to that in [7] (starting with the first level in our construction, any FO-level, and only them, corresponds to an encoding level in increasing order).

Security Issues. To show that our scheme defeats the backtracking attack we remark first that the "migration" of a value g_i^α associated to an input wire w_1 of a logic gate Γ_1 to an input wire w_2 of another logic gate Γ_2 is possible only if w_1 and w_2 are output wires of some FO-gate Γ. If w is the input wire of Γ, the value associated to w cannot be computed from g_i^α (because of the one-wayness property of the chained multi-linear map), whereas the value of w_1 can be computed only by using the value associated to w. Therefore, to compute the value for w_2, one has to evaluate bottom-up the circuit and to obtain first the value of w.

The decisional MDH problem can be formulated for chained multi-linear maps as well, with generators as in Remark 1. Then we have:

Theorem 2. *The KP-ABE_Scheme is secure in the selective model under the decisional MDH assumption.*

Proof. It can be found in Appendix B.   □

5   Complexity of the Construction

We will discuss in this section the complexity of our KP-ABE_Scheme in terms of size of the decryption key and chained multi-linear map, and we will compare it with the complexity of the construction provided in [7].

The approach in [7] associates two keys to each input wire, four keys to each OR-gate output wire, and three keys to each AND-gate output wire. Therefore, the total number of keys is bounded from below by $2n + 3q$ and from above by $2n + 4q$, where n is the number of inputs and q is the number of gates of the Boolean circuit. If $depth(\mathcal{C}) = \ell$, then the size of the leveled multi-linear map is $\ell(\ell + 1)/2$ and its graded encoding multiplication depth is $\ell + 1$ [6].

Assuming that the Boolean circuit in our approach has n inputs, r FO-levels, and the total number of outputs of the FO-gates is f, our KP-ABE_Scheme involves $n+r+f$ decryption key components and $r+1$ bilinear maps. To compare the two approaches (the one in [7] and ours), we need to examine the complexity of the conversion of Boolean circuits as used in [7] to Boolean circuits as used in our paper. Assume that $\mathcal{C}$ is a Boolean circuit as considered in [7], with n inputs and q logic gates. Let $n = n_1 + n_2$ and $q = q_1 + q_2$, where n_1 (q_1) is the number of input (logic) gates of fan-out one (called *type 1 input (logic) gates*) and n_2 (q_2) is the number of input (logic) gates of fan-out greater than one (called *type 2 input (logic) gates*). Each type 1 input gate "consumes" one input wire and "produces" one output wire, each type 2 input gate "consumes" one input wire and "produces" at least two output wires, each logic gate "consumes" two input wires and "produces" one output wire, and each type 2 logic gate "consumes" two input wires and "produces" at least two output wires. As $\mathcal{C}$ has n input wires and one output wire, it follows

$$n - n_2 - q_1 - 2q_2 + f = 1,$$

where f is the total number of output wires of type 2 input and logic gates. We can easily transform $\mathcal{C}$ into a Boolean circuit $\mathcal{C}'$ according to our notation by simply adding a FO-gate to each type 2 input and logic gate. This leads to n_2+q_2 FO-gates with a total of f output wires. This FO-gates may be distributed on at least two levels and on at most $1+q_2$ levels (remark that the FO-gates associated to input gates are all on the 0th level). Therefore, the number of decryption key components (that is, $n + r + f$) satisfies

$$n_2 + q + q_2 + 3 \le \text{number of key components } \le n_2 + q + 2q_2 + 2$$

Now, let us estimate the depth ℓ of a Boolean circuit as in [7]. The number of logic gates needed to "consume" n input wires and to generate just one input wire is at least $\log n$ and at most $n - 1$. If the Boolean circuit has n_2 type 2 input gates and q_2 type 2 logic gates (see the notation above), then the wires produced by them is

$$n - n_2 - 2q_2 + f = n_1 - 2q_2 + f = q_1 + 1$$

To consume these wires by type 1 logic gates, at least $\log(q_1 + 1)$ and at most q_1 levels are needed. The q_2 type 2 logic gates can be distributed on at least one level and at most q_2 levels. Therefore, the number ℓ satisfies

$$1 + \log(q_1 + 1) \le \ell \le q_1 + q_2 = q \text{ (remark that } q_1 \ge n + n_2)$$

Our constructions, using the notation above, needs a chained multi-linear map with $r + 1$ components, where r is the number of FO-levels. According to the estimate above, $1 \le r \le q_2$ if $n_2 = 0$, and $2 \le r \le q_2 + 1$ if $n_2 \ne 0$. Moreover, $r \le \ell - 2$.

Another main difference between our KP-ABE_Scheme and the one in [7] is with respect to the multi-linear map these schemes use. Given k multiplicative groups of the same prime order p, any $k - 1$ bilinear maps $e_i : G_1 \times G_1 \to G_{i+1}$, $1 \le i \le k - 1$, define a chained multi-linear map. This is simply seen by taking any arbitrary generator g_1 of G_1 and recursively defining $g_{i+1} = e_i(g_i, g_1)$, for any $1 \le i \le k - 2$. On the contrary, not any $k(k - 1)/2$ bilinear maps $e_{i,j} : G_i \times G_j \to G_{i+j}$ define a leveled multi-linear map. This is because of the constraint $e_{i,j}(g_i, g_j) = g_{i+j}$, for all $i, j \ge 1$ with $i + j \le k - 1$.

The graded encoding multiplicative depth of the leveled multi-linear map in [7] is $\ell + 1$, while in our scheme is $r + 1$, which does not depend on the circuit depth ℓ. Therefore, a chained multi-linear map of multiplicative depth $r + 1$ can be used with all Boolean circuits with r FO-levels. This is not possible for the construction in [7] where the depth of the Boolean circuits dictates the multiplicative depth of the leveled multi-linear map.

More on the complexity of our construction will be provided in the table in the next section.

6   Extensions and Improvements

It is straightforward to see that our scheme can be extended to Boolean circuits with logic gates of fan-in more than two, without increasing the size of the decryption key or of the chained mutilinear map. Such an extension could be useful in order to reduce the size of the Boolean circuit, resulting in a possible smaller decryption key.

Our KP-ABE_Scheme is defined for a fixed number r of FO-levels. However, we can easily extend it to correspond to an arbitrary but upper bounded number of such levels. The main idea is to add FO-level-keys for the "missing FO-levels". More precisely, let r be an upper bound of the number of FO-levels.

Define two procedure *Share'* and *Recon'* by modifying *Share* and *Recon* as follows:

1. *Share'*(y, C) outputs (S, P, L, H) and it is obtained from *Share* by changing the second and third steps into

   "2 '. For each FO-level i, $0 \leq i \leq depth(C) - 3$, choose uniformly at random $a_i \in \mathbb{Z}_p$ and assign $L(i) := g_1^{a_i}$. For each $1 \leq i \leq h$, where $h = r - r'$ and r' is the number of FO-levels in C, choose uniformy at random $c_i \in \mathbb{Z}_p$ and assign $H(i) := g_1^{c_i}$, $1 \leq i \leq r - r'$;"

   "3 '. $S(o) := y c_1^{-1} \cdots c_h^{-1} \bmod p$ if $h > 0$, and $S(o) = y$, otherwise;"

2. *Recon'*(C, P, L, H, A, V_A) is obtained from *Recon* by simply adding one more step

   "7. $R(o) := Shift(R(o), h \cdots 1, H)$"

The new scheme is the next one:

KP-ABE_Scheme_1

Setup(λ, n, r): the same as in KP-ABE_Scheme;

Encrypt(m, A, PP): the same as in KP-ABE_Scheme;

KeyGen(C, MSK): the decryption key generation algorithm generates a decryption key D for a Boolean circuit C with n input wires and $r' \leq r$ FO-levels, as follows:

   − $(S, P, L, H) \leftarrow$ *Share'*(y, C);
   − $D = ((D(i) | i \in \mathcal{U}), P, L, H)$, where $D(i) = g_1^{S(i)/t_i}$, for all i;

Decrypt(E, D): given E and D as above, the decryption works as follows:
   − compute $V_A = (V_A(i) | i \in \mathcal{U})$, where

$$V_A(i) = e_1(E_i, D(i)) = e_1\left(g_1^{t_i s}, g_1^{S(i)/t_i}\right) = g_2^{S(i)s}$$

   for all $i \in A$, and $V_A(i) = \perp$ for all $i \in \mathcal{U} - A$;
   − $R := $ *Recon'*(C, P, L, H, A, V_A);
   − compute $m := E'/R(o)$.

An important improvement of our scheme consists of using the FO-level-key of a FO-level as a FO-key for the first output wire of each FO-gate on that level. More precisely, define the procedure *Share''* by modifying the fifth step of *Share* into:

5'. If $\Gamma = (w, FO, w_1, \ldots, w_j)$ is an unmarked FO-gate and $S(w_i) = x_i$ for all $1 \leq i \leq j$, then mark Γ and do the followings:
   (a) compute x such that $x_1 = x a_{level(\Gamma)} \bmod p$;
   (b) compute b_i such that $x_i = x b_i \bmod p$, for all $2 \leq i \leq j$;
   (c) assign $S(w) := x$, $P(w_1) = g_1^{a_{level(\Gamma)}}$, and $P(w_i) := g_1^{b_i}$, for all $2 \leq i \leq j$;

Now, define the scheme KP-ABE_Scheme_2 as the scheme obtained by replacing *Share* by *Share''* in KP-ABE_Scheme.

The main benefit of this new KP-ABE scheme consists of the fact that the number of decryption key components is decreased by the number of FO-gates. Thus, according to our notation in Sect. 5, the size of the key provided by KP-ABE_Scheme_2 is

$$n_2 + q + 3 \leq \text{number of key components} \leq n_2 + q + q_2 + 2$$

Of course, the extensions and the improvement above can be combined. Their security can be proved as for the KP-ABE_Scheme.

The efficiency of our scheme (the improved version), in comparison with the scheme in [7] which falls in the same class of schemes as ours, is presented in the following table.

Boolean circuits with − n_1 input gates of fan-out 1 − n_2 input gates of fan-out > 1 − q_1 logic gates of fan-out > 1 − q_2 logic gates of fan-out > 1 − r FO-levels and depth ℓ	No of keys	Multi-linear map (type, size, and mult. depth)
KP-ABE scheme in [7]	$2(n_1 + n_2) + 3(q_1 + q_2) \leq$ $no.\,keys \leq$ $2(n_1 + n_2) + 4(q_1 + q_2)$	• leveled • $\dfrac{\ell(\ell+1)}{2}$ • $\ell + 1$
Our KP-ABE_Scheme_2	$n_2 + q_1 + q_2 + 3 \leq no.\,keys \leq$ $n_2 + q_1 + 2q_2 + 2$	• chained • $r + 1 < \ell$ • $r + 1$

7   Conclusions

We have proposed in this paper a KP-ABE scheme for general Boolean circuits. The scheme is based on secret sharing and a particular and special form of leveled multi-linear maps, called *chained multi-linear maps*. It can be viewed as a bridge between the approach in [9] based on secret sharing and just one bilinear map (but limited to Boolean formulas), and the more complex one in [7] based only on leveled multi-linear maps (which works for general Boolean circuits). We have shown that our scheme is more efficient than the one in [7], both in terms of the decryption key size and of the multi-linear map size and graded encoding multiplication depth. We have stressed several times in the paper that the use of FO-gates is just for the sake of clarity. We can avoid these gates by merging two consecutive steps of the *Share* and *Recon* procedures whenever they are to be applied to logic gates of fan-out more than one (the details can be easily fixed).

A   Appendix 1

This appendix illustrates the *Share* and *Recon* procedures on the Boolean circuit in Fig. 1.

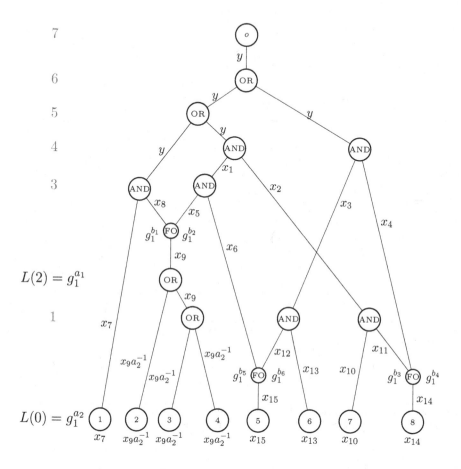

$$x_5 + x_6a_1 \equiv x_1 \bmod p, \qquad x_1 + x_2a_1 \equiv y \bmod p, \qquad x_3a_1 + x_4a_1 \equiv y \bmod p,$$

$$x_7a_1a_2 + x_8 \equiv y \bmod p, \qquad x_{12} + x_{13}a_2 \equiv x_3 \bmod p, \qquad x_{10}a_2 + x_{11} \equiv x_2 \bmod p,$$

$$x_8 \equiv x_9b_1 \bmod p, \qquad x_6 \equiv x_{15}b_5 \bmod p, \qquad x_{11} \equiv x_{14}b_3 \bmod p,$$

$$x_5 \equiv x_9b_2 \bmod p, \qquad x_{12} \equiv x_{15}b_6 \bmod p, \qquad x_4 \equiv x_{14}b_4 \bmod p,$$

Fig. 2. *Share*$(y, \mathcal{C})$

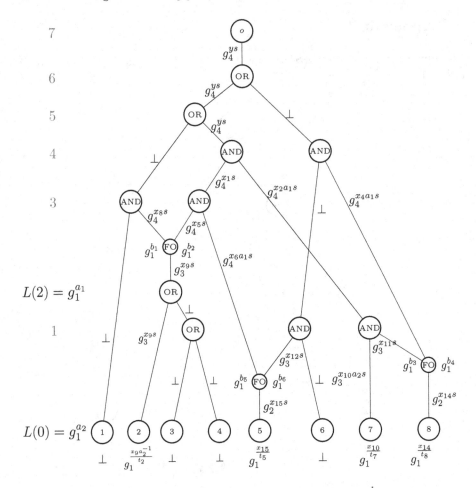

Fig. 3. $Recon(\mathcal{C}, P, L, A, V_A)$, where $A = \{2, 5, 7, 8\}$, $V_A(2) = g_2^{x_9 a_2^{-1} s}$, $V_A(5) = g_2^{x_{15} s}$, $V_A(7) = g_2^{x_{10} s}$, and $V_A(8) = g_2^{x_{14} s}$ (V_A is $\perp$ for all the other values)

B   Appendix 2

In this appendix we prove the security of our KP-ABE_Scheme.

Theorem 2. *The KP-ABE_Scheme is secure in the selective model under the decisional MDH assumption.*

Proof. It is sufficient to prove that for any adversary $\mathcal{A}$ with an advantage η in the selective game for KP-ABE_Scheme, a PPT algorithm $\mathcal{B}$ can be defined, with the advantage $\eta/2$ over the decisional MDH problem. The algorithm $\mathcal{B}$ plays the role of challenger for $\mathcal{A}$ in the selective game for KP-ABE_Scheme. Taking into account that

1. any leveled multilinear map $\{e_{i,j} | i, j \geq 1, \ i + j \leq k\}$ includes a chained multilinear map $(e_{i,1} | 1 \leq i < k)$;
2. if some PPT algorithm can decide the decisional MDH problem with chained multilinear map instances then it can decide, with at least the same advantage, the decisional MDH problem with leveled multilinear map instances,

we conclude that it is sufficient to give the algorithm $\mathcal{B}$ a chained multilinear map instance of the decisional MDH problem consisting of $r + 2$ multiplicative groups $G_1, \ldots, G_{r+2}$ of the same prime order p, $r + 2$ generators $g_1, \ldots, g_{r+2}$ of these groups, respectively, $r + 1$ bilinear maps $e_i : G_i \times G_1 \rightarrow G_{i+1}$ such that $e_i(g_i^a, g_1^b) = g_{i+1}^{ab}$ for all $1 \leq i \leq r + 1$ and $a, b \in \mathbb{Z}_p$, and the values g_1^s, $g_1^{c_1}, \ldots, g_1^{c_{r+2}}$, $Z_0 = g_{r+2}^{sc_1 \cdots c_{r+2}}$, and $Z_1 = g_{r+2}^z$, where $s, c_1, \ldots, c_{r+2}, z$ are chosen uniformly at random from $\mathbb{Z}_p$.

Now, the algorithm $\mathcal{B}$ runs $\mathcal{A}$ acting as a challenger for it.

Init. Let A be a non-empty set of attributes the adversary $\mathcal{A}$ wishes to be challenged upon.

Setup. $\mathcal{B}$ chooses at random $r_i \in \mathbb{Z}_p$ for all $i \in \mathcal{U}$, and computes $Y = g_{r+2}^{c_1 \cdots c_{r+2}}$ and $T_i = g_1^{t_i}$ for all $i \in \mathcal{U}$, where

$$t_i = \begin{cases} r_i, & \text{if } i \in A \\ c_2 r_i, & \text{otherwise} \end{cases}$$

($\mathcal{B}$ can compute Y by using $g_1^{c_1}, \ldots, g_1^{c_{r+2}}$ and $e_1, \ldots, e_{r+1}$, as well as T_i by using r_i and $g_1^{c_2}$). Then, $\mathcal{B}$ publishes the public parameters

$$PP = (n, r, p, G_1, \ldots, G_{r+2}, g_1, e_1, \ldots, e_{r+1}, Y, (T_i | i \in \mathcal{U}))$$

The choice of T_i in this way will be transparent in the next step.

Phase 1. The adversary is granted oracle access to the decryption key generation oracle for all queries $\mathcal{C}$ with n input wires and r FANOUT-levels and $\mathcal{C}(A) = 0$. Given such a query, the decryption key is computed by the following general methodology. First, the algorithm $\mathcal{B}$ uses a procedure *FakeShare* which shares $g_1^{c_1}$ by taking into account a set A of attributes and using FANOUT-level-keys based on $g_1^{c_3}, \ldots, g_1^{c_{r+2}}$. Then, $\mathcal{B}$ delivers decryption keys based on $g_1^{c_2}$. Two requirements are to be fulfilled:

1. from the adversary's point of view, the secret sharing and distribution of decryption keys should look as in the original scheme;
2. the reconstruction procedure *Recon*, starting from the decryption keys and an authorized set of attributes, should return $g_{r+2}^{c_1 \cdots c_{r+2} s}$.

In order to describe the procedure *FakeShare* we adopt the following notation: given a wire w of $\mathcal{C}$, denote by $\mathcal{C}_w(A)$ the truth value at w when the circuit $\mathcal{C}$ is evaluated for A. The main idea in *FakeShare* is the following:

1. if the output wire w of a logic gate $\Gamma = (w_1, w_2, X, w)$ satisfies $C_w(A) = 0$, where X stands for "OR" or "AND", then the value to be shared at this wire is of the form g_1^x, for some $x \in \mathbb{Z}_p$; otherwise, the value to be shared at this wire is an element $x \in \mathbb{Z}_p$;
2. the shares obtained by sharing the value associated to w, and distributed to the input wires of Γ, should satisfy the same constraints as above. For instance, if $C_{w_1}(A) = 0$ and $C_{w_2}(A) = 1$, then the share distributed to w_1 should be of the form $g_1^{x_1}$ while the share distributed to w_2 should be of the form x_2;
3. the same policy applies to FANOUT-gates as well.

The procedure $FakeShare$ is as follows (for the sake of simplicity we adopt the convention $a_{i_1} \cdots a_{i_u} = 1 = a_{i_1}^{-1} \cdots a_{i_u}^{-1}$ whenever $i_1 \cdots i_u$ is the empty sequence):

$FakeShare(g_1^{c_1}, g_1^{c_3} \ldots, g_1^{c_{r+2}}, \mathcal{C}, A)$

1. Initially, all gates of $\mathcal{C}$ are unmarked;
2. Assuming that the FANOUT-levels in $\mathcal{C}$ are $h_1 < \cdots < h_r$, we denote c_j by $c'_{h_{j-2}}$, for all $3 \leq j \leq r + 2$. The aim of this notation is just technical, in order to have a correspondence between the c's and the FANOUT-levels (see below).
   Now, for each FANOUT-level i, $0 \leq i < depth(\mathcal{C}) - 2$, choose uniformly at random $a_i \in \mathbb{Z}_p$ and assign $L(i) := g_1^{a_i c'_i}$;
3. $S(o) := g_1^{c_1}$;
4. If $\Gamma = (w_1, w_2, OR, w)$ is an unmarked OR-gate and $S(w)$ was defined, then mark Γ and do the followings:
   (a) compute $i_1 \cdots i_u$ and $j_1 \cdots j_v$ the left and right FANOUT-level sequences of Γ, respectively;
   (b) if $C_w(A) = C_{w_1}(A) = C_{w_2}(A) = 0$, then $S(w_1) := S(w)^{a_{i_1}^{-1} \cdots a_{i_u}^{-1}}$ and $S(w_2) := S(w)^{a_{j_1}^{-1} \cdots a_{j_v}^{-1}}$;
   (c) if $C_w(A) = C_{w_1}(A) = C_{w_2}(A) = 1$, then $S(w_1) := S(w) \cdot a_{i_1}^{-1} \cdots a_{i_u}^{-1}$ and $S(w_2) := S(w) \cdot a_{j_1}^{-1} \cdots a_{j_v}^{-1}$;
   (d) if $C_w(A) = 1 = C_{w_1}(A)$ and $C_{w_2}(A) = 0$, then $S(w_1) := S(w) \cdot a_{i_1}^{-1} \cdots a_{i_u}^{-1}$ and $S(w_2) := g_1^{S(w) \cdot a_{j_1}^{-1} \cdots a_{j_v}^{-1}}$;
   (e) if $C_w(A) = 1 = C_{w_2}(A)$ and $C_{w_1}(A) = 0$, then $S(w_1) := g_1^{S(w) \cdot a_{i_1}^{-1} \cdots a_{i_u}^{-1}}$ and $S(w_2) := S(w) \cdot a_{j_1}^{-1} \cdots a_{j_v}^{-1}$.
   Remark that $S(w) \in \mathbb{Z}_p$ in the cases (c), (d), and (e);
5. If $\Gamma = (w_1, w_2, AND, w)$ is an unmarked AND-gate and $S(w)$ was defined, then mark Γ and do the followings:
   (a) compute $i_1 \cdots i_u$ the left FANOUT-level sequence of Γ and $j_1 \cdots j_v$ the right FANOUT-level sequence of Γ;
   (b) choose x_1 uniformly at random from $\mathbb{Z}_p$;
   (c) if $C_w(A) = 1$, then:

i. compute x_2 such that

$$S(w) = (x_1 a_{i_1} \cdots a_{i_u} + x_2 a_{j_1} \cdots a_{j_v}) \bmod p;$$

ii. assign $S(w_1) := x_1$ and $S(w_2) := x_2$;

(d) if $\mathcal{C}_w(A) = 0 = \mathcal{C}_{w_2}(A)$ and $\mathcal{C}_{w_1}(A) = 1$ then assign $S(w_1) := x_1$ and

$$S(w_2) = \left(S(w)/g_1^{x_1 a_{i_1} \cdots a_{i_u}} \right)^{a_{j_1}^{-1} \cdots a_{j_v}^{-1}}$$

(e) if $\mathcal{C}_w(A) = 0 = \mathcal{C}_{w_1}(A)$ and $\mathcal{C}_{w_2}(A) = 1$ then do as above by switching w_1 and w_2;

(f) if $\mathcal{C}_w(A) = \mathcal{C}_{w_1}(A) = \mathcal{C}_{w_2}(A) = 0$ then $S(w_1) := g_1^{x_1}$ and $S(w_2)$ is computed as in the case (d).

6. If $\Gamma = (w, FANOUT, w_1, \ldots, w_j)$ is an unmarked FANOUT-gate and $S(w_i)$ was defined for all $1 \le i \le j$, then mark Γ and do the followings:

(a) choose uniformly at random $x \in \mathbb{Z}_p$;

(b) if $\mathcal{C}_w(A) = \mathcal{C}_{w_1}(A) = \cdots = \mathcal{C}_{w_j}(A) = 1$ then $S(w) := x$ and

$$P(w_i) := g_1^{c'_{level(\Gamma)} S(w_i) x^{-1}}$$

for all $1 \le i \le j$;

(c) if $\mathcal{C}_w(A) = \mathcal{C}_{w_1}(A) = \cdots = \mathcal{C}_{w_j}(A) = 0$ then $S(w) := g_1^{c'_{level(\Gamma)} x}$ and $P(w_i) := S(w_i)^{x^{-1}}$, for all $1 \le i \le j$;

7. repeat the last three steps above until all gates get marked.

Let $(S, P, L) \leftarrow FakeShare(g_1^{c_1}, g_1^{c_3}, \ldots, g_1^{c_{r+2}}, \mathcal{C}, A)$. The algorithm $\mathcal{B}$ delivers to $\mathcal{A}$ the decryption key $D = ((D(i)|i \in \mathcal{U}), P, L)$, where

$$D(i) = \begin{cases} (g_1^{c_2})^{S(i)/r_i}, & \text{if } i \in A \\ S(i)^{1/r_i}, & \text{if } i \notin A \end{cases}$$

for any $i \in \mathcal{U}$. The key component $D(i)$ is of the form $g_1^{y_i/r_i} = g_1^{c_2 y_i/c_2 r_i}$ for all $i \notin A$ (for some $y_i \in \mathbb{Z}_p$) because the shares of $i \notin A$ are all powers of g_1 (remark that $C_i(A) = 0$).

The distribution of this decryption key is identical to that in the original scheme. Moreover, it is straightforward to see that the reconstruction procedure $Recon$, applied to $V_A(i) = g_2^{S(i)c_2 s}$ for all $i \in A$, where A is an authorized set, returns $g_{r+2}^{c_1 \cdots c_{r+2} s}$. Indeed, in the reconstruction process each FANOUT-level h_j changes the generator (by applying a bilinear map) and multiplies the exponent by c'_{h_j}. As $c_3 \cdots c_{r+2} = c'_{h_1} \cdots c'_{h_r}$, the claim follows.

Challenge. The adversary $\mathcal{A}$ selects two messages m_0 and m_1 (of the same length) and sends them to $\mathcal{B}$. The algorithm $\mathcal{B}$ encrypts m_u with Z_v, where $u \leftarrow \{0,1\}$, and sends it back to the adversary (recall that Z_v was randomly chosen from $\{Z_0, Z_1\}$). The ciphertext is

$$E = (A, E' = m_u Z_v, \{E_i = T_i^s = g_1^{sr_i}\}_{i \in A})$$

If $v = 0$, E is a valid encryption of m_u; if $v = 1$, E' is a random element from G_2.

Phase 2. The adversary may receive again oracle access to the decryption key generation oracle (with the same constraint as in *Phase 1*).

Guess. Let u' be the guess of $\mathcal{A}$. If $u' = u$, then $\mathcal{B}$ outputs $v' = 0$; otherwise, it outputs $v' = 1$.

We compute now the advantage of $\mathcal{B}$. Clearly,

$$P(v' = v) - \frac{1}{2} = P(v' = v|v = 0) \cdot P(v = 0) + P(v' = v|v = 1) \cdot P(v = 1) - \frac{1}{2}$$

Both $P(v = 0)$ and $P(v = 1)$ are $1/2$. Then, remark that

$$P(v' = v|v = 0) = P(u' = u|v = 0) = \frac{1}{2} + \eta$$

and $P(v' = v|v = 1) = P(u' \neq u|v = 1) = \frac{1}{2}$. Putting all together we obtain that the advantage of $\mathcal{B}$ is $P(v' = v) - \frac{1}{2} = \frac{1}{2}\eta$. □

References

1. Bellare, M., Hoang, VT., Rogaway, P.: Foundations of garbled circuits. In: Proceedings of the 2012 ACM Conference on Computer and Communications Security, CCS 2012, pp. 784–796. ACM, New York, USA (2012)
2. Bethencourt, J., Sahai, A., Waters, B.: Ciphertext-policy attribute-based encryption. In: IEEE Symposium on Security and Privacy, SP 2007, pp. 321–334. IEEE Computer Society (2007)
3. Boneh, D., Nikolaenko, V., Halevi, S., Vaikuntanathan, V., Vinayagamurthy, D., Gentry, C., Gorbunov, S., Segev, G.: Fully key-homomorphic encryption, arithmetic circuit ABE and compact garbled circuits. In: Nguyen, P.Q., Oswald, E. (eds.) EUROCRYPT 2014. LNCS, vol. 8441, pp. 533–556. Springer, Heidelberg (2014)
4. Coron, J.-S., Lepoint, T., Tibouchi, M.: New multilinear maps over the integers. Cryptology ePrint Archive, Report 2015/162 (2015). (Accepted at CRYPTO 2015)
5. Drăgan, C.C., Ţiplea, F.L.: Key-policy attribute-based encryption for boolean circuits from bilinear maps. In: Ors, B., Preneel, B. (eds.) BalkanCryptSec 2014. LNCS, vol. 9024, pp. 175–193. Springer, Heidelberg (2015)
6. Gentry, C., Halevi, S., Garg, S.: Candidate multilinear maps from ideal lattices. In: Johansson, T., Nguyen, P.Q. (eds.) EUROCRYPT 2013. LNCS, vol. 7881, pp. 1–17. Springer, Heidelberg (2013)
7. Waters, B., Garg, S., Gentry, C., Halevi, S., Sahai, A.: Attribute-based encryption for circuits from multilinear maps. In: Canetti, R., Garay, J.A. (eds.) CRYPTO 2013, Part II. LNCS, vol. 8043, pp. 479–499. Springer, Heidelberg (2013)
8. Gorbunov, S., Vaikuntanathan, V., Wee, H.: Attribute-based encryption for circuits. In: Boneh, D., Roughgarden, T., Feigenbaum, J. (eds) STOC, pp. 545–554. ACM (2013)
9. Goyal, V., Pandey, O., Sahai, A., Waters, B.: Attribute-based encryption for fine-grained access control of encypted data. In: ACM Conference on Computer and Communications Security, pp. 89–98. ACM (2006)

10. Ostrovsky, R., Sahai, A., Waters, B.: Attribute-based encryption with non-monotonic access structures. In: ACM Conference on Computer and Communications Security, pp. 195–203. ACM (2007)
11. Sahai, A., Waters, B.: Fuzzy identity-based encryption. In: Cramer, R. (ed.) EUROCRYPT 2005. LNCS, vol. 3494, pp. 457–473. Springer, Heidelberg (2005)
12. Shamir, Adi: Identity-based cryptosystems and signature schemes. In: Blakely, G.R., Chaum, David (eds.) CRYPTO 1984. LNCS, vol. 196, pp. 47–53. Springer, Heidelberg (1985)
13. Stinson, D.R.: Cryptography: Theory and Practice, 3rd edn. Chapman and Hall/CRC, Boca Raton (2005)

Closing the Gap: A Universal Privacy Framework for Outsourced Data

Dirk Achenbach[1]([⊠]), Matthias Huber[2], Jörn Müller-Quade[1], and Jochen Rill[2]

[1] Karlsruhe Institute of Technology (KIT), Karlsruhe, Germany
{dirk.achenbach,joern.mueller-quade}@kit.edu
[2] FZI Forschungszentrum Informatik, Karlsruhe, Germany
{mhuber,rill}@fzi.de

Abstract. We study formal privacy notions for data outsourcing schemes. The aim of our efforts is to define a security framework that is applicable to highly elaborate as well as practical constructions. First, we define the privacy objectives *data privacy*, *query privacy*, and *result privacy*. We then investigate fundamental relations among them. Second, to make them applicable to practical constructions, we define generalisations of our basic notions. Lastly, we show how various notions from the literature fit into our framework. Data privacy and query privacy are independent concepts, while result privacy is consequential to them. The generalised notions allow for a restriction on the number of the adversary's oracle calls, as well as a "leakage relation" that restricts the adversary's choice of challenges. We apply the generalised notions to existing security notions from the fields of searchable encryption, private information retrieval, and secure database outsourcing. Some are direct instantiations of our notions, others intertwine the concepts. This work provides a privacy framework for data outsourcing schemes from various cryptographic fields with an unified view, from which several new interesting research questions emerge.

Keywords: Formal security notions · Searchable encryption · Private information retrieval · Database outsourcing

1 Introduction

The IT industry has seen numerous trends in the last two decades, yet a majority of them seem to revolve around a common paradigm shift: Data is stored less and less locally, but is outsourced to a data processing centre and accessed over the Internet. To retrieve parts of the outsourced data, clients submit queries to the servers which then execute them and return the result. Applications that fit into this paradigm are not restricted to relational databases, but to any information that can be structured meaningfully—be it searchable documents, SQL

The full version of this paper can be found at https://crypto.iti.kit.edu/fileadmin/User/Achenbach/AHMR15.pdf.

© Springer International Publishing Switzerland 2016
E. Pasalic and L.R. Knudsen (Eds.): BalkanCryptSec 2015, LNCS 9540, pp. 134–151, 2016.
DOI: 10.1007/978-3-319-29172-7_9

databases, or image archives. Data outsourcing promises significant advantages, particularly for organisations that do not specialise in data management. But entrusting private data to a service provider also introduces a security risk. While an IT service provider can be trusted to provide the contractually agreed-on services faithfully, one can easily imagine that a curious employee might try to learn confidential information from the outsourced data. Cryptographic methods promise to secure confidentiality in such a scenario.

Many cryptographic schemes have a custom security notion. While a tailored security notion helps accurately express a scheme's security properties, it makes comparing security properties difficult. This work introduces a framework that allows for modelling the privacy guarantees of data outsourcing schemes on a common level of abstraction. We identify three conceptually different privacy goals: keeping the outsourced data itself private, keeping the queries to the data private, and keeping the result of the query private. Our results are applicable to constructions from seemingly disparate fields of cryptographic research, e.g. private information retrieval, searchable encryption, and secure database outsourcing.

We show that data privacy and query privacy are independent concepts, while result privacy is consequential to them. What is more, we found that many existing privacy notions, e.g. for searchable encryption, mix these concepts.

In general, strong privacy can be bought with communication and computation complexity or a non cost efficient distribution among many servers. Such schemes find no use in practice, however. On the other hand, existing formal security notions are often not applicable to schemes used in practice. Thus, we want to design security notions applicable to both practical (i.e. $O(\log(n))$) complexity, single server, single client) and highly elaborate (i.e. PIR, ORAM) outsourcing schemes. Therefore our framework allows to independently specify bounds for the level of privacy for queries, the outsourced data, and the query result. We showcase the applicability of our formal notions by expressing existing notions in our framework.

1.1 A Model for Outsourced Data

Our basic object of interest is a *data set*—be it a database, an e-mail archive or a collection of images. One can execute *queries* on this data. The *result* of the execution of a query on a data set can be any function of the data.

In this work, we focus on queries that only return a function of the data they are executed on. Note, however, that updating data is also an area worthy of investigation.

In an outsourcing scenario, a *client* transfers the data to a *server* for storage. Before the data is transferred, the client *encrypts* it using a private key. Instead of executing queries locally, the client transforms them into an interactive *protocol* that it runs with the server. The client's input into the protocol is its private key, the server's input is the encrypted data. See Fig. 1 for an illustration of our outsourcing model.

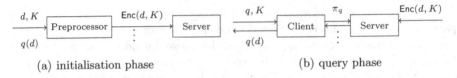

(a) initialisation phase   (b) query phase

Fig. 1. We model the interaction of the client with the server in two phases. In the initialisation phase (a) a preprocessing agent receives a data set d and an encryption key K, prepares the encrypted data $\mathsf{Enc}(d, K)$ and uploads it to the server. In the query phase (b) the client issues queries q using encryption key K by running protocol π_q with the server. The server's input is the encryption $\mathsf{Enc}(d, K)$. After the interaction the client outputs the query result $q(d)$.

We assume the server may be under adversarial influence. We restrict the adversary to honest-but-curious behaviour however—he may not deviate from the protocol as to interfere with its correct execution, but he may try to learn private information from the interaction.

Efficiency. We are particularly interested in capturing the security properties of *efficient* schemes within our framework. In practice, the size of outsourced data sets can easily measure terabytes. Since data is uploaded to the server only once while queries get executed repeatedly, it is not practical to use encryption schemes which process the whole data set on each query—or even a fraction of it. Therefore, we consider schemes efficient which have strictly logarithmic *communication and computation complexities* per query—for the client as well as for the server. This is in contrast to many schemes in the literature which are considered efficient even though they have a polynomial overhead.

Privacy. There are three privacy objectives: Keeping the data private, keeping the queries private, and keeping the results private.

Keeping the Data Private. Bob runs an e-mail service. Alice uses the service and is concerned Bob might snoop through her private e-mail. *Data Privacy* guarantees that Bob does not learn anything about the content of Alice's e-mail.

Keeping the Queries Private. In this scenario, Bob runs a patent search service. Clients can submit construction plans and Bob's service looks for any patents the construction is infringing. Alice is worried that Bob might learn her ideas and register them as patents himself. If the query protocol has *query privacy*, Bob cannot learn the content of Alice's requests.

Keeping the Results Private. Bob also owns a database of DNA markers that are a sign of genetic diseases. He offers his customers the possibility to check blood samples against the database. Alice runs a clinic and is interested in Bob's services. She has no interest in disclosing to Bob whether her patients suffer from any genetic diseases. If the method of accessing Bob's database has *result privacy*, the results to Alice's requests are hidden from Bob. As we will show, result privacy implies database privacy as well as query privacy and vice versa.

1.2 Related Work

In this work, we distinguish between data privacy, query privacy, and result privacy, the latter implying the former two. Therefore, we divide the related work concerning security notions for data outsourcing schemes into three categories: notions which only consider the privacy of the outsourced data, notions which only consider the privacy of the queries, and those which intertwine both.

Security Notions for Data Privacy. There is a rich body of literature on data outsourcing schemes which only consider the privacy of the outsourced data in both static and adaptive settings. There are game-based notions [10,12,16], simulation-based notions [4,5,17], and notions that use the Universal Composability framework [3,19,24]. A well-known example for an adaptive security notion is IND-CKA established by Goh [12]. The intuition is that an adversary should not be able to distinguish two sets of data of his choosing based on the generated index even if he can issue and observe queries. However, in Goh's notion, the queries the adversary can choose are strongly restricted: he is not allowed to query for words that are exclusive two one of the two sets he chooses as challenge.

An example for a notion which only considers static security is Huber et al.'s IND-ICP [16]. Here, the idea is that an adversary should not be able to distinguish the encryptions of two databases. However, the databases the adversary is challenged on are restricted to being independent permutations of one another.

Security Notions for Query Privacy. Hiding queries on outsourced data on a single server has been studied in the context of Single-Server Private Information Retrieval [7] (PIR). The PIR notion requires that an adversary who observes access patterns cannot distinguish any two queries. PIR does not guarantee that the data itself is kept private [7] There is a rich body of literature on PIR schemes which have sublinear *communication complexity* ([2,11,20]). However, all PIR schemes inherently have a *computational complexity* for the server which is linear in the size of the data [23]. The PIR security notion is thus not applicable to efficient schemes.

The privacy of queries on data has also been investigated in the context of Oblivious RAMs (ORAMs) first introduced by Goldreich and Ostrovsky [13] and further explored and improved upon by others [9,21,22]. Similar to PIR, an "oblivious" RAM is one that cannot distinguish access patterns—the data itself is not required to be private. As is the case with PIR, all ORAM constructions can not be considered efficient in our sense. They either have polylogarithmic computation cost while requiring the client to store a constant amount of data [22] or have logarithmic computation cost, but require the client to store at least a sublinear amount of data dependent on the size of the RAM [14].

Security Notions for Data Privacy as well as Query Privacy. There are security notions in the literature which consider both data privacy as well as query privacy. Chase et al. [6] introduce the simulation-based notion of "chosen query attacks" which models both the privacy of queries and that of the data. However, in their notion, the concepts of privacy for data and privacy for queries are intertwined. Haynberg et al. [15] try to separate both properties: they introduce the notion of "data privacy" and complement it with "pattern privacy", which is similar to PIR. However, their notion for data privacy only allows the adversary to observe the execution of one query. While the notion works for their scheme, this limitation is too strict for other schemes.

Modeling Information Leakage. A reoccurring pattern in security notions for practical schemes is the use of a *leakage function* which describes the information the scheme leaks to the adversary during execution. A certain amount of leakage seems necessary in order for schemes to be efficient. Cash et al. investigate the construction of efficient and practical schemes that also have a formal security analysis [4,5]. Their analyses follow a simulation-based approach. The constructions leak information about the plaintext and the query which they explicitly model by a *leakage function* $\mathcal{L}$. This is similar to Chase et al. [6], whose notion allows to describe the information that leaks through the encryption itself ($\mathcal{L}_1$) and the information about the ciphertext *and* the queries combined that is leaked by evaluating queries ($\mathcal{L}_2$). Stefanov et al. [24] employ the same technique in the Universal Composability Framework. In game-based notions such leakage is modelled by restricting the challenges the adversary can choose. Thus, in our framework we define "leakage relations" that model information leakage.

1.3 Our Contribution

In this paper, we investigate formal security notions for data outsourcing. We close the gap between strict formal security notions (e.g. PIR) which are not applicable to schemes used in practice and security notions for practical schemes that are tailored specifically to the scheme. To that end, we first precisely define security notions for three seemingly disparate privacy objectives: data privacy, query privacy, and result privacy. We show how these notions are related. Second, we give generalisations of these notions to make them applicable to both highly elaborate and practical schemes. We show that several notions from the literature are specialisations of one of our notions, others intertwine them. Our framework allows to express and compare the security of outsourcing schemes from diverse areas of cryptographic research. We hope to inspire future work in this direction of research as we believe a common umbrella for various outsourcing schemes is an important aid in constructing, selecting, and implementing protocols for practical applications.

2 Security Notions for Data Outsourcing Schemes

In this section we define precise terminology for securely outsourcing data and establish fundamental relations.

2.1   Notation and Conventions

We use the probabilistic-polynomial time (PPT) model, i.e. we assume all machines, algorithms, parties and adversaries to be restricted to a polynomial number of computation steps (in the security parameter). We denote the set of all PPT two-party protocols with Π. Our definitions can be extended to allow for the interaction of multiple servers with multiple clients. For the sake of clarity, we focus on the single-server-single-client case and leave a further generalisation of the definitions for future work.

We define our algorithms and protocols to operate on a *domain*. In this work, a domain is the set of all possible values in the given context—for example, in a database context, a domain would be the set of all databases. Our algorithms and protocols operate on three domains: a domain of the data to be encrypted (i.e. plaintexts) Δ, a domain of ciphertexts Γ, and a domain of results P.

2.2   Outsourcing Data

In this section, we define the elementary concepts used in the rest of the paper.

Definition 1. *A* data set *$d \in \Delta$ is an element of a domain Δ. By $|d|$ we denote the length of its (unique) binary representation.*

For example, in the scenario of an outsourced e-mail archive, Δ is the set of all mailboxes and a concrete data set (mailbox) $d \in \Delta$ is a set of e-mail messages. To outsource data, one requires an algorithm that makes the data ready to be uploaded to a server. We call this process "encrypting" the data, as we will require later that no adversary can learn the original data from the outsourced data.

Definition 2. *An* outsourcing scheme *for data sets is a tuple* (Gen, Enc) *such that*

$$\text{Gen} : 1^k \to \{0,1\}^n$$
$$\text{Enc} : \Delta \times \{0,1\}^n \to \Gamma$$

We call an outsourcing scheme for a data set retrievable *if there is a function* Dec $: \Gamma \times \{0,1\}^n \to \Delta$ *such that* $\forall K \in \{0,1\}^n, d \in \Delta : \text{Dec}(\text{Enc}(d,K),K) = d$.

We do not require that encrypted data sets be decryptable. The main purpose of outsourcing data in this work is to remotely execute queries on it.

Definition 3. *A* query q *is a PPT algorithm that, on input of a data set $d \in \Delta$ returns a* result set $q(d) \in P$ *and an updated data set $d_q \in \Delta$.*

We point out that, to simplify notation, we do not model parameters for queries explicitly. Our model supports parameterised queries nevertheless, as for each pair of a query q with parameters p, there is an equivalent query $q(p)$ that has the parameters "hard coded". Without loss of generality we assume that queries are functions of the data, i.e. $\forall q \exists d_1, d_2 \in \Delta : q(d_1) \neq q(d_2)$, and the query result is the same if evaluated twice.

Our idea of the "correctness" of a protocol is relative to a given query q.

Definition 4. *A two-party protocol* $\pi_q \in \Pi$ *between a Server* $\mathfrak{S}$ *and Client* $\mathfrak{C}$ *executes a query* q *for a outsourced data set* $\mathsf{Enc}(d, K)$ *if*

- *The Client, on input of a key* K, *outputs the result set* $q(d) = \pi_q^{\mathfrak{C}}(K, \mathsf{Enc}(d, K))$.
- *The Server, on input the outsourced data set* $\mathsf{Enc}(d, K)$, *outputs an updated outsourced data set* $\mathsf{Enc}(d_q, K) = \pi_q^{\mathfrak{S}}(\mathsf{Enc}(d, K))$.

Note that although "update" queries are outside the scope of this work, Definition 4 also models protocols that update the outsourced data set.

Definition 5. *A* queryable outsourcing scheme *for data sets is a tuple* $(\mathsf{Gen}, \mathsf{Enc}, \mathsf{Q})$ *such that*

- $(\mathsf{Gen}, \mathsf{Enc})$ *is an outsourcing scheme for data sets, and*
- $\mathsf{Q} \subseteq \Pi$ *is a non-empty set of efficient two-party protocols that execute a query for outsourced data sets.*

We stress that the client has no direct access to the data when interacting with the server in order to execute a query. To be able to argue about privacy in the presence of queries to outsourced data, we require a notion of what a protocol party "sees" during the execution of a protocol.

Definition 6. *A* view *of a protocol party is the totality of its inputs, received messages, sent messages and outputs. To denote the view of protocol party* $\mathfrak{P} \in \{\mathfrak{C}, \mathfrak{S}\}$ *in protocol* π *with inputs* c *and* K, *we write*

$$\mathsf{view}_{\mathfrak{P}}^{\pi}(c, K).$$

In particular, the encrypted data is part of the server's view.

2.3   Privacy Notions for Outsourced Data Sets

Static Security. The static notion of privacy for outsourced data captures the intuition that no adversary may deduce any information about the data from its ciphertext alone. We model it closely after the IND-CPA [18] notion. Due to space constraints, we omit it here. See the full version for the definition.

Privacy in the Presence of Queries. When outsourced data sets are queried three conceptually different privacy goals can be distinguished: keeping the data private, keeping the queries private, and keeping the results private. We model these privacy goals as security games. The adversary is supplied an oracle for views on the interaction between client and server and tries to discern the challenge bit b. In all three security experiments, in addition to a challenge oracle, the adversary is supplied with an "open" view oracle. The oracle provides views for arbitrary queries executed on an encryption of arbitrary data sets *using the challenge key*. It implies that the scheme must have a probabilistic property in the sense that two identical queries on two different encryptions of the same plaintext will not access the same parts of the ciphertext. This can either be done by randomizing the structure of the encrypted ciphertext (as in the work of Haynberg et al. [15]) or by randomizing the protocol which realises the query.

Security Game 1 (D-IND$^{\mathcal{A}}_{(\mathsf{Gen},\mathsf{Enc},\mathsf{Q})}(k)$)

1. The experiment chooses a key $K \leftarrow \mathsf{Gen}(1^k)$.
2. $\mathcal{A}$ receives access to an oracle for $\mathrm{view}^{\pi}_{\mathfrak{S}}(\mathsf{Enc}(\cdot, K))$, and continues to have access to it. The oracle takes a query q and a data set d as input and returns $\mathrm{view}^{\pi_q}_{\mathfrak{S}}(\mathsf{Enc}(d, K))$.
3. $\mathcal{A}$ outputs two data sets d_0 and d_1 of equal length to the experiment.
4. The experiment draws a random bit $b \leftarrow \{0, 1\}$.
5. Challenge oracle: $\mathcal{A}$ is given access to an oracle for $\mathrm{view}^{\pi}_{\mathfrak{S}}(\mathsf{Enc}(d_b, K))$. That is, the oracle takes any query q such that $\pi_q \in \mathcal{Q}$ as input, internally runs the protocol π_q on $\mathsf{Enc}(d_b, K)$, and outputs $\mathrm{view}^{\pi_q}_{\mathfrak{S}}(\mathsf{Enc}(d_b, K))$ to the adversary.
6. $\mathcal{A}$ outputs a guess b' for b.

The result of the experiment is 1 if $b' = b$ and 0 else.

Security Game 2 (Q-IND$^{\mathcal{A}}_{(\mathsf{Gen},\mathsf{Enc},\mathsf{Q})}(k)$)

1. The experiment chooses a key $K \leftarrow \mathsf{Gen}(1^k)$.
2. $\mathcal{A}$ receives access to an oracle for $\mathrm{view}^{\pi}_{\mathfrak{S}}(\mathsf{Enc}(\cdot, K))$, and continues to have access to it. The oracle takes a query q and a data set d as input and returns $\mathrm{view}^{\pi_q}_{\mathfrak{S}}(\mathsf{Enc}(d, K))$.
3. $\mathcal{A}$ outputs two queries q_0 and q_1 to the experiment. q_0 and q_1 must yield protocols π_{q_0} and π_{q_1} with the same number of protocol messages.
4. The experiment draws a random bit $b \leftarrow \{0, 1\}$.
5. Challenge oracle: $\mathcal{A}$ is given access to an oracle for $\mathrm{view}^{\pi_{q_b}}_{\mathfrak{S}}(\mathsf{Enc}(\cdot, K))$. That is, the oracle takes any data set $d \in \Delta$ as input, internally runs the protocol π_{q_b} on $\mathsf{Enc}(d, K)$, and outputs $\mathrm{view}^{\pi_{q_b}}_{\mathfrak{S}}(\mathsf{Enc}(d, K))$ to the adversary.
6. $\mathcal{A}$ outputs a guess b' for b.

The result of the experiment is 1 if $b' = b$ and 0 else.

Definition 7 (Data Privacy). *An outsourcing scheme* $(\mathsf{Gen}, \mathsf{Enc}, \mathsf{Q})$ *has Data Privacy, if*

$$\forall \mathcal{A}, c \in \mathbb{N} \, \exists k \in \mathbb{N} : |\mathrm{Pr}[\text{D-IND}^{\mathcal{A}, R_d}_{(\mathsf{Gen},\mathsf{Enc},\mathsf{Q})}(k) = 1]| \leq \frac{1}{2} + k^{-c}$$

The privacy notion of Query Privacy captures the goal of hiding the queries themselves from the server. The notion is equivalent to Private Information Retrieval (see Sect. 4.1 for a discussion and proof).

Definition 8 (Query Privacy). *An outsourcing scheme* $(\mathsf{Gen}, \mathsf{Enc}, \mathsf{Q})$ *has Query Privacy, if*

$$\forall \mathcal{A}, c \in \mathbb{N} \, \exists k \in \mathbb{N} : |\mathrm{Pr}[\text{Q-IND}^{\mathcal{A}, R_q}_{(\mathsf{Gen},\mathsf{Enc},\mathsf{Q})}(k) = 1]| \leq \frac{1}{2} + k^{-c}$$

The third privacy goal, Result Privacy, captures the idea that the adversary must not learn the result of any query executed on any data. To formulate this idea formally, we allow the adversary to output two data-set-query pairs (d_0, q_0) and (d_1, q_1), as a result is always determined by a query and a data set on which it is evaluated. We then challenge the adversary on the view of query q_b executed on data set d_b.

Security Game 3 $(\text{R-IND}^{\mathcal{A}}_{(\text{Gen},\text{Enc},Q)}(k))$

1. The experiment chooses a key $K \leftarrow \text{Gen}(1^k)$.
2. $\mathcal{A}$ receives access to an oracle for $\text{view}^{\pi_{\cdot}}_{\mathbb{G}}(\text{Enc}(\cdot, K))$, and continues to have access to it. The oracle takes a query q and a data set d as input and returns $\text{view}^{\pi_q}_{\mathbb{G}}(\text{Enc}(d, K))$.
3. $\mathcal{A}$ outputs two data-set-query pairs (d_0, q_0) and (d_1, q_1) to the experiment. ($|d_0| = |d_1|$ and q_0 and q_1 must yield protocols π_{q_0} and π_{q_1} with the same number of protocol messages).
4. The experiment draws a random bit $b \leftarrow \{0, 1\}$.
5. Challenge: The experiment runs the protocol π_{q_b} on $\text{Enc}(d_b, K)$ and outputs $\text{view}^{\pi_{q_b}}_{\mathbb{G}}(\text{Enc}(d_b, K))$ to the adversary.
6. $\mathcal{A}$ receives oracle access to $\text{view}^{\pi_{\cdot}}_{\mathbb{G}}(\text{Enc}(d_b, K))$ and $\text{view}^{\pi_{q_b}}_{\mathbb{G}}(\text{Enc}(\cdot, K))$.
7. $\mathcal{A}$ outputs a guess b' for b.

The result of the experiment is 1 if $b' = b$ and 0 else.

Definition 9 (Result Privacy). *An outsourcing scheme* $(\text{Gen}, \text{Enc}, Q)$ *has Result Privacy, if*

$$\forall \mathcal{A}, c \in \mathbb{N} \, \exists k \in \mathbb{N} : |\Pr[\text{R-IND}^{\mathcal{A}, R_d, R_q}_{(\text{Gen}, \text{Enc}, Q)}(k) = 1]| \leq \frac{1}{2} + k^{-c}$$

Fundamental Relations among the Basic Security Notions. We establish fundamental relations among the three concepts of Data Privacy, Query Privacy, and Result Privacy.

Theorem 1 (D-IND $\not\Rightarrow$ Q-IND). *If a data outsourcing scheme that has Data Privacy exists, there is a data outsourcing scheme that has Data Privacy but no Query Privacy.*

Proof. Let $(\text{Gen}, \text{Enc}, Q)$ be a data outsourcing scheme that has Data Privacy. We modify it in a way that we violate Query Privacy, but keep Data Privacy intact. To this end, we amend the protocols that execute queries to have the client transmit the executed query in the clear after the actual protocol is complete. We have to show that the modification violates Query Privacy, but does not violate Data Privacy.

With the modification, the adversary in experiment Q-IND can easily extract the executed query from any view and thus determine the challenge bit with certainty. Thus the modification violates Query Privacy. To see that this modification does not violate Data Privacy, first note that the modified scheme retains its Data Privacy up until the point of the modification. We argue that the transmission of the query in the clear does not break Data Privacy. Consider experiment D-IND. Because the experiment draws the key K after the scheme is fixed, the scheme is independent of the actual key used to encrypt the data set d. Further, because the query is supplied by the adversary in the experiment and the adversary has learned neither d_b nor K up to this point, the query is also independent of d_b and K. This concludes the argument. ∎

Theorem 2 (Q-IND $\not\Rightarrow$ D-IND). *If there is a retrievable data outsourcing scheme that has Static Security, there is a data outsourcing scheme that has Query Privacy and Static Security, but no Data Privacy.*

Proof. Let $(\mathsf{Gen}, \mathsf{Enc}, \mathsf{Q})$ be a retrievable data outsourcing scheme that has Static Security. We construct a modified scheme $(\mathsf{Gen}, \mathsf{Enc}, \mathsf{Q}')$ that suits our purposes. By adopting Gen and Enc, we retain static security. We design Q' such that it has Query Privacy, but trivially loses Data Privacy. Q' is constructed iteratively, starting with an empty set. For each protocol $\pi_q \in \mathsf{Q}$ that realises a query q, we define a protocol π_q' to Q' as follows:

1. Client: Transfer K to the Server.
2. Server: Decrypt $\mathsf{Enc}(d, K)$ and send $d = \mathsf{Dec}(\mathsf{Enc}(d, K), K)$ back to the Client.
3. Client: Execute query q locally on d and output $q(d)$.

Protocol π' transmits the data set d in the open, violating Data Privacy. Because the client executes q locally and never transmits any information that depends on q, π' does have Query Privacy. ∎

The following theorems show that Result Privacy is equivalent to both Data Privacy and Query Privacy (at the same time).

Theorem 3 (R-IND $\Longrightarrow$ D-IND). *There is no data outsourcing scheme that has Result Privacy but no Data Privacy.*

Proof. Assume a data outsourcing scheme $(\mathsf{Gen}, \mathsf{Enc}, \mathsf{Q})$ for which there is an efficient adversary $\mathcal{A}$ against experiment D-IND. We give an efficient reduction for $\mathcal{A}$ that breaks the Result Privacy (experiment R-IND) of the scheme, contradicting the assumption. The reduction is straightforward. It has to provide a challenge oracle $\mathsf{view}_{\mathfrak{S}}^{\pi}(\mathsf{Enc}(d_b, K))$. Such an oracle is provided by experiment R-IND and only has to be "passed through". ∎

Theorem 4 (R-IND $\Longrightarrow$ Q-IND). *There is no data outsourcing scheme that has Result Privacy but no Query Privacy.*

The proof of Theorem 4 is similar to the proof of Theorem 3 and omitted here.

Theorem 5 (D-IND $\wedge$ Q-IND $\Longrightarrow$ R-IND). *Data Privacy and Query Privacy together imply Result Privacy, i.e. there is no data outsourcing scheme that has Data Privacy and Query Privacy but no Result Privacy.*

We prove the statement using a game-hopping technique. Assume any adversary against R-IND. We replace both view oracles for d_b and q_b, respectively, with an oracle for fixed challenges d_0 and q_0. We argue the indistinguishability of these steps with Data Privacy and Query Privacy. Finally, in the now-transformed experiment, the adversary has no advantage since his input is independent of b. Concluding, given a scheme with Data Privacy and Query Privacy, no adversary against Result Privacy has a non-negligible advantage.

Proof. We define two game transformations, R-IND$'$ and R-IND$''$, starting from the Result Privacy experiment R-IND. In the unmodified experiment R-IND, the adversary is supplied with two view oracles $\mathrm{view}_{\mathbb{G}}^{\pi_{\cdot}}(\mathrm{Enc}(d_b, K))$ and $\mathrm{view}_{\mathbb{G}}^{\pi_{q_b}}(\mathrm{Enc}(\cdot, K))$. In R-IND$'$ we replace the $\mathrm{view}_{\mathbb{G}}^{\pi_{\cdot}}(\mathrm{Enc}(d_b, K))$ oracle by an $\mathrm{view}_{\mathbb{G}}^{\pi_{\cdot}}(\mathrm{Enc}(d_0, K))$ oracle. In R-IND$''$ we further replace $\mathrm{view}_{\mathbb{G}}^{\pi_{q_b}}(\mathrm{Enc}(\cdot, K))$ by $\mathrm{view}_{\mathbb{G}}^{\pi_{q_0}}(\mathrm{Enc}(\cdot, K))$. In R-IND$''$ the adversary receives no input that is dependent on the challenge bit b. He thus has no advantage over guessing b. We have to argue that R-IND$''$ is indistinguishable from R-IND for the adversary. To this end, we prove the indistinguishability of R-IND from R-IND$'$ in Lemma 1 and the indistinguishability of R-IND$'$ from R-IND$''$ in Lemma 2.   ∎

Lemma 1. *An adversary who can distinguish between running in experiment* R-IND *and experiment* R-IND$'$ *yields a successful adversary against database privacy.*

The proof of Lemma 1 is omitted here. It is included in the full version.

Lemma 2. *An adversary who can distinguish between* R-IND$'$ *and* R-IND$''$ *is also a successful adversary on Query Privacy.*

The proof of Lemma 2 is analogous to that of Lemma 1. We omit it.

Corollary 1 (R-IND $\iff$ D-IND $\wedge$ Q-IND)**.** *Result Privacy is equivalent to both Data Privacy and Query Privacy (at the same time).*

3   Generalised Security Notions for Data Outsourcing Schemes

In this section, we generalise the security notions introduced in Sect. 2 to make them applicable to practical schemes. Protocols that—for the sake of efficiency—base decisions on the content of the queried data are bound to leak information about it [4–6] or are only secure for a limited number of queries [15]. Therefore, we first introduce bounds for the number of oracle calls. A special case is a bound of 1 that renders the notions non-adaptive.

Second, we define "leakage relations" R_d and R_q. Challenges the adversary can choose are subject to equivalence under these relations. This way, one can explicitly rule out specific distinction advantages. To model the leakage of the length of a data set for example, one would define $R_d \subset \Delta^2$ as the set of all data set pairs with equal length.

Third, we explicitly model the issuing of queries independently of handing out the results. This allows us to capture security notions where the adversary can alter the state of the database, but can not see the immediate result (e.g. he can only observe the result of the last issued query).

Goh [12] introduces restricting parameters into his security notion as well. They allow for a bound on the running time, the advantage, and the number of oracle calls. Our work in this section can be seen as a generalisation of his concept.

We only give the security definitions here and defer discussion to Sect. 4 where we showcase case studies that are direct applications of our generalised notions.

Security Game 4 ($\text{IND-CDA}^{\mathcal{A},R_d}_{(\text{Gen},\text{Enc})}(k)$)

1. The experiment chooses a key $K \leftarrow \text{Gen}(1^k)$ and a random bit $b \leftarrow \{0,1\}$.
2. The adversary $\mathcal{A}$ is given input 1^k and oracle access to $\text{Enc}(\cdot, K)$.
3. $\mathcal{A}$ outputs two data sets d_0 and d_1 to the experiment. The choice of d_0 and d_1 is restricted to data set pairs that are equivalent with regard to equivalence relation $R_d \subseteq \Delta^2$, i.e. $(d_0, d_1) \in R_d$.
4. $\mathcal{A}$ is given $\text{Enc}(m_b, K)$.
5. $\mathcal{A}$ outputs a guess b' for b.

The result of the experiment is 1 if $b' = b$ and 0 else.

Definition 10 (Static Security). *An outsourcing scheme* (Gen, Enc) *has* indistinguishable encryptions under chosen-data-attacks (IND-CDA) *or* static security *with respect to* R_d, *if*

$$\forall \mathcal{A}, c \in \mathbb{N} \exists k \in \mathbb{N} : |\text{Pr}[\text{IND-CDA}^{\mathcal{A},R_d}_{(\text{Gen},\text{Enc})} = 1]| \leq \frac{1}{2} + k^{-c}$$

Definition 11 (n_1, n_2, n_3-Data Privacy). *An outsourcing scheme* (Gen, Enc, Q) *has* n_1, n_2, n_3-Data Privacy *with respect to* R_d, *if*

$$\forall \mathcal{A}, c \in \mathbb{N} \exists k \in \mathbb{N} : |\text{Pr}[\text{D-IND}^{\mathcal{A},R_d,n_1,n_2,n_3}_{(\text{Gen},\text{Enc},\text{Q})}(k) = 1]| \leq \frac{1}{2} + k^{-c}$$

Definition 12 (n_1, n_2, n_3-Query Privacy). *An outsourcing scheme* (Gen, Enc, Q) *has* n_1, n_2, n_3-Query Privacy *with respect to* R_q, *if*

$$\forall \mathcal{A}, c \in \mathbb{N} \exists k \in \mathbb{N} : |\text{Pr}[\text{Q-IND}^{\mathcal{A},R_q,n_1,n_2,n_3}_{(\text{Gen},\text{Enc},\text{Q})}(k) = 1]| \leq \frac{1}{2} + k^{-c}$$

Result Privacy can be generalised in the same way. As we do not investigate Result Privacy any further, we defer the definition to the full version.

4 Case Studies

In this section we review security notions from the literature and examine how they fit into our framework. To that end, we translate these notions to our formalisms. We discuss Private Information Retrieval, a privacy notion for searchable encryption and a notion for secure database outsourcing. We refer to the appendix for a discussion of the well established security notions IND-CKA [12] and $\text{Ind}^*_{\text{SSE}}$ [8].

Security Game 5
$$(\text{D-IND}_{(\text{Gen},\text{Enc},Q)}^{\mathcal{A},R_d,n_1,n_2,n_3}(k))$$

1. The experiment chooses a key $K \leftarrow \text{Gen}(1^k)$.
2. $\mathcal{A}$ receives access to an oracle for $\text{view}_{\mathfrak{S}}^{\pi}(\text{Enc}(\cdot, K))$, and continues to have access to it. $\mathcal{A}$ is only allowed to query the oracle for a total number of n_1 times.
3. $\mathcal{A}$ outputs two data sets d_0 and d_1 to the experiment. The choice of d_0 and d_1 is restricted to pairs of data sets that are equivalent with regard to equivalence relation $R_d \subseteq \Delta^2$, i.e. $(d_0, d_1) \in R_d$.
4. The experiment draws a random bit $b \leftarrow \{0, 1\}$.
5. Challenge oracle: $\mathcal{A}$ is given access to an oracle for $\text{view}_{\mathfrak{S}}^{\pi}(\text{Enc}(d_b, K))$, and continues to have access to it. $\mathcal{A}$ may call the challenge oracle for a total number of n_2 times.
6. Run oracle: $\mathcal{A}$ is given access to an oracle $\text{run}_{\mathfrak{S}}^{\pi}(\text{Enc}(d_b, K))$. The run oracle executes queries just as the view oracle does, but has no output. $\mathcal{A}$ is allowed to call the run oracle for a total number of n_3 times.
7. $\mathcal{A}$ outputs a guess b' for b.

The result of the experiment is 1 if $b' = b$ and 0 else.

Security Game 6
$$(\text{Q-IND}_{(\text{Gen},\text{Enc},Q)}^{\mathcal{A},R_q,n_1,n_2,n_3}(k))$$

1. The experiment chooses a key $K \leftarrow \text{Gen}(1^k)$.
2. $\mathcal{A}$ receives access to an oracle for $\text{view}_{\mathfrak{S}}^{\pi}(\text{Enc}(\cdot, K))$, and continues to have access to it. $\mathcal{A}$ is only allowed to query the oracle for a total number of n_1 times.
3. $\mathcal{A}$ outputs two queries q_0 and q_1 to the experiment. The choice of q_0 and q_1 is restricted to query pairs that are equivalent with regard to equivalence relation $R_q \subseteq \Pi^2$, i.e. $(q_0, q_1) \in R_q$.
4. The experiment draws a random bit $b \leftarrow \{0, 1\}$.
5. Challenge oracle: $\mathcal{A}$ is given access to an oracle for $\text{view}_{\mathfrak{S}}^{\pi_{q_b}}(\text{Enc}(\cdot, K))$. $\mathcal{A}$ may call the challenge oracle for a total number of n_2 times.
6. Run oracle: $\mathcal{A}$ is given access to an oracle $\text{run}_{\mathfrak{S}}^{\pi_b}(\text{Enc}(\cdot, K))$, and continues to have access to it. The run oracle executes queries just as the view oracle does, but has no output. $\mathcal{A}$ is allowed to call the run oracle for a total number of n_3 times.
7. $\mathcal{A}$ outputs a guess b' for b.

The result of the experiment is 1 if $b' = b$ and 0 else.

4.1 Private Information Retrieval

We give a definition of the original (single-server) Computational Private Information Retrieval (cPIR) [20] notion using our conventions.

Definition 13 (Private Information Retrieval). *A queryable outsourcing scheme* $(\text{Gen}, \text{Enc}, \text{Dec}, \{\pi\})$ *exhibits* Computational Single-Server Private Information Retrieval *(PIR) when two conditions hold for any* $n \in \mathbb{N}$, *any security parameter* $k \in \mathbb{N}$, *and any data set* d *over* $\Sigma = \{0, 1\}^n$:

1. *Correctness:* $\forall i \in \{0, \ldots, n-1\} : \pi_i^{\mathfrak{C}}(d) = d[i]$.
2. *Privacy:* $\forall c \in \mathbb{N}, i, j \in \{0, \ldots, n-1\}, \forall \mathcal{A} \exists K \in \mathbb{N}$ *such that* $\forall k > K$

$$|\Pr[\mathcal{A}(\text{view}_{\mathfrak{S}}^{\pi_i}(\text{Enc}(d, K))) = 1] - \Pr[\mathcal{A}(\text{view}_{\mathfrak{S}}^{\pi_j}(\text{Enc}(d, K))) = 1]| < \frac{1}{\max(k, n)^c}.$$

Theorem 6. *Private Information Retrieval is equivalent to Query Privacy.*

Due to space constraints, we refer to the full version for the proof.

4.2 Searchable Encryption Using Directed Acyclic Word Graphs

Haynberg et al. [15] construct an efficient scheme for symmetric searchable encryption and a corresponding security notion. Their construction is not based on a dictionary, but realises incremental pattern matching.

Security Game 7 $(\text{PrivK}^{\text{cppa}}_{\mathcal{A},\text{Enc}}(k))$

1. The experiment chooses a key $K \leftarrow \text{Gen}(1^k)$ and a random bit $b \leftarrow \{0,1\}$.
2. The adversary receives oracle access to $\text{view}^{\pi\cdot}_{\mathcal{G}}(\text{Enc}(\cdot, K))$, and continues to have access to it.
3. $\mathcal{A}$ outputs two plaintexts m_0 and m_1 of the same length to the experiment.
4. $\mathcal{A}$ outputs a number of queries $x_0, \ldots, x_q$ and an integer $i \in \{0, \ldots, q\}$ to the experiment.
5. The queries $x_0, \ldots, x_q$ are evaluated in that order.
6. $\mathcal{A}$ is given the view on the challenge ciphertext to query i: $\text{view}^{\pi_{x_i}}_{\mathcal{G}}(\text{Enc}(m_b, K))$.
7. $\mathcal{A}$ submits a guess b' for b.

The result of the experiment is 1 if $b' = b$ and 0 else.

The security notion can be directly instantiated in our framework.

Theorem 7. $\text{PrivK}^{\text{cppa}}$ *is equivalent to Data Privacy.*

Proof. $\text{PrivK}^{\text{cppa}}_{\mathcal{A},\text{Enc}}(k)$ can be directly instantiated from $\text{D-IND}^{\mathcal{A},R_d,n_1,n_2,n_3}_{(\text{Gen},\text{Enc},\mathsf{Q})}(k)$ with parameters $R_d = \{d_0, d_1\}$, $|d_0| = |d_1|$, $n_1 = \text{poly}(k)$, $n_2 = 1$, and $n_3 = \text{poly}(k)$. ∎

4.3 Indistinguishability Under Independent Column Permutations

Huber et al. [16] present a provably-secure database outsourcing scheme which is es efficient as the underlying database. In their notion the encryptions of two databases must be indistinguishable if they can be transformed into each other by permuting attribute values within columns. Since our generalised notions allow for defining a restriction on the plaintexts, this database-specific security notion also fits into our framework.

Definition 14 (Independent Column Permutation [16]). *Let Φ be the set of database functions $\mathfrak{p} : \Delta \to \Delta$ such that each $\mathfrak{p} \in \Phi$ permutes the entries within each column of a database. We call $\mathfrak{p}$ an* independent column permutation.

Security Game 8 $(\mathsf{IND}\text{-}\mathsf{ICP}^{\mathcal{A}}_{\mathsf{Gen},\mathsf{Enc},\Phi}(k))$

1. The experiment chooses a key $K \leftarrow \mathsf{Gen}(1^k)$.
2. $\mathcal{A}$ outputs one plaintext m and an independent column permutation $\mathfrak{p} \in \Phi$ to the experiment.
3. The experiment chooses $m_0 := m$ and $m_1 := \mathfrak{p}(m)$ draws $b \leftarrow \{0,1\}$ uniformly at random.
4. $\mathcal{A}$ is given $\mathsf{Enc}(m_b, K)$.
5. $\mathcal{A}$ submits a guess b' for b.

Theorem 8. $\mathsf{IND}\text{-}\mathsf{ICP}$ *is equivalent to static security.*

Proof. $\mathsf{IND}\text{-}\mathsf{ICP}$ is a direct instantiation of $\mathsf{IND}\text{-}\mathsf{CDA}^{\mathcal{A},R_{\mathrm{ICP}}}_{(\mathsf{Gen},\mathsf{Enc})}(k)$, where $R_{\mathrm{ICP}} \subset \Delta^2$ is the set of all pairs of databases that are independent column permutations of each other: We set $\Delta = DB$ and $R_{\mathrm{ICP}} = \Delta_{/\Phi(\Delta)}$. Then, each adversary that has a non-negligible advantage in $\mathsf{IND}\text{-}\mathsf{ICP}^{\mathcal{A}}_{\mathsf{Gen},\mathsf{Enc},\Phi}(k)$ can efficiently be reduced to an adversary that has non negligible advantage in $\mathsf{IND}\text{-}\mathsf{CDA}^{\mathcal{A},R_{\mathrm{ICP}}}_{(\mathsf{Gen},\mathsf{Enc})}(k)$ and vice versa. The reduction from $\mathsf{IND}\text{-}\mathsf{ICP}$ to $\mathsf{IND}\text{-}\mathsf{CDA}^{\mathcal{A},R_{\mathrm{ICP}}}_{(\mathsf{Gen},\mathsf{Enc})}(k)$ sets $m_0 := m$ and $m_1 := \mathfrak{p}(m)$, while the reduction from $\mathsf{IND}\text{-}\mathsf{CDA}^{\mathcal{A},R_{\mathrm{ICP}}}_{(\mathsf{Gen},\mathsf{Enc})}(k)$ to $\mathsf{IND}\text{-}\mathsf{ICP}$ determines $\mathfrak{p}$ with $\mathfrak{p}(m_0) = m_1$. ∎

5   Conclusion and Future Work

We presented a framework that unifies the security notions of outsourcing schemes. To this end we precisely defined outsourcing schemes with queries and introduced the security notions *Data Privacy*, *Query Privacy*, and *Result Privacy*. While Data Privacy and Query Privacy capture independent objectives, we showed that both Data Privacy and Query Privacy are necessary for keeping the *results* of a query to an outsourced data set private. We defined generalised versions of these notions to capture constructions with weaker security properties. Finally, we showcased how security notions for existing outsourcing schemes fit into our framework.

Our work provides directions for several interesting new research topics. In particular, the relations between concrete instantiations of our generalised security notions (e.g., if a weaker instantiation of Data Privacy is still strictly separable from a weaker instantiation of Query Privacy) remain an open question, as well as giving a complete hierarchy of instantiations of one security notion (e.g., if Data Privacy with two queries is weaker than Data privacy with three queries). In particular, a precise characterisation of schemes which fit into each hierarchy class would be of interest.

Further, our security notions are game-based. Investigating simulation-based techniques for our purposes might lead to further insights. Since game-based and simulation-based formulations of the same security notion are not necessarily equivalent (as it is in the case with Selective Opening Security [1]), analysing the relations between our framework and a simulation-based variant could further deepen the understanding security notions for outsourcing schemes.

A   Further Case Studies

A.1   Semantic Security against Adaptive Chosen Keyword Attacks

Goh [12] presents a security notion for index-based searchable encryption schemes. We give a translation into our formalisms. Trapdoors are translated to a view oracle.

Security Game 9 ($\mathsf{IND\text{-}CKA}^{\mathcal{A}}_{(\mathsf{Gen},\mathsf{Enc},\mathsf{Q})}$)

1. The experiment chooses a key $K \leftarrow \mathsf{Gen}(1^k)$ and a random bit $b \leftarrow \{0,1\}$.
2. The adversary $\mathcal{A}$ is given input 1^k and access to an oracle $\mathsf{view}^{\pi\cdot}_{\mathfrak{G}}(\mathsf{Enc}(\cdot, K))$.
3. $\mathcal{A}$ outputs two plaintexts m_0 and m_1 of the same length to the experiment. The adversary must not have queried the oracle for words that are only in one of the two plaintexts.
4. $\mathcal{A}$ is given $\mathsf{Enc}_K(m_b)$ and access to an oracle $\mathsf{view}^{\pi\cdot}_{\mathfrak{G}}(\mathsf{Enc}(m_b, K))$.
5. $\mathcal{A}$ submits a guess b' for b.

The result of the experiment is 1 if $b' = b$ and 0 else.

$\mathsf{IND\text{-}CKA}$ is a weaker form of Data Privacy. Were the adversary not restricted in choosing queries (Line 3. in Security Game 9), the notions would be equivalent. As in the case of Curtmola et al.'s notion (Sect. A.2), we prove the relation of Goh's notion to our model without considering this restriction. Our security notions could easily be further generalised to include this restriction, however, we decided against this, as the applications of such restrictions seem limited.

Theorem 9. $\mathsf{IND\text{-}CKA}$ *implies static security.*

The proof is a straightforward reduction and we omit it here.

Theorem 10. *Database privacy implies* $\mathsf{IND\text{-}CKA}$.

Due to space constraints, the proof is only included in the full version.

A.2   Adaptive Security for Symmetric Searchable Encryption

Curtmola et al.'s notion *adaptive indistinguishability security for SSE* [8] is also a security notion for symmetric searchable encryption based on indices.

Security Game 10 ($\mathsf{Ind}^*_{\mathsf{SSE},\mathcal{A},(\mathsf{Gen},\mathsf{Enc},\mathsf{Q})}(k)$ [8])

1. The experiment chooses a key $K \leftarrow \mathsf{Gen}(1^k)$ and a random bit $b \leftarrow \{0,1\}$.
2. The adversary $\mathcal{A}$ is given input 1^k and outputs two plaintexts m_0 and m_1 of the same length to the experiment.
3. $\mathcal{A}$ is given $\mathsf{Enc}_K(m_b)$.
4. $\mathcal{A}$ can output polynomially many pairs of queries (q_0, q_1) and is given $\mathsf{view}^{\pi_{q_b}}_{\mathfrak{G}}(\mathsf{Enc}(d_b, K))$.
5. $\mathcal{A}$ submits a guess b' for b.

The result of the experiment is 1 if $b' = b$ and 0 else. Note that in Curtmola et al.'s notion, Query Privacy and Data Privacy are intertwined. Thus, it can not be directly instantiated from our framework. We instead show how his notion relates to our notions. $\mathsf{Ind}^*_{\mathrm{SSE}}$ also requires the adversary to only choose plaintexts and corresponding search queries which have the same views for both databases. This is a very strict restriction which we do not take into consideration here. We instead focus on the more general notion.

Theorem 11. (Q-IND∧D-IND $\implies$ Ind^*_{SSE}). *If a queryable outsourcing scheme has Query Privacy, Data Privacy implies* Ind^*_{SSE}.

Theorem 12. ($\mathsf{Ind}^*_{SSE} \implies$ D-IND). Ind^*_{SSE} *implies database privacy.*

Due to space constraints, the proofs are omitted here. They are included in the full version.

References

1. Böhl, F., Hofheinz, D., Kraschewski, D.: On definitions of selective opening security. Cryptology ePrint Archive, Report 2011/678 (2011). http://eprint.iacr.org/2011/678
2. Cachin, C., Micali, S., Stadler, M.A.: Computationally private information retrieval with polylogarithmic communication. In: Stern, J. (ed.) EURO-CRYPT 1999. LNCS, vol. 1592, pp. 402–414. Springer, Heidelberg (1999). http://dx.doi.org/10.1007/3-540-48910-X_28
3. Canetti, R.: Universally composable security: a new paradigm for cryptographic protocols. In: Proceedings of the 42nd IEEE Symposium on Foundations of Computer Science, pp. 136–145. IEEE (2001)
4. Cash, D., Jaeger, J., Jarecki, S., Jutla, C., Krawczyk, H., Rosu, M., Steiner, M.: Dynamic searchable encryption in very-large databases: data structures and implementation. In: Network and Distributed System Security Symposium, NDSS, vol. 14 (2014)
5. Krawczyk, H., Jarecki, S., Steiner, M., Jutla, C., Cash, D., Roşu, M.-C.: Highly-scalable searchable symmetric encryption with support for boolean queries. In: Canetti, R., Garay, J.A. (eds.) CRYPTO 2013, Part I. LNCS, vol. 8042, pp. 353–373. Springer, Heidelberg (2013)
6. Chase, M., Shen, E.: Pattern matching encryption. Cryptology ePrint Archive, Report 2014/638 (2014). http://eprint.iacr.org/2014/638
7. Chor, B., Kushilevitz, E., Goldreich, O., Sudan, M.: Private information retrieval. J. ACM 45(6), 965–981 (1998). http://doi.acm.org/10.1145/293347.293350
8. Curtmola, R., Garay, J., Kamara, S., Ostrovsky, R.: Searchable symmetric encryption: improved definitions and efficient constructions. In: Proceedings of the 13th ACM Conference on Computer and Communications Security, CCS 2006, pp. 79–88. ACM, New York (2006). Full version available at https://eprint.iacr.org/2006/210
9. Damgård, I., Nielsen, J.B., Meldgaard, S.: Perfectly secure oblivious RAM without random oracles. In: Ishai, Y. (ed.) TCC 2011. LNCS, vol. 6597, pp. 144–163. Springer, Heidelberg (2011)

10. Evdokimov, S., Fischmann, M., Gunther, O.: Provable security for outsourcing database operations. In: Proceedings of the 22nd International Conference on Data Engineering, ICDE 2006, p. 117. IEEE (2006)
11. Gentry, C., Ramzan, Z.: Single-database private information retrieval with constant communication rate. In: Caires, L., Italiano, G.F., Monteiro, L., Palamidessi, C., Yung, M. (eds.) ICALP 2005. LNCS, vol. 3580, pp. 803–815. Springer, Heidelberg (2005). http://dx.doi.org/10.1007/11523468_65
12. Goh, E.J.: Secure indexes. IACR Cryptology ePrint Archive 2003, 216 (2003). https://eprint.iacr.org/2003/216/
13. Goldreich, O., Ostrovsky, R.: Software protection and simulation on oblivious RAMs. J. ACM 43(3), 431–473 (1996). http://doi.acm.org/10.1145/233551.233553
14. Goodrich, M.T., Mitzenmacher, M., Ohrimenko, O., Tamassia, R.: Oblivious ram simulation with efficient worst-case access overhead. In: Proceedings of the 3rd ACM Workshop on Cloud Computing Security Workshop, pp. 95–100. ACM (2011)
15. Haynberg, R., Rill, J., Achenbach, D., Müller-Quade, J.: Symmetric searchable encryption for exact pattern matching using directed acyclic word graphs. In: SECRYPT, pp. 403–410 (2013)
16. Gabel, M., Schulze, M., Huber, M., Bieber, A.: Cumulus4j: a provably secure database abstraction layer. In: Cuzzocrea, A., Kittl, C., Simos, D.E., Weippl, E., Xu, L. (eds.) CD-ARES Workshops 2013. LNCS, vol. 8128, pp. 180–193. Springer, Heidelberg (2013)
17. Kamara, S., Papamanthou, C.: Parallel and dynamic searchable symmetric encryption. In: Sadeghi, A.-R. (ed.) FC 2013. LNCS, vol. 7859, pp. 258–274. Springer, Heidelberg (2013)
18. Katz, J., Lindell, Y.: Introduction to Modern Cryptography. Chapman & Hall/CRC Cryptography and Network Security Series. Chapman & Hall/CRC, New York/Boca Raton (2007)
19. Kurosawa, K., Ohtaki, Y.: How to construct uc-secure searchable symmetric encryption scheme. Cryptology ePrint Archive, Report 2015/251 (2015). http://eprint.iacr.org/2015/251
20. Kushilevitz, E., Ostrovsky, R.: Replication is not needed: single database, computationally-private information retrieval. In: 2013 IEEE 54th Annual Symposium on Foundations of Computer Science, p. 364. IEEE Computer Society (1997)
21. Reinman, T., Pinkas, B.: Oblivious RAM revisited. In: Rabin, T. (ed.) CRYPTO 2010. LNCS, vol. 6223, pp. 502–519. Springer, Heidelberg (2010)
22. Shi, E., Stefanov, E., Li, M., Chan, T.-H.H.: Oblivious RAM with $O((\log n)^3)$ worst-case cost. In: Lee, D.H., Wang, X. (eds.) ASIACRYPT 2011. LNCS, vol. 7073, pp. 197–214. Springer, Heidelberg (2011)
23. Sion, R., Carbunar, B.: On the computational practicality of private information retrieval. In: Proceedings of the Network and Distributed Systems Security Symposium (2007)
24. Stefanov, E., Papamanthou, C., Shi, E.: Practical dynamic searchable encryption with small leakage. Cryptology ePrint Archive, Report 2013/832 (2013). http://eprint.iacr.org/2013/832

Implementation and Verifiable Encryption

On the Efficiency of Polynomial Multiplication for Lattice-Based Cryptography on GPUs Using CUDA

Sedat Akleylek[1,2]($\boxtimes$), Özgur Dağdelen[3], and Zaliha Yüce Tok[4]

[1] Department of Computer Engineering, Ondokuz Mayıs University, Samsun, Turkey
akleylek@gmail.com
[2] Cryptography and Computer Algebra Group, TU Darmstadt, Darmstadt, Germany
[3] BridgingIT GmbH, Mannheim, Germany
oezdagdelen@googlemail.com
[4] Institute of Applied Mathematics, METU, Ankara, Turkey
zalihayuce@gmail.com

Abstract. Polynomial multiplication is the most time-consuming part of cryptographic schemes whose security is based on ideal lattices. Thus, any efficiency improvement on this building block has great impact on the practicability of lattice-based cryptography. In this work, we investigate several algorithms for polynomial multiplication on a graphical processing unit (GPU), and implement them in both serial and parallel way on the GPU using the compute unified device architecture (CUDA) platform. Moreover, we focus on the quotient ring $(\mathbb{Z}/p\mathbb{Z})[x]/(x^n + 1)$, where p is a prime number and n is a power of 2. We stress that this ring constitutes the most common setting in lattice-based cryptography for efficiency reasons. As an application we integrate the different implementations of polynomial multiplications into a lattice-based signature scheme proposed by Güneysu et al. (CHES 2012) and identify which algorithm is the preferable choice with respect to the ring of degree n.

Keywords: Lattice-based cryptography · GPU implementation · CUDA platform · Polynomial multiplication · Fast Fourier transform · cuFFT · NTT · Schönhage-Strassen

1 Introduction

Lattice-based cryptography has gained a lot of attention since the breakthrough work by Gentry [10] who constructed the very first fully homomorphic encryption scheme, answering a problem posed in 1978 and thought by many to be impossible to resolve. The security of lattice-based cryptographic schemes depends on the hardness of lattice problems which are believed to be intractable even against quantum attacks, as opposed to classical cryptographic schemes which are based on the hardness of factoring or computing discrete logarithms. Indeed, Shor [26] has shown that quantum computers can solve the latter computational

© Springer International Publishing Switzerland 2016
E. Pasalic and L.R. Knudsen (Eds.): BalkanCryptSec 2015, LNCS 9540, pp. 155–168, 2016.
DOI: 10.1007/978-3-319-29172-7_10

problems in polynomial time, and thus making it plain to the community that alternatives are necessary once efficient quantum computers are omnipresent.

Additional reasons for the current popularity of lattice-based cryptography lies in their asymptotic efficiency. While classical cryptographic schemes deal with very large finite fields and/or require to perform expensive exponentiations, the efficiency of lattice-based schemes is dominated mainly by "cheap" matrix-vector multiplications. Moreover, even more efficient instantiations of lattice-based cryptographic schemes are derived if they are based on ideal lattices corresponding to ideals in rings of the form $\mathbb{Z}[x]/(f)$, where f is a degree n irreducible polynomial (usually $f = x^n + 1$). The most common ring used in lattice-based cryptography (e.g., [6,12,17]) is the quotient ring $(\mathbb{Z}/p\mathbb{Z})[x]/(x^n + 1)$ for which we know quasi-logarithmic multiplication algorithms, namely via the Fast Fourier Transform (FFT). We stress that polynomial multiplication still constitutes the bottleneck of lattice-based cryptography with respect to its performance. Hence, efficient implementations of the multiplication operation impact positively and directly the performance of lattice-based cryptosystems.

In the past there has been a great interest for the implementation of lattice-based cryptography on FPGAs [4,11–14,21–23,25]. The main inducement lies here in running the arithmetic operations in parallel. Pöppelmann et al. [20] showed how the arithmetic involved in lattice-based cryptography can be efficiently implemented on FPGAs. Specifically, they gave the details on the implementation of how to parallelize the Number Theoretic Transform (NTT) algorithm for the precomputed values. Due to the memory requirements of finding those values, the precomputation step was not performed on the FPGA but were given to the system directly. In [4], Aysu et al. presented a low-cost and area efficient hardware architecture for polynomial multiplication via NTT with applications in lattice-based cryptographic schemes. In contrast to [20], Aysu et al. computed all values for precomputation also on the FPGA.

Interestingly, the literature offers far less studies on the efficiency of polynomial multiplication on graphical processing units (GPU) in the quotient ring $(\mathbb{Z}/p\mathbb{Z})[x]/(x^n + 1)$. While GPUs are already a tool to cryptanalyze lattice problems [15,16,24], only few works use GPUs to accelerate lattice-based cryptosystems [5,28]. To the best of our knowledge, Emeliyanenko [8], Akleylek and Tok [1–3] are the only ones dealing with the efficiency of algorithms for polynomial multiplication on GPUs from which only the latter emphasizes on settings relevant for lattice-based cryptography.

Our Contribution. The contribution of this paper is three-fold: We propose modified FFT algorithm for sparse polynomial multiplication. With the proposed method we improve the complexity results almost 34 % for the sparse polynomial multiplication in the lattice-based signature scheme by Güneysu et al. [12]. Second, we provide the first efficient implementation of the Schönhage-Strassen polynomial multiplication algorithm on GPU using the CUDA platform and discuss its efficiency in comparison with well-known polynomial multiplication algorithms, namely iterative/parallel NTT and cuFFT. Our implementations are designed to the given GPU, namely the NVIDIA Geforce GT 555M GPU. Last, as an application we have implemented the lattice-based signature scheme by Güneysu et al. [12] on GPU and measured running times of the signature and verification algorithm while using different polynomial multiplication methods. Originally, this signature scheme was implemented on FPGAs [12].

Roadmap. In Sect. 2 we recall well-known algorithms for polynomial multiplication, show their efficient implementations in GPU and modify FFT algorithm to be used in sparse polynomial multiplication efficiently. In Sect. 3 we recall the lattice-based signature scheme by Güneysu et al.. We show the experimental results of our implementations in Sect. 4. We also show the performance of the selected lattice-based signature scheme with respect to the chosen algorithm for polynomial multiplication. In Sect. 5 we impose further discussion on our observation. We conclude in Sect. 6.

2 Multiplication over the Ring $(\mathbb{Z}/p\mathbb{Z})[x]/(x^n + 1)$

In this section, we give an overview of selected algorithms for polynomial multiplication, namely NTT in serial and parallel type, and CUDA-based FFT (cuFFT). We also discuss improved version of FFT for sparse polynomial multiplication. We focus on the arithmetic over the quotient ring $(\mathbb{Z}/p\mathbb{Z})[x]/(x^n + 1)$ whose importance in lattice-based cryptography that we emphasized in the previous section. Recall that polynomial multiplication by using FFT mainly consists of three steps:

- conversion of coefficients of polynomials to Fourier domain with FFT algorithm having $O(n \log(n))$ complexity,
- coefficient wise multiplication of elements in Fourier domain having $O(n)$ complexity,
- converting the result into the integer domain with inverse FFT algorithm having $O(n \log(n))$ complexity.

2.1 Number Theoretic Transform

The NTT algorithm was proposed in [19] to avoid rounding errors in FFT. NTT is a discrete Fourier transform defined over a ring or a finite field and is used to multiply two integers without requiring arithmetic operations on complex numbers. The multiplication complexity is quasi-linear (i.e., $O(n \log n)$).

The NTT algorithm can be applied if both of the following requirements are fulfilled:

- The degree n of the quotient ring $(\mathbb{Z}/p\mathbb{Z})[x]/(x^n + 1)$ must divide $(p-1)$.
- $\exists w \in (\mathbb{Z}/p\mathbb{Z})$ such that $w^n \equiv 1 \pmod{p}$ and for each $i < n$ it holds $w^n \neq 1 \pmod{p}$.

In order to multiply two ring elements via NTT, those elements have to transformed into NTT form. Let w be the primitive n-th root of unity, and $a(x) = \sum_{i=0}^{n-1} a_i x^i \in (\mathbb{Z}/p\mathbb{Z})[x]$ be given. The ring element a is transformed into the NTT form by algorithm $NTT_w(a)$ which is defined as follows:

$$NTT_w(a) := (A_0, \ldots, A_{n-1}) \text{ where } A_i = \sum_{j=0}^{n-1} a_j w^{ij} \pmod{p},$$

for $i \in \{0, 1, \ldots, n-1\}$. The inverse transform $NTT_w^{-1}(A)$ for $A = (A_0, \ldots, A_{n-1})$ is given as:

$$NTT_w^{-1}(A) := (a_0, \ldots, a_{n-1}) \text{ where } a_i = n^{-1} \sum_{j=0}^{n-1} A_j w^{-ij} \pmod{p},$$

with $i \in \{0, 1, \ldots, n-1\}$. By using the Convolution theorem, arbitrary polynomials can be multiplied and then reduced according to chosen reduction polynomial. However, appending n 0's to the inputs doubles the size of the transform. To use NTT for the multiplication of two elements in $(\mathbb{Z}/p\mathbb{Z})[x]/(x^n + 1)$ the condition is that $p \equiv 1 \pmod{2n}$ due to wrapped convolution approach. In Algorithm 1 the parallel version of the iterative NTT method is given. To make it efficient, we make use of "for" loops in the algorithm. Parallelization is achieved by determining the required number of threads. This algorithm needs data transfer between CPU and GPU. This may cause a delay and potentially defined the bottleneck in the performance. In Algorithm 2 we show how the parallelism is performed.

Algorithm 1. Parallelized iterative NTT method (CPU and GPU side)

Input: $a(x) = \sum_{i=0}^{n-1} a_i x^i$, $b(x) = \sum_{i=0}^{n-1} b_i x^i \in (\mathbb{Z}/p\mathbb{Z})[x]/(x^n + 1)$
Output: $c(x) = a(x) \cdot b(x) = \sum_{i=0}^{n-1} c_i x^i$
1: $f = \mathsf{BitReverseCopy}(a)$
2: $f = \mathsf{SumDiff}(f)$
3: $r_n = \mathsf{Element\_of\_order}(n)$
4: **if** reverse NTT **then**
5:     $r_n = r_n^{-1} \pmod{p}$
6: **end if**
7: **for** $i = 2$ to $\log(n)$ **do**
8:     $m = 2^i$
9:     $m_h = m/2$
10:    $d_w = r_n^{2^{\log(n)-i}}$
11:    Create block and grids
12:    Call the GPU_NTT procedure (grids, blocks) (f, d_w)
13: **end for**
14: Return f

Algorithm 2. GPU procedure

1: $thread\_idx = block\_id.x \cdot block\_dimension.x + threadidx.x$
2: $thread\_idy = block\_id.y \cdot block\_dimension.y + threadidx.y$
3: **if** $thread\_idx > 0$ or $thread\_idy = 0$ **then**
4:    Return
5: **end if**
6: **for** $i = 2$ to $thread\_idy$ **do**
7:    $w = w \cdot d_w \pmod{p}$
8: **end for**
9: $t_1 = thread\_idx \cdot m_h + thread\_idy$
10: $t_2 = t_1 \cdot m_h$
11: $v = at_2 \cdot w \pmod{p}$
12: $u = at_1$
13: $at_1 = (u + v) \pmod{p}$
14: $at_2 = (u - v) \pmod{p}$

2.2 Modified Fast Fourier Transform for Sparse Polynomial Multiplication

In this section, we present FFT algorithm for sparse polynomials. In Algorithm 6 multiplications in Step 3 and 4 can be considered as sparse polynomial multiplication since the coefficients of s_1 and s_2 are in the set $\{-1, 0, 1\}$ and the number of nonzero coefficients with $\{-1, 1\}$ is at most 32 in c. Thus, it's important to find such a specialized method for that kind of multiplications to improve the timing results. The most time consuming part in FFT-based polynomial multiplication is FFT, i.e., conversion of coefficients of polynomials to Fourier domain. Therefore, we focus on modifying FFT algorithm for sparse polynomials. In Algorithm 3 we modify FFT algorithm [19] for sparse polynomials.

Remark 1. Our observation is that in original FFT algorithm in [19] for each coefficient of polynomial is used in each step. Moreover, computing the powers of w (n–th root of unity) is computed in each step. There is no need to compute the corresponding power of w for the 0 coefficients.

In Table 1, we compare FFT and Algorithm 3 in view of the required number of arithmetic operations. n is the number of elements in the polynomial to be converted in Fourier domain. The parameter $m << n$ depends on the number of nonzero coefficients in the polynomial. ℓ stands for the number of nonzero elements in the polynomial. According to Table 1, the required number of arithmetic operations is significantly reduced. Improvement is almost same for each operation for a fixed $n = 1024$. So, by using Algorithm 3 one can improve the conversion operation to/from FFT with the given percentages in Improvement column in Table 1.

2.3 CUDA Fast Fourier Transform Based Multiplication

The NVIDIA CUDA Fast Fourier Transform (cuFFT) library enables the users to have very fast FFT computations with an interface on the GPU by using

---

Algorithm 3. Modified FFT for sparse polynomials

Input: $a(x) = \sum_{i=0}^{n-1} a_i x^i \in (\mathbb{Z}/p\mathbb{Z})[x]/(x^n + 1)$, size of n and forward or inverse. $w^{2n} \equiv 1 \pmod{p}$.

Output: $FFT_w(a)$

1: $a = \mathsf{BitReverseCopy}(a)$
2: **for** $i = 0$ to $\log(n) - 1$ **do**
3:      Compute the positions of all nonzero elements of a and d is an array of the position of nonzero elements. ℓ is the number of elements in d.
4:      **for** $j = 0$ to $\ell - 1$ **do**
5:          **if** $d[j]$ is even **then**
6:              $P_{id[j]/2} \leftarrow \lfloor \frac{d[j]/2}{2^{\log(n)-1-i}} \rfloor 2^{\log(n)-1-i}$
7:              $A_{\frac{d[j]}{2}} \leftarrow a_{d[j]} + a_{d[j]+1} w^{P_{id[j]/2}} \pmod{p}$
8:              $A_{\frac{d[j]}{2}+\frac{n}{2}} \leftarrow a_{d[j]} - a_{d[j]+1} w^{P_{id[j]/2}} \pmod{p}$
9:          **else**
10:             **if** $a_{d[j]-1} = 0$ **then**
11:                 $P_{i(d[j]-1)/2} \leftarrow \lfloor \frac{(d[j]-1)/2}{2^{\log(n)-1-i}} \rfloor 2^{\log(n)-1-i}$
12:                 $A_{\frac{d[j]-1}{2}} \leftarrow a_{d[j]-1} + a_{d[j]} w^{P_{i(d[j]-1)/2}} \pmod{p}$
13:                 $A_{\frac{d[j]-1}{2}+\frac{n}{2}} \leftarrow a_{d[j]-1} - a_{d[j]} w^{P_{i(d[j]-1)/2}} \pmod{p}$
14:             **end if**
15:         **end if**
16:     **end for**
17:     **if** $i \neq \log(n) - 1$ **then**
18:         $a \leftarrow A$
19:     **end if**
20: **end for**
21: Return A

Table 1. Complexity comparison of FFT and modified FFT for sparse polynomials

Operation	[7] and [19]	Algorithm 3	Improvement	
Multiplication	$\frac{3n}{2} \log(n)$	$\frac{3m}{2} \log(n)$	$\ell = 32$	$m = 338$, 34%
			$\ell = 64$	$m = 391$, 24%
Add/Sub	$n \log(n)$	$m \log(n)$	$\ell = 128$	$m = 440$, 14%
Mod p	$n \log(n)$	$m \log(n)$	$\ell = 256$	$m = 484$, 5%

the CUDA platform [18]. cuFFT is optimized for a wide range of application areas from computational physics to signal processing. Unlike previous parallel programming languages, CUDA provides an alternative way for an easy development of parallel computing and finding application on different fields such as in cryptographic protocols. In this work, we use cuFFT to obtain an efficient polynomial multiplication over the quotient ring. In Algorithm 4 we give the parallel version of the polynomial multiplication method using CUDA. In Step 5 the schedule is planned to have FFT value on GPU and then in Step 6 and 7 the computed values are stored. The component-wise multiplication is performed in

---

Algorithm 4. cuFFT-based multiplication

Input: $a(x) = \sum_{i=0}^{n-1} a_i x^i$, $b(x) = \sum_{i=0}^{n-1} b_i x^i \in (\mathbb{Z}/p\mathbb{Z})[x]/(x^n + 1)$
Output: $c(x) = a(x) \cdot b(x) = \sum_{i=0}^{n-1} c_i x^i$
  1: allocate_cuda_memory(cuda_a)
  2: allocate_cuda_memory(cuda_b)
  3: cuda_copy(a, cuda_a)
  4: cuda_copy(b, cuda_b)
  5: cufftPlanId(planForward, n, CUFFT_D2Z, 1)
  6: cufftExecD2Z(planForward, cuda_a, cuda_a)
  7: cufftExecD2Z(planForward, cuda_b, cuda_b)
  8: multiply_complex(cuda_a, cuda_b, cuda_a)
  9: cufftPlanId(planInverse, n, CUFFT_Z2D, 1)
 10: cufftExecD2Z(planInverse, cuda_a, cuda_a)
 11: Copy the results form GPU to host
 12: cuda_copy(cuda_a, c)
 13: **for** $i = 0$ to n **do**
 14:     $c_i = c_i/n$
 15: **end for**
 16: Return c

---

parallel in Step 8. Forward FFT is achieved in Step 9. The result is sent to host in Step 11. From Step 13 to Step 15 normalization of the computed values is performed by simply dividing the result to the polynomial degree n.

2.4   Schönhage-Strassen Polynomial Multiplication

In Algorithm 5 we describe the Schönhage-Strassen polynomial multiplication algorithm in $(\mathbb{Z}/p\mathbb{Z})[x]/(x^n + 1)$ where n is of the form $n = 2^k$. This algorithm has complexity $O(n \log n \log \log n)$ [9]. The main idea of this approach is to split the input polynomials into t blocks of length m. This allows us to obtain convolution properties of the quotient ring $(\mathbb{Z}/p\mathbb{Z})[x]/(x^n + 1)$. These relatively small size polynomials are then multiplied with an efficient polynomial multiplication method such as FFT-based techniques. From Step 5 to 12, the polynomials are decomposed. In Step 18–21, the elements are prepared for the multiplication operation; it can also be considered as change of variables. Note that there is no computational cost for this mapping.

3   An Application: The Signature Scheme by Güneysu et al.

In the following we recall the construction of the lattice-based signature scheme proposed by Güneysu et al. [12]. A signature scheme consists of three algorithms, namely a key-generation algorithm, a signature, and a verification algorithm. In key-generation phase, secret keys s_1, s_2 are chosen uniformly from $(\mathbb{Z}/p\mathbb{Z})[x]/(x^n + 1)$ with coefficients in the set $\{-1, 0, 1\}$ and the public key is

---

Algorithm 5. Schönhage-Strassen polynomial multiplication

Input: $a(x) = \sum_{i=0}^{n-1} a_i x^i$, $b(x) = \sum_{i=0}^{n-1} b_i x^i \in (\mathbb{Z}/p\mathbb{Z})[x]/(x^n + 1)$, with $n = 2^k$
Output: $c(x) = a(x) \cdot b(x) = \sum_{i=0}^{n-1} c_i x^i \pmod{(x^n + 1)}$
1: Set coefficients of $a(x)$ to a
2: Set coefficients of $b(x)$ to b
3: $m = 2^{\lfloor \frac{k}{2} \rfloor}$
4: $t = \frac{n}{m}$
5: **for** $i = 0$ to $t - 1$ **do**
6:     $A[i] = 0$
7:     $B[i] = 0$
8:     **for** $j = 0$ to $m - 1$ **do**
9:         $A[i] = A[i] + a[i \cdot m + j]x^j$
10:        $B[i] = B[i] + b[i \cdot m + j]x^j$
11:    **end for**
12: **end for**
13: **if** $t = 2m$ **then**
14:    $w = x$
15: **else**
16:    $w = x^2$
17: **end if**
18: **for** $i = 0$ to $t - 1$ **do**
19:    $\tilde{A} = \tilde{A} + A[i]w^i y^i \pmod{(x^{2m} + 1)}$
20:    $\tilde{B} = \tilde{B} + B[i]w^i y^i \pmod{(x^{2m} + 1)}$
21: **end for**
22: $\tilde{C} = Polynomial\_multiplication(\tilde{A}, \tilde{B}) \pmod{(x^{2m} + 1)} \pmod{(y^t - 1)}$
23: **for** $i = 0$ to $t - 1$ **do**
24:    **for** $j = 0$ to $m - 1$ **do**
25:        $c = c + \tilde{C}[i \cdot m + j]x^j$
26:    **end for**
27: **end for**
28: $c = c \pmod{(x^n + 1)}$
29: Return c

---

a uniformly chosen polynomial $a \leftarrow (\mathbb{Z}/p\mathbb{Z})[x]/(x^n + 1)$ and polynomial t where $t \leftarrow a \cdot s_1 + s_2$. We note that parameters p, n are determined beforehand to satisfy a certain security level. The signature scheme makes use of a the hash function H and its security is shown in the random oracle model which assumes that hash function H behaves ideally.

The signature algorithm is presented in Algorithm 6. Note that multiplications in Step 3 and 4 can be considered as sparse polynomial multiplication since the coefficients of s_1 and s_2 are in the set $\{-1, 0, 1\}$ and the number of nonzero coefficients with $\{-1, 1\}$ is at most 32 in c. Since Step 3 and Step 4 are independent operations, these can be performed in parallel. As discussed in [12], k is a power of 2 with $k \approx \sqrt{p}$. For sake of simplicity we omit the presentation of the compression step.

Algorithm 6. The signature generation algorithm

Input: $s_1(x) = \sum_{i=0}^{n-1} s_{1_i} x^i$, $s_2(x) = \sum_{i=0}^{n-1} s_{2_i} x^i \in (\mathbb{Z}/p\mathbb{Z})[x]/(x^n + 1)$ where $s_{1_i}, s_{2_i} \in$
$\{-1, 0, 1\}$ and a message $m \in \{0, 1\}^*$
Output: $z_1(x) = \sum_{i=0}^{n-1} z_{1_i} x^i$, $z_2(x) = \sum_{i=0}^{n-1} z_{2_i} x^i \in (\mathbb{Z}/p\mathbb{Z})[x]/(x^n + 1)$ where
$z_{1_i}, z_{2_i} \in \{-(k-32), \dots, (k-32)\}$ and hash value $c \in \{-1, 0, 1\}$ (c has at most 32
$\{-1, 1\}$)
1: Sample $y_1, y_2 \leftarrow (\mathbb{Z}/p\mathbb{Z})[x]/(x^n + 1)$ whose coefficients are in the set $\{-(k-32), \dots, (k-32)\}$.
2: $c \leftarrow H(a \cdot y_1 + y_2, m)$
3: $z_1 \leftarrow s_1 \cdot c + y_1$ //sparse polynomial multiplication ($s_1 \cdot c$)
4: $z_2 \leftarrow s_2 \cdot c + y_2$ //sparse polynomial multiplication ($s_2 \cdot c$)
5: **if** any coefficients of z_1 or z_2 are not in the set $\{-(k-32), \dots, (k-32)\}$ **then**
6:    goto Step 1.
7: **end if**
8: Return (z_1, z_2, c)

The verification algorithm is presented in Algorithm 7. The control of coefficients of z_1, z_2 and the multiplication $t \cdot c$ can be performed in parallel. We refer the reader to [12] for the proof of correctness and security of the signature scheme.

Algorithm 7. The verification algorithm

Input: $z_1(x) = \sum_{i=0}^{n-1} z_{1_i} x^i$, $z_2(x) = \sum_{i=0}^{n-1} z_{2_i} x^i \in (\mathbb{Z}/p\mathbb{Z})[x]/(x^n + 1)$ where $z_{1_i}, z_{2_i} \in$
$\{-(k-32), \dots, (k-32)\}$, $a, t \in (\mathbb{Z}/p\mathbb{Z})[x]/(x^n + 1)$, hash value $c \in \{-1, 0, 1\}$ and
a message $m \in \{0, 1\}^*$
Output: valid or invalid
1: **if** the coefficients of z_1 and z_2 are in the set $\{-(k-32), \dots, (k-32)\}$ and $c = H(a \cdot z_1 + z_2 - t \cdot c, m)$ **then**
2:    Return "valid"
3: **else**
4:    Return "invalid"
5: **end if**

---

4   Experimental Results

In this section, we give cycle counts of the multiplication algorithms and signature generation and verification processes. To obtain more consistent results the algorithms are run 1000 times for the uniformly random polynomials in the multiplication operation. To compare the multiplication operation on the GPU using CUDA platform we fix $p = 8383489$ satisfying $p \equiv 1 \pmod{2n}$. We implement the algorithms using the NVIDIA Geforce GT 555M GPU having 144 CUDA cores on a notebook with the Intel Core i7-2670QM processor and 4GB memory.

4.1 Experimental Results for Polynomial Multiplication

In Table 2 we list the performance results of different multiplication algorithms which multiply two elements in $(\mathbb{Z}/p\mathbb{Z})[x]/(x^n + 1)$ for $n = 2^k$ with $k \in \{8, \dots, 13\}$. The polynomials are generated randomly whose coefficients are in the set $\{-1, 0, 1\}$. For NTT-based implementations, we prefer to compute w and related values online in contrast to [20]. This, of course, gives a timing penalty.

Table 2. Timings for different multiplication methods

Degree n	256	512	1024	2048	4096	8192
Iterative NTT	11475	24524	54407	125332	274217	719816
Parallelized iterative NTT	16589	32569	72713	231960	689075	1860731
cuFFT-based multiplication	13970	26885	61089	134909	245964	450917
Schönhage-Strassen method	14684	29163	75942	167857	331857	799078

According to the timing results, we observe that for the polynomials of degree $n \in \{256, 512, 1024, 2048\}$, the iterative NTT method is the most efficient one. However, for $n > 2048$, there is enough workload such that cuFFT-based multiplication outperforms the other methods since the library is designed to work with large data sets. The parallelization of cuFFT library is very effective when working with large data sets. Note that other parallelized methods, such as iterative NTT, do not give the expected improvement since the data transfer between CPU and GPU happens multiple times and increases the execution time affecting the efficiency negatively. cuFFT-based multiplication has a better performance since data transfer is performed merely once. This decreases the latency versus the other methods. Recall that cuFFT is an optimized library for GPU. The Schönhage-Strassen method improves in performance with larger n since we prefer to use cuFFT-based multiplication for decomposed polynomials instead of schoolbook multiplication.

4.2 Experimental Results for the Signature Scheme

Here, we give the timing results of our implementation of the signature scheme proposed in [12] and described in Sect. 3. It is defined over the polynomial ring $(\mathbb{Z}/p\mathbb{Z})[x]/(x^n + 1)$. Again, we run the signature generation and verification algorithm 1000 times and list in Table 3 our respective timing results under consideration of various multiplication algorithms. In the signature generation process the most time-consuming part is the polynomial multiplication. Hence, we make similar observations as in the previous section. That is, according to the timing results, the signature generation process with iterative NTT for polynomial multiplication performs best for $n < 4096$ as in Table 2. For $n \in \{4096, 8192\}$ the signature generation with cuFFT-based multiplication is most efficient.

Table 3. Cycle counts for the signature generation algorithm with different multiplication methods

Degree n	256	512	1024	2048	4096	8192
Iterative NTT	73866	158703	325530	702773	1534303	3808258
Parallelized iterative NTT	102804	234901	472159	1850947	4975280	19548904
cuFFT-based multiplication	92816	206719	359664	726804	1371674	2561705
Schönhage-Strassen method	97085	219485	405977	857904	1964071	5081130

Table 4. Cycle counts for the signature verification algorithm with different multiplication methods

Degree n	256	512	1024	2048	4096	8192
Iterative NTT	40746	82331	171857	366431	815838	1971789
Parallelized iterative NTT	58015	114089	295402	856910	2142230	1097502
cuFFT-based multiplication	53618	90526	201976	424451	707590	1239700
Schönhage-Strassen method	56419	99217	218006	480731	824003	2698207

The Schönhage-Strassen method is of the same magnitude as the cuFFT-based multiplication and is a preferable choice for higher security levels where the degree n is chosen large. The timing results of the signature verification process with various multiplication algorithms is given in Table 4.

5 Further Discussion

In the following we list some of potential ideas which may yield better performance and are subject of future work:

– The general method of polynomial multiplication is to first multiply the polynomials and then reduce the coefficients according to the prime p. In this work, we focus on the polynomial multiplication modulo $(x^n + 1)$. Therefore, we merely use CUDA's modular reduction function. However, one might speed up the modular reduction step by choosing prime numbers in a special form such as pseudo Mersenne prime or generalized Mersenne prime. Those primes enable very efficient modular reduction with merely additions [27].
– We precompute the n-th root of unity w and other related values if needed in NTT or FFT conversion. On the other hand, if we proceed without a precomputation phase, the computation of w and its powers could be done online. Since there is no need to compute them in each round, this decreases the performance.
– In the Schönhage-Strassen method, we use cuFFT-based multiplication method for the multiplication operation in Step 22 of Algorithm 5, i.e., $\tilde{C} = \mathsf{Polynomial\_multiplication}(\tilde{A}, \tilde{B})$ (mod $x^{2m}+1$ and y^t-1). We believe that this multiplication can be optimized in this method. Note that this method

uses the benefit of a divide-and-conquer idea. Thus, these polynomials multiplied have low degrees compared with the first form. Moreover, a specific structure for the convolution phase might be used.

- The GPU used for our experiments has far less cores than, for example, NVIDIA Geforce GTX980 having 2048 cores, NVIDIA Geforce TITAN Z having 5760 cores. The performance of our implemented algorithms will be improved if run on those GPUs due to the large number of CUDA cores. However, there is a trade-off between the number used cores and efficiency. If the number of transactions between GPU and CPU is relatively large, then the use of so many cores maybe counterproductive. Moreover, GPUs differ significantly with respect to the latency between GPU and CPU. Therefore, one should implement these algorithms preferably almost without data transfer between GPU and CPU.
- The algorithms discussed in this paper are generic. That is, they work with any polynomials with essentially the same running time. In [12, 20, 21], polynomials with low Hamming weight are considered as required by their signature scheme. Thus, if we are able to find an efficient method for sparse polynomial multiplication like Algorithm 3, we might outperform all the generic polynomial multiplication methods we analyzed in this work.

6   Conclusion

In this paper, we propose modified FFT algorithm for sparse polynomial multiplication with applications in the lattice-based cryptography. We improve the complexity results by 34 % with the proposed method. Then, we discuss the computational aspects of polynomial multiplication algorithms for lattice-based cryptographic schemes. Specifically, we investigate how these algorithms perform when run on GPU. We show that some of the multiplication methods which efficiently run in the CPU platform do not give the expected performance on GPU. Data latency between CPU and GPU causes inefficient implementations, in particular, for small data sets since the CUDA platform is designed to work with large data sets. Every kernel call causes latency since kernel initialization is done for each call specific to CUDA platform. We obtain the highest efficiency of cuFFT-based multiplication method for the polynomial degree larger than 4096. We conclude that for an efficient GPU implementation of cryptographic schemes using the CUDA platform more effort is required to optimize modular arithmetic operations.

Acknowledgments. Sedat Akleylek was partially supported by TÜBITAK under 2219-Postdoctoral Research Program Grant.

References

1. Akleylek, S., Tok, Z.Y.: Efficient arithmetic for lattice-based cryptography on GPU using the CUDA platform. In: 22nd Signal Processing and Communications Applications Conference (SIU 2014), pp. 854–857. IEEE Press (2014)
2. Akleylek, S., Tok, Z.Y.: Efficient interleaved montgomery modular multiplication for lattice-based cryptography. IEICE Electron. Express **11**(22), 1–6 (2014)
3. Akleylek, S., Tok, Z.Y.: Computational aspects of lattice-based cryptography on graphical processing unit. In: El Sayed, M.S., El-Alfy, M.H., (eds.) Improving Information Security Practices through Computational Intelligence, pp. 255–284. IGI Global (2015)
4. Aysu, A., Patterson, C., Schaumont, P.: Low-cost and area efficient FPGA implementations of lattice-based cryptography. In: IEEE HOST 2013, pp. 81–86. IEEE Press (2013)
5. Bai, T., Davis, S., Li, J., Jiang, H.: Analysis and acceleration of NTRU lattice-based cryptographic system. In: SNPD, pp. 1–6. IEEE Press (2014)
6. Banerjee, A., Peikert, C., Rosen, A.: Pseudorandom functions and lattices. In: Pointcheval, D., Johansson, T. (eds.) EUROCRYPT 2012. LNCS, vol. 7237, pp. 719–737. Springer, Heidelberg (2012)
7. Chen, D.D., Mentens, N., Vercauteren, F., Roy, S.S., Cheung, R.C.C., Pao, D., Verbauwhede, I.: High-speed polynomial multiplication architecture for ring-LWE and SHE cryptosystems. IEEE Trans. Circ. Syst. I: Regul. Pap. **62**(1), 157–166 (2015)
8. Emeliyanenko, P.: Efficient multiplication of polynomials on graphics hardware. In: Dou, Y., Gruber, R., Joller, J.M. (eds.) APPT 2009. LNCS, vol. 5737, pp. 134–149. Springer, Heidelberg (2009)
9. Gathen, J.V.Z., Gerhard, J.: Modern Computer Algebra, 3rd edn. Cambridge University Press, Cambridge (2013)
10. Gentry, C.: Fully homomorphic encryption using ideal lattices. In: Proceedings of the Forty-First Annual ACM Symposium on Theory of Computing (STOC), pp. 169–178. ACM, NY (2009)
11. Göttert, N., Feller, T., Schneider, M., Buchmann, J., Huss, S.: On the design of hardware building blocks for modern lattice-based encryption schemes. In: Prouff, E., Schaumont, P. (eds.) CHES 2012. LNCS, vol. 7428, pp. 512–529. Springer, Heidelberg (2012)
12. Güneysu, T., Lyubashevsky, V., Pöppelmann, T.: Lattice-based signatures: optimization and implementation on reconfigurable hardware. IEEE Trans. Comput. **64**, 1954–1967 (2014). doi:10.1109/TC.2014.2346177
13. Györfi, T., Cret, O., Borsos, Z.: Implementing modular FFTs in FPGAs - a basic block for lattice-based cryptography. In: Euromicro Conference on Digital System Design (DSD 2013), pp. 305–308. IEEE Press (2013)
14. Györfi, T., Cret, O., Hanrot, G., Brisebarre, N.: High-throughput Hardware Architecture for the (SWIFFT)/(SWIFFTX) Hash Functions. In: IACR, Cryptology ePrint Archive 2012, p. 343 (2012)
15. Hermans, J., Schneider, M., Buchmann, J., Vercauteren, F., Preneel, B.: Parallel shortest lattice vector enumeration on graphics cards. In: Bernstein, D.J., Lange, T. (eds.) AFRICACRYPT 2010. LNCS, vol. 6055, pp. 52–68. Springer, Heidelberg (2010)
16. Kuo, P.-C., Schneider, M., Dagdelen, Ö., Reichelt, J., Buchmann, J., Cheng, C.-M., Yang, B.-Y.: Extreme enumeration on GPU and in clouds. In: Preneel, B., Takagi, T. (eds.) CHES 2011. LNCS, vol. 6917, pp. 176–191. Springer, Heidelberg (2011)

17. Lyubashevsky, V., Micciancio, D., Peikert, C., Rosen, A.: SWIFFT: a modest proposal for FFT hashing. In: Nyberg, K. (ed.) FSE 2008. LNCS, vol. 5086, pp. 54–72. Springer, Heidelberg (2008)

18. NVIDIA CUDA Toolkit Documentation (2014). http://docs.nvidia.com/cuda/eula/index.html

19. Pollard, J.M.: The fast fourier transform in a finite field. Math. Comput. **25**(114), 365–374 (1971)

20. Güneysu, T., Pöppelmann, T.: Towards efficient arithmetic for lattice-based cryptography on reconfigurable hardware. In: Hevia, A., Neven, G. (eds.) LatinCrypt 2012. LNCS, vol. 7533, pp. 139–158. Springer, Heidelberg (2012)

21. Pöppelmann, T., Ducas, L., Güneysu, T.: Enhanced lattice-based signatures on reconfigurable hardware. In: Batina, L., Robshaw, M. (eds.) CHES 2014. LNCS, vol. 8731, pp. 353–370. Springer, Heidelberg (2014)

22. Pöppelmann, T., Güneysu, T.: Towards practical lattice-based public-key encryption on reconfigurable hardware. In: Lange, T., Lauter, K., Lisoněk, P. (eds.) SAC 2013. LNCS, vol. 8282, pp. 68–86. Springer, Heidelberg (2014)

23. Pöppelmann, T., Güneysu, T.: Area optimization of lightweight lattice-based encryption on reconfigurable hardware. In: IEEE International Symposium on Circuits and Systems (ISCAS 2014), pp. 2796–2799. IEEE Press (2014)

24. Qiao, S.: A jacobi method for lattice basis reduction. In: Spring Congress on Engineering and Technology (S-CET 2012), pp. 1–4 (2012)

25. Roy, S.S., Vercauteren, F., Mentens, N., Chen, D.D., Verbauwhede, I.: Compact ring-LWE cryptoprocessor. In: Batina, L., Robshaw, M. (eds.) CHES 2014. LNCS, vol. 8731, pp. 371–391. Springer, Heidelberg (2014)

26. Shor, P.: Polynomial-time algorithms for prime factorization and discrete logarithms on a quantum computer. SIAM J. Comput. **26**(5), 1484–1509 (1997)

27. Solinas, J.A.: Generalized Mersenne Numbers. Technical report CORR99-39, Center for Applied Cryptographic Research, University of Waterloo (1999)

28. Wang, W., Chen, Z., Huang, X.: Accelerating leveled fully homomorphic encryption using GPU. In: IEEE International Symposium on Circuits and Systems (ISCAS 2014), pp. 2800–2803. IEEE Press (2014)

cuHE: A Homomorphic Encryption Accelerator Library

Wei Dai$^{(\boxtimes)}$ and Berk Sunar

Worcester Polytechnic Institute, Worcester, MA, USA
wdai@wpi.edu

Abstract. We introduce a CUDA GPU library to accelerate evaluations with homomorphic schemes defined over polynomial rings enabled with a number of optimizations including algebraic techniques for efficient evaluation, memory minimization techniques, memory and thread scheduling and low level CUDA hand-tuned assembly optimizations to take full advantage of the mass parallelism and high memory bandwidth GPUs offer. The arithmetic functions constructed to handle very large polynomial operands using number-theoretic transform (NTT) and Chinese remainder theorem (CRT) based methods are then extended to implement the primitives of the leveled homomorphic encryption scheme proposed by López-Alt, Tromer and Vaikuntanathan. To compare the performance of the proposed CUDA library we implemented two applications: the Prince block cipher and homomorphic sorting algorithms on two GPU platforms in single GPU and multiple GPU configurations. We observed a speedup of 25 times and 51 times over the best previous GPU implementation for Prince with single and triple GPUs, respectively. Similarly for homomorphic sorting we obtained 12–41 times speedup depending on the number and size of the sorted elements.

Keywords: Homomorphic evaluation · GPU acceleration · Large polynomial arithmetic

1 Introduction

Fully homomorphic encryption (FHE) has gained increasing attention from cryptographers ever since its first plausible secure construction was introduced by Gentry [18] in 2009. FHE allows one to perform arbitrary computation on encrypted data without the need of a secret key, hence without knowledge of original data. That feature would have invaluable implications for the way we utilize computing services. For instance, FHE is capable of protecting the privacy of sensitive data on cloud computing platforms. We have witnessed amazing number of improvements in fully and somewhat homomorphic encryption schemes (SWHE) over the past few years [2–4,11,19,20]. In [21] Gentry, Halevi and Smart (GHS) proposed the first homomorphic evaluation of a complex circuit, i.e. a full AES block. The implementation makes use of batching [32,33], key switching [2] and modulus switching techniques to efficiently evaluate a leveled circuit.

© Springer International Publishing Switzerland 2016
E. Pasalic and L.R. Knudsen (Eds.): BalkanCryptSec 2015, LNCS 9540, pp. 169–186, 2016.
DOI: 10.1007/978-3-319-29172-7_11

In [28] a leveled NTRU [25, 34] based FHE scheme was introduced by López-Alt, Tromer and Vaikuntanathan (LTV), featuring much slower growth of noise during homomorphic computation. Later Doröz, Hu and Sunar (DHS) [12] used an LTV SWHE variant to evaluate AES more efficiently. More recently, Ducas and Micciancio [16] presented an efficient implementation of the bootstrapping algorithm.

At the same time researchers have also started investigating how to best put these new homomorphic evaluation tools to use in privatizing applications. In particular, in [29] Lauter et al. analyzed the problems of evaluating averages, standard deviations, and logistical regressions which provide basic tools for a number of real-world applications in the medical, financial, and advertising domains. Later in [26], Lauter et al. demonstrated the viability of privatized computation of genomic data. In [15], Doröz et al. used an NTRU based SWHE scheme to construct a bandwidth efficient private information retrieval scheme. Bos et al. in [1] showed how to privately perform predictive analysis tasks on encrypted medical data. Graepel et al. in [22] showed that it is possible to execute machine learning algorithms on privatized data. Cheon et al. [7] presented an implementation to homomorphically evaluate dynamic programming algorithms such as Hamming distance, edit distance, and the Smith-Waterman algorithm on encrypted genomic data. Çetin et al. [6] analyzed the complexity and provided implementation results for homomorphic sorting.

Despite the rapid advances, HE evaluation efficiency remains as one of the obstacles preventing it from deployment in real-life applications. Given the computation and bandwidth complexity of HE schemes, alternative platforms such as FPGAs, application-specific integrated circuits (ASIC) and graphics processor units (GPU) need to be employed. Over the last decade GPUs have evolved to highly parallel, multi-threaded, many-core processor systems with tremendous computing power. Compared to FPGA and ASIC platforms, general-purpose computing on GPUs (GPGPU) yields higher efficiency when normalized by price. For example, in [13] an NTT conversion costs 0.05 ms on a $5,000 FPGA, whereas takes only 0.15 ms on a $200 GPU (NVIDIA GTX 770). The results of [9,10,35] demonstrate the power of GPU-accelerated HE evaluations. Another critical advantage of GPUs is the strong memory architecture and high communication bandwidth. Bandwidth is crucial for HE evaluation due to very large evaluation keys and ciphertexts. In contrast, FPGAs feature much simpler and more limited memory architectures and unless supplied with a custom memory I/O interface design the bandwidth suffers greatly.

For CPU platforms Halevi and Shoup published the HElib [23], a C++ library for HE that is based on Brakerski-Gentry-Vaikuntanathan (BGV) cryptosystem [2]. More recently, Ducas and Micciancio [16] published FHEW, another CPU library which features encryption and bootstrapping. In this paper, we propose cuHE: a GPU-accelerated optimized SWHE library in CUDA/C++. The library is designed to boost polynomial based HE schemes such as LTV, BGV and DHS. Our aim is to accelerate homomorphic circuit evaluations of leveled circuits via CUDA GPUs. To demonstrate the performance gain achieved with cuHE, by employing the DHS scheme [12], along with many optimizations, to implement the Prince block cipher and a homomorphic sorting algorithm on integers.

Our Contributions

- The cuHE library offers the feasibility of accelerating polynomial based homomorphic encryption and various circuit evaluations with CUDA GPUs.
- We incorporated various optimizations and design alternative methods to exploit the memory organization and bandwidth of CUDA GPUs. In particular, we adapted our parameter selection process to optimally map HE evaluation keys and precomputed values into the right storage type from fastest and more frequently used to slowest least accessed. Moreover, we also utilized OpenMP and CUDA hybrid programming for simultaneous computation on multiple GPUs.
- We attain the fastest homomorphic block cipher implementation, i.e. Prince at 51 ms (1 GPU), using the cuHE library which is 25 times faster than the previously reported fastest implementation [9]. Further, our library is able to evaluate homomorphic sorting on an integer array of various sizes 12–41 times faster compared to a CPU implementation [6].

2   Background

2.1   The LTV SWHE Scheme

In this section we briefly explain the LTV SWHE [28] with specializations introduced in [12]. We work with polynomials in ring $R = \mathbb{Z}[x]/(m(x))$ where $\deg m(x) = n$. All operations are performed in $R_q = R/qR$ where q is an odd modulus. Elements of $\mathbb{Z}_q$ are associated with elements of $\{-\lfloor \frac{q}{2} \rfloor, \ldots, \lfloor \frac{q}{2} \rfloor\}$. A truncated discrete Gaussian distribution χ is used as an error distribution from which we can sample random small B-bounded polynomials. The primitives of the public key encryption scheme are Keygen, Enc, Dec and Eval.

Keygen. We generate a decreasing sequence of odd moduli $q_0 > q_1 > \cdots > q_{d-1}$ where d denotes the circuit depth and a monic polynomial $m(x)$. They define the ring for each level. $m(x)$ is the product of l monic polynomials each of which defines a message slot. In [12] more details about batching are explained. Keys are generated for the 0-th level, and are updated for every other level.

   The 0-th level Sample $\alpha, \beta \leftarrow \chi$, and set $sk^{(0)} = 2\alpha + 1$ and $pk^{(0)} = 2\beta(sk^{(0)})^{-1}$ in ring $R_{q_0} = \mathbb{Z}_{q_0}[x]/\langle m \rangle$ (re-sample if $sk^{(0)}$ is not invertible in the this ring). Then for $\tau \in \mathbb{Z}_{\lceil \lceil \log q_0 \rceil / w \rceil}$ where $w \leqslant \log q_{d-1}$ is a preset value, sample $s_\tau^{(0)}, e_\tau^{(0)} \leftarrow \chi$ and publish evaluation key $\{ek_\tau^{(0)} \mid \tau \in \mathbb{Z}_{\lceil \lceil \log q_0 \rceil / w \rceil}\}$ where $ek_\tau^{(0)} = pk^{(0)} s_\tau^{(0)} + 2e_\tau^{(0)} + 2^{w\tau} sk^{(0)}$. *The i-th level* Compute $sk^{(i)} = sk^{(0)} \pmod{q_i}$ and $pk^{(i)} = pk^{(0)} \pmod{q_i}$ in ring $R_{q_i} = \mathbb{Z}_{q_i}[x]/\langle m \rangle$. Then compute evaluation key $\{ek_\tau^{(i)} \mid \tau \in \mathbb{Z}_{\lceil \lceil \log q_i \rceil / w \rceil}\}$ where $ek_\tau^{(i)} = ek_\tau^{(0)} \pmod{q_i}$.

Enc. To encrypt a bit $b \in \{0,1\}$ with public key $(pk^{(0)}, q_0)$, sample $s, e \leftarrow \chi$, and set $c^{(0)} = pk^{(0)} s + 2e + b$ in R_{q_0}.

Dec. To decrypt a ciphertext $c^{(i)}$, multiply the ciphertext with the corresponding private key $sk^{(i)}$ in R_{q_i} and then compute the message by modulo two: $b = c^{(i)}sk^{(i)} \pmod{2}$.

Eval. We perform arithmetic operations directly on ciphertexts. Suppose $c_1^{(i)} = \mathsf{Enc}(b_1) \pmod{q_i}$ and $c_2^{(i)} = \mathsf{Enc}(b_2) \pmod{q_i}$. The XOR gate is realized by adding ciphertexts: $b_1 + b_2 = \mathsf{Dec}(c_1^{(i)} + c_2^{(i)})$. The AND gate is realized by multiplying ciphertexts. However, polynomial multiplication incurs a much greater growth in the noise. So each multiplication step is followed by relinearization and modulus switching. First we compute $\tilde{c}^{(i)} = c_1^{(i)} \times c_2^{(i)}$ in R_{q_i}. To obtain $\tilde{c}^{(i+1)}$ from $\tilde{c}^{(i)}$, we perform relinearization on $\tilde{c}^{(i)}$. We expand it as $\tilde{c}^{(i)} = \sum_{\tau=0}^{\lceil \log q_i \rceil / w} 2^{\tau} \tilde{c}_{\tau}^{(i)}$ where $\tilde{c}_{\tau}^{(i)}$ takes its coefficients from $\mathbb{Z}_{2^w}$. Then set $\tilde{c}^{(i+1)} = \sum_{\tau=0}^{\lceil \log q_i \rceil / w} ek_{\tau}^{(i)} \tilde{c}_{\tau}^{(i)}$ in R_{q_i}. To obtain $c^{(i+1)}$ in $R_{q_{i+1}}$, we perform modulus switching: $c^{(i+1)} = \left\lfloor \frac{q_{i+1}}{q_i} c^{(i)} \right\rceil_2$ and then we have $m_1 \times m_2 = \mathsf{Dec}(c^{(i+1)})$.

2.2   Arithmetic Tools

Schönhage-Strassen's Multiplication. Here we very briefly introduce the polynomial multiplication scheme by Schönhage-Strassen [30]. Given two polynomials $f = \sum_{k=0}^{n-1} a_k x^k$ and $g = \sum_{k=0}^{n-1} b_k x^k$, we compute $\hat{f} = \sum_{k=0}^{2n-1} \hat{a}_k x^k$, where $[\hat{a}_0, \hat{a}_1, \ldots, \hat{a}_{2n-1}] = \mathsf{NTT}\left([a_0, a_1, \ldots, a_{n-1}, 0, \ldots, 0]\right)$. One multiplication of two degree n polynomials consists of two $2n$-point NTTs, one coefficient-wise multiplication and one $2n$-point inverse transform (INTT):

- Inputs: $f = \sum_{k=0}^{n-1} a_k x^k$, $g = \sum_{k=0}^{n-1} b_k x^k$;
- NTT Conversion: $f \to \hat{f} = \sum_{k=0}^{2n-1} \hat{a}_k x^k$, $g \to \hat{g} = \sum_{k=0}^{2n-1} \hat{b}_k x^k$;
- Output: $f \times g = \mathsf{INTT}\left(\sum_{k=0}^{2n-1} \hat{a}_k \hat{b}_k x^k\right)$.

CRT. We introduce the CRT to handle large integer computation. We generate t prime numbers $\{p_0, p_1, \ldots, p_{t-1}\}$ with $B_p < 32$ bits. We further compute, for each level, $q_i = p_0 p_1 \cdots p_{t_i}$ where $0 < t_i < t_{i-1} < t$ as in [21]. Then, we have $R_{q_i} \cong R_{p_0} \times \cdots \times R_{p_{t_i}}$. Given a polynomial $f = \sum_{k=0}^{n-1} a_k x^k$ in ring R_{q_i}, we compute a vector of polynomials $\mathcal{F} = [f_{(0)}, f_{(1)}, \ldots, f_{(t_i-1)}]$ as its CRT representation: $f_{(j)} = \sum_{k=0}^{n-1} a_{k(j)} x^k \in R_{p_j}$, where $a_{k(j)} = a_k \pmod{p_j}$, $j \in \mathbb{Z}_{t_i}$. For all $f, g \in R_{q_i}$ where $i \in \mathbb{Z}_d$, and $\mathcal{F} = \mathsf{CRT}(f)$, $\mathcal{G} = \mathsf{CRT}(g)$, we have $f \circ g = \mathsf{ICRT}(\mathcal{F} \circ \mathcal{G})$, where $\mathcal{F} \circ \mathcal{G} = [f_{(0)} \circ g_{(0)}, \ldots, f_{(t_i-1)} \circ g_{(t_i-1)}]$. Given a polynomial modulus m and $\mathcal{M} = \mathsf{CRT}(m)$, for all f, we have $f \pmod{m} = \mathsf{ICRT}(\mathcal{F} \pmod{\mathcal{M}})$. Other than CRT and ICRT, no large integer operation is needed.

2.3   CRT, NTT

In our implementations, the degree of modulus m is 8192, 16384 or 32768. And q_0 has more than 256, 512 or 1024 bits, respectively. Coefficient independent operations, e.g. polynomial addition, can provide sufficient parallelism for a GPU realization. Still, two problems remain to be solved: how to compute large integers on CUDA GPUs; and how to efficiently implement operations that are not coefficient independent, e.g. polynomial multiplication. Those problems are handled by using CRT and NTT together.

3   GPU Basics

GPUs are powerful but highly specialized devices that require careful coding to take full advantage of the massive parallelism offered. Specifically, the programming model and memory organization is much different from in CPUs. Here we present a concise overview.

3.1   Programming Model

In general, a GPU-accelerated scheme offloads compute-intensive portions of the application to the GPU, while the remainder of the code still runs on the CPU. A GPU has its own on-chip memory. We call the CPU and memory "host", while GPU and its on-chip memory "device". A normal GPU computational task includes 3 operations: copying essential data from host to device (memcpy_h2d), initializing computation (a kernel) on device, copying result from device to host (memcpy_d2h) when necessary. A CUDA kernel is executed by an array of sequential threads. All threads run the same code, with an ID to compute memory addresses and make control decisions. On a GPU with warp size of 32, the kernel is executed in groups of 32 threads. Threads are further grouped into blocks. Only threads within a block can cooperate or synchronize. A kernel launch defines a grid of thread blocks. The dimension of a grid and that of each block determine how computing resource is assigned to program. The computation complexity of a kernel and the amount of data transferred between host and device depend on the details of an implementation.

3.2   Stream Management

A stream is a sequence of operations that execute in issue-order on the device. A default stream is created by CUDA on each device when no stream is specified. On a single stream, any operation will wait until the previous one completes. However, some operations, e.g. a kernel and a memcpy (without data dependency), are not necessarily sequential. We create extra streams so that operations on different streams can run concurrently and be interleaved. This not only allows a more flexible execution order, but also improves performance. Figure 1 gives an example of how using multiple streams makes a difference. We can hide the latency of memcpy behind a kernel execution. Alternatively, we may further break down one kernel launch into several parts in order to create concurrency. Every stream belongs to its own device. To have streams on different devices run concurrently and synchronize as needed is multi-GPU computing.

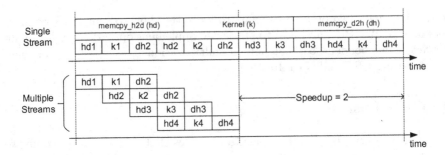

Fig. 1. Improving performance by using multiple streams

Table 1. GPU memory organization

Memory	Cached	Access	Scope	Lifetime
Register	N/A	R/W	One thread	Thread
Constant	Yes	R	All thread + host	Application
Texture	Yes	R	All thread + host	Application
Shared	N/A	R/W	All threads in a block	Block
Local	No	R/W	One thread	Thread
Global	No	R/W	All thread + host	Application

However, merely using streams to launch tasks on different devices creates expensive latency. Using OpenMP along with streams is a better solution. The goal of stream management is to achieve the best possible utilization of computing resources.

3.3 Memory Management

A significant ingredient to the performance of a program is memory management. The effect is particularly strong on GPUs since there are many different types of memory to store data and since the GPU-CPU interface tends to be slow. The GPU memory architecture is represented in Table 1. Memory types are listed from top to bottom by access speed from fast to slow. Before executing a kernel, we need to feed constant memory and global memory with data, and bind texture memory if needed. Other than using streams to overlap data transfer and computation, we optimize these data transfers in following methods: minimizing the amount of data transferred between host and device when possible, batching many small transfers into one larger transfer, using page-locked (or pinned) memory to achieve a higher bandwidth. Towards an efficient application, kernels should be designed to take advantage of the memory hierarchy properties:

- Constant memory is cached and fast. Due to its limited size, e.g. 64 KB, it is only suitable for repeatedly requested data.

- Global memory is not cached, expensive to access, and huge in size, e.g. 2 GB. Data that is only read once, or is updated by kernels is better allocated in global memory. The pattern of memory access in kernels also matters. If each thread in a warp accesses memory contiguously from the same 128 B chunk, it is called coalesced memory access. A non-coalesced (strided) memory access could make a kernel hundreds of times slower.
- Texture memory is designed for this scenario: a thread is likely to read from an address near the ones that nearby threads read (non-coalesced). It is better to use texture memory when the data is updated rarely but read often, especially when the read access pattern exhibits a spatial locality.
- Shared memory is allocated for all threads in a block. It offers better performance than local or global memory and allows all threads in a block to communicate. Thus it is often used as a buffer to hold intermediate data, or to re-order strided global memory accesses to a coalesced pattern. However, only a limited size of shared memory can be allocated per block. Typically one configures the number of threads per block according to shared memory size. The shared memory is accessed by many threads, so that it is divided into banks. Since each bank can serve only one address per cycle, multiple simultaneous accesses to a bank result in a bank conflict. If all threads of a half-warp access a different bank (no bank conflict), the shared memory may become as fast as the registers.

4 Our Contribution: A CUDA Polynomial Arithmetic Library

In this section we explain how the basic polynomial arithmetic operations, such as multiplication, addition and polynomial modular reduction are implemented efficiently on CUDA GPUs. Our design is optimized for the device NVIDIA Geforce GTX 680, one of the Kepler architecture GPUs. It has 1536 CUDA cores, 2 GB memory, 64 KB constant memory, 48 KB shared memory per block, CUDA Capability 3.0 and warp size of 32. On a device with better specifications, the program is believed to provide a better performance, yet has room to improve if configured and customized for the device.

4.1 Overview

Interfacing with NTL. We build our library to interface with the NTL library by Shoup [31]. Most implementations of polynomial based HE schemes are built on NTL. We provide an interface to NTL data types, in particular to the polynomial class ZZX so that GPU acceleration can be achieved with very little modification to a program. Another reason is that we only support very limited types of polynomial operations. Therefore, until non performance critical operations, e.g. a polynomial inversion in a polynomial ring, are implemented we may still utilize the NTL library.

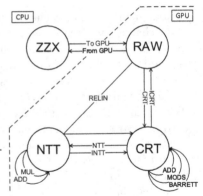

Fig. 2. Four representation domains for polynomials

Table 2. Polynomial representation on a GPU.

Domain	Word type	# of words
RAW	unsigned int 32-bit	$n \lceil \lceil \log q_i \rceil /32 \rceil$
CRT	unsigned int 32-bit	nt_i
NTT	unsigned int 64-bit	nt_i

Polynomial Representation. Suppose we work within the i-th level of a circuit. To store an n-degree polynomial in R_{q_i} in GPU memory, we use an array of $n \lceil \lceil \log q_i \rceil /32 \rceil$ 32-bit unsigned integers, where every $\lceil \lceil \log q_i \rceil /32 \rceil$ integers denote a polynomial coefficient. We call a polynomial of this form in RAW domain. In the background section, we introduced two techniques: CRT and NTT, which give a polynomial CRT and NTT domain representations. Table 2 lists the structure and storage size of a polynomial in each domain. Figure 2 illustrates basic routines of operations on polynomials. Due to mathematical properties, each domain supports certain operations more efficiently as shown in Fig. 2. In other words, to perform a certain operation, the polynomial should first be converted to a specific domain unless it is already in the desired domain. As shown in Table 2, the CRT domain representation requires more space than the RAW domain. However, having polynomials stay in the CRT domain saves one CRT conversion in every polynomial operation and one ICRT conversion in every operations except relinearization. Moreover, the sequence of operations might also create unnecessary latency if there are conversions that could have been spared.

4.2 CRT/ICRT

CRT prime numbers are precomputed based on the application settings and are stored in constant memory. ICRT conversion for a coefficient x is $x = \sum_{j=0}^{t_i-1} \frac{q_i}{p_j} \cdot ((\frac{q_i}{p_j})^{-1} \cdot x_{(j)} \pmod{p_j}) \pmod{q_i}$ where $q_i = \prod_{j=0}^{t_i-1} p_j$. To efficiently compute ICRT, constants: q_i, $\{\frac{q_i}{p_j}\}$ and $\{(\frac{q_i}{p_j})^{-1} \pmod{p_j}\}$, where $j \in \mathbb{Z}_{t_i}$, are also precomputed and stored in constant memory. Given the coefficients of a RAW domain polynomial $[a_0, \ldots, a_{n-1}]$, the number of 32-bit unsigned integers we use to represent each coefficient $a_k \in \mathbb{Z}_{q_i}$ is $|a_k| = n \lceil \lceil \log q_i \rceil /32 \rceil$. Its CRT domain representation is $\{[a_{0(j)}, \ldots, a_{n-1(j)}] \mid j \in \mathbb{Z}_{t_i}\}$. A straightforward CRT_kernel design is to have every thread handle the CRT of one coefficient a_k, as in Fig. 3a. However, that exhibits strided global memory access. Instead, we use shared memory to build a

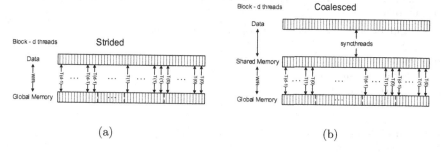

Fig. 3. Using shared memory to avoid strided access to global memory.

buffer as in Fig. 3b. Not only do we reorder all accesses to global memory as coalesced, but also we avoid bank conflicts when reading or writing to shared memory. The ICRT_kernel operation is designed similarly. Moreover, we make wide use of registers in ICRT_kernel with assembly code for a better performance.

4.3 NTT/INTT

NTT is performed on a polynomial in R_{p_j}. We take an array of $2n$ elements, $A = [a_0, \ldots, a_{n-1}, 0, \ldots, 0]$, which are n coefficients appended with n zeros, as input. We obtain a new array $\hat{A} = [\hat{a}_0, \ldots, \hat{a}_{2n-1}]$ by performing a $2n$-point NTT on A. Given t_i CRT prime numbers, to convert a CRT domain polynomial to NTT domain, we need t_i NTTs. We follow the approach of Dai et al. [9] to build an NTT scheme on GPU. According to FHE scheme settings, we only support NTTs of 16384, 32768 and 65536 points. Let $N = 2n$ be the size of NTT. We construct three CUDA kernels to adopt the four-step Cooley-Tukey algorithm [8]. As shown in Algorithm 1, an N-point NTT is computed with several smaller size NTTs. What is not shown in Algorithm 1 is that a 64-point NTT is computed with 8-point NTTs. In [17] the benefit of working in finite field $\mathbb{F}_P$ is demonstrated where $P = \text{0xFFFFFFFF00000001}$. In such a field, modulo P operations may be computed efficiently. Besides, 8 is a 64-th primitive root of P. By using $\langle 8 \rangle \subset \mathbb{F}_P$, 64-point NTTs can be done with shifts rather than requiring 64-bit by 64-bit multiplications. We build inline device functions for arithmetic operations in $\mathbb{F}_P$ in assembly code. In kernels we use shared memory to store those points. That ensures coalesced global memory accesses and fast transpose computation. We precompute $2N$ twiddle factors and bind them to texture memory since they are constant and are too large for constant memory. INTT is basically an NTT with extra steps. Given $\hat{A} = [\hat{a}_0, \ldots, \hat{a}_{2n-1}]$, we first re-order the array as $\hat{A}' = [\hat{a}_0, \hat{a}_{2n-1}, \hat{a}_{2n-2}, \ldots, \hat{a}_1]$. Then we compute $A = \frac{1}{N}\text{NTT}(\hat{A}') \pmod{p_j}$.

Algorithm 1. N-point NTT

1: N samples: 4096 rows (consecutive) by $N/4096$ columns
2: **for** $N/4096$ columns **do**   ▷ 1st kernel
3:     4096 samples: 64 rows by 64 columns
4:     **for** 64 columns **do**
5:         64-point NTT
6:     **end for**
7:     Transpose
8:     Multiply twiddle factors of 4096-point NTT
9:     **for** 64 columns **do**   ▷ 2nd kernel
10:         64-point NTT
11:     **end for**
12: **end for**
13: Transpose
14: Multiply twiddle factors of N-point NTT
15: **for** 4096 columns **do**   ▷ 3rd kernel
16:     $N/4096$-point NTT
17: **end for**

Algorithm 2. Polynomial Multiplication

1: Input NTT domain polynomials $\hat{\mathcal{F}}$ and $\hat{\mathcal{G}}$
2: $\hat{\mathcal{H}} = \hat{\mathcal{F}} \cdot \hat{\mathcal{G}}$ ▷ coefficient-wise multiplication
3: $\mathcal{H} \leftarrow \mathsf{INTT}(\hat{\mathcal{H}})$ ▷ convert to CRT domain
4: Output $\mathcal{H} \pmod{M}$ ▷ polynomial modular reduction

---

4.4 Polynomial Multiplication

Polynomial multiplication takes NTT domain inputs or first converts inputs to NTT domain. Algorithm 2 shows the four steps needed to compute a multiplication. The coefficient-wise multiplication DOTMUL has high parallelism, which is very suitable for GPU computing. Compared to NTTs and INTTs, DOTMUL is almost negligible in terms of overhead. Since the product is a $(2n - 2)$-degree polynomial in CRT domain, it is followed by modular reductions over R_{p_j}, for all $j \in \mathbb{Z}_t$.

4.5 Polynomial Addition

Polynomial addition is essential for two functions in homomorphic circuit evaluation. One is in the homomorphic evaluation of an XOR gate which is simply implemented as a polynomial addition. For this the addition operation is carried out in the CRT domain. It provides sufficient parallelism for a GPU to process and also yields a result in the ring R_{q_i} without the need of coefficient modular reduction. The other computation that needs polynomial addition is in the accumulation part of relinearization. We will discuss this in detail later.

Algorithm 3. Polynomial Barrett Reduction

1: **procedure** PRECOMPUTATION(m)
2:     $u = \lfloor x^{2n-1}/m \rfloor$
3:     Store $\mathcal{M} = \mathsf{CRT}(m)$
4:     Store $\hat{\mathcal{M}} = \mathsf{NTT}(\mathcal{M})$
5:     Store $\hat{\mathcal{U}} = \mathsf{NTT}(CRT(u))$
6: **end procedure**
7: **procedure** BARRETTREDUCTION($\mathcal{F}$)
8:     $\mathcal{Q} = \mathsf{trunc}(\mathcal{F},\ n-1)$ ▷ input in CRT domain
9:     $\hat{\mathcal{Q}} = \mathsf{NTT}(\mathcal{Q})$ ▷ 1st multiplication
10:     $\hat{\mathcal{Q}} = \hat{\mathcal{Q}} * \hat{\mathcal{U}}$
11:     $\mathcal{Q} = \mathsf{INTT}(\hat{\mathcal{Q}})$
12:     $\mathcal{Q} = \mathsf{trunc}(\mathcal{Q},\ n)$
13:     $\hat{\mathcal{Q}} = \mathsf{NTT}(\mathcal{Q})$ ▷ 2nd multiplication
14:     $\hat{\mathcal{Q}} = \hat{\mathcal{Q}} * \hat{\mathcal{M}}$
15:     $\mathcal{Q} = \mathsf{INTT}(\hat{\mathcal{Q}})$
16:     $\mathcal{R} = \mathcal{F} - \mathcal{Q}$ ▷ subtraction
17:     **if** $\deg \mathcal{R} \geqslant \deg \mathcal{M}$ **then**
18:         $\mathcal{R} = \mathcal{R} - \mathcal{M}$
19:     **end if**
20:     Return $\mathcal{R}$ ▷ output in CRT domain
21: **end procedure**

4.6 Polynomial Barrett Reduction

Polynomial computation is in ring $R_{q_i} = \mathbb{Z}_{q_i}/m$, where $\deg m = n$. Given a computation result f with $\deg f \geqslant n$, a polynomial reduction modulo m is needed. In fact, $\deg f \leqslant 2n - 2$ always holds in our construction. We implement a customized Barrett reduction on polynomials by using our polynomial multiplication schemes as in Algorithm 3. We precomputed all constant polynomials generated from the modulus, and stored them in the GPU memory as described in the procedure "Precomputation". The goal of Barrett reduction is to compute $r = f \pmod{m}$. We take the CRT domain polynomial as input and return CRT domain polynomial as output.

4.7 Supporting HE Operations

To evaluate a leveled circuit, besides operations introduced above, we need other processes to reduce the introduced noise, e.g. by multiplication. An AND gate is followed by a relinearization. All ciphertexts are processed with modulus switching to be ready for next level. In our implementation Keygen is modified for a faster relinearization and parameters are selected to accommodate our GPU implementation.

Relinearization. A relinearization computes products of ciphertexts and evaluation keys. It then accumulates the products. By operating additions in the NTT domain we reduce the overhead of INTT in each multiplication. Given

---

Algorithm 4. Modulus Switching

1: $\mathcal{A} = \{a_{(0)}, \ldots, a_{(t_i-1)}\} \leftarrow \mathsf{CRT}(a^{(i)})$
2: **for** $k \leftarrow 1$, **do**
3: $\quad a^* \leftarrow a_{(t_i-k)}$
4: $\quad$ **if** $a^* = 1 \pmod 2$ **then**
5: $\quad\quad$ **if** $a^* > (p_{t_i-k} - 1)/2$ **then**
6: $\quad\quad\quad a^* = a^* - p_{t_i-k}$
7: $\quad\quad$ **else**
8: $\quad\quad\quad a^* = a^* + p_{t_i-k}$
9: $\quad\quad$ **end if**
10: $\quad$ **end if**
11: $\quad \mathcal{A} = (\mathcal{A} - a^*)/p_{t_i-k} \pmod{p_{t_i-k}}$
12: **end for**
13: $a^{(i+1)} = \mathsf{ICRT}(\mathcal{A}) = \mathsf{ICRT}(\{a_{(0)}, \ldots, a_{(t_{i+1}-1)}\})$

---

a polynomial $c^{(i)}$ in RAW domain we first expand it to $\tilde{c}_\tau^{(i)}$ where $\tau \in \mathbb{Z}_{\eta_i}$ and $\eta_i = \lceil \lceil \log q_i \rceil / w \rceil$. We call w the size of relinearization window. Then we need to compute $\tilde{c}^{(i+1)} = \sum_{\tau=0}^{\eta_i} ek_\tau^{(i)} \tilde{c}_\tau^{(i)}$ in R_{q_i} which is equivalent to computing $\tilde{\mathcal{C}}^{(i+1)} = \mathsf{INTT}\left(\sum_{\tau=0}^{\eta_i} \hat{\mathcal{E}K}_\tau^{(i)} \hat{\tilde{\mathcal{C}}}^{(i)}\right)$. We find a way to precompute and store evaluation keys for all levels. In Keygen, we convert evaluation keys of the 0-th level to NTT domain and store them. For every $\tau \in \mathbb{Z}_{\eta_0}$ compute $ek_\tau^{(0)} \xrightarrow{CRT} \mathcal{E}K_\tau^{(0)} \xrightarrow{NTT} \hat{\mathcal{E}K}_\tau^{(0)}$. Then $\{\hat{\mathcal{E}K}_\tau^{(0)} \mid \tau \in \mathbb{Z}_{\eta_0}\}$ is stored in GPU global memory. We no longer need to update the evaluation keys for any other level, observing that $\hat{\mathcal{E}K}_\tau^{(i)} \subseteq \hat{\mathcal{E}K}_\tau^{(0)}$, for all $i \in \mathbb{Z}_d$ and $\tau \in \mathbb{Z}_{\eta_i}$. Here what matters the most is the overhead of expanding and converting the ciphertexts. To convert $\tilde{c}_\tau^{(i)}$ to $\hat{\tilde{\mathcal{C}}}_\tau^{(i)}$ for all $\tau \in \mathbb{Z}_{\eta_i}$, we need η_i CRTs and $\eta_i t_i$ NTTs. However, if we set $w < \log p_j$, then for all $j \in \mathbb{Z}_{t_0}$ we have $\tilde{c}_\tau^{(i)} \in R_{2^w} \subset R_{p_j}$, i.e. $\tilde{\mathcal{C}}_\tau^{(i)} = \{\tilde{c}_\tau^{(i)}\}$. In such a setting, we only need η_i NTTs to convert $\tilde{c}_\tau^{(i)}$ to the NTT domain.

Based on these optimizations, we build a *multiplier and accumulator* for NTT domain polynomials. Suppose we have sufficient memory on GPU to hold all $\hat{\mathcal{E}K}_\tau^{(0)}$. Only one kernel that uses the shared memory to load all $\hat{\tilde{\mathcal{C}}}_\tau^{(i)}$ will suffice. We also provide solutions when the evaluation keys are too large for the GPU memory to hold. On a multi-GPU system, we evenly distribute the keys on devices. When the keys on another device are requested, copy them from that device to the current device. This is the best solution for two reasons: the bandwidth between devices is much larger than that between the device and host; accesses to memory on another device in a kernel yield roughly 3 times less overhead, compared to accessing the current device's memory.

Double-CRT Setting. According to [12], to correctly evaluate a circuit of depth d and to reach a desired security level, we can determine the lower bounds of n and $\log q_0$, and that $\delta_q \leqslant \log \frac{q_i}{q_{i+1}} = \prod_{j=t_i}^{t_i-1} p_j$ where $i \in \mathbb{Z}_d$. Let B_p be the size of CRT prime numbers, i.e. $B_p = \log p_j$. Then we know that $2^{B_p} < \sqrt{P/n} < 2^{32}$.

To simplify, we set $t_i = d - i - 1$, $B_p \geqslant \delta_q$. Then we have $\delta_q \leqslant B_p < \log \sqrt{P/n}$. We select $B_p = \delta_q$. Then we select the relinearization window size such as $w < B_p$. In these settings, we reach the desired security level with minimal computation.

Modulus Switching. In [21] Gentry et al. proposed a method to perform modulus switching on ciphertexts in CRT domain (double-CRT), by generating $q_i = p_0 p_1 \cdots p_{t_i - 1}$ where $i \in \mathbb{Z}_d$. Since modulus switching is a coefficient independent operation, to simplify, we represent it on a single coefficient. Given a coefficient $a^{(i)} \in \mathbb{Z}_{q_i}$ where $i \in \mathbb{Z}_d$, modulus switching is designed as in Algorithm 4 to obtain $a^{(i+1)} \in \mathbb{Z}_{q_{i+1}}$ such that $a^{(i+1)} = a^{(i)} \pmod 2$ and $\epsilon = |a^{(i+1)} - \frac{q_{i+1}}{q_i} a^{(i)}|$ where $-1 \leqslant \epsilon \leqslant 1$ always holds. We precompute $p_j^{-1} \pmod{p_k}$ for all $k \in \mathbb{Z}_{t_0} \setminus \mathbb{Z}_{t_{d-1}}$ and $j \in \mathbb{Z}_k$. These values are stored as a lookup table in constant memory.

Table 3. Precomputation

Item	Memory type	Size (Bytes)			
		Equation	Prince	Sorting(8)	Sorting(32)
$\mathcal{P}$	constant	$4d$	100	52	60
q_i	constant	$4\lceil (d-i)B_p/32 \rceil$	$\leqslant 80$	$\leqslant 36$	$\leqslant 44$
$\mathcal{Q}_i^*$	constant	$4(d-i)\lceil (d-i-1)B_p/32 \rceil$	$\leqslant 1,900$	$\leqslant 416$	$\leqslant 600$
$\mathcal{Q}_i^\dagger$	constant	$4(d-i)$	$\leqslant 100$	$\leqslant 52$	$\leqslant 60$
$\mathcal{P}^{-1}$	constant	$2d(d-1)$	$1,200$	312	420
$\mathcal{M}$	texture	$4dn$	$1,638,400$	$425,984$	$491,520$
$\hat{\mathcal{M}}$	texture	$16dn$	$6,553,600$	$1,703,936$	$1,966,080$
$\hat{\mathcal{U}}$	texture	$16dn$	$6,553,600$	$1,703,936$	$1,966,080$
$\hat{\mathcal{EK}}_\tau^{(i)}$	global	$16dn\lceil dB_p/w \rceil$	$262,144,000$	$28,966,912$	$41,287,680$

Precomputation Routine. For a circuit with depth d, we select parameters with a sequence of constraints: $d \to n \to \delta_q \to B_p \to w$. We generate a set of d prime numbers with B_p bits $\mathcal{P} = \{p_0, \ldots, p_{d-1}\}$ as CRT constants. For each level $i \in \mathbb{Z}_d$ of the circuit we generate ICRT constants: $q_i = \prod_{j=0}^{i-1} p_j$, $\mathcal{Q}_i^* = \{\frac{q_i}{p_j} \mid j \in \mathbb{Z}_i\}$ and $\mathcal{Q}_i^\dagger = \{(\frac{q_i}{p_j})^{-1} \pmod{p_j} \mid j \in \mathbb{Z}_i\}$. We also generate Modulus Switching constants for all levels: $\mathcal{P}^{-1} = \{p_{j,k}^{-1} = p_k^{-1} \pmod{p_j} \mid j \in \mathbb{Z}_i \setminus \{0\}, k \in \mathbb{Z}_j\}$. $\mathcal{P}$ and $\mathcal{P}^{-1}$ are stored in GPU constant memory. However, we store $\mathcal{Q} = \{q_i \mid i \in \mathbb{Z}_d\}$, $\mathcal{Q}^* = \{\mathcal{Q}_i^* \mid i \in \mathbb{Z}_d\}$ and $\mathcal{Q}^\dagger = \{\mathcal{Q}_i^\dagger \mid i \in \mathbb{Z}_d\}$ in CPU memory at first. We update ICRT constants for ICRT conversions in a new level by copying q_i, $\mathcal{Q}_i^*$ and $\mathcal{Q}_i^\dagger$ to GPU constant memory. We generate an n degree monic polynomial m as polynomial modulus and compute $u = x^{2n-1}/m \in R_{q_0}$ for Barrett reduction. Their CRT and NTT domain representations $\mathcal{M}$, $\hat{\mathcal{M}}$ and $\hat{\mathcal{U}}$ are computed and bound to GPU texture memory. Table 3 is a summary of precomputed data, showing storage memory types and sizes. Besides general expressions of size in bytes, we also list the memory usage of three target circuits: Prince stands for the Prince block cipher that has $[d = 25,\ n = 16384,\ B_p = 25,\ w = 16]$. Sorting(8) is a sorting circuit of 8 unsigned 32-bit integers, with parameters set to $[13,\ 8192,\ 20,\ 16]$. Similarly, Sorting(32) sorts 32 unsigned integers and has parameters $[15,\ 8192,\ 22,\ 16]$.

Keygen. As explained in background, for all levels, we generate secret keys $sk^{(i)}$ and public keys $pk^{(i)}$. Based on those, we compute $ek_{\tau^{(i)}}$ as evaluation keys. We then convert and store their NTT domain representations $\mathcal{EK}_{\tau^{(i)}}$ in GPU memory.

5   Implementation Results

We implemented the proposed algorithms on two target GPU platforms: NVIDIA GeForce GTX770 and GTX690. Note that the GTX690 consists of two GTX680 GPUs. We programmed the GTX690 in both single GPU, i.e. GTX 680, and in multi-GPU modes. The testing environment is summarized in Table 4. We show performance of our library and compare it to CPU implementations using the NTL library (v9.2.0) which is adopted by DHS-HE [12] and HELib [24].

Table 4. Testing Environment

Item	Specification	Item	Specification
CPU	Intel core i7-3770K	GPU	NVIDIA GeForce GTX690
# of cores	4	# of cores	1536×2
# of threads	8	GPU core freq	1020 MHz
CPU freq	3.50 GHz	GPU memory	$2\,\text{GB} \times 2$
Cache	8 MB	GPU	NVIDIA GeForce GTX770
System memory	32 GB DDR3	# of cores	1536
NTL	9.2.0	GPU core freq	1163 MHz
GMP	6.0.0a	GPU memory	2 GB

5.1   Performance of GPU Library Primitives

Table 5 shows the latency of the basic polynomial operations. MULADD stands for the *multiplier and accumulator* for NTT domain polynomials. ADD denotes polynomial addition in CRT domain. The latencies in the table of NTT conversions, whose speed is solely affected by n, consist of d iterations. Figure 4a shows the performance of relinearization. Doröz et al. [12] use the NTL library with an optimized polynomial reduction method. As shown in Fig. 4b, the speedup is at least 20 times, and increases as the coefficient size increases, up to 160 times for

Table 5. Performance of basic operations on polynomials (d, n, dB_p) where $B_p = 24$

Functions	Latency (ms)		
	(15, 8192, 360)	(25, 16384, 600)	(40, 32768, 960)
CRT / ICRT	0.70 / 0.54	4.00 / 3.73	21.31 / 17.94
NTT / INTT	0.84 / 0.98	1.78 / 2.09	6.24 / 6.86
MULADD	0.06	0.11	0.19
BARRETT	5.10	10.00	32.63
ADD	0.10	0.67	0.92

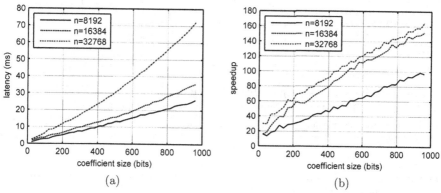

(a)   (b)

Fig. 4. Performance of relinearization (a) latency with growing coefficient size (b) speedup over [12]

960 bit coefficients. Note that Dai et al. [9] did not fully implement relinearization on the GPU but rather relies on NTL/CPU for coefficient and polynomial
reduction. For instance, for Prince parameters with coefficient size of 575 bits,
our relinearization takes only 18.3 ms whereas Dai et al.'s takes 890 ms on GPU
plus an additional 363 ms for reduction on the CPU. This yields a speedup of
68 times.

5.2 Performance of Sample Algorithms

To demonstrate the performance gain obtained by the cuHE library we implemented the Prince block cipher, and homomorphic sorting algorithms with array
sizes $4, 8, 16, 32$. The homomorphic evaluation performance is summarized in
Table 6. We updated and reran Doröz et al.'s homomorphic Prince [14] with a
16-bit relinearization window. With cuHE library, we achieve 40 times speedup
on a single GPU, 135 times on three GPUs simultaneously, over the Doröz et al.
CPU implementation. Also compared to Dai et al.'s [9] the speedup is 25 times
on the same GPU device.

Finally we would like to note that the proposed Prince implementation is
the *fastest homomorphic block cipher implementation* currently available. For

Table 6. Performance of Implemented Algorithms ("1/1024" means this is an amortized performance achieved by computing 1024 operands simultaneously, so does "1/630"; "×" marks the speedup achieved)

Platform	Prince		Sorting 8		Sorting 16		Sorting 32	
	1/1024	×	1/630	×	1/630	×	1/630	×
CPU (1-bit) [14]	3.3 s	1	n/a	n/a	n/a	n/a	n/a	n/a
GTX 680 (1-bit) [9]	1.28 s	2.6	n/a	n/a	n/a	n/a	n/a	n/a
CPU (16-bit) [5,14]	1.98 s	1.7	944 ms	1	4.28 s	1	18.60 s	1
GTX 680 (1 GPU)	51 ms	64	62 ms	15	291 ms	15	1.52 s	12
GTX 770 (1 GPU)	45 ms	72	55 ms	17	256 ms	17	1.35 s	14
GTX 690 (2 GPUs)	32 ms	103	34 ms	27	162 ms	26	864 ms	22
GTX 690/770 (3 GPUs)	24 ms	134	23 ms	41	108 ms	39	678 ms	27

instance, Lepoint and Naehrig evaluated homomorphic SIMON-64/128 in 2.04 s with 4 cores on Intel Core i7-2600 at 3.4 GHz [27] for the $n = 32,768$ setting. Our homomorphic Prince is 40 times faster for $n = 16,384$, and 20 times for $n = 32,768$.

Acknowledgment. Funding for this research was in part provided by the US National Science Foundation CNS Award #1319130.

References

1. Bos, J.W., Lauter, K., Naehrig, M.: Private predictive analysis on encrypted medical data. J. Biomed. Inf. **50**, 234–243 (2014)
2. Brakerski, Z., Gentry, C., Vaikuntanathan, V.: (leveled) fully homomorphic encryption without bootstrapping. In: Proceedings of the 3rd Innovations in Theoretical Computer Science Conference, pp. 309–325. ACM (2012)
3. Vaikuntanathan, V., Brakerski, Z.: Fully homomorphic encryption from ring-LWE and security for key dependent messages. In: Rogaway, P. (ed.) CRYPTO 2011. LNCS, vol. 6841, pp. 505–524. Springer, Heidelberg (2011)
4. Brakerski, Z., Vaikuntanathan, V.: Efficient fully homomorphic encryption from (standard) LWE. SIAM J. Comput. **43**(2), 831–871 (2014)
5. Sunar, B., Savaş, E., Çetin, G.S., Doröz, Y.: Depth optimized efficient homomorphic sorting. In: Lauter, K., Rodríguez-Henríquez, F. (eds.) LatinCrypt 2015. LNCS, vol. 9230, pp. 61–80. Springer, Heidelberg (2015)
6. Sengupta, I., Kaushal, M., Chatterjee, A.: Accelerating sorting of fully homomorphic encrypted data. In: Paul, G., Vaudenay, S. (eds.) INDOCRYPT 2013. LNCS, vol. 8250, pp. 262–273. Springer, Heidelberg (2013)
7. Cheon, J.H., Kim, M., Lauter, K.: Homomorphic computation of edit distance. In: Brenner, M., Christin, N., Johnson, B., Rohloff, K. (eds.) FC 2015 Workshops. LNCS, vol. 8976, pp. 194–212. Springer, Heidelberg (2015)
8. Cooley, J.W., Tukey, J.W.: An algorithm for the machine calculation of complex fourier series. Math. Comput. **19**(90), 297–301 (1965)

9. Dai, W., Doröz, Y., Sunar, B.: Accelerating NTRU based homomorphic encryption using GPUs. In: 2014 IEEE High Performance Extreme Computing Conference (HPEC), pp. 1–6 (2014)

10. Dai, W., Doröz, Y., Sunar, B.: Accelerating SWHE based PIRs using GPUs. In: Brenner, M., Christin, N., Johnson, B., Rohloff, K. (eds.) FC 2015 Workshops. LNCS, vol. 8976, pp. 160–171. Springer, Heidelberg (2015)

11. van Dijk, M., Gentry, C., Vaikuntanathan, V., Halevi, S.: Fully homomorphic encryption over the integers. In: Gilbert, H. (ed.) EUROCRYPT 2010. LNCS, vol. 6110, pp. 24–43. Springer, Heidelberg (2010)

12. Doröz, Y., Hu, Y., Sunar, B.: Homomorphic AES evaluation using the modified LTV scheme. In: Designs, Codes and Cryptography, pp. 1–26 (2015)

13. Sunar, B., Doröz, Y., Savaş, E., Öztürk, E.: Accelerating LTV based homomorphic encryption in reconfigurable hardware. In: Güneysu, T., Handschuh, H. (eds.) CHES 2015. LNCS, vol. 9293, pp. 185–204. Springer, Heidelberg (2015)

14. Shahverdi, A., Sunar, B., Eisenbarth, T., Doröz, Y.: Toward practical homomorphic evaluation of block ciphers using prince. In: Böhme, R., Brenner, M., Moore, T., Smith, M. (eds.) FC 2014 Workshops. LNCS, vol. 8438, pp. 208–220. Springer, Heidelberg (2014)

15. Doröz, Y., Sunar, B., Hammouri, G.: Bandwidth efficient PIR from NTRU. In: Böhme, R., Brenner, M., Moore, T., Smith, M. (eds.) FC 2014 Workshops. LNCS, vol. 8438, pp. 195–207. Springer, Heidelberg (2014)

16. Ducas, L., Micciancio, D.: FHEW: bootstrapping homomorphic encryption in less than a second. In: Oswald, E., Fischlin, M. (eds.) EUROCRYPT 2015. LNCS, vol. 9056, pp. 617–640. Springer, Heidelberg (2015)

17. Emmart, N., Weems, C.C.: High precision integer multiplication with a GPU using Strassen's algorithm with multiple FFT sizes. Parallel Process. Lett. **21**(03), 359–375 (2011)

18. Gentry, C.: A Fully Homomorphic Encryption Scheme. Ph.D. thesis, Stanford University (2009)

19. Gentry, C.: Fully homomorphic encryption using ideal lattices. In: Proceedings of the Forty-First Annual ACM Symposium on Theory of Computing, STOC 2009, pp. 169–178. ACM (2009)

20. Gentry, C., Halevi, S.: Fully homomorphic encryption without squashing using depth-3 arithmetic circuits. In: 2011 IEEE 52nd Annual Symposium on Foundations of Computer Science (FOCS), pp. 107–109 (2011)

21. Gentry, C., Halevi, S., Smart, N.P.: Homomorphic evaluation of the AES circuit (updated implementation). Technical report, IACR Cryptology ePrint Archive: Report 2012/099 (2015). https://eprint.iacr.org/2012/099.pdf

22. Lauter, K., Naehrig, M., Graepel, T.: ML confidential: machine learning on encrypted data. In: Kwon, T., Lee, M.-K., Kwon, D. (eds.) ICISC 2012. LNCS, vol. 7839, pp. 1–21. Springer, Heidelberg (2013)

23. Halevi, S., Shoup, V.: Design and implementation of a homomorphic-encryption library. Technical report, IBM Technical Report (2013)

24. Halevi, S., Shoup, V.: HElib - an implementation of homomorphic encryption (2014). https://github.com/shaih/HElib

25. Hoffstein, J., Pipher, J., Silverman, J.H.: NTRU: a ring-based public key cryptosystem. In: Buhler, J.P. (ed.) ANTS 1998. LNCS, vol. 1423, pp. 267–288. Springer, Heidelberg (1998)

26. Lauter, K., Naehrig, M., López-Alt, A.: Private computation on encrypted genomic data. In: Aranha, D.F., Menezes, A. (eds.) LATINCRYPT 2014. LNCS, vol. 8895, pp. 3–27. Springer, Heidelberg (2015)

27. Lepoint, T., Naehrig, M.: A comparison of the homomorphic encryption schemes FV and YASHE. In: Pointcheval, D., Vergnaud, D. (eds.) AFRICACRYPT. LNCS, vol. 8469, pp. 318–335. Springer, Heidelberg (2014)

28. López-Alt, A., Tromer, E., Vaikuntanathan, V.: On-the-fly multiparty computation on the cloud via multikey fully homomorphic encryption. In: Proceedings of the Forty-Fourth Annual ACM Symposium on Theory of Computing, STOC 2012, pp. 1219–1234. ACM (2012)

29. Naehrig, M., Lauter, K., Vaikuntanathan, V.: Can homomorphic encryption be practical? In: Proceedings of the 3rd ACM Workshop on Cloud Computing Security Workshop, CCSW 2011, pp. 113–124. ACM (2011)

30. Schönhage, D.D.A., Strassen, V.: Schnelle multiplikation grosser zahlen. Computing 7(3–4), 281–292 (1971)

31. Shoup, V.: NTL: A library for doing number theory (2001). http://www.shoup.net/ntl/

32. Smart, N.P., Vercauteren, F.: Fully homomorphic encryption with relatively small key and ciphertext sizes. In: Nguyen, P.Q., Pointcheval, D. (eds.) PKC 2010. LNCS, vol. 6056, pp. 420–443. Springer, Heidelberg (2010)

33. Smart, N.P., Vercauteren, F.: Fully homomorphic SIMD operations. Des. Codes Crypt. 71(1), 57–81 (2014)

34. Stehlée, D., Steinfeld, R.: Making NTRU as secure as worst-case problems overideal lattices. In: Paterson, K.G. (ed.) EUROCRYPT 2011. LNCS, vol. 6632, pp. 27–47. Springer, Heidelberg (2011)

35. Wang, W., Hu, Y., Chen, L., Huang, X., Sunar, B.: Accelerating fully homomorphic encryption using GPU. In: 2012 IEEE Conference on High Performance Extreme Computing (HPEC), pp. 1–5 (2012)

Extended Functionality in Verifiable Searchable Encryption

James Alderman, Christian Janson, Keith M. Martin,
and Sarah Louise Renwick[✉]

Information Security Group, Royal Holloway, University of London,
Egham, Surrey TW20 0EX, UK
{James.Alderman,Keith.Martin}@rhul.ac.uk,
{Christian.Janson.2012,SarahLouise.Renwick.2012}@live.rhul.ac.uk

Abstract. When outsourcing the storage of sensitive data to an (untrusted) remote server, a data owner may choose to encrypt the data beforehand to preserve confidentiality. However, it is then difficult to efficiently retrieve specific portions of the data as the server is unable to identify the relevant information. Searchable encryption well studied as a solution to this problem, allowing data owners and other authorised users to generate search queries which the server may execute over the *encrypted* data to identify relevant data portions.

However, many current schemes lack two important properties: verifiability of search results, and expressive queries. We introduce Extended Verifiable Searchable Encryption (eVSE) that permits a user to verify that search results are correct and complete. We also permit verifiable computational queries over keywords and specific data values, that go beyond the standard keyword matching queries to allow functions such as averaging or counting operations. We formally define the notion of eVSE within relevant security models and give a provably secure instantiation.

1 Introduction

It is now common for data owners to outsource their data to public servers providing storage on a pay-as-you-go basis. This can reduce the costs of data storage compared with that of running a private data center (e.g. hardware, construction, air conditioning and security costs), making this a cost effective solution. If the server is not fully trusted and the data is of a sensitive nature, the data owner may wish to encrypt it to ensure confidentiality. This, however, prevents the efficient retrieval of specific portions of the data as the server is unable to identify the relevant information.

J. Alderman—Supported by the European Commission under project H2020-644024 "CLARUS" and acknowledges support from BAE Systems Advanced Technology Centre.

S.L. Renwick—Supported by Thales UK and EPSRC under a CASE Award.

E. Pasalic and L.R. Knudsen (Eds.): BalkanCryptSec 2015, LNCS 9540, pp. 187–205, 2016.
DOI: 10.1007/978-3-319-29172-7_12

Searchable Encryption (SE) [11,16,19,21,22,24,26,32] addresses this issue by indexing the encrypted data in such a way as to allow a server to execute a search query (formed by the data owner or an authorised data user) over the encrypted data and return the identifiers of any file that satisfies the query.

To preserve confidentiality of the data, the server must not learn anything about the underlying data from the encrypted data and the data indexes; namely *ciphertext indistinguishability* and *index indistinguishability*. In the presence of a search query the only information leaked to the server is the search results. *Query indistinguishability* is also a desirable property although, due to the *offline keyword guessing attack* [12], this is not always easy to achieve in the public key setting (where indexes are generated using the data owner's public key).

The majority of existing work on SE focusses on efficiently preserving confidentiality in the presence of an *honest-but-curious* server. This means that the server is trusted to follow the search protocol honestly but may try to infer information about data or search queries that it is unauthorised to know.

Verifiable Searchable Encryption (VSE) [13,25,30,35,37] assumes a stronger *semi-honest-but-curious* adversarial model in which the server might execute only a fraction of the search, or return a fraction of the search results in order to preserve its resources. To ensure the completeness and correctness of search results in this scenario, it is required that the server is able to prove to the querier that the search was computed honestly.

The current approaches to VSE in the literature do not support a wide range of expressive search queries. We address this issue by extending the types of queries that can be executed and verified by a VSE scheme to include more expressive search queries, as well as some computations. Most VSE schemes in the literature also require that the verification of query results be performed by the entity that issued the query whereas eVSE is publicly and blindly verifiable.

1.1   Our Contributions

We adapt and apply new techniques from the area of Publicly Verifiable Outsourced Computation to VSE in a novel way to enable a wider family of queries, and some types of computations, to be performed over outsourced encrypted data with verifiable query results. In summary, our contributions are:

- More expressive queries: Our scheme supports queries such as boolean formulae involving conjunctions, disjunctions and negations, threshold operations, polynomials, arbitrary CNF and DNF formulae, and fuzzy search[1].
- Evaluation of computations: Our scheme supports the evaluation of some computations over the encrypted data, such as averaging and counting operations. As well as assigning keywords to label data, we propose to also assign keywords representing certain data values that may be computed over (either in the form of single keywords or as a string of keywords encoding binary data, see Sect. 3.3).

---

[1] Depending on the choice of underlying ABE scheme; see Sect. 4.1.

– Blind public verifiability of query results: Any entity is able to verify the correctness and completeness of query results without any knowledge of either the underlying query or the results themselves.

The remainder of this paper is organised as follows. Section 2 gives some background information on SE and verifiable computation. Section 3 formally defines eVSE and its security model, Sect. 4 gives an instantiation of eVSE and Sect. 5 concludes the paper, highlighting possible avenues of future research. The Appendix provides more details on the security models and gives a security proof sketch as well as a discussion comparing our scheme with the ones in the literature. Additional details can be found in the full version [3].

2   Background

Searchable Encryption (SE) allows data to be outsourced in encrypted form and for keyword search queries to be performed remotely. Methods based on oblivious RAM [20] provide a high level of security (hiding both the access and search patterns) at the expense of slow search times and high communication costs. Song et al. [28] achieve a scheme with fewer rounds of communication, but which leaks the access pattern and requires each word of a document to be encrypted separately, so compression is not possible. Goh [19] introduced meta data (indexes) describing the content of each document, and enabled constant time searches using Bloom filters over the index only. Curtmola et al. [16] extended the system model to allow multiple users to query the data, using broadcast encryption to manage user access privileges. SE schemes that allow many users to upload data can be built using public key encryption, however the data can only be searched by the holder of the corresponding secret key (or a derivative thereof) [11]. Most SE schemes assume an honest-but-curious server model.

Verifiable Searchable Encryption (VSE) schemes assume a semi-honest-but-curious server model. The first VSE scheme was presented by Chai et al. [13], where they extend the paradigm of searchable symmetric encryption (SSE) [16] to create a verifiable SSE (VSSE) scheme that allows verification of search results from a single keyword equality query. Another approach by [25] extends a public key encryption with keyword search scheme [11] to support verification of search results from a single keyword equality query, where the indexes are created using a public key. Sun et al. [30] and Wang et al. [34] detail VSE schemes with enhanced functionality; verifiable multi-keyword ranked search and verifiable fuzzy keyword search, respectively.

Verifiable Computation (VC) allows a client with limited resources to efficiently outsource a computation to a more powerful server, and to verify the correctness of results. Gennaro et al. [18] considered the use of garbled circuits, whilst Parno et al. [27] introduced *publicly* verifiable computation (PVC) built from key policy attribute based encryption (KP-ABE), where a single client computes an evaluation key for the server and publishes information enabling other clients to outsource computation to the server. *Any* client may verify the correctness of a result. Alderman et al. [2] considered an alternative system model that used ciphertext policy attribute based encryption (CP-ABE) to allow clients to query computations on data held by the server (or initially outsourced by a client) called *Verifiable Delegable Computation* (VDC). This can naturally be applied to problems like querying on remote data, as well as MapReduce. Data remains statically stored on the server and may be embedded in a server's secret key, whilst the computation of many different functions can be requested by creating ciphertexts using *only* public information. Other notable approaches in the realm of querying remote data can be found in [4–6, 8–10, 15].

3   Extended Verifiable Searchable Encryption

3.1   System Model

We consider a system comprising a *data owner*, a remote storage *server*, and a set of authorised *data users*. The data owner sets up the system to generate a master secret and holds a set of data D (e.g. a database) that they wish to encrypt and outsource to the remote server. The data owner controls which additional users are able to query their encrypted data. Queries may be formulated over these keywords (e.g. to identify records associated with a given set of keywords) as usual in SE, but we also allow *computational queries* of functions in the class NC^1, which consists of Boolean functions computable by circuits of depth $\mathcal{O}(\log n)$ where each gate has a fan-in of two, over encoded data values.

For example consider workgroups within an organisation. The manager or system administrator acts as the data owner for the organisation and outsources a shared database to a remote server. Authorisation is granted by issuing a secret key to each user, which is required when creating a query token QT_Q for a particular query Q. The token is sent to the server who performs the query on the encoded index to generate a result R. We allow *any* entity to verify the correctness and completeness of the result[2], but we restrict the ability to read the value of the result to only authorised data users (holding a retrieval key).

Throughout this work, we assume a strict separation between *queriers* (the data owner and users) and the remote server – the server may not issue queries itself, else it will trivially be able to learn the encoding of the index and queries (legitimate queriers must know this encoding to gain meaningful results).

3.2   Formal Definition

We now formally define a scheme for eVSE. We use the following notation. Data to be outsourced is denoted D and is considered to be a collection of

---

[2] We also permit the server to verify correctness to avoid the rejection problem, where a server may learn some useful information by observing if results are accepted.

n documents. Prior to outsourcing, the data owner specifies a *pre-index* for D, denoted $\delta(D)$, which assigns a set of descriptive labels to each document e.g. keywords contained in the document or specific data values that may be computed upon. The encoded form of the data, including the descriptive labels, is referred to as the *index* of D, denoted $\mathcal{I}_D$, and is stored by the server. Queries for functions in the class NC^1 are denoted by Q and to make such a query, a data user creates a query token QT_Q for Q, a verification key VK_Q which allows *any* entity to blindly verify the result, R, of the query, and a retrieval key RK_Q which is issued to authorised data users to enable the query result to be learnt.

Definition 1. *An* Extended Verifiable Searchable Encryption (eVSE) *scheme comprises the following algorithms:*

- $(\text{MK}, \text{PP}) \xleftarrow{\$} \text{Setup}(1^\kappa, \mathcal{U})$: Run by the data owner and takes as input the security parameter and a universe of attributes (keywords and data values). It outputs the data owner's master secret key MK that is used for further administrative tasks and public parameters PP, both of which are provided to the remaining algorithms where required.
- $(\mathcal{I}_D, st_s, st_o) \xleftarrow{\$} \text{BuildIndex}(\delta(D), G, \text{MK}, \text{PP})$: Run by the data owner and takes as input the pre-index of the data $\delta(D)$ and the set G of authorised users, and outputs a searchable index $\mathcal{I}_D$ for the data D, as well as a server and data owner state.
- $(SK_{\text{ID}}, st_s) \xleftarrow{\$} \text{AddUser}(\text{ID}, G, \text{MK}, \text{PP})$: Run by the data owner to authorise a user ID to perform queries by issuing them a secret key SK_{ID} and outputs an updated server state.
- $(QT_Q, VK_Q, RK_Q) \xleftarrow{\$} \text{Query}(Q, st_s, st_o, SK_{\text{ID}}, \text{PP})$: Run by a data user using its secret key and both states to generate a query token QT_Q for a query Q, a verification key VK_Q and an output retrieval key RK_Q.
- $R \xleftarrow{\$} \text{Search}(\mathcal{I}_D, QT_Q, st_s, SK_S, \text{PP})$: Run by the server to execute a query given in the query token QT_Q on the index $\mathcal{I}_D$. It generates a result R which can be returned to the querying user or published.
- $r \leftarrow \text{Verify}(R, VK_Q, RT_Q, RK_Q, \text{PP})$: Verification consists of two steps:
  1. $RT_Q \leftarrow \text{BVerif}(R, VK_Q, \text{PP})$: Run by *any* party to verify the correctness and completeness of the result R. It takes the verification key VK_Q and, if the result is accepted, it outputs a retrieval token RT_Q which can be used to learn the result. Otherwise a distinguished failure symbol $RT_Q = \perp$ is returned.
  2. $r \leftarrow \text{Retrieve}(VK_Q, RT_Q, RK_Q, \text{PP})$: Run by a data user to read the value of the result. It takes as input the retrieval token RT_Q, the retrieval key RK_Q and the user's secret key. If the user holds a valid retrieval key for Q and the computation was performed correctly, then it returns the actual result $r = Q(\mathcal{I}_D)$, otherwise it returns $r = \perp$.
- $(st_s, st_o) \xleftarrow{\$} \text{RevokeUser}(\text{ID}, G, \text{MK}, \text{PP})$: Run by the data owner using its master secret key to revoke a user's authorisation to make queries and read results. It does so by updating the server and data owner state.

An eVSE is *correct* if there is a negligible probability that verification does not suceed when all algorithms are run honestly. A formal definition can be found in [3].

3.3 Types of Query

We consider a broader range of verifiable queries than many prior schemes. In particular, we consider two main types:

– **Keyword matching queries**: Queries of this type have formed the basis of most prior work in SE. Suppose there exists a universe (dictionary) of keywords. Each encrypted data item is associated with an *index* of one or more keywords to describe the contents. Queries are formed over the same universe of keywords. In this work, we permit Boolean formulae over sets of keywords (e.g. $((a \wedge b) \vee c)$ where a, b, c are keywords). We return an identifier for each file whose associated keywords in the index satisfy this formula. Thus we can perform very expressive search queries over keywords.

– **Computational queries**: Queries of this type are similar to the operations commonly discussed in the context of outsourced computation. We allow statistical queries over keywords (e.g. counting the number of data items that satisfy a keyword matching query), as well as operations over selected data values that have been encoded using additional portions of the keyword universe. It is possible to encode the entire database in such a way as to enable computations over all data fields, but it would usually be more efficient to select a (small) subset of fields that are most useful or most frequently queried. Clearly, keyword matching queries can be seen as a special case of computational queries where the function operator is equality testing.

– **Mixed queries**: Queries of this type combine both the functionalities of the aforementioned query types (e.g. finding the average of data values contained in all documents associated with a particular keyword).

All types of query are performed in a verifiable manner to ensure that results are correct and complete.

3.4 Security Model

We now formalise several notions of security as a series of cryptographic games. The adversary against each notion is modelled as a probabilistic polynomial time (PPT) algorithm $\mathcal{A}$ run by a challenger, with input parameters chosen to represent the knowledge of a real attacker as well as the security parameter κ. The adversary algorithm may maintain state and be multi-stage; we refer to each stage as $\mathcal{A}$ for ease of notation. The notation $\mathcal{A}^{\mathcal{O}}$ denotes the adversary being provided with oracle access to the following algorithms: $\mathsf{BuildIndex}(\cdot, \cdot, \mathrm{MK}, \mathrm{PP})$, $\mathsf{AddUser}(\cdot, \cdot, \mathrm{MK}, \mathrm{PP})$, $\mathsf{Query}(\cdot, \cdot, \cdot, \cdot, \mathrm{PP})$ and $\mathsf{Search}(\cdot, \cdot, \cdot, \cdot, \mathrm{PP})$. We assume that oracle queries are performed in a logical order such that all required information is generated from previous queries. For each game, we define the *advantage* and *security* of $\mathcal{A}$ as:

Game 1. $\mathbf{Exp}_{\mathcal{A}}^{PubVerif}[e\mathcal{VSE}, 1^{\kappa}]$:

1: $(Q, \delta(D^{\star})) \leftarrow \mathcal{A}(1^{\kappa})$
2: $(PP, MK)F \leftarrow \mathsf{Setup}(1^{\kappa}, \mathcal{U})$
3: $G \leftarrow \emptyset$
4: $ID \xleftarrow{\$} \mathsf{Users}$
5: $(SK_{ID}, st_s) \leftarrow \mathsf{AddUser}(ID, G, MK, PP)$
6: $(\mathcal{I}_{D^{\star}}, st_s, st_o) \leftarrow \mathsf{BuildIndex}(\delta(D^{\star}), G, MK, PP)$
7: $(QT_Q, VK_Q, RK_Q) \leftarrow \mathsf{Query}(Q, st_s, st_o, SK_{ID}, PP)$
8: $R^{\star} \leftarrow \mathcal{A}^{\mathcal{O}}(QT_Q, VK_Q, RK_Q, \mathcal{I}_{D^{\star}}, PP)$
9: $RT_Q \leftarrow \mathsf{BVerif}(R^{\star}, VK_Q, PP)$
10: $r \leftarrow \mathsf{Retrieve}(VK_Q, RT_Q, RK_Q, PP)$
11: **if** $(r \neq \perp)$ **and** $(r \neq Q(\mathcal{I}_{D^{\star}}))$ **then return** 1
12: **else return** 0

Definition 2. *The advantage of a PPT adversary $\mathcal{A}$ is defined as follows, where* $\mathbf{X} \in \{PubVerif, IndPriv, QueryPriv\}$:

$$Adv_{\mathcal{A}}^{\mathbf{X}}(e\mathcal{VSE}, 1^{\kappa}) = \Pr[\mathbf{Exp}_{\mathcal{A}}^{\mathbf{X}}[e\mathcal{VSE}, 1^{\kappa}] = 1].$$

An eVSE scheme is secure against Game $\mathbf{X}$ *if for all PPT adversaries $\mathcal{A}$,* $Adv_{\mathcal{A}}^{\mathbf{X}}(e\mathcal{VSE}, 1^{\kappa}) \leq \mathrm{negl}(\kappa)$ *where* negl *is a negligible function.*

Public Verifiability. In Game 1, we capture the notion of *public verifiability* such that a server may not cheat by returning an incorrect result without being detected. This is a selective notion of security where, at the beginning of the game, the adversary chooses the challenge query and pre-index. The challenger then initialises the system, runs AddUser for a randomly chosen ID from the userspace, runs BuildIndex for the challenge pre-index to create the index, and finally runs Query. The adversary is given the resulting parameters, as well as access to the above specified oracle queries, and outputs $R^{\star}$, which it believes to be an incorrect result that will, nevertheless, be accepted by the verifier. The challenger runs the verification steps on this output. The adversary wins if verification succeeds, yet the result is not $Q(\mathcal{I}_{D^{\star}})$.

Index Privacy and Query Privacy. In Appendix A, we provide notions of *index indistinguishability* against a selective chosen keyword attack and *query privacy*, which ensure that no information regarding the keywords is leaked from the index or query tokens respectively.

4   Construction

4.1   Overview

We base our instantiation on a CP-ABE scheme. As shown by Alderman et al. [2], CP-ABE can be used to verifiably request computations to be performed on data held by a server, referred to as VDC. In VDC, a trusted Key

Distribution Center (KDC) initialises the system and issues a CP-ABE decryption key to the server pertaining to the data it holds. We use a similar technique, but have the data owner act as the KDC (so the data need not be revealed to an external KDC, as in VDC). The index for a set of data is a CP-ABE decryption key for a set of attributes encoding the pre-index, and is sent to the server. The method of encoding is described in Sect. 4.2.

We consider the family $\mathcal{B}$ of Boolean functions closed under complement – that is, if $F \in \mathcal{B}$ then $\overline{F}$, where $\overline{F}(x) = F(x) \oplus 1$, is also in $\mathcal{B}$. A function $F : \{0,1\}^n \to \{0,1\}$ is *monotonic* if $x \leqslant y$ implies $F(x) \leqslant F(y)$, where $x = (x_1, \ldots, x_n) \leq y = (y_1, \ldots, y_n)$ if and only if $x_i \leqslant y_i$ for all i. For a monotonic function F, the set $\mathbb{A}_F = \{x : F(x) = 1\}$ defines a monotonic access structure.

A query Q is represented as a Boolean function of keywords and computational data points. If a monotonic CP-ABE scheme is used then queries can be comprised of AND and OR gates (and negation can inefficiently be handled by including both a positively and negatively labelled attribute in the universe and requiring the presence of exactly one of them). A non-monotonic CP-ABE scheme enables queries formed from AND, OR and NOT gates, which is a universal set of gates, and fuzzy CP-ABE enables fuzzy keyword search. We can achieve all functions in the class NC^1, which includes common arithmetic and comparison operators useful in queries. An n-bit result can be formed by performing n Boolean queries, each of which returns the ith bit of the output.

The query token for a Boolean function $Q \in \mathcal{B}$ comprises two CP-ABE ciphertexts for access structures representing Q and $\overline{Q} \in \mathcal{B}$ respectively. To perform the search, the server attempts to decrypt each ciphertext under the secret key (associated with the pre-index) and outputs the result. Each decryption succeeds if and only if the query evaluates to True on the index. Any entity may perform the blind verification operation using the verification key to learn only whether the operation was performed correctly or not. Only entities holding the retrieval token can read the value of the result.

4.2   Data Encoding

Defining the Index. Suppose the data D to be outsourced comprises n documents. We now discuss how to form a *pre-index* $\delta(D)$, which represents the keywords and data fields that may be queried over.

Let $\mathcal{D}$ be a dictionary of keywords that describe the documents. $\mathcal{D}$ alone suffices for keyword matching queries but for computational queries, we also need to be able to encode data values such that they can be input to queries represented as access structures encoding Boolean functions.

For each data field x that may be input to a computational query, let the maximum size of the data value be m_x bits. We define m_x additional attributes $A_{x,1}, A_{x,2}, \ldots, A_{x,m_x}$, and define the universe $\mathcal{C} = \bigcup_{x \in D} \cup_{i=1}^{m_x} A_{x,i}$ to be the union of these attributes over all data fields. Let y be a value stored in the data field x and let the binary representation of y be $y_1, \ldots, y_{m_x}$. We view y as a *characteristic tuple* of an attribute set $A_y \subseteq \mathcal{C}$, where $A_y = \{A_{x,i} : y_i = 1\}$ – we include an attribute for position i in the set if and only if the ith bit of y is 1.

Finally, to enable the index for all n documents to be encoded within a single CP-ABE key (and hence for computations to be performed simultaneously on all documents), and to ensure that the correct index data is used for each query, we must encode a labelling of the document that each attribute pertains to. We define our attribute universe $\mathcal{U}$ for the CP-ABE scheme to be $\mathcal{U} = \{\mathcal{D} \cup \mathcal{C}\} \times [n]$. Thats is, we take n copies of $\mathcal{D}$ and $\mathcal{C}$. Each element of $\{\mathcal{D} \cup \mathcal{C}\}$ describes a particular keyword or data value, and each copy relates to a different document in D - if we index each copy of an attribute $w \in \{\mathcal{D} \cup \mathcal{C}\}$ as $\{w_i\}_{i=1}^n$, then w_i denotes the presence of w in document i. In practice, it may be desirable to use a 'large universe' CP-ABE scheme, wherein arbitrary textual strings are mapped to attributes (group elements), e.g. using a hash function H. Thus, for a keyword or data value w in document i, the attribute could be defined as $\mathsf{H}(w\|i)$.[3]

The pre-index of the data D is a set of attributes $\delta(D) \subseteq \mathcal{U}$. The index that is outsourced will be a CP-ABE key generated over this attribute set.

Hiding the Index. In general, CP-ABE schemes do not hide the attributes within the decryption key. This is usually expected behaviour since CP-ABE is often used to cryptographically enforce access control policies and it is natural to assume that an entity is aware of their access rights.

However, in this setting we are using CP-ABE not to protect objects from unauthorised access, but instead to prove the outcome of a function evaluation. The keys in our setting are formed over attributes encoding the index of outsourced data, as opposed to encoding access rights. Since the server should not learn any information about the data, *including* the index, we must implement a mechanism by which the decryption key hides the associated attributes.

In many CP-ABE schemes, the public parameters comprise an ordered set of group elements [36], each associated with an attribute from the universe; that is, $\forall i \in \mathcal{U}$, choose $t_i \xleftarrow{\$} \mathbb{Z}_p$, then form the encoded attribute set $\{g^{t_i}\}_{i \in \mathcal{U}}$. Thus, given a key (or ciphertext) that comprises g^{t_i}, it is possible, based on the ordering of this set, to determine the attribute $i \in \mathcal{U}$ it relates to. In addition, the attributes may be listed in the clear, and attached to keys and ciphertexts to indicate which group elements should be applied at each point. Clearly, this is unsuitable for our requirement for a hidden index.

To this end, we first apply a random permutation to $\mathcal{U}$ such that the position of the group elements within the ordered set does not reveal the attribute string (unless the permutation is known). We then use a symmetric encryption scheme to encrypt each attribute $x \in \mathcal{U}$ under a key k, and then instantiate the CP-ABE scheme on this universe of *encrypted* attributes. Thus, without knowledge of the key k, the server should be unable to determine the attribute string x. We assume that only the keywords or data items being computed over are considered sensitive, and not the logical makeup of the Boolean function (in terms of gates).

---

[3] In this case, it may be possible to avoid the use of symmetric encryption in our construction by letting the secret k be the key for this cryptographic hash function.

4.3   Formal Details

The data owner initialises the system and encodes the data as an index which is pushed to the server. Each (authorised) user will be issued with a personalised secret key enabling them to form queries. To make a query Q, a user chooses a random message from the message space $\mathcal{M}$ to act as a verification token, and encrypt this using the CP-ABE scheme under the access structure encoding Q. The server attempts to decrypt the ciphertext and recovers the chosen message if and only if $Q(\mathcal{I}_D) = 1$. By the indistinguishability security of the CP-ABE scheme, the server learns nothing about the message if $Q(\mathcal{I}_D) = 0$ since this corresponds to an access structure not being satisfied. Thus, if a server returns the correct message, the user is assured that the query evaluated to 1 on the data. If, however, $Q(\mathcal{I}_D) = 0$, then decryption will return $\perp$. This is insufficient for verification purposes since the server can return $\perp$ to convince a user of a false negative search result. Thus, the user must, in fact, produce two CP-ABE ciphertexts. As above, one corresponds to the function Q, whilst the other corresponds to $\overline{Q}$, the complement query of Q. Hence, the server's key will decrypt *exactly one* ciphertext and the returned message will distinguish whether Q or $\overline{Q}$ was satisfied, and therefore the value of $Q(\mathcal{I}_D)$. A well-formed response (d_0, d_1) from a server, therefore, satisfies the following:

$$(d_0, d_1) = \begin{cases} (m_0, \perp), & \text{if } Q(\mathcal{I}_D) = 1 \\ (\perp, m_1), & \text{if } Q(\mathcal{I}_D) = 0. \end{cases} \tag{1}$$

Public Verifiability is achieved by publishing a token comprising a one-way function g applied to both plaintexts. Any entity can apply g to the server's response and compare with this token to check correctness. To achieve blind verification, a random bit b permutes the order of the ciphertexts. Thus, verifiers that do not know b cannot determine whether a plaintext is associated with Q or $\overline{Q}$.

Our adversarial model allows the adversary (and hence servers in our system) to hold more than one key (for multiple datasets); we must ensure that a key cannot produce a valid looking response to a query on a different index. We achieve this by labelling each pre-index with a label $l(\delta(D))$ and define an attribute for each label. Then, for a pre-index $\delta(D)$, the decryption key is formed over the attribute set $(\delta(D) \cup l(\delta(D)))$. Recall that encoded data stored on the server's side is a collection of n documents, which we label $D_1, \ldots, D_n$. When making a query $Q(\mathcal{I}_D)$, a sub-query Q_i may be formed for each document (e.g. to check if a given keyword is contained in each document). In this case, the encryption algorithm takes the access structure encoding of the conjunction $(D_i \wedge l(\delta(D)))$ for $i \in [n]$. A valid result can only be formed by applying the sub-query to the specified document, which is also labelled by $D_i \in \mathcal{D}$ – decryption succeeds if and only if the function is satisfied *and* the label $l(\delta(D))$ is matched in the key and ciphertext. Note that a key for a different pre-index will not include the correct label. Inputs to the Query algorithm are assumed to be in this form.

Let $\mathcal{CPABE} = $ (ABE.Setup, ABE.KeyGen, ABE.Encrypt, ABE.Decrypt) define a CP-ABE encryption scheme over the universe $\mathcal{U}$. Let $\mathcal{SE} = $ (SE.KeyGen,

SE.Encrypt, SE.Decrypt) be an authenticated symmetric encryption scheme secure [7] in the sense of IND-CPA. Let $\mathcal{BE} = ($BE.KeyGen, BE.Encrypt, BE.Add, BE.Decrypt$)$ be a broadcast encryption scheme that retains IND-CPA security against a coalition of revoked users. Finally, let g be a one-way function and let Π and ϕ be pseudo-random permutations (PRPs) (which pad their inputs if required). Then Algorithms 1–8 define an eVSE scheme for a class of queries $\mathcal{Q}$.

Algorithm 1. $(MK, PP) \leftarrow \mathsf{Setup}(1^\kappa, \mathcal{U})$

1: $mk \leftarrow$ BE.KeyGen(1^κ)
2: $k \leftarrow$ SE.KeyGen(1^κ)
3: **for** $i \in \mathcal{U}$ **do**
4:    $u_i \leftarrow$ SE.Encrypt(i, k)
5: $\mathcal{U}' \leftarrow \{u_i\}_{i \in \mathcal{U}}$
6: $\tilde{\mathcal{U}} \leftarrow \Pi(\mathcal{U}')$
7: $(MSK_{\mathrm{ABE}}, MPK_{\mathrm{ABE}}) \leftarrow$ ABE.Setup$(1^\kappa, \tilde{\mathcal{U}})$
8: $PP \leftarrow (MPK_{\mathrm{ABE}}, \tilde{\mathcal{U}})$
9: $MK \leftarrow (MSK_{\mathrm{ABE}}, mk, k, \Pi)$

Algorithm 2. $(\mathcal{I}_D, st_s, st_o) \leftarrow \mathsf{BuildIndex}(\delta(D), G, MK, PP)$

1: $\mathcal{I}_D \leftarrow$ ABE.KeyGen$((\delta(D) \cup l(\delta(D))), MSK_{\mathrm{ABE}}, MPK_{\mathrm{ABE}})$
2: $j \xleftarrow{\$} \{0,1\}^\kappa$
3: $st_s \leftarrow$ BE.Encrypt(G, j, mk)
4: $st_o \leftarrow j$

Algorithm 3. $(SK_{ID}, st_s) \leftarrow \mathsf{AddUser}(ID, G, MK, PP)$

1: $uk_{ID} \leftarrow$ BE.Add(ID, mk)
2: **if** ID is a user **then** $SK_{\mathrm{ID}} \leftarrow (uk_{\mathrm{ID}}, k, \Pi)$
3: **else** $SK_{\mathrm{ID}} \leftarrow uk_{\mathrm{ID}}$
4: $st_s \leftarrow$ BE.Encrypt$(G \cup \mathrm{ID}, \mathrm{j}, \mathrm{mk})$

Algorithm 4. $(QT_Q, VK_Q, RK_Q) \leftarrow \mathsf{Query}(Q = \{Q_i\}, st_s, st_o, SK_{\mathrm{u}}, PP)$

1: $\widetilde{j} \leftarrow$ BE.Decrypt(st_s, uk_{ID})
2: **if** $(\widetilde{j} \neq st_o)$ **then** return $\perp$
3: **for** $i = 1$ **to** $|Q|$ **do**
4:    $(m_{0_i}, m_{1_i}) \xleftarrow{\$} \mathcal{M} \times \mathcal{M}$
5:    $b_i \xleftarrow{\$} \{0,1\}$
6:    $c_{b_i} \leftarrow$ ABE.Encrypt$(m_{b_i}, Q_i, MPK_{\mathrm{ABE}})$
7:    $c_{1-b_i} \leftarrow$ ABE.Encrypt$(m_{1-b_i}, \overline{Q_i}, MPK_{\mathrm{ABE}})$
8:    $QT_{Q_i} \leftarrow (c_{b_i}, c_{1-b_i})$
9:    $\gamma_i \leftarrow \phi_j(c_{b_i} \| c_{1-b_i})$
10:   $VK_{Q_i} \leftarrow (g(m_{0_i}), g(m_{1_i}))$
11:   $RK_{Q_i} \leftarrow b_i$
12: $QT_Q \leftarrow \{\gamma_i\}, VK_Q \leftarrow \{VK_{Q_i}\}, RK_Q \leftarrow \{RK_{Q_i}\}$

Algorithm 5. $R \leftarrow \mathsf{Search}(\mathcal{I}_D, QT_Q = \{\gamma_i\}, st_s, SK_S, \mathrm{PP})$

1: $\widetilde{j} \leftarrow \mathsf{BE.Decrypt}(st_s, uk_S)$
2: **if** $(\widetilde{j} \neq st_s)$ **then return** $\perp$
3: **for** $i = 1$ **to** $|Q|$ **do**
4:    $(c_{b_i} \| c_{1-b_i}) \leftarrow \phi_{\widetilde{j}}^{-1}(\gamma_i)$
5:    $d_{b_i} \leftarrow \mathsf{ABE.Decrypt}(c_{b_i}, \mathcal{I}_D, MPK_{\mathrm{ABE}})$
6:    $d_{1-b_i} \leftarrow \mathsf{ABE.Decrypt}(c_{1-b_i}, \mathcal{I}_D, MPK_{\mathrm{ABE}})$
7:    $R_i = (d_{b_i}, d_{1-b_i})$
8: $R = \{R_i\}$

Algorithm 6. $RT_Q \leftarrow \mathsf{BVerif}(R = \{(d_i, d_i')\}, VK_Q = \{(VK_i, VK_i')\}, \mathrm{PP})$

1: **for** $i = 1$ **to** $|Q|$ **do**
2:    **if** $VK_i = g(d_i)$ **then** $RT_{Q_i} = d_i$
3:    **else if** $VK_i' = g(d_i')$ **then** $RT_{Q_i} = d_i'$
4:    **else** $RT_{Q_i} = \perp$
5: $RT_Q = \{RT_{Q_i}\}$

Algorithm 7. $r \leftarrow \mathsf{Retrieve}(VK_Q = \{(g(m_{b_i}), g(m_{1-b_i}))\}, RT_Q = \{RT_{Q_i}\}, RK_Q = \{b_i\}, \mathrm{PP})$

1: **for** $i = 1$ **to** $|Q|$ **do**
2:    **if** $g(RT_{Q_i}) = g(m_0)$ **then** $r_i = 1$
3:    **else if** $g(RT_{Q_i}) = g(m_1)$ **then** $r_i = 0$
4:    **else** $r_i = \perp$
5: $r = \{r_i\}$

Algorithm 8. $(st_s, st_o) \leftarrow \mathsf{RevokeUser}(\mathrm{ID}, G, \mathrm{MK}, \mathrm{PP})$

1: $j' \xleftarrow{\$} \{0,1\}^\kappa$
2: $st_s \leftarrow \mathsf{BE.Encrypt}(G \setminus \mathrm{ID}, j', \mathrm{mk})$
3: $st_o \leftarrow j'$

Theorem 1. *Given a selective* IND-CPA *secure CP-ABE scheme, an authenticated symmetric encryption scheme and a broadcast encryption scheme, both secure in the sense of* IND-CPA, *pseudo-random permutations* Π *and* ϕ, *and a one-way function* g. *Let* $e\mathcal{VSE}$ *be the extended verifiable searchable encryption scheme defined in Algorithms 1–8. Then* $e\mathcal{VSE}$ *is secure in the sense of Public Verifiability, Index Privacy and Query Privacy.*

In Appendix A.1 we provide a proof sketch. Full proofs can be found in [3]. In Appendix B we discuss the trade-off between efficiency and functionality of our scheme. Note that we can add additional contextual access control following Alderman et al. [1] by replacing ϕ with a *key assignment scheme*.

5   Conclusion

With this work we have begun to consider the application of VC techniques in the setting of searchable encryption. On the searchable encryption side, this enables additional functionality in the form of computational queries (e.g. computing the average of outsourced data fields that are linked to a specific set of keywords), whilst on the VC side, this introduces additional privacy concerns regarding the outsourced data and computations. The choice of using VC techniques based on ABE stems from the natural correspondence between attributes and keywords in an index. However, future work should investigate other forms of VC to achieve different classes of functionality and (especially) improve efficiency.

In future work, we would like to consider a model whereby multiple data owners can store data on a server without each having to initialise their own scheme. In practice, this could result in the Key Distribution Center from VDC [2] setting up the system and publishing public parameters that any data owner can use, but enabling each data owner to generate their own CP-ABE decryption keys for the data they hold.

A   Security Models

Index Privacy. In Game 2, we formalise the notion of index indistinguishability against a selective chosen keyword attack, which ensures no information regarding the keywords is leaked from the index. Firstly the adversary outputs two sets of attributes $(D_0, D_1 \subseteq \mathcal{U})$ that they wish to be challenged on, with the restriction that $|D_0| = |D_1|$ (this is required as the CP-ABE used to produce the index does not conceal the index length). The challenger runs Setup to produce the public and secret parameters. The challenger selects a bit $b \in \{0, 1\}$ uniformly at random to select which set of attributes to encode into the index. Before the index is created, the challenger needs to create the pre-index from the set of attributes D_b (line 4 of Game 2). This is done using an Encode mechanism that takes the elements of D_b as input and outputs the pre-index $\delta(D_b)$. Encode is not required in our instantiation as the pre-indexes can be chosen directly from $\tilde{U}$ as the user knows the mapping from $\mathcal{U}$ to $\mathcal{U}'$ and the permutation Π; the adversary however does not. The challenger then runs BuildIndex using $\delta(D_b)$ to produce the index $\mathcal{I}_{D_b}$, which is given to $\mathcal{A}$. The adversary is then given PP and oracle access, with the restriction that the query results are identical for each index $\mathcal{I}_{D_0}, \mathcal{I}_{D_1}$, i.e. if $R_0 \leftarrow \mathsf{Search}(\mathcal{I}_{D_0}, QT_Q, st_s, SK_S, PP)$ and $R_1 \leftarrow \mathsf{Search}(\mathcal{I}_{D_1}, QT_Q, st_s, SK_S, PP)$ then we need $R_0 = R_1$. After this query phase, $\mathcal{A}$ outputs a guess b' and wins the game if the comparison operator $==$ returns 1 which indicates that $b' = b$. Hence $\mathcal{A}$ wins the game if they can identify which attribute set (D_0 or D_1) was encoded into the index $\mathcal{I}_{D_b}$.

Query Privacy. The queries themselves should not leak any information about the corresponding keywords that make up the query. Our construction of the queries leaks the gates, but not the keywords themselves. This notion of

Game 2. $\mathbf{Exp}_{\mathcal{A}}^{IndPriv}[e\mathcal{VSE}, 1^\kappa]$:

1: $(D_0, D_1, Q) \leftarrow \mathcal{A}(1^\kappa, \mathcal{U})$
2: **if** $(|D_0| \neq |D_1|)$ **then return** $\bot$
3: $b \xleftarrow{\$} \{0, 1\}$
4: $(\mathrm{MK}, \mathrm{PP}) \leftarrow \mathsf{Setup}(1^\kappa, \mathcal{U})$
5: $G \leftarrow \emptyset$
6: $\mathrm{ID} \xleftarrow{\$} \mathsf{Users}$
7: $(SK_{\mathrm{ID}}, st_s) \leftarrow \mathsf{AddUser}(\mathrm{ID}, G, \mathrm{MK}, \mathrm{PP})$
8: $\delta(D_b) \leftarrow \mathsf{Encode}(D_b)$
9: $(\mathcal{I}_{D_b}, st_s, st_o) \leftarrow \mathsf{BuildIndex}(\delta(D_b), G, \mathrm{MK}, \mathrm{PP})$
10: $b' \leftarrow \mathcal{A}^{\mathcal{O}}(\mathcal{I}_{D_b}, st_s, \mathrm{PP})$
11: **return** $(b' == b)$

Game 3. $\mathbf{Exp}_{\mathcal{A}}^{QueryPriv}[e\mathcal{VSE}, 1^\kappa]$:

1: $(Q_0, Q_1) \leftarrow \mathcal{A}(1^\kappa, \mathcal{U})$
2: **if** $(\mathcal{G}_{Q_0} \neq \mathcal{G}_{Q_1})$ **then return** $\bot$
3: $b \xleftarrow{\$} \{0, 1\}$
4: $(\mathrm{MK}, \mathrm{PP}) \leftarrow \mathsf{Setup}(1^\kappa, \mathcal{U})$
5: $G \leftarrow \emptyset$
6: $\mathrm{ID} \xleftarrow{\$} \mathsf{Users}$
7: $(SK_{\mathrm{ID}}, st_s) \leftarrow \mathsf{AddUser}(\mathrm{ID}, G, \mathrm{MK}, \mathrm{PP})$
8: $\delta(D_b) \xleftarrow{\$} \tilde{\mathcal{U}}$
9: $(\mathcal{I}_D, st_s, st_o) \leftarrow \mathsf{BuildIndex}(\delta(D), G, \mathrm{MK}, \mathrm{PP})$
10: $\tilde{Q}_b \leftarrow \mathsf{Encode}(Q_b)$
11: $(QT_{Q_b}, VK_{Q_b}, RK_{Q_b}) \leftarrow \mathsf{Query}(\tilde{Q}_b, st_s, st_o, SK_{\mathrm{ID}}, \mathrm{PP})$
12: $b' \leftarrow \mathcal{A}^{\mathcal{O}}(QT_{Q_b}, VK_{Q_b}, RK_{Q_b}, \mathcal{I}_D, st_s, \mathrm{PP})$
13: **return** $(b' == b)$

query indistinguishability against a selective chosen query attack is formalised in Game 3. The game runs similarly to that of Game 2, subject to the following restrictions: the challenge queries (Q_0, Q_1) must use the same gates. We denote the gate structure of a query Q by $\mathcal{G}_Q$, and hence require that $\mathcal{G}_{Q_0} = \mathcal{G}_{Q_1}$.

A.1   Security Proofs

Proof (Public Verifiability). Here we provide a proof sketch; full details can be found in [3]. We start by assuming that $\mathcal{A}_{eVSE}$ is an adversary with non-negligible advantage δ. We begin by defining the following three games:

– **Game A.** This is the selective Public Verifiability game as defined in Game 1.
– **Game B.** This is the same as **Game A** with the modification that in Query, we no longer return an encryption of m_0 and m_1.
  Instead, we choose another random message $m' \neq m_0, m_1$ and, if $Q(\mathcal{I}_D) = 1$, we replace c_1 by $\mathsf{ABE.Encrypt}(\overline{Q}, m', MPK_{\mathrm{ABE}})$. Otherwise, we replace c_0 by $\mathsf{ABE.Encrypt}(Q, m', MPK_{\mathrm{ABE}})$.
– **Game C.** This is the same as **Game B** with the exception that instead of choosing a random message m', we implicitly set m' to be the challenge input w in the one-way function game.

We show that an adversary with non-negligible advantage against the selective Public Verifiability game can be used to construct an adversary that may invert the one-way function g.

We begin by showing that there is a negligible distinguishing advantage between **Game A** and **Game B**. We construct an adversary $\mathcal{A}_{ABE}$ that creates an eVSE instance by executing Algorithms 1–8 and uses $\mathcal{A}_{eVSE}$ as a sub-routine to break the selective IND-CPA security of the CP-ABE scheme. The advantage of our constructed adversary is $Adv_{\mathcal{A}_{ABE}} \geqslant \frac{\delta}{2}$. Hence, if $\mathcal{A}_{eVSE}$ has advantage δ at distinguishing these games then $\mathcal{A}_{ABE}$ can win the sIND-CPA game for CP-ABE with non-negligible probability. Thus since we assumed the CP-ABE scheme to be secure, we conclude that $\mathcal{A}_{eVSE}$ cannot distinguish the games with non-negligible probability. The transition from **Game B** to **Game C** is simply to set the value of m'_i to no longer be random but instead to correspond to the challenge w in the one-way function inversion game. We argue that the adversary has no distinguishing advantage between these games since the new value is independent of anything else in the system bar the verification key $g(w)$ and hence looks random to an adversary with no additional information. Finally we show that using $\mathcal{A}_{eVSE}$ in **Game C**, $\mathcal{A}_{ABE}$ can invert the one-way function g – that is, given a challenge $z = g(w)$ we can recover w. Now, if $\mathcal{A}_{eVSE}$ is successful, it will output a forgery comprising the plaintext encrypted under the unsatisfied query (Q or $\overline{Q}$). By construction, this will be w and $\mathcal{A}_{ABE}$ can therefore forward this result to $\mathcal{C}$ in order to invert the one-way function with the same non-negligible probability that $\mathcal{A}_{eVSE}$ has against the public verifiability game.

We conclude that if the ABE scheme is sIND-CPA secure and the one-way function is hard-to-invert, then $e\mathcal{VSE}$ as defined by Algorithms 1–8 is secure in the sense of selective Public Verifiability. □

The remaining proofs can be found in the full version [3].

B   Discussion

Our scheme extends the expressiveness of queries that can be achieved in VSE. No other VSE schemes to our knowledge are able to perform the range of search queries or include negation of keywords in their search queries. Additionally our scheme leaks neither the access pattern (AP) or the search pattern (SP) to the server whilst executing a search. Our combination of search queries with computational queries is also a novel functionality in the field of VSE.

The search time and size of the queries are both linear in n (the amount of data items stored on the remote server). Due to this eVSE may be more suited to smaller databases to prevent these features from being prohibitively expensive. The VSE scheme of [13] has a search time that is linear in the number of letters in the queried keyword (which is usually much smaller than n). This faster search is achieved using a tree-based index, however only a single keyword equality search can be performed. Another scheme built using ABE [37] is able to achieve multi-level access, where users can be restricted to searching only certain parts of the

Table 1. Comparison of schemes

Scheme	Data type	Query type	Publicly Verifiable	Leakage	Computations
[33]	Static	Ranked equality	No	AP,SP	No
[23]	Dynamic	Equality	No	AP	No
[30]	Static	Conjunctive, Disjunctive	No	AP	No
[31]	Dynamic	Conjunctive	No	AP	No
[29]	Dynamic	Equality	No	AP, SP	No
[37]	Static	Equality	No	AP	No
[34]	Static	Fuzzy	No	AP, SP	No
[17]	Static	Semantic	No	AP, SP	No
[13]	Static	Equality	No	AP, SP	No
[14]	Static	Conjunctive	Yes	AP, SP	No
Our scheme	Static	Conjunctive, Disjunctive, Arbitrary CNF/DNF formulae, NC^1	Yes	None	Yes

database. Keywords are grouped with respect to their access control policies, and the search time is linear in the number of groups. This scheme also only achieves a single keyword equality search. The scheme of [35] achieves verifiable fuzzy keyword search with a search time that is linear in the size of the fuzzy keyword set (which varies depending on the level of fuzziness required i.e. searching for data items that contain keywords of edit distance two will require a larger fuzzy keyword set than searching for keywords with an edit distance of one from the queried keyword [24]). Again, this is likely to be less than n. In terms of the number of rounds of communication required per search, our scheme is optimal requiring only one round of communication. The size of the search results in our scheme is also linear in n. Most VSE schemes in the literature return results of a size that is linear in the number of data items that match the query, however this method leaks the access pattern which in turn may leak information about the query. Our scheme hides the access pattern as all search results are of the same form, regardless of what query was submitted.

Our scheme achieves public verifiability, index privacy and query privacy (in terms of the keywords searched for), which is comparable to the security of other VSE schemes. Overall, our scheme sacrifices efficiency when compared to existing VSE schemes, but gains much increased functionality and query expressiveness.

Table 1 gives a brief comparison between our scheme and those in the literature as discussed above and throughout the paper.

References

1. Alderman, J., Janson, C., Cid, C., Crampton, J.: Access control in publicly verifiable outsourced computation. In: Bao, F., Miller, S., Zhou, J., Ahn, G. (eds.) Proceedings of the 10th ACM Symposium on Information, Computer and Communications Security, ASIA CCS 2015. ACM, pp. 657–662 (2015)
2. Alderman, J., Janson, C., Cid, C., Crampton, J.: Hybrid publicly verifiable computation. IACR Cryptol. ePrint Arch. **2015**, 320 (2015)
3. Alderman, J., Janson, C., Martin, K.M., Renwick, S.L.: Extended functionality in verifiable searchable encryption. IACR Cryptol. ePrint Arch. (2015)
4. Apon, D., Katz, J., Shi, E., Thiruvengadam, A.: Verifiable oblivious storage. In: Krawczyk, H. (ed.) PKC 2014. LNCS, vol. 8383, pp. 131–148. Springer, Heidelberg (2014)
5. Backes, M., Barbosa, M., Fiore, D., Reischuk, R.M.: ADSNARK: nearly practical and privacy-preserving proofs on authenticated data. In: 2015 IEEE Symposium on Security and Privacy, SP 2015, pp. 271–286. IEEE Computer Society (2015)
6. Backes, M., Fiore, D., Reischuk, R.M.: Verifiable delegation of computation on outsourced data. In: Sadeghi, A., Gligor, V.D., Yung, M. (eds.) 2013 ACM SIGSAC Conference on Computer and Communications Security, CCS 2013, pp. 863–874. ACM (2013)
7. Bellare, M., Namprempre, C.: Authenticated encryption: relations among notions and analysis of the generic composition paradigm. J. Cryptol. **21**(4), 469–491 (2008)
8. Ben-Sasson, E., Chiesa, A., Genkin, D., Tromer, E.: Fast reductions from rams to delegatable succinct constraint satisfaction problems: extended abstract. In: Kleinberg, R.D. (ed.) Innovations in Theoretical Computer Science, ITCS 2013, pp. 401–414. ACM (2013)
9. Benabbas, S., Gennaro, R., Vahlis, Y.: Verifiable delegation of computation over large datasets. In: Rogaway, P. (ed.) CRYPTO 2011. LNCS, vol. 6841, pp. 111–131. Springer, Heidelberg (2011)
10. Bitansky, N., Canetti, R., Chiesa, A., Tromer, E.: From extractable collision resistance to succinct non-interactive arguments of knowledge, and back again. In: Goldwasser, S. (ed.) Innovations in Theoretical Computer Science 2012, pp. 326–349. ACM (2012)
11. Boneh, D., Persiano, G., Di Crescenzo, G., Ostrovsky, R.: Public key encryption with keyword search. In: Cachin, C., Camenisch, J.L. (eds.) EUROCRYPT 2004. LNCS, vol. 3027, pp. 506–522. Springer, Heidelberg (2004)
12. Park, H.-A., Rhee, H.S., Lee, D.-H., Byun, J.W.: Off-line keyword guessing attacks on recent keyword search schemes over encrypted data. In: Jonker, W., Petković, M. (eds.) SDM 2006. LNCS, vol. 4165, pp. 75–83. Springer, Heidelberg (2006)
13. Chai, Q., Gong, G.: Verifiable symmetric searchable encryption for semi-honest-but-curious cloud servers. In: Proceedings of IEEE International Conference on Communications, ICC 2012, pp. 917–922. IEEE (2012)
14. Cheng, R., Yan, J., Guan, C., Zhang, F., Ren, K.: Verifiable searchable symmetric encryption from indistinguishability obfuscation. In: Proceedings of the 10th ACM Symposium on Information, Computer and Communications Security, ASIA CCS '15, pp. 621–626. ACM (2015)
15. Kalai, Y.T., Raz, R., Chung, K.-M., Liu, F.-H.: Memory delegation. In: Rogaway, P. (ed.) CRYPTO 2011. LNCS, vol. 6841, pp. 151–168. Springer, Heidelberg (2011)

16. Curtmola, R., Garay, J.A., Kamara, S., Ostrovsky, R.: Searchable symmetric encryption: improved definitions and efficient constructions. In: 3th ACM Conference on Computer and Communications Security, pp. 79–88. ACM (2006)

17. Fu, Z., Shu, J., Sun, X., Linge, N.: Smart cloud search services: verifiable keyword-based semantic search over encrypted cloud data. IEEE Trans. Consum. Electron. **60**(4), 762–770 (2014)

18. Gennaro, R., Gentry, C., Parno, B.: Non-interactive verifiable computing: outsourcing computation to untrusted workers. In: Rabin, T. (ed.) CRYPTO 2010. LNCS, vol. 6223, pp. 465–482. Springer, Heidelberg (2010)

19. Goh, E.: Secure indexes. IACR Cryptol. ePrint Arch. **2003**, 216 (2003)

20. Goldreich, O., Ostrovsky, R.: Software protection and simulation on oblivious rams. J. Assoc. Comput. Mach. **43**, 431–473 (1996)

21. Kamara, S., Papamonthou, C., Roeder, T.: Dynamic searchable symmetric encryption. In: Conference on Computer and Communications Security, pp. 965–976. ACM (2012)

22. Sahai, A., Waters, B., Katz, J.: Predicate encryption supporting disjunctions, polynomial equations, and inner products. In: Smart, N.P. (ed.) EUROCRYPT 2008. LNCS, vol. 4965, pp. 146–162. Springer, Heidelberg (2008)

23. Kurosawa, K., Ohtaki, Y.: How to update documents *verifiably* in searchable symmetric encryption. In: Abdalla, M., Nita-Rotaru, C., Dahab, R. (eds.) CANS 2013. LNCS, vol. 8257, pp. 309–328. Springer, Heidelberg (2013)

24. Li, J., Wang, Q., Wang, C., Cao, N., Ren, K., Lou, W.: Fuzzy keyword search over encrypted data in cloud computing. In: 29th IEEE International Conference on Computer Communications, Joint Conference of the IEEE Computer and Communications Societies. INFOCOM 2010, pp. 441–445. IEEE (2010)

25. Liu, P., Wang, J., Ma, H., Nie, H.: Efficient verifiable public key encryption with keyword search based on KP-ABE. In: Ninth International Conference on Broadband and Wireless Computing, Communication and Applications, BWCCA 2014, pp. 584–589. IEEE (2014)

26. Park, D.J., Kim, K., Lee, P.J.: Public key encryption with conjunctive field keyword search. In: Lim, C.H., Yung, M. (eds.) WISA 2004. LNCS, vol. 3325, pp. 73–86. Springer, Heidelberg (2005)

27. Vaikuntanathan, V., Parno, B., Raykova, M.: How to delegate and verify in public: verifiable computation from attribute-based encryption. In: Cramer, R. (ed.) TCC 2012. LNCS, vol. 7194, pp. 422–439. Springer, Heidelberg (2012)

28. Song, D.X., Wagner, D., Perrig, A.: Practical techniques for searches on encrypted data. In: IEEE Symposium on Security and Privacy, pp. 44–55. IEEE (2000)

29. Stefanov, E., Papamonthou, C., Shi, E.: Practical dynamic searchable encryption with small leakage. In: 21st Annual Network and Distributed System Security Symposium, NDSS 2014. The Internet Society (2014)

30. Sun, W., Wang, B., Cao, N., Li, M., Lou, W., Hou, Y.T., Li, H.: Verifiable privacy-preserving multi-keyword text search in the cloud supporting similarity-based ranking. IEEE Trans. Parallel Distrib. Syst. **25**(11), 3025–3035 (2014)

31. Sun, W., Yu, S., Lou, W., Hou, T., Li, H.: Protecting your right: verifiable attribute-based keyword search with fine-grainedowner-enforced search authorization in the cloud. IEEE Trans. Parallel Distrib. Syst. 99 (2013)

32. Wang, C., Cao, N., Li, J., Lou, W.: Secure ranked keyword search over encrypted cloud data. In: International Conference on Distributed Computing Systems, ICDCS 2010, pp. 253–262. IEEE Computer Society (2010)

33. Wang, C., Cao, N., Ren, K., Lou, W.: Enabling secure and efficient ranked keyword search over outsourced cloud data. IEEE Trans. Parallel Distrib. Syst. **23**(8), 1467–1479 (2012)

34. Wang, J., Ma, H., Li, J., Zhu, H., Ma, S., Chen, X.: Efficient verifiable fuzzy keyword search over encrypted data in cloud computing. Comput. Sci. Inf. Syst. **10**(2), 667–684 (2013)

35. Wang, J., Ma, H., Tang, Q., Li, J., Zhu, H., Ma, S., Chen, X.: Efficient verifiable fuzzy keyword search over encrypted data in cloud computing. Comput. Sci. Inf. Syst. **10**(2), 667–684 (2013)

36. Waters, B.: Ciphertext-policy attribute-based encryption: an expressive, efficient, and provably secure realization. In: Catalano, D., Fazio, N., Gennaro, R., Nicolosi, A. (eds.) PKC 2011. LNCS, vol. 6571, pp. 53–70. Springer, Heidelberg (2011)

37. Zheng, Q., Xu, S., Ateniese, G.: VABKS: verifiable attribute-based keyword search over outsourced encrypted data. In: 2014 IEEE Conference on Computer Communications, INFOCOM 2014, pp. 522–530. IEEE (2014)

Author Index

Printed in the United States
By Bookmasters